Outlaw Lead

Outlaw Lead

KENNETH R. HUGHEY

Page 151

ISBN: 1511736062
ISBN 13: 9781511736060
Library of Congress Control Number: 2015905939
CreateSpace Independent Publishing Platform
North Charleston, South Carolina

Prelude

THE BATTLE GROUND

At some time in her literary life, Emily Dickinson referred to her work as "...my letter to the world." I don't expect the world to react to this memoir with the same intensity, admiration, and appreciation finally lavished on Emily Dickinson's poems, but hope that at least a few people might be interested.

A good bit of this memoir is the result of eight years of my life spent dealing with what we commonly refer to as the Viet Nam War, even though there was never a declaration of war by any of the participants.

Note that I wrote Viet Nam as two words. The Viet language is monosyllabic. For all Viet words and names I may use, I will follow this convention, even though in common American English parlance most people don't. You will notice in most publications, Sai Gon, Ha Noi, and Da Nang, for example, show up as Saigon, Hanoi, and Danang. I only learned a few words of the Viet language working with the South Viet Namese people, but, I learned to respect their language. For that reason, even though I can't include the diacritical markings that determine the tonal quality of their language, I can at least follow the monosyllabic feature.

On the subject of Ha Noi, it might be interesting to some to include a bit of trivia about the current Capitol of Viet Nam. There were originally five towns in North Viet Nam bearing the proper name *Ha*. In English these towns were Central Ha, surrounded by North, South, East, and West Ha. Thus the City of Ha Noi is literally Central Ha, and, Ha Bac, Ha Nam, Ha Dong, and Ha Tay are North, South, East, and West Ha, respectively, and are grouped, as you might expect, around Ha Noi. At least one of these has been assimilated into what is now the city of Ha Noi.

To follow the "action" during combat operations, one needs to understand the military divisions of the country. For purposes of planning air strikes, North Viet Nam was divided into seven areas designated as *Route Packages*, commonly referred to as *Packages* or *Packs*. The Packages were numbered I through VIA and VIB. The southern part of Package I was sometimes referred to as *Tally-Ho* and was specially targeted in attempting to interrupt the flow of supplies and personnel to South Viet Nam. (Figure 1, Upper Half)

Refueling routes are shown as straight colored lines and are referred to as "Anchors." Brown and Tan Anchors are over the South China Sea. Red, White, and Blue Anchors extend from Northern Thailand into Northern Laos.

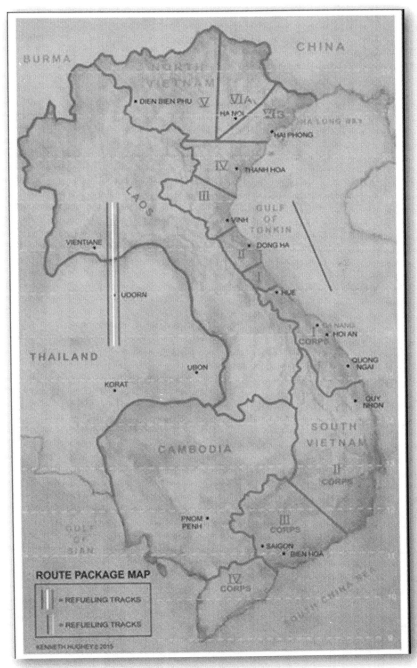

Figure 1

South Viet Nam was divided into four areas denoted as Corps--Roman numerals I though IV, and sometimes spelled out. The First Corps, usually written as *I Corps* and pronounced "Eye Corps," was the northernmost Corps. The other Corps were usually written with the Roman numeral and pronounced as *Two Corps, Three Corps*, and *Four Corps*. The corps numbers ran from north to south, IV Corps being the southernmost. (See the Lower Part of Figure 1.) The locations of the border lines between the Corps are approximate.)

Each of the Corps had at least two divisions. I am most intimately familiar with I Corps. The 1st Infantry Division covered the northern part of I Corps from near Da Nang north to the DMZ, and the 2nd Infantry Division covered the area from near Da Nang to south of the city of Quang Ngai. As a Forward Air Controller, I flew exclusively in I Corps in the area covered by the 2nd division.

The Bridge

With the exceptions of a relatively few major targets, often personally approved by the President of the United States and designated as "JCS" (Joint Chiefs of Staff) targets on our operations orders, there were very few targets anywhere in Viet Nam worth the risk and expense. For example, in South Viet Nam, we always estimated the number of "structures" destroyed in those areas controlled by the maquis, which we commonly referred to as the VC (Viet Cong) Viet Namese Communists. These "structures" were thatched huts made of bamboo poles with thatching of local materials. The local villagers could knock these things together quicker than it takes me to tell you about them. We could burn each of them with a short burst of 20 mm cannon fire and could burn a large number with a 5 minute strike.

Look at the risk. One round from an AK-47 could easily bring down one of our highly sophisticated and very expensive fighter aircraft. The betting odds, when reduced to poker terms, are terrible. A poker player wouldn't bother.

Some of our targets in North Viet Nam appeared to have better trade value. The question has to be reduced to what effect will damage to any selected target have on the outcome of the "war" we are waging in Viet Nam. If we push the clock forward from early 1965 to 1975, when our involvement is over, one could make a case that nothing we did in North Viet Nam affected the final outcome. We came here to save South Viet Nam from the ravages of Communism. We threw everything we had into that effort only to witness the most ignominious failure one could imagine in 1975 when the "Commies" achieved their objective, and we ran like thieves while trying to take some of the faithful with us.

I had the privilege of flying a total of 564 combat sorties in South East Asia during two combat tours in Viet Nam. 106 of those were over North Viet Nam; the remainder was over South Viet Nam and Laos. At no point in those tours, and at no point in the additional five plus years as a POW in North Viet Nam, was there ever any real prospect of success. However that may be, there were many missions that were relatively economical to carry out in terms of risk/benefit considerations, and which were fun and satisfying in term of strategic results with minimum risk to innocent bystanders. I will take you along on one of those.

It's 02:30 on January 19, 1967. We are as close to tree top level as we can safely fly at eight nautical miles per minute in the middle of the night running blacked out over the tropical jungle of Northern Laos heading 020 degrees--generally North by Northeast. Sam Bakke and a new PSO, whose name I can't remember at the moment, are in trail with us, following with their radar. To them, we are a blip on their radar screen five miles ahead at their 12 o'clock position. Note that in flight, we use clock positions to communicate positions. Thus 12 o'clock is straight ahead and at the same altitude; twelve o'clock high is straight ahead and above; six o'clock low is directly behind and low; and nine o'clock would be directly left and level, etc. In this case Sam Bakke would see us on his radar scope at what would be 12 o'clock if his scope were a clock.

The terrain here is rolling, tropical jungle. We are flying low to use the hilly terrain to shield us from the North Viet Nam early warning system and any SAM sites located in the western part of their country, especially Lead-54, located in Package Five in North Viet Nam, who could have a shot at us if we get high enough to be above their horizon. We are listening and watching for SAM activity on our Radar Warning equipment. Nothing so far.

We have the benefit of a quarter moon just far enough above the horizon to provide enough light for us to remain low and to use visual geographical references to assist in navigation. There are no lights in sight anywhere on the ground--only the jungle canopy--a dark sea of endless undulating wasteland. We vary our heading and altitude as we weave our way to a geographic point where we will pull up to 9,000 feet to establish a 45 degree diving attack on a railroad bridge spanning a tributary of the Red River, about forty miles from of Ha Noi.

At this low altitude--we won't be much above 1,000 feet above sea level as we cruise the tree tops--our speed indicators are very close. Our Calibrated Airspeed (CAS) is the airspeed that we read on the Airspeed Indicator (AI)--like reading the speedometer in a car. If we were flying at sea level on a standard day with no wind, what we see on the AI would be our true airspeed and would also be our ground speed. Since we are not much above sea level, there is little or no wind, and the temperature here is very close the 59 degrees Fahrenheit of a standard day, the AI reading is very close to our ground speed.

For more accurate navigation, we use the ground speed reading from our Inertial Navigation System (INS), which uses a set of very accurate accelerometers to keep track of how fast we are moving in relation to the earth's surface; i.e., ground speed. The INS says that we are moving at 480 knots (532 mph) over the earth's surface--eight nautical miles per minute. Because we are not at sea level and other standard day conditions, the AI shows a bit less than 480 knots.

We are here because our intelligence efforts have revealed sufficient traffic from the China border through North Nam via a combination of motorable roads and trails, along with segments of railroad, to warrant some attention. One of the links in this supply chain is a bridge across a tributary of the Red River about forty miles Northwest of Ha Noi. Our response is to take it out. This is not the equivalent of the Paul Doumer Bridge spanning the Red River in Ha Noi, but its removal would put a big dent in the supply line from China.

Sam Bakke is assigned to the Wing Staff. His duties include sifting through intelligence data to identify important targets and to plan missions to damage or destroy them. Sam played a major role in planning every aspect of this mission tonight.

We left Da Nang an hour or so ago carrying six Mark 117, 750 pound bombs each, taking off singly from Runway 35 Right. At 1000 feet I made a shallow 90 degree turn to head West. Sam slid into formation on my left wing, and we climbed out to 20,000 feet and headed for the south end of the tanker track that reaches from central Thailand to the 19th parallel over Northern Laos. After we tanked up, we doused our running lights, dropped down to tree top level, and Sam and company took their position in trail by locking their radar on us. Since that moment, just minutes ago, we have been wending our, hopefully secret, way toward this short, but important, railroad bridge.

A quarter moon is just about perfect for visual low level flying. We can see enough detail to remain low and not be concerned with colliding with a tree. "Tree Top" means that sometimes we may cross a hill or ravine, and, for a few seconds, the tree tops fall away and then rise to meet us as we move along. We make no attempt to maintain an exact altitude above the trees. At times we have only a few feet clearance from the jungle canopy, and sometimes we might be at 300 feet or more. The quarter moon provides enough light to make this possible, but not enough for us to be visible from the ground.

We continue northward and soon cross the border into North Viet Nam into Package V. Ha Noi is not far away--just in the southwestern corner of Package VI-A. (Figure 1) We are nearing the target, and I set up the armament delivery panel to ripple off the six M117 bombs.

As we close in on the pull-up point, Ha Noi appears just off our right wing tip lit up like New York City. In a few seconds it's time to pull. I push the throttles to the firewall and haul the airplane into a steep climb, look off to our right and spot the target easily. As we rise, Ha Noi becomes more impressive. I roll right and position for a forty five degree diving attack to cut the bridge at a thirty degree angle. The bridge is beautiful in the sight picture, just like the photographs that we are carrying. The water running under the bridge glints from the moonlight, and the span crossing the stream appears as a dark straight line from bank to bank.

I position the pipper--a small dot of light in the gun sight that indicates the aiming point--just short of the release point and make the minute corrections necessary to coordinate our dive angle, airspeed, altitude, and sight picture. It all comes together, and when I press and hold the pickle button on the stick, the six bombs ripple away from the airplane. I lay enough back pressure on the control stick to hold six plus g's, and watch the nose rise toward the horizon as my G-suit squeezes my legs and waist to help me resist blacking out.

As the G-Suit pressurizes my lower body, the lights in North Viet Nam go out!! Just as if Uncle Ho had a guy throwing a big Master Switch hooked up to the whole country.

As our nose approaches the horizon, I roll into a steep right turn, ease off the g's, descend in a shallow dive, and roll into level flight just above the tree tops. If Ho's switchman knows we're here, so does Lead 54, and any other SAM sites that we don't know about. Our Radar Warning

(RAW) gear is quiet, but, if we stayed high, Lead 54 would be looking for us soon, and we would hear the high pitched tone of his Radar search signal.

We ease down as low as we can comfortably go, and the dark jungle canopy rushes by at 600 plus miles per hour as we settle into a south-westerly escape route and continue mixing it up with rural rolling hills and jungle while maintaining a heading for the Laotian border. Lead 54 passes off our left wing tip, and we are soon out of their range. The same dark geography that we traversed inbound recedes to our six o'clock, and, in minutes we are in Lao airspace and ease up to a comfortable altitude.

On a more "ordinary" daylight mission we would head for the tanker track and fuel up before going home. Tonight we will climb to cruise altitude, skip the tanker, and take the short way home. We will be on the ground at Da Nang by the time we could finish tanking.

We turn on our running lights, and in a few minutes, Sam pulls up on my left wing. We turn due south and soon cross the Thai border. As Da Nang approaches our left wing tip, we turn left, cross the narrow part of Laos, and are soon talking to Da Nang tower.

The weather has cooperated with us during this mission. The past week or so has been typical winter monsoon weather--rain, clouds all over the place, and weather diversions to Thailand. Tonight we can see Da Nang from miles out. We get a clearance to enter the traffic pattern for Runway 35 Right and level off at 1500 feet with Sam on our right wing as we line up on initial approach at 325 knots. Over the numbers I break left, reduce power, and put out the speed brakes. When we roll out on the downwind leg, I drop the gear and flaps and set up "on speed" for landing. The F-4 is easier to handle in the traffic pattern than a Piper Cub. It is totally impervious to turbulence--just watch those on-speed indicators and aim for the end of the runway.

When the airplane touches down, I retard the throttles to idle and deploy the drogue chute by pulling up the handle located just left of the throttles. The drogue chute handle locks in the up position, and we slow down as the airplane rolls down the runway. Approaching the opposite end of the runway, I tap the brakes to make sure they are working, and engage the nose wheel steering to turn off the runway. When we clear the runway we turn so that our tail faces the infield and release the drogue chute with a slight throttle burst. Later, ground crews will drive out and pick it up.

We taxi into the de-arming area and park. Our canopies are open, and we watch the ordnance crews crawl under our airplanes and place safety pins in the appropriate places. When they are finished, the chief armorer signals that we are cleared to taxi.

We taxi to the revetment area and park.

The mission is over. We stroll across the flight line at a little before 04:00 and wind up in the command post for a cold beer and de-briefing. There is not a lot to report. No SAMs. No AAA. No signals from any of the Sam sites. No Migs. No Problems. We separate and head to our quarters for a shower.

This was my 32nd mission over North Viet Nam, and number 466 total in Southeast Asia (SEA).

Two days later, I bump into one of my favorite Viet Namese Army officers--Major Nguyen Noc Sau--who is stationed here in Da Nang. We met on my previous tour as a Forward Air Controller (FAC) with the Viet Namese 2nd Infantry division. We greet each other on the flight line and he tells me that he has seen the post-strike photos of our mission against the bridge and is impressed that the bridge is no more. I am pleased to hear this news. Major Sau reiterates an invitation to come to his home for dinner. I am pleased to hear that as well. I would like to go to Major Sau's house for dinner immediately, and resolve to make that date ASAP. This war is not always escapable, and I will not have dinner with Major Sau and his family until March 11, 1967, nearly two months from now.

Photo 1

The man on the right is Major Nguyen Ngoc Sau in the Tactical Operations Center at 2nd Division Headquarters--Summer 1965. Major Sau's name is pronounced approximately as follows. Nguyen is pronounced "Win." Ngoc is pronounced Knock." Sau is pronounced "Sow" like a Pig mother.

Sometimes I think about the question: "How did I get here in this strange country in a crazy war?"

Part I

The Eviction

Sunday February 22, 1930.

Sunday--a day of rest--has replaced the Sabbath in that duty in the Christian world in that one Jesus, believed by many to be the long promised Messiah of the Jewish world, was allegedly crucified on Friday, visited Hell and did who knows what other things on Saturday--the traditional Sabbath--and then was resurrected on what is now Sunday, the first day of the week. It's chilly--as the weather goes--but endurable. There are clouds in the sky--a medium to high light stratus overcast--sheltering the earth from the heat of the sun--a sun that would be welcomed by nearly anybody who chose to walk outside on Sunday, February 22, 1930.

It's the kind of a day that is uncomfortable no matter what you would like to do. Not much sunshine--not enough to make you comfortably warm--not cold enough to bundle up--just an in-between uncomfortable chilly day.

1

Whatever kind of day it is matters little or nothing to two men who are walking the Mississippi River Delta very near to the mouth of the Obion River. The ground is not frozen as it had been just a few days earlier, but is cold, and its state of having been only roughly cleared makes an uncomfortable walk.

The two men making this walk probably care little for such a mild--to them, at least--inconvenience. Both have endured hardships and trauma that make a slightly uncomfortable walk seem like a pleasant stroll.

From a few yards away, an observer would discern two men, darkly dressed, hatted, moving steadily across the towhead created by the strange deliberations, violent actions, whimsies, and, sometimes seemingly malicious action of nature attempting to even the score with mere men who were arrogant enough to attempt to assert some authority over her, and, by doing so, to wrest a profit. Is Nature concerned by profit? Does Nature care if men, who woo her in their clumsy, forceful, greedy, needy, and necessary way, win any of their objectives, even those who attempt to contest Nature for their own survival? Do these two men care a whit for the forces of Nature, except for Nature's effect on their enterprises?

Who are these men whom nature observes from her omniscient and omnipresent perch? As we, from our observation point just at their rear, watch them, their movement is little handicapped by the rough, cleared yet unplowed terrain. A short time ago--within the last two years--this land was primeval forest--having never been exposed to any kind of planned agricultural activity. The indigenous population, if there was one, left this land undisturbed. The two who strolled here today are disturbers. Both are frontiersmen, a rapidly disappearing breed.

We move closer. The man on the left is rangy, lanky, and thin. He moves easily with an athletic swing of his legs as he places each foot to the ground with just enough authority to keep it there as he swings the other foot ahead to another authoritative placement and thus propels himself forward. He wears a sweat stained felt hat, dark, not only from its initial dyeing and shaping, but from hard use. It has been worn on unendurably hot and humid days, in rain, snow or sleet, as well as days like today, a day more comfortably endured in the shelter of an enclosed bungalow near a big cast iron, load-the-wood-from-the top stove, perhaps accompanied with home grown popcorn, popped in a big iron skillet on the hearth or on top of the stove itself, with lots of salt and butter.

Along with, or maybe because of, the way he moves, we perceive that this man has a purpose. There is nothing in the surroundings, other than the slightly difficult terrain, to challenge his progress, yet he moves as if he is pushing something out of his way. We wonder what it is.

He wears a cotton jumper, originally dyed and finished in dark Levi Strauss blue, but is now weathered, faded, and a good deal softer to the touch than when he wore it for the first time. A close observation would reveal a bit of a bulge in the right hand pocket of the jumper--a .32 caliber Colt semi-automatic pistol--8 rounds in the clip, none in the chamber--standard accoutrement for this particular man. It's only use, up until today, has been for occasional target practice. The source of the bulge adds to the equation defining this, now more interesting man, forces a mental pause and, combined with the initial perception of him, cautions us to keep our distance--don't get in his way.

The second man walks with ease also, but we perceive that ease, for him, requires more effort. He is a bit shorter than his companion. Where his companion is somewhat swart, and bears the indelible scars of some kind of pox, and whose face is not only more weathered, but also scarred by at least one encounter with a sharp object, such as a straight razor wielded in anger, this second man is smoother, jowlier. With heavier brows and a somewhat rotund figure, he is also lighter in complexion, and looks better fed. His companion's countenance could pass for containing a bit of Cherokee or Chickasaw influence, while his own is ruddy; light eyes, as opposed to dark, lighter hair and a nose from somewhere in Europe.

He also wears a jumper, but no sign of a weapon. He seems strong and able, and we discern that he is a part of a team of two today, but in a supporting role.

Perceived singly, we might have missed something very important about these two men. Together, they project, just with this momentary glimpse, that neither is in any way ordinary--alone or with the other--or with other company. We are wary, but not afraid. These men do not project fear with the way they move, but they do project an aura that engenders respect. We want them on our side.

If we knew them better, we would know who they are. The rangy, swart, pox scarred man is Aught Hughey. He is called Aught (sometimes written as Ought) as diminutive for Arthur. No one would ever call this man Art. Not that he would object--just that Art wouldn't "go" with him. He is also called "Ot" by many--usually when referred to as "old man Ot--" a complimentary reference. Ot is a strange mixture of personalities. He is very generous. On one occasion he purchased a virtually worthless car from a brother-in-law for several times its value as a way of concealing badly needed financial assistance. He is tougher than nails, and can be cruel when baited. He left home when he was sixteen years old to work in a portable saw mill for fifty cents a day. By the time he was 21, he owned and operated his own saw mill.

Saw milling on the Mississippi River around the turn of the 20th Century was hard and dangerous work. The business plan was to find available timber to cut and then to plant your saw mill down-stream from the trees. Next step--cut the trees and snake them into the river--usually with oxen, but also with mules or horses. Once in the river, tie the logs together to form rafts. Then, pole the rafts out into the three miles per hour river channel, and, eventually, pole them to the river bank close to your mill. The ox, mule, or horse teams would then snake the logs up the river bank to the mill. The saws were great circular saws turned by a steam engine connected to the saw axis via a belt. The product--barrel staves, rail road ties, or construction lumber.

The second man is Charlie Morgan. He and Aught are long-time friends. Both possess the tough constituents of character necessary to survive in the rural Mississippi River Delta--good health, physical strength, honesty, total trustworthiness, common sense, and all the other unnamable virtues necessary to succeed in a tough, unforgiving environment. Each was willing to take big risks for the other in time of need, and "time of need" could occur frequently in the world they live in. Both of these men have families and have stood by a spouse who had mothered their children and had suffered untimely deaths sharing the demands of their near-frontier existence. These men needed no talk to share these experiences as common bonds, but rather gestalted into an understanding of trust and friendship.

Today Aught needs a friend. He has a mission that could be done alone, but loneliness is never a substantial companion. Charlie Morgan's presence, even in total silence, is a comfort--a crutch, a support, an exterior endorphin--in time of need and stress.

Last fall a cypress clapboard house that Aught hoped would accommodate a future hand or share-cropper to help with next year's crop was empty. A young man approached Aught explaining that he had a wife and was looking for a place to winter. Aught had a glimmer of hope that this young man might join him as a hand, or maybe share a part of the crop. The young man was not interested in staying--he only begged for a place to stay for the winter and then to move on to some undefined place.

Aught explained that he would be willing to allow the young man and his wife to occupy the vacant house, but only until Aught could locate a more permanent resident who could work a crop, and that he might be required to move on a moment's notice. The young man agreed to the terms and moved into the house.

The young couple has now occupied the house for five months, and Aught has made an agreement with a family to cross the river from Arkansas in hopes of improving their lot. It is now time for the young man and his wife to move on. Evicting this putant family is a grievous task for Aught--a dreadful task for a man who could, and had, faced down the old grim reaper several times with no more than a casual shrug--a man who had, among other things, not totally side stepped the slashing attack of a straight razor, and had almost casually gunned down an assailant set on taking his life--a task for which he needs the support of a friend who understands its heartrending nature without the need for discourse. That friend is Charlie Morgan.

The two approach the clapboard house. It is little more than a shack, but has a mantel on the wall that now holds a double barreled shotgun. Aught steps up onto the porch to the front door. Charlie Morgan hovers nearby as Aught knocks on the door. The young man opens the door and a brief conversation begins. We can't hear all the words, but suddenly the door swings wide open as the young man wheels and steps rapidly across the room and reaches for the shot gun. Charlie shouts to the young man: "I wouldn't do that if I was you--Mr. Hughey has a gun and he knows how to use it--you'll never get that shot gun off the wall."

Aught's hand is in his jumper pocket. We cannot see the little .32 Colt that it now holds. The young man hesitates. All are silent for a long moment. The young man steps slowly to the middle of the room and mumbles some unintelligible words aimed at Aught. Aught and

Charlie turn slowly, step down the steps and move back across the newly cleared field they just crossed. The door to the clapboard house closes slowly.

It's now a warm late spring day in 1939. The backwater is rising all around our house. I am six years old--almost seven, and still haven't learned to swim. Our front yard slopes such that a short wade will take me into water plenty deep for a swim. I am a little afraid, but it's time to try. My teacher addresses me as "Kennel." He is one of my favorite people and has volunteered to help me learn to swim. He explains the motions required to paddle much like a dog, and encourages me to give it a try. I wade in. He lets me know that it's o.k., and that if I get in trouble, he will be there. I try several times to paddle. I hold my breath and flail about, trying to do what my instructor is telling me. Then, finally, I'm staying afloat, and even moving a little. My confidence soars, and I soon realize that if I just relax and do what my teacher tells me that I can really swim. I keep at it. My life will never be the same after today. I can swim.

I tire, and my instructor and I take a break and sit down on our front steps which are, for the moment at least, high and dry. At the moment, my brother Jack and my Dad and Mother, are not in earshot. My instructor says to me: "Kennel, did I ever tell you about the time your Dad had to run off a fellow who was living in one of his houses down at the mouth?"

TRICYCLE

One of my earliest recollections of being in this world is the spring of 1935. I will soon be three years old, and we are moving from a house that I remember well. I am on the front porch with my brother, Jack, who is twenty years older than I. I live at home with Jack and my parents. I am very concerned about this move, mainly because my tricycle is on the front porch, and I am fearful that we might leave it behind. I let Jack know in no uncertain terms that I want my tricycle to travel with me. Jack assuages my fears by picking up my tricycle, carrying it down the long, steep steps, and placing it in our car.

The tricycle has a wood seat painted bright red--my favorite color. It has two small wheels fitted on an axle bolted to the rear underside of the wood seat. The steering mechanism is a set of handle bars and a larger front wheel connected to the front of the board. This is my favorite toy. We are inseparable.

The tricycle makes it to our new home, about two miles up the road. I ride it every day. Then, one day, I get careless and leave it under the big Cottonwood tree in our side yard where we sometimes park our car. My Dad comes home from a busy day and parks the car right on top of my tricycle. From now on, I will use the remains of my tricycle as best I can to entertain myself, but will never ride it again.

NAP
In the summer of 1936, another day etches itself into my memory.

Nap is Nip's team-mate and is a rather large bay mule.

It is a hot August day in the Mississippi River Delta about 76 miles up the river from Memphis. The Western boundary of our farm is the River. Nap spent his young life as a teammate with Nip. Nip is a smaller, more close-knit version of a mule, with the smoother bay finish of a horse. Only Nip's ears and general demeanor give him away from horse-dom. Nap is rangier and, for lack of a better word, *mulier* than Nip.

This morning everything on our farm has gone normally so far. Everybody, except for me (I am a spoiled little brat) has been up since before daylight. My mother was probably first up to fire the stove and begin preparing breakfast. The others divide the chores between feeding the livestock, milking the cows, pumping fresh water, and waiting for breakfast. Breakfast. Ham right out of the smokehouse, fresh eggs, less than a day old, biscuits worked by my mother's arthritic hands, saw mill gravy and red eye gravy to go with the biscuits, and hot coffee percolated with two eggs nestled among the grounds for a treat for somebody later in the day.

After breakfast, something unusual. Nap died yesterday. His death was sudden and mysterious and fearsome in the mystery. Colic usually didn't kill a grown mule. He had exhibited the symptoms of a belly ache, and then gradually settled into a malaise and laid down, groaning and whimpering and begging for his life, and then…, he died.

Grown men don't usually cry, but the four who are present here for Nap's funeral are having an awfully hard time lurking around, hiding behind each other's back, or just disappearing out of sight, to let their eyeballs leak in solitude. I am too young to be bothered at that level. I am just confused about it all, and sad that Nip no longer has a team mate. My mother is mostly out of sight during the day, thinking her own thoughts. I later learn that she had suffered trauma at various times in her life that would make Nap's demise seem like a party of some kind rather than a funeral.

After breakfast, morning wears on at a slow pace. Lum Williams, an old friend of my father, is living at our house. He leads the slow parade to activity by gathering up the shovels we have and beginning to lay out the outline of a large, rectangular grave that would house Nap before sundown. My brothers, Jack and Earl, soon join in, and the sand laden loam just west of our garden begins to pile up along the east side of Nap's soon-to-be resting place. My Dad mans a shovel from time to time between other chores. By noon the hole that will soon hold Nap's remains is well developed in form, but is far from deep enough to hold his large muscular tawny body.

My mother has fixed her usual noon meal we call "Dinner." Corn bread, lots of fresh vegetables, including sliced tomatoes, asparagus, bell peppers, green onions, ham from the smoke house, a fried chicken, and plenty of potatoes--mashed and skin on. All eat a hearty meal, take a short rest in the shade on the porch and soon resume the dig.

As the digging progresses, the stuffy, breath-stealing heat of August increases. Soon, all the diggers are soaked with sweat, and consuming plenty of water from the jugs that I carry from our front porch pump with frequent regularity. Mid-afternoon approaches and dark clouds begin forming on all horizons. The heat intensifies.

Then, an occasional zephyr of cool air sweeps by with considerable relief. Soon the rumble of distant thunder interferes with the rhythm of the shovels tossing the damp sandy loam out of Nap's deep home. The thunder producing clouds move near, and large jagged streaks of lightning precede the authoritative cracks of some ear splitting thunderbolts. There soon follows some large drops of rain--like fluid quail eggs--kicking up the loose, freshly shoveled dirt. Larger and larger lightning strikes and a sudden downpour of driving rain sends the digging crew running for the shelter of our front porch.

In seconds, my brother Earl is standing alone at the south end of our long front porch, while my brother Jack, Mr. Lum, myself, and my Dad stand just under the eaves watching the down pour and wonder at the lightning bolts now splitting the horizon with ferocious regularity and occasionally laying waste to one of our pecan trees. In a few minutes, the whole thing turns into a steady downpour punctuated with a sprinkling of modest sized hail.

The rain is noisy on our tin roof. Conversation requires a bit of volume. I notice that my brother, Earl, appears to be singing from his isolated position at the south end of the porch. I move down close to him--curious about the song. The only words I hear are: "I'm going to Colorado…" I have never heard of Colorado before and want to know all about it. I ask a lot of questions and am inculcated with curiosity about Colorado.

After the interrogation, I move away from Earl and join my Dad, my brother Jack, and Lum Williams (Mr. Lum to me) several feet away near the porch steps. The air has become cool and fresh. The rain gradually drips to a halt, leaving puddles in the yard as steadily diminishing drops from the wet roof spatter the rapidly disappearing run-off. Soon the scene segues into a steadily brightening day, and we see the long arc of a beautiful rainbow spanning the sky.

From Mr. Lum I hear: "Kennet, see over yonder at the end of the rainbow? There's a pot of gold right there at the end. All you've gotta do is march over there and pick it up." The end of the rainbow appears to be near the bank of the river—not far at all. I want to go immediately, but Nap's unfinished new home beckons all of us. The men return to their shovels, and I switch my attention to watch the digging proceed. At first, it's messy and muddy, but soon the hill of damp sandy loam begins to increase as the shovelers do their job. Nap's large, prone body is darker from the wetting.

Nap! Nap! Wouldn't it be wonderful if you could roll over on the damp ground, pull your feet up under yourself like mules and horses do, rise and shake the wetness off your coat, and walk back into the lot from whence you were dragged here for your funeral? I would gladly trade my pot of gold to see you alive!

AIRPLANES

The first time I ever saw an airplane it was in the sky overhead our farm on the Mississippi River sometime before 1937. The engine was noisy and it was very high in the sky and appeared to be moving very slowly. It looked a fraction of the speed that Dr. Tipton drove when he scattered chickens, guineas, dogs, and debris on his way to a house call along the single concrete slab road that ran by our house, 22 miles from Dr. Tipton's home in Dyersburg. In fact, it was moving so slowly that it seemed to take all day to get from where I first picked it up to go out of sight as it headed down the River to somewhere south of us, maybe New Orleans. I was an inquisitive little cuss and must have driven my big brother, Jack, and my Dad crazy asking questions about airplanes.

Later I saw another airplane in a grass field between Finley and Dyersburg--about three miles outside Dyersburg on the way from our home in Chic. This airplane was nothing like the slow one that I saw occasionally going up and down the river and always high in the sky, far away, and very slow. This airplane had one engine in the nose and didn't make a lot of noise, but was much faster than the noisy one. I wanted to fly it, but it never worked out.

One day we were going to town (Dyersburg, Tennessee) and, as we passed through Rush Slough, about ten miles from our house, there was an airplane parked in someone's yard on the left side of the road. The yard was shaded by four or five big pecan trees, and the silver airplane with two wings and a round engine sat there like it belonged. We later learned that the engine had quit, and the pilot had landed in a nearby field, and that some people from Rush Slough had helped the pilot push the airplane to this front yard, and there it sat.

It was beautiful. The silver paint glittered in the sunlight filtering through the tall trees. I desperately wanted to stop and touch it. We passed it again on the way home and never saw it after that. We heard that the pilot had gone somewhere for a part and had returned with some help and, after the repairs, he took off from the same field where he'd landed.

THE 1937 FLOOD

Floods are always a threat to our existence on the river. Every spring the Mississippi River rises. Some years the rise can be contained within the bounds of the river--the river gets full, but remains within its banks. Some years the river overflows and floods our land early and then recedes in time for us to make a crop.

Such a time is the 1937 flood. In January the tributaries that feed the Mississippi River are swollen and continue to rise. In late January the weather is cold and blustery and the Mississippi River is bursting out of its banks. Our farm slowly goes underwater. As the water rises, we keep thinking (hoping?) the flood will crest and begin to recede. It doesn't always work that way.

We have two barns. One is small and sits on a mound. We move our car into the center section of the mound just before the water covers our yard. Our milk cows are already there and we move the remainder of our stock there while we still can. The water continues to rise, and we are fearful that it will come into our house sitting on blocks, which has never been flooded before. My brother, Jack, my father, Mr. Lum, Hollis Reagor and others, nail together several saw horses and make platforms with planks for our heavy furniture, including my mother's piano. We move smaller lighter furniture upstairs, and some furniture won't fit on the make shift platforms and remains on the floor.

The water keeps rising and is soon level with our floor. I am sitting on the staircase that runs up our dining room wall to the upstairs floor watching these last minute preparations when my Father walks into the kitchen/dining area carrying a two inch auger. He is wearing hip boots, as are all of the others. The center point in the floor of the house is in the doorway that connects the dining room to the living room. My Dad places the auger upright and starts turning it to drill a two inch diameter hole in the floor to let the water in before our house starts to float. In a minute the hole is done and the muddy water burbles up through the hole, and, as the water continues to rise, we all move upstairs.

The water is soon a foot deep in our house and continues to rise. Jack and my Father remove the kitchen window that faces the staircase, and we have direct access to the stairs by placing a bateau through the window such that its passengers can duck through the window opening from that part of the boat that extends outside and step upstairs.

The water continues to rise. My mother cries as the water level downstairs is soon deeper than the platforms, and her piano is partially submerged.

A cottonwood tree stands on the south side of our yard, between our house and our shop and harness house. As the weather gets colder, a Shanty Boat ties up between the Cottonwood Tree and our house, and its sole occupant and owner joins those who now live temporarily upstairs. There is a wood burning stove upstairs and my mother manages to keep us fed.

Mid-morning, the day after the Shanty Boat arrives; Jack lets us know that my mother and I will be evacuated. He steps down the stairs and ducks through the window to the outside. My mother and I step down the stairs, duck through the window, and step into a big Diesel powered boat parked broadside to the outside end of the bateau. The power boat is painted gray with the name *Sequoia* in black lettering on the sides. It is a big beautiful boat--much bigger than our skiff--and holds about ten people seated on benches behind the driver who stands up in front behind a big steering wheel and operates the various controls. We drive down the highway in about six feet of water for several miles and finally unload near Finley, Tennessee where cars pick us up and take us to the Commercial Hotel in Dyersburg.

Several people from Chic are there, including two of my playmates who are older than I--Bill Fronabarger and Ralph "Boy" Williams. We are sort of trapped in the hotel, so we cook up our own diversions, some of which get unfavorable reviews from the adult population.

Bill shows me how to fold notebook paper into paper airplanes. I soon master the art, and we go up the stairs to the second floor to launch our air force over the heads of whoever happens to be on the first floor. I explain to Bill that our airplanes are much too fast--that the airplane I saw going up and down the river was much slower. Since I can't get my paper airplane to go that slow in flight, I demonstrate the whole thing by creeping through the lobby holding the airplane aloft over my head and providing sound effects as best I can. Bill tries to explain that airplanes have to go fast to fly, but it just doesn't sink in--I have seen that noisy distant airplane creep from horizon to horizon too many times.

I eventually learn enough about airplanes to understand how they work. Then World War II breaks out, and for four years the world is inundated with war news. I, along with nearly all my buddies, follow the war news, especially the part about our fighter aces. As their reputations develop, their names and records become part of our lives. We follow the "scores" of our favorites as the war progresses, and several of us aspire to be fighter pilots. Of my cronies during that time, I am the only one who succumbs to that calling.

We spend two weeks in the Commercial Hotel waiting for the water to recede. When my mother and I get back home, we discover a mess. Jack, my Father and other neighbors assist in cleaning up. My Dad and Jack patch the hole in the floor and all begin excavating mud from every corner downstairs. The closet under the stairwell is three inches deep in smelly river mud. My mother's Piano is history, and she cries some more.

While my Mother and I were in Dyersburg, a strong wind pushed the Shanty Boat around and before the owner could disconnect the tie down ropes, the Cottonwood tree broke and fell into the water. It now lies on its side in the yard. The helpers cut it into pieces and remove the roots. Later in the spring, my Father replaces the lost tree with a cottonwood pole he cuts from the river bank. The pole soon sprouts, and by 1940, I can climb the replacement tree to a point level with the upstairs window in our house.

Our small mound went under water during the flood. The animals must have been very uncomfortable wading constantly in the cold flood water, but they had plenty to eat and were sheltered from the cold as much as possible. The water was about hub cap deep on our car.

As soon as we get things cleaned up and begin farming operations, a new tractor shows up. John A. Johnson sends us a new 1936 F-20 Farm-All from his last year's inventory. 1936 is the last year that International-Harvester produced a black tractor.

As soon as crops are in, and neighbors have time to help, we begin digging a pond and use the dirt to build a mound that rises above the 1937 flood level. As soon as the mound is finished and settles, we build a barn on it.

Two Ton Tony

All the men in Chic are fight fans, particularly the heavy weight division. Joe Louis is a household word. We always listen to his fights as he mows down the "Bum of the Month" with apparent ease.

On June 28, 1939 Joe's opponent is Two Ton Tony Galento, a tough brawler, but a distinct underdog that everybody thought would go down fast. On fight day, our radio is either out of commission or our battery is dead. Our neighbor, Simon Bizzle, lives on the farm that joins our farm to the north. Late in the day, Jack, our Dad, and some other neighbors congregate at Mr. Bizzle's house and listen to the fight.

On summer days, particularly the sultry, sweaty kind, radio reception can be filled with static, and fade in and out. June 28 is such a day. We listen intently with the volume high as the signal wavers from almost nothing to very loud reception filled with static. It is an exciting fight. Nobody thought that Galento could get near Joe Louis, but in the second round, Galento lands one of his famous deadly left hooks and floors Joe. When Louis goes down, the announcer goes wild--screaming into the microphone at the top of his lungs to out-volume the screaming crowd. No one in the room makes a peep.

We have trouble figuring out exactly what happened, and soon the fight continues into round three, with the announcer's excitement and the noisy crowd infecting the room. In round four, Joe punishes Galento severely, and the referee stops the carnage. We listen to the recap to piece together the parts we missed.

MURDER IN CHIC
We make a good crop in 1938 and 1939. Jack and my Dad are busy all the time and we sometimes hire neighbors as we need extra labor. One of those neighbors is Clay Nelson--"Mr. Clay" to me. We still use a mule-powered mower to cut hay, and Clay usually gets that job. I sometimes ride with "Mr. Clay" on the mower and hang out with him when he does other things. He is good fisherman, and sometimes walks across our farm to the River and, on the return trip, shows us his catch. He always catches something to eat and occasionally has a good sized catfish to show off. He gives us fish from time to time. My mother deep fries catfish in a big kettle and it's a real treat.

Clay and his wife, Lottie, live in a tent in the primeval forest that stretches from the eastern boundary of our farm for three miles to the Obion River. Their tent is near the Chic Cemetery. Miss Lottie visits us frequently and sometimes helps my mother with canning and household chores. The Nelsons appear to be a perfect couple. Clay is soft spoken, gentle, and a pleasure to be around. I look forward to "working" with him. Miss Lottie is quiet and a very sweet woman.

Frank Boyd is another of our neighbors. Mr. Frank owns a farm that joins our farm on the south, and my Dad bought most of the land we now own from him. He has two teen age daughters, Helen and Juanita, and one young adult son, George. He lost an infant daughter in 1926, and his wife, Lexie, died at home in 1928. Juanita and Helen live with him at his home near us, and George is married and lives in a tenant house on another farm.

December 8, 1939 is a warm, sunny day--like a late Indian summer. In the early afternoon, a neighbor stops by to tell us that Clay Nelson has just shot and killed Frank Boyd. His news is filled with a graphic description of what happened. Juanita, Helen, and Mr. Boyd were sitting at the dinner table for their noon meal when Mr. Clay knocked on their porch. Mr. Boyd went to the door with his daughters huddled behind him. Clay was standing in the yard as Frank greeted him. Clay's response was: "Frank is your insurance paid up?" When Frank said yes, it was, Clay pulled his .38 Smith & Wesson revolver from his jumper pocket and fired five shots into Frank's chest from about ten feet away.

Frank fell dead on his front porch. His daughters drug his body into the house, and Helen ran to their nearest neighbor's place for help. Clay walked away and has not been seen since. Another neighbor went to Dyersburg to summon an ambulance.

Our neighborhood is suddenly in turmoil. We soon hear that Frank had confronted Clay a day or so before the shooting, had accused Clay of stealing his pecans, and they had argued. At nightfall, we are confused and afraid. My Dad and Frank Boyd were long time good friends, and my mother fears that Clay might come looking for my Dad. In the evening we light our kerosene lamps as usual, except that my mother turns the lamps down low and pulls all of our window curtains.

The next day we hear that Clay's brother, Jack Nelson, and Clay crossed the river to Arkansas either yesterday or last night, and that Jack is back home with his wife, Callie.

For the next few months, Clay Nelson is a fugitive. We hear rumors that posters have been placed in several Post Offices. Then in the late spring Clay is arrested in a small town in Arkansas and is soon in the Dyer County Jail awaiting trial for murder.

The trial is quick. Helen and Juanita Boyd testify, and that's about all there is to it. Clay is found guilty of murder and sentenced to death. He is then transferred to the State Prison in Nashville to await his execution date. Eventually, he is sentenced to die on September 4, 1940, not quite nine months after the murder.

September 4, 1940 is a very pleasant sunny day. My mother is busy canning vegetables, and Lottie Nelson (Miss Lottie to me) comes to our house to help. She comes up our back steps into the kitchen and is hardly in the door when she says softly: "They're a' killin' Clay today," and takes a seat at our kitchen table. She is frail and cries quietly. Our kitchen is very still for a few minutes as my mother sits silently and cries with Lottie. I step out into our enclosed porch and stay out of the way. Lottie spends the day, busy with the canning process, and then goes home to her tent in the forest.

JOE'S LAST FIGHT
Since his fight with Galento in 1939, Joe Louis has been heavily favored in all his bouts. We always listen, but none are very exciting.

Then in 1941 along comes a great light heavyweight boxer with a lot of class--Billy Conn. Conn is supposedly so fast and so technically skilled, that he has a good chance to beat Joe. June 18 comes around and all the male members of the Chic community that I know are tuned in on tonight's fight between Louis and Conn.

Our radio battery has run dead, and we haven't had a chance to make the 25 mile trip to Dyersburg to replace it, so as the sun gets low, we walk up the road to visit Mr. Alec Williams. When we arrive, Mr. Alec greets us at the door and we enter with alacrity to avoid the cloud of mosquito's intent on eating us alive. As soon as the door is closed, Miss Trixie, Alec's wife, sprays the inside of the house with what smells like pure kerosene to discourage the squadrons that squeezed in with us.

The radio reception is better than the Galento fight, but still loaded with static and swells and troughs in volume. These impediments to fidelity amplify our attention as we listen to a great boxing match.

From the outset I am waiting for Joe Louis to somehow stay even or ahead of this upstart, Billy Conn. Twelve rounds come and go, and Joe is losing the fight. There's no way that Conn is going to kayo Joe Louis, but Conn's fight plan and execution are certainly working. Then, there is round thirteen. The room I am in is quiet. It's sounding like more of the same. As the round progresses, Conn seems to be gaining more ground, exchanging blows with Joe as Conn increases the tempo. Then the announcer's voice rises as Joe's offence suddenly comes alive and Joe connects with a trademark jack hammer punch and Conn hits the mat. Joe steps into a neutral corner and the fight is over. We walk home escorted by two squadrons of determined mosquitoes.

We get our crops in, including the corn crop from the Miss Kelly place that includes a three mile trip through the primeval woods, sometimes in sight of coons and horned owls on patrol in the post dusk darkening.

The *Miss Kelly* place is a tract of land bounded on the east by the Obion River and on the other three sides by land holdings that are still mostly uncleared. My father leased this small tract of partly cleared land from its owners, some of the Kelly matriarch's heirs, with the agreement that he would clear the remainder that was still primeval woods.

We had to clear our own access to Miss Kelly by cutting a three mile trail through the woods directly from our house due east to the Obion River that parallels the course of the Mississippi. Preparing the trail was roughly equivalent to clearing a strip of land 12 feet wide by three miles long.

AND THEN THERE WAS WAR

Sunday, December 7, 1941 is a bright sunny day. It is pleasantly warm, and my Mother and I attend Sunday School in the Chic Schoolhouse. There are no churches in this rural community, so the Dyer County School System allows the use of the schoolhouse that sits about one hundred yards from our house for church services. Baptist and Methodist "Circuit Riding" preachers take turns coming to Chic to preach to us. If there are no preachers available, we have Sunday School and leave it at that. Today, after Sunday School, my Mother and I come home, and my mother fixes her usual Sunday dinner--fried chicken, cornbread plenty of cooked vegetables, and something sweet for dessert. Dinner occurs at noon here in Chic, and Supper is the evening meal.

After dinner, I am playing in the yard, and my brother Jack and my father are reading the Sunday Paper. I have finished my part of the paper--the comics, and my mother turns on the radio that sits on a table in our living room. Since we have no electricity, we buy large dry cell batteries that look like a package crudely wrapped with cardboard, weigh about a ton, and are advertised to last for 1,000 hours. Because the battery has to serve us a long time, we ration the time we listen. I don't know what my Mother intended to listen to this Sunday afternoon, but whatever it was, she never hears. The instant the Radio crackles to life, there is nothing but the news from Hawaii.

In a few minutes we are all glued to the radio in stunned disbelief. My mother cries. There isn't much conversation the rest of the day.

All of the draft age males have registered for the draft. We now wait for the next shoe to fall.

One evening just before sunset in late February, 1942, several draft age young men show up in our yard. In a few minutes after the first arrival, there are several pickup trucks nosed around our house and a yard full of hunting hounds milling and talking their own peculiar language to each other. My brother Jack, Hollis Reagor, R.V. Fortner, John Fronabarger, and some others are on our front porch filling their carbide lights in preparation for an all-night coon hunt. Soon after dark, they are on their way. I want to go, but the attitude shared by my mother and the hunters freeze me out. I go to bed and sleep well, and get up the next morning to discover the hunt produced no coons.

I didn't know it at the time, but no coons was probably no surprise to the "real" coon hunters who lived in Chic--most notably two of the Smith brothers, John and Walt. When the Smiths took to the woods looking for coons, the coons were in some difficulty. With my brother and his cohorts, the coons probably enjoyed the show, knowing they were safe.

In March, 1942, my brother Jack and his fellow coon hunters gather once more on our front porch before dawn on a chilly morning and leave for Dyersburg to begin their military careers. One other "boy" from Chic, Man-Boy Bowles, barely of draft age, leaves a few days later. The War takes its toll on these five from Chic. Man-Boy dies on Salerno Beach; John Fronabarger loses a big chunk of his right hand courtesy of a Nazi machine gunner; Hollis Reagor and R.V. Fortner are captured and spend time as Prisoners of War in Germany; my brother Jack is wounded at Monte Casino and then wounded again shortly after and spends a year in an Army Hospital in Rome, Georgia before he is discharged in 1945.

From March, 1942, I do the best I can to help my parents run our farm.

PECANS

In the late Fall of 1942, I am ten years old and have lived all of my cognitive life on this farm in Chic, Tennessee on the Mississippi river. I live here with my father, my mother--my brother Jack was living here but is now in the Army. I have only scant memories of any other place. Incursions from outside of these environs occur, but are seldom and me-teoric, much like an asteroid shower interrupting the sky with an unusual display. While these displays are beautiful and unusual, mostly visits from my sisters who are adults, they remain just that--beautiful and unusual, but in the everyday lives of those who work, grovel, sweat, bleed, and struggle to stay alive, are mere.

My mother and I are picking up pecans today. For those who have no familiarity with the nut called "pecan," there is no *can* in pecan, but rather it rhymes with the *con* in con man or the first syllable of the word *continent*. Some prefer to pronounce pecan like the word for a container into which one might urinate--how disgusting!

There are more than eighty pecan trees on our farm. If you show me a pecan from our farm, I can take you to the tree that produced it. Each of these wild pecan trees produces a unique nut--easily identifiable. We have our favorite trees, based on size, shape, coloration of the hull, yield, and quality of the meat inside the pecan.

My mother is fifty years old. She might be considered overweight by some, but to me, she is just right. She is my mother, and that's all that matters. She is broad shouldered and strong for a woman. She has a matronly feminine figure--waist much smaller than shoulders and a shapely derriere--when she was younger and more svelte, she could easily have posed for a Callipygian Venus. She wears spectacles with horn rims. Today, she is bundled up in the warmest clothes she has--a heavy dress, old thick wool coat, wool tartan plaid scarf tied around her head and neck, and cotton gloves with the finger tips removed to facilitate the dexterity needed to pick up individual nuts.

It is bitter cold. We have experienced several frosts, and now a particularly hard frost has frozen the pecan hulls into total submission. All the hulls have given up their grip, have opened their arms in complete release and the nuts in their bare shells, minus their leather-like coating, lie scattered about on the ground. To us, this is manna from heaven--a gift to be harvested to assure our survival. Pecans are worth nine cents per pound on our front porch--the rare gift of cash to purchase necessities.

We know from experience about how many pounds each pecan tree produces. The tree we are under today produces about 150 pounds per year. Wild pecans produce fruit that is all over the place in terms of size, shape, and shell coloration. Some pecans have very distinctive shapes. One of our trees produces a pecan that is shaped like a very stubby baseball bat--a long slender hull with a bulbous end. This particular pecan is also unusual in coloration. The shell is very light with contrasting darker brown markings. The small end is a light tan with virtually no markings, while the bulbous end appears darker because of distinctive flower-like striping. It is a bit small with a softer shell than most wild pecans, but still crisply hard unlike tame soft shell pecans.

Wild pecans are more prized than tame paper shells. They have a stronger taste and the meat is oilier and fuller than soft shells. A bag of wild pecans will weigh more than the same sized bag of tame. We are very proud of our trees.

This land was cleared from its primeval condition not so long ago by a man named Frank Boyd--the same Frank Boyd that Clay Nelson murdered a while ago. Like others who bought "new ground" and cleared it for cultivation, he left the pecan trees standing. When he cleared it of all other trees, he sold the trees that would make lumber--oak, walnut, hickory, and cypress, for the most part. Oak, Walnut and Hickory also made good firewood--the other woods being too soft and fast burning for fire wood. Also, the Hickory would be set aside and, during hog killing time would find their way into the smoke houses of every farm in Chic, Tennessee.

During the clearing process, the various vines, including Possum Grape and Muscadine, and all the other underbrush and trimmings from felled trees, simply went up in smoke. When I survey the landscape of our farm, I see only the Pecan trees, fences which separate our pastures, our home, and our two barns. Otherwise, the land is all under cultivation and on this day is essentially bare, except for some remnants of corn stalks waiting to be plowed under in the spring.

We have raked up some twigs and debris and made a fire that burns nearby. The pecans are cold to touch--much like picking up small pieces of ice--and our hands become so cold and stiff that we need to warm them occasionally. Each of us has a bucket to collect the nuts. As we fill our buckets--a slow process because the pecans are scattered over a large area--we pour them into a burlap bag. When we finish for the day, we will carry the bag and our buckets to the front porch of our house where this bag will join several other bags that are already full. As the bags fill, my mother sews them closed with a huge needle threaded with heavy twine.

But we are not finished. The sun, still high in the sky, seems to be spewing out cold instead of heat, and several pounds of these hard little pieces of ice remain scattered about. We will never get them all today, but will continue until the cold winter sun gives up and sinks too far below the horizon to light our way.

My mother uses the proceeds from the pecans she gathers to buy clothes for me. She is able to gather only a small part of the total crop. Other people, mostly Mr. Lum Williams, come and thrash the trees and gather them for a percentage, and those profits go toward other farm expenses.

J. IS FOR JUSTICE

During the summers I work with my father doing fencing and maintenance and driving our tractor cultivating cotton and corn and cutting hay. My father is the local magistrate and I get to see him in action from time to time. I don't know it now, but later in life, I will become a lawyer and will run for a judgeship in California. A part of my election propaganda will be a memoir about him:

The best bench officer I have ever known is my Father. As I was growing up, my father was a country magistrate. His bench was sometimes a 500 gallon cylindrical kerosene tank welded horizontally onto sled-like runners and parked in our yard. He stood there, with his magistrate's book opened on the tank, calling the court to order and conducting trials, sometimes in a hot mid-day sun.

Some of my colleagues have referred to me as the ICEMAN, loosely based on the Top Gun movie--the acronym ICE standing for Integrity, Courage, and Experience. I like the flattery, but my father was the real epitome of these qualities--I am a mere imitation. He had about a 6th grade education and left home when he was 16 years old to make his way in the world. By the time he was 21, he owned and operated a portable saw mill.

The modus operandi of saw milling was to set up the saw mill on solid ground on the bank of the Mississippi river, and then to cut timber upstream from the mill, roll the logs into the river and form rafts, and float the rafts downstream and tie them up to the bank near the mill. He used oxen to "snake" the logs to the river and then from their tied up position from the river to the mill. Hard and dangerous work. He wound up in the river more than once, and more than once, he cheated death by a narrow margin. He was tough. He was also very fair, honest to a fault, and considerate of his work force, particularly the animals. Later, long after his sawmilling days, I witnessed him firing a field hand and ordering him off our farm for mistreating one of our mules. I also witnessed several elopement weddings conducted under the light of a kerosene lamp in our living room.

The most memorable trial I have ever witnessed in my life involved a game law violation. We lived 25 miles from the nearest town--Dyersburg--in a farm community named Chic. The game warden was the undertaker in Dyersburg, and was probably the wealthiest man in town. He liked to hunt and was a stickler regarding game laws. He showed up in our yard on a hot August day in 1943, driving a 1942 Buick Roadmaster--roughly equivalent to a Rolls Royce Silver Cloud in our neck of the woods. Two young men, our neighbors, were in the car with him. The game warden parked his car near our 500 gallon kerosene tank, got out of the car and approached my father and me. He addressed my father: "Squire Hughey, can you do a trial?" My Dad said that he could, and asked about the subject matter. The game warden explained that he had two defendants in the car with him who had been shooting rabbits out of season, and that the rabbits were in his car. With that, the trial proceeded.

The warden opened the trunk and laid five rabbits in the hot dust near the kerosene tank. My Dad retrieved his books from the house and opened the record book on top of the tank and called the court to order. The game warden presented the defendants and the evidence--five dead rabbits--and explained the case. My

Dad listened intently and made some notes in his record book. When the game warden finished his case, my Dad asked the defendants a few questions. They admitted that they had killed the rabbits, and the rabbits they killed were those five rabbits lying there in the dust. My dad noted that, in that case, he had no choice but to find them guilty. He then pronounced sentence per the game law: $50.00 fine. The warden was on the verge of exultation, when my Dad popped his book closed and said: "sentence suspended."

With that, the warden scooped up the rabbits, threw them into the trunk of his Buick Roadmaster, cranked up and sped out of our yard in a cloud of dust. He apparently never realized, thought about, or cared that these young men lived in different circumstances than he did. They didn't shoot the rabbits for sport. They shot them because their mother did not have meat for her table. There were plenty of rabbits in Chic. These young men, and, of course, my Dad, knew more about the practicalities of game conservation than did the game warden.

I was 11 years old when I stood there beside my Dad at that brief little trial. I can still recall the aroma of tobacco and sweat, my father's cologne. I knew at that moment that my Dad had just done something special, but, at that time I couldn't define what it was. We call it justice.

BACCALAUREATE SUNDAY, 1949

I finished High School in 1949 and was a pretty good student until I got to be about ten years old, and innate laziness and other diversions infected my soul and from then on, for a long time I was a poor scholar. In high school, the only homework I really bothered with was math, chemistry, and physics, except I worked pretty hard in the agriculture class, largely because our Ag instructor, Sam Reed, kept us challenged and busy.

I am sorry that I did so poorly in several classes, particularly in the English classes with Miss Alleen Park and Miss Julia Sheaffer. I have to say that that I loved Miss Park. She was the sweetest among all that I cared for a lot. She was very tall and stately and very patient. Miss Sheaffer was a tyrant, but lovable anyway. Her tyranny had a good purpose--she believed in her product and was a faithful exemplar. One of my regrets in life is that I never took the effort to let Miss Sheaffer know that I had earned an M.A. in English with very nearly a 4.0 GPA. (On second thought, it might be just as well, as she may have had a heart seizure at the news, assuming she believed it.)

Our graduation baccalaureate is on my birthday, May 22, 1945. I am driving my mother's 1940 Chevrolet business coupe, the one an old man saw who lived in a house on Neely's Chapel Road, and who happened to be sitting on his front porch whittling as I approached his house at about 70 miles per hour. He watched me attempt to dodge around one of his hens who was crossing the gravel road with her chicks as I approached, and then watched, no doubt in astonished amazement, as that little coupe suddenly turned sideways in the road and started rolling over and over with Billy Stafford and me inside, and then plunged head-on into a gully. That one.

Sue Austin, the one who will someday be my wife, and about whom you will hear more as we go along, is with me. We are soon parked in front of 317 Light Street in Dyersburg to pick up one of the most important people in my life--Mrs. Clara Ward.

When I was in the seventh and eighth grade, my mother saw to it that I attended the best grade school in the county--Central Grammar School. Central grammar was a 7th and 8th grade school and was part of the Dyersburg City School System. The only way I could go to school there was to board in Dyersburg. In the seventh grade, I boarded at the same Commercial Hotel where we stayed during the 1937 flood. My mother didn't like me staying in the hotel, so she somehow found Mrs. Ward. Mrs. Ward is an Angel. She is like a grandmother to me.

Today, a flood of memories splash through my head, as I re-live the 1944-45 school year living on 317 Light Street in Dyersburg. I was a better student that year than the year before, and Mrs. Ward was largely responsible for the improvement. She took over my "raising" as best she could. She set aside time for me to study and expected me to use it wisely. She had other people living in her house. A middle aged couple lived in the apartment upstairs, and young couples whose husbands were B-17 pilot trainees at Halls Air Base near here, shared the downstairs with Mrs. Ward and me.

One of our diversions was the "table up" game. Four of us--usually myself, Mrs. Ward, and one other of the rest--would sit on three sides of a card table, place our hands palm down on the table in front of us, and quietly chant together: "table up, table up, table up…, until the unoccupied side of the table lifted, and the table stood on two legs with the other pair of legs suspended two or three inches above the floor.

We would then ask the table questions. Along with the question, the asker had to instruct the table how to answer. For example, if the question required a yes or no answer, the asker could say: "Table, tap once for yes, two for no." Or, if the question demanded a number, as "When will the war end?" the instruction might be: "Table, tap once for each month." I sat on all sides of that table a lot of times, and I have no explanation other than it works like a Ouija board. The couple who lived upstairs swore the person who sat opposite the unoccupied side maneuvered the table. I sat on that side of the table as often as the others and can testify that the table was "honest."

Mrs. Ward is ready to go when we get to her house. We ride together to the baccalaureate. The proceedings are soon over and we return Mrs. Ward to her home. I say good bye to Mrs. Ward and enjoy a grandmotherly hug.

(I don't know it today, but I will never see her again on this planet. In the fall of 1953, I open a letter from my mother while sitting on my bunk in

the Aviation Cadet barracks at Williams AFB, Arizona. In a few weeks I will graduate from the Jet Fighter School with a commission as a Second Lieutenant, and will go home to marry the girl of my dreams who accompanied me on my Baccalaureate Sunday. I read the letter. It is not long. My heart breaks as I read that Mrs. Clara Ward has died. Would that she had survived long enough to be at our wedding. Is that a selfish thought? Yes, in a way, it is. A lot of that wish is for myself to preen my feathers in front of a wonderful woman who will always be in my heart.)

Part II

My Mother's struggle

For several months prior to graduation, I discuss with my Mother the fact that my personal plan is to join the Air Force the day after my 17th birthday. There is a catch--my mother has to sign the enlistment papers, and she steadfastly maintains that she will not do that.

After graduation, I have a job for nine days doing a survey with the Department of Agriculture. Two of my classmates and I set up shop in various county school houses and the local farmers come there to fill out DOA forms regarding their crop plans. After that, the only thing left to do is field work for three dollars per day. Field work means chopping cotton with a hoe. I become a bum. I go to the fields sometimes, and sometimes I leave and just goof off. By the end of June, my Mother gives up. She agrees to sign me up the day after the 4th of July. The 4th is on Monday and is a horrible day for me and a lot worse day for my Mother. I go to the river for a swim on a sandbar with my brother, Earl, and his wife O'Neil, and then spend all the time I can with Sue. Nobody is happy.

At this time in my life at age 17, there's too much about life that I don't know and understand. If I could live some of my life over, I might do something different today, but it is impossible for me to fully know and understand is the agony that my Mother has suffered.

In 1923 Flora Lewis was living on Island 26 in the Mississippi River, just north of Osceola Arkansas, with her first husband, John Burgher, and four children, age six to infancy. Her children were Johnny, age six years; Nancy five years; Louise three, and Earl, about a year old. That summer, John Burgher died. As he lay dying, and knew the end was near, he asked my mother to bring each of his children to his bedside to say good bye. Louise was three when my mother placed her in bed with her Papa. John died soon after. My mother began making arrangements to leave the island and move to Luxora, Arkansas to live with her mother--"Big Mammy" to the children.

About three weeks after John Burgher died, my mother was giving Johnny a bath, when he collapsed in her arms. She wrapped him in a towel and held him in her lap. As she held him, he said to her: "Mama, I'm dying. I see Papa." These were his last words as he died in his mother's arms.

My mother soon discovered the cause of Johnny's death. When she searched his pockets after he died, she found a small attractive pill box that was empty. She routinely kept this little box in a cabinet high above the kitchen work space. Apparently, Johnny liked the box and wanted it for his own. He somehow used a chair or stepstool and recovered the box. Noticing that there were some small pills in the box, he swallowed them and kept the empty box in his pocket. The pills were strychnine, prescribed to my mother for an irregular heartbeat.

Beginning an Air Force Career

On July 5, 1949, I ride a Greyhound bus from Dyersburg to Memphis and report to the Air force recruiting office in Memphis with paperwork from the Dyersburg recruiter, who has briefed me well on what to expect. I know that I have to take a long comprehensive test, that is basically an I.Q. test, and that the results are important. I didn't do all that well on the short preliminary test that I took in Dyersburg, and I'm a bit concerned about how this longer exam will go.

In Memphis, I meet four other recruits in the recruiting office. The recruiting office has arranged for us to spend the night in the Memphis YMCA, and we will go there together when we leave the recruiting office. Meanwhile, we complete the required paperwork and learn that we will take the test tomorrow morning at 08:00.

On July 6, the five of us get some breakfast at a local coffee shop and walk to the recruiting office. An Air Force Sergeant briefs us on the test procedure and we spend the morning taking the multiple choice test. There are no general knowledge questions; just hypothetical situations with choices as to best solutions. The test seems very difficult. We have just over a minute to dope out each question and mark the answer sheet. I approach this test with an intensity and purpose that I didn't know I had. My heart is racing, and I'm totally absorbed in the task.

At one point, I see a question that puzzles me. Until now, I have at least understood each question and have been able to pick what I believe to be the best response. But now I face a puzzle. There is a stack of bricks with some bricks missing. If no bricks were missing the stack would contain 1728 bricks--12 layers with 12 bricks on each side of each layer. The problem is to figure out how many bricks are missing. At first, I can't figure out how to count the missing bricks in the three dimensional drawing, and I almost panic. I know this problem has to be solvable, but I also know that it will take much too long to count those spaces as individual spaces. I can answer several other questions in that amount of time. In a trice, I decide to go on to questions that I can answer.

After I finish the remainder of the test, I go back to the bricks. I take one look, and the answer literally leaps out at me. In seconds I know how many bricks are missing, and wonder what questions I answered incorrectly out of poor logic.

When the time is up for the test, we take a break. The staff scores our answers and in a few minutes the Sergeant comes out to the break room where we are waiting and asks me to come back to his office inside. I follow him through the locked door into the secure area where his office is located. He sits down, looks up at me and asks if I have taken this test before. I answer no. He asks if I have ever seen the test before. I answer no. He asks: "Are you sure?" I am puzzled by his inquiry, but I tell him that I never saw this test before this morning when he handed it to me.

He finally tells me why the questions. I have just turned in a very high score, one of the highest he has seen. I am surprised, happy, and stunned all at once. He then tells me that the five of us will be leaving shortly for San Antonio, Texas where we will begin Basic Training tomorrow and, that their policy is to put the one with the highest score in charge of each group of recruits. He then briefs me on my duties and gathers us together to explain all this to the other four.

We leave for the train station. As the one in charge, I have our orders, our train tickets, and our meal tickets in a packet, and we do everything together from now until another Sergeant greets us at the train station in San Antonio late that night and takes us to Lackland Air force Base for thirteen weeks of Basic Military Training, commonly referred to as "Hell."

Thirteen weeks later we all look a lot better in our uniforms and are justifiably proud of ourselves. We have trained as a Flight of 60 and form up outside the Squadron Orderly Room to hear our next assignments. I am assigned to Keesler Air Force Base in Biloxi Mississippi for Ground Radar Maintenance School--a one year technical school.

The next day I am on a train home for a ten day leave and then on to Keesler. The year at Keesler flies by, and in October 1950, I transfer to Langley AFB, Virginia to a real "line" organization. The barracks I move into is salted heavily with more senior enlisted men. Three of the sixty are Technical Sergeants--"Tech" Sergeants in vernacular.

The organization is a Radar Calibration Squadron--one of two that travel wherever we have early warning radar sites to check on their coverage capability. The squadron puts together Calibration Teams headed by an Officer and a senior Non Commissioned Officer (NCO). Each Team is only together long enough to calibrate one radar site and prepare a report. The Team then dissolves and waits for the next job. In between each calibration assignment, the team members study electronics with the tutelage of civilian Technical Representatives (TechReps), officers, and senior NCOs.

We travel to Radar Sites all over the country, particularly the northern part of the U.S. and some of Canada and Greenland. These Radar sites form our early warning network.

The Calibration process goes like this:

The Air Defense Command (ADC) selects a site for calibration and sends orders to our squadron to go there and calibrate the site. Our squadron appoints an officer to head the team and a senior Non Commissioned Officer (NCO) to assist. The next step is to select the team. Two members will be Radar Mechanics, like me. One member will be a surveyor. At least two will be radar operators and one will be a radio operator. One member will be a civilian TechRep, who is an electrical engineer trained on each of the types of Radar we encounter. Each of these members has a specific duty to perform.

The first step upon arriving at a site is to assure that the Radar set is working at peak performance. The surveyor goes to work checking the orientation of the Site by taking shots of Polaris through the antenna to assure that the presentation on the Radar screens are in synchronization with the antenna. The surveyor also takes a panoramic view of the horizon line as viewed by the Radar antenna. For a day or two, the team is getting ready for the real test.

The performance test is done with B-29s as targets. Our squadron owns five B-29s that fly specific patterns at varying altitudes as the radar operators track them on the screens and take down information on the strength of returns as seen by the radar. We leave with a stack of data and return home to prepare a report on what we found. We are usually at a site a week or so and it takes about a month to prepare a report based on the data we have collected. When these reports are put together, ADC knows what our early warning coverage is like and takes steps to place new sites or to replace and modify existing sites to plug any holes. We are busy year round making the rounds of the system.

We make several trips while I am with the squadron at Langley, and then we transfer to Griffiss AFB in Rome, New York in September, 1951. The job is the same. One major difference is that we have a hanger at Griffiss that houses all five of the B-29s plus a C-45. Four of the B-29s are backed into each corner with their noses facing the center of the hanger. The fifth airplane sits in the middle with the C-45 in the interstitial space. It's a tricky job moving these airplanes around, and fun to watch the ground crews choreograph their musical shuffle. All of the airplanes are seldom hangered at one time, and sometimes the hanger is almost empty.

We maintain Strategic Air Command level of security for these airplanes, which means 24 hours of armed protection. During the day, the Air Police Force security is sufficient, but at night and on all other off duty hours, we post guards 24 hours. The enlisted population furnishes these armed guards and all of us take our turn. About twenty enlisted men are always assigned to guard duty and serve for seven days. My turn comes up in January 1952.

Those who serve guard duty move into a special barracks the week before guard duty and undergo thorough training regarding clothing, weapons handling, and security procedures. All who are assigned must be current with the weapon--the M-1911-a-1, .45 Caliber Semiautomatic Pistol. The bulk of the training is a review of general guard duty procedures and responsibilities and how to handle varying situations. We are also issued cold weather clothing because some of shifts require walking an assigned post outdoors, and it's bloody cold in Rome New York in January.

My week goes by with only one memorable incident.

The fire department at Griffiss AFB is made up of very professional civilian Department of Defense (DOD) employees. One of their duties is to conduct regular inspections of everything on the base. One night I am manning my post inside the hanger with five B-29s. The only unlocked entry to the hanger opens, and a man in a civilian fire department uniform steps through the door. As per my instructions, I call for him to halt. He halts. I approach to within ten steps of him with my .45 at port arms in my right hand. He watches me warily. I ask him who he is. He says that he is a Captain in the fire Department. A part of our training was a comprehensive review of proper identifications and uniforms. He looks legit, but my orders are to verify his identification by a certain procedure. If he really is a fire Department employee, he will be carrying an Identification Card that I will recognize.

I ask him if he has ID. He says yes. I ask him where is ID is located. He tells me that it is in an inside pocket of his jacket in his billfold. I ask him to remove his billfold from his inside pocket, open it and place it on the floor with his picture ID facing up. He complies. I ask him to move to a certain area about 15 feet away and remain standing there. He complies. As he moves away, I approach his billfold while watching his every move.

If he does anything suspicious, I have orders to shoot him, and he apparently knows that. I retrieve the billfold without taking my eyes off him. He stands patiently. I hold the billfold at my eye level so that I can see him and his ID, and move slowly toward him. I ask him his name and ID #. His response matches the ID card and the picture looks good. I holster my piece, smile, and hand him his billfold. Maybe I was being too friendly. In the movies, he could have pulled out a gun and shot me dead while I was putting my pistol away. But he doesn't. He goes about his business of looking around the hanger, smiles and bids me good night as he leaves.

(Retrospective: I was 19 years old when this incident occurred, and looked about 15. I sometimes wonder what this mature, intelligent, professional man thought when a kid stepped out from behind the landing gear of a B-29 with a .45 at port arms and asked him to halt. There is a good chance that he had been through this drill before and expected a grown man to stop him.)

OPPORTUNITY KNOCKS

My original enlistment in the Air Force for three years will end in July, 1952--six months from now. Because of the Korean War, the Air Force has extended my enlistment for six months--until January 6, 1953. When I enlisted, Sue and I knew that someday we would marry. I now know that I need an education and our plans are that I will leave the Air Force when my enlistment expires, that we will marry in December, and that I will enroll at the University of Tennessee, join the ROTC, and use the

GI bill to get through school. Sue agrees that we can make it on the GI bill, and she is willing to work as well. This is the direction we are headed in early 1952. I now know that if I am ever to become a fighter pilot, I have to become an officer first--those are the rules. Then a bombshell falls into the middle of things.

The Air Force announces that it is reopening the Aviation Cadet program for pilots and navigators. The criteria for selection are: age; minimum nineteen and a half; education; high school plus two years of college or passing a two year college equivalency exam; physically fit, 20/20 eyesight, 28 teeth, etc. I am more than interested. If I can get into the Cadet program, it would take five years off the waiting time to become a fighter pilot. Whatever the outcome, I have to apply.

Soon after submitting my application, I am told that I must meet a board of officers who will determine whether or not to forward my application to Samson AFB for the physical and mental examinations. The board will determine if I am suitable officer material.

In a few days a board of three officers summons me for a hearing in a meeting room at Base Headquarters. I have a new haircut, am dressed for inspection, and am terrified as I salute the board and address the President, an Air force Major who is flanked by two Captains--all rated officers, two pilots, and one navigator: "Sir, Sergeant Kenneth R. Hughey reporting as ordered." The major returns my salute and asks me to have a seat. I sit; my heart is pushing a pounding surf through my inner ears. I hope I don't exhibit any outward symptoms.

The Major begins with some questions about my career so far and about my origins. In a few moments he, and the other two members are smiling, and I begin to feel at ease. I soon perceive that this is not an inquisition, and that these three officers are on my side. They are all on the young side for their rank and are immaculate in their Class A uniforms. I hope that their view of me is the same.

Soon the questions steer toward my decision to try to be a rated officer, and the Captain on my left reminds me that the Air Force is looking for "Rated" officers, not just Pilots, but Navigators as well, and asks what my reaction would be to being selected for a rated crew position other than Pilot. This question worries me a lot--largely because it has never occurred to me that I wouldn't be selected for Pilot training, but might instead be selected to become a Navigator. I know that to be an officer and leader, being a "team player" will be a necessity. I begin by saying, "I want to be Pilot, but I also want to be an officer. If I am chosen for another crew position, I will do it."

The Navigator then has some fun with the two Pilots with a couple of follow ups. "Have you thought about what it might be like to be in the airplane with no access to the controls, but responsible for other crew duties? Would you wish you were up front?" The Major smiles and rescues me. The Major wants to know if I have thought about what type of airplane I would like to fly. I tell him that I want to fly fighters. The three look at each other and the Major continues: "Along the lines that my friend here just started, what would you think if, after you finish Pilot training, you are assigned to fly transports?" I will never forget my response. Without thinking: "I would wish to be flying fighters."

I think this final response, straight from my innocent, childish heart, sealed my fate. The three men chuckle and thank me for joining them. I stand, salute, execute a perfect about face, and march out of the room. Soon after this interview in March 1952, I am scheduled to go to Samson AFB in central upstate New York for three days to take the series of physical and mental examinations.

The tests are grueling. Several parts of the physical hand-eye co-ordination tests worry me, and I am fearful that I'm not doing well enough to pass. When the tests are finished, the applicants disappear in all directions.

I return to Griffiss AFB and go about my business, and in about two weeks the personnel clerk notifies me that I have been accepted as a candidate for Pilot Training and will be called up within a few months for assignment to a class. Along with this notification, I am instructed to check in with the Dental Office at Griffiss for essential repair to my teeth.

I go to the Dental office at the base hospital the next day with the written notification in hand. In a few minutes, I am ushered into the office of the head of the Dental department--an Air force Major. He is cordial and explains to me that I must have twenty eight of my own teeth in perfect working order to become a pilot trainee. He immediately examines my teeth and tells me that we will be spending some time together for the next few weeks. The next day I begin a series of visits with the head of the Dental department that result in twenty seven restorations and two extractions. I have two molars that he could not salvage. One of the extracted molars comes out in seven pieces that he reconstructs on his operative pallet to be sure he has it all. Except for once when I had an abscessed tooth, I had never been in a dentist's office for treatment, but now I have thirty perfect teeth.

My acceptance into the Aviation Cadet program is a complication to my life. Sue and I have planned to be married during the Christmas holidays this year--1952. The Air Force has extended my enlistment for six months, so, with any luck, I can be enrolled at the University of Tennessee in the Spring Semester beginning in January. But now I have an opportunity to cut five years off the wait to become a fighter jock. I know that later this year I will be assigned to a class and fifteen months later (assuming I succeed), I will be an Air Force Pilot. The problem is that Cadets must be single, and if I wind up in Pilot training, we can't be married this coming December.

LES

One of our Calibration trips takes us to a Radar Site in Vermont. The man in charge of maintaining the Radar system is Chief Warrant Officer (CWO) Marshall D. Lester. All of our team on this trip know Mr. Lester as "Les." He is nearly everybody's favorite person.

When I joined the 7th Radar Calibration Unit in 1950, less than two years ago, Les was a Staff Sergeant and the senior NCO on all of our Calibration exercises. He had served in WWII as a Pilot and flew the "Hump" on a regular basis. When the war ended, he left the Air Corps as a Captain, and took a job flying for TACA Airlines. In 1948, the original TACA found itself involved in a series of trades that eventually led to a consolidation of several airlines in South America. One of the results was that Les found himself living in South Florida, unemployed, with his only possessions a 1947 Lincoln Zephyr Coupe, a wardrobe, and a toilet kit.

Jobs were scarce and Les's search included asking the Air Force to recall him as a commissioned officer. The Air Force wasn't hiring officers just then, but as an alternative, offered to allow him to enlist as a Non-commissioned Officer (NCO). He accepted and came on active duty as a Staff Sergeant. He is now famous in the small world that I live in.

Because of his background, knowledge, experience, and outstanding performance as an NCO, Les moved up quickly. He was promoted to Technical Sergeant just after I joined the organization at Langley AFB, and within a year, he was promoted to Master Sergeant--as far as he can go in the enlisted ranks. Six months later, he was eligible to apply for a Warrant Officers position, and soon became a Warrant Officer (WO), Grade Four (W-4). There are four steps in the WO grade structure, and

Les moved up right away. Having an opportunity to consult with him regarding my plans is a windfall.

As soon as we get to the site, I speak to Les and ask him to set aside some time for me to talk about my career. He agrees, and promises to find some time that we can talk privately. During our stay, there is a lull in activity, and Les snags me and invites me for a walk outside. The countryside in Vermont is a perfect scene for a confidential meeting. We walk a ways from the site and there is a stone fence that's a good spot to sit and talk. I brief Les on what has happened to me since he left the Calibration Squadron. Les then briefs me on how I might proceed.

He begins by telling me that most likely when I finish Pilot Training, I will be commissioned as a Reserve Officer, and details the steps that I must take as soon as possible to obtain a "regular" commission. He describes the application process in great detail. I will need several special Officer Effectiveness Reports (OERs). Routinely, an Officer is rated by his/her superiors once each year, but for purposes of certain applications, he/she can request a special OER covering much shorter periods, without direct supervision. Les says to get at least ten to include in the application, and to start working this problem as soon as I arrive at a permanent duty assignment after being commissioned.

Step two is to get a college degree as soon as I can. He briefs me on the details of an Air force organization at Wright-Patterson AFB, Ohio, called the Air Force Institute of Technology (AFIT). AFIT sponsors Air Force Officers to attend college full time for the last two years of most technical undergraduate degrees. This means that after commissioning I will have to go to school at night to pick up two years of college credit, including math through calculus. The Air Force also has a program called "Operation Bootstrap" that arranges for near-by colleges to send professors to Air force Bases to instruct classes on a demand basis.

Operation Bootstrap also arranges for correspondence courses. The bottom line--"where there is a will, there is a way."

Les follows up with suggestions as to how to proceed with AFIT. He reminds me that by the time I am doing these things that I need to do to secure a regular commission and a college degree, I will be a pilot and will have access to airplanes to fulfill one hundred hours per year required cross country proficiency time, and can fly to Wright-Patterson AFB and visit the AFIT office any time I wish. So, as soon as I am situated in a plan that will lead me to completion of the two year requirement, I should pay a personal visit to AFIT to introduce myself and provide AFIT with my plan. AFIT will then become a willing partner in my quest for higher education.

I leave this visit to Vermont with Mr. Lester's briefing firmly engraved in my head and heart.

Inside me, unknown to anyone else, my soul is in turmoil. I don't know it now, but I need maturity. I am facing an issue that takes a man to face, not an immature boy. For several weeks, I stew, and then come to the conclusion that I really have no choice other than plan A, the original plan to leave the Air Force when this enlistment is up, marry my sweetheart, enroll at the University of Tennessee, join the ROTC Corps, graduate from UT, and go to Pilot Training as an Officer. Even if something sidetracks Pilot training, I will have an education and can make a living for my future family.

The personnel clerk in our squadron is Sergeant Sexton--a friend and fellow poker player. He's from Kentucky, is an all-around good guy, and is far more mature than I. Having made my decision, I make it a point to cruise by the orderly room and inform Sergeant Sexton that I wish to withdraw my application for Pilot Training. I tell him. He is always busy behind his typewriter and always smiling. He stops typing long enough to smile and say: "Don't worry about it, it's a done deal." I stop worrying about it--it's a done deal.

Summer 1952 passes and in September I am at Ernest Harmon AFB in Newfoundland as a member of a Calibration Team waiting for a C-124 to take us to Thule, Greenland to calibrate our most distant early warning site. We have been delayed due to weather and availability of an airplane.

The Officer in Charge (OIC) of this team is Lt. Carpenter. After breakfast today we have congregated at the Airman's club to play cribbage, table tennis, shuffle board, or maybe pinochle, to pass the time. I am in the middle of a cribbage game when the public address systems pages Lt. Carpenter, who is watching the cribbage game. He walks over to a wall phone to take the incoming call, and, after a brief conversation, he puts his hand over the phone microphone, calls my name, and waves for me to come over and join him.

I approach him, and he says to me that my orders to report for my next assignment as an Aviation Cadet for pilot training have arrived at our headquarters at Griffiss AFB. He is talking to our squadron First Sergeant who is about to begin the process of arranging for my immediate return to Griffiss to be processed out and transferred to Lackland AFB to join a Pilot training Class. Lt. Carpenter knows my plans and knows that I had requested our personnel NCO to withdraw my application. With his hand over the phone mike so our first soldier can't hear us, he asks me what I want to do--do I want to return and go to Pilot training, or do I want to tell the First Sergeant to cancel the assignment?

I am suddenly in a quandary. At the moment, I am committed to a wedding date in December; my future wife has made all the plans-- the date, the place, the ceremony. It never once occurred to me that Sergeant Sexton hadn't cancelled my application. Now, the prospect of a commission and pilot's wings by the end of next year is overwhelming. Lt. Carpenter knows what is going through my head. He says: "What have you got to lose; you can bow out after you get to Griffiss." I ask: "How much time do I have to make up my mind?" He looks at his watch, looks at me, and says: "Ten seconds." I tell him I want to take the assignment.

Lt. Carpenter spends the next few minutes talking to the First Sergeant. When he hangs up, we sit down and talk. In a few minutes, the personnel section here at Ernest Harmon will issue me a set of orders to return to Griffiss AFB immediately. These orders will include a Number 1 priority, which means I can't be bumped from any flight by other than a General Officer or an Emergency Leave.

I am a mess inside. I am excited at the prospect of Pilot Training, but am bleeding inside at even bringing up this subject with Sue. I think about the briefing from Les, the long travail through a four year college program on the GI Bill, Sue's feelings, and my own ambiguous feelings.

I am soon packed, and Lt. Carpenter and I are at Base Operations. We go to the Operations Counter and show the dispatcher my orders. There is a C-97 on the flight line now that is scheduled to load a group of civilian construction workers from Thule, who are on their way home to spend the winter. Since the airplane has no Generals or Emergency leaves, I will have a seat on this airplane that will get me to Otis AFB in about three hours.

Later that day I disembark at Otis AFB and am not surprised that there are no flights going anywhere near Rome, New York. I remember the days at Keesler when I hitch hiked home for weekends. I haven't hitch hiked lately, but I have no hesitation about it. I grab a local bus and am soon standing on the side of the main highway heading west-north-west toward Rome, New York and am soon in Rome.

My next stop is home in Finley, Tennessee. I have spoken to Sue several times before I get my bags completely packed and have cleared out of Griffiss. The ride home by train is tedious. I finally make it to Dyersburg on the Illinois Central City of New Orleans for a week's visit before reporting to Lackland. Sue and I agree that the best thing we can do for our future is to postpone our marriage for one year so that we can have some financial security sooner than later. We make this decision together. She listens carefully to my career plan regarding the whole scenario outlined by Les Lester and believes it's the best we can do. Neither of us is overjoyed by the delay in our marriage, but we are willing to do it. I am assigned to Class 53-H scheduled to graduate on December 16, 1953. Our new wedding date is December 26, 1953.

Retrospective: This decision was the most painful thing that Sue and I have ever done. As it turned out, the plan worked. We married on December 16, 1953 and we successfully executed the rest of the plan. I began my education at my first permanent assignment at Tyndall AFB near Panama City, Florida. I went to school three or four nights a week, and Sue had a good job all the time we were there. We worked hard, but we also had a lot of fun. We had good friends there and went home to visit our families regularly. The drives from Panama City to Tennessee and later from Valdosta, Georgia to Tennessee weren't that long, and going home was always a treat.

Just as planned, when I arrived at Tyndall, I began my application for a regular commission, and submitted it in 1956. After getting enrolled in extension classes conducted by Florida State University on Tyndall AFB and later at Moody AFB, I did exactly what Les Lester suggested: I checked out a T-33 and made the 2 hour flight to Wright-Patterson AFB to visit AFIT. I was a Second Lieutenant in a flight suit when I walked into AFIT headquarters and approached the counter in the reception area. The receptionist treated me like a General, and in a few minutes I was in the inner sanctum sitting in an office with an Air Force Major, planning my curriculum and preparing a file with my name on it. As I completed each semester of work, AFIT updated that file until my application was complete.

In May, 1957, I was sworn into the regular Air Force. In early 1959, AFIT notified me that I would be going to school somewhere in pursuit of a degree in Aeronautical Engineering. Soon they sent me a list of schools to consider as choices, with the caveat that I might not get my first choice, but they would try. I chose the University of Colorado, and was assigned there, and eventually earned a B.S. in Aeronautical Engineering.

Thank you, Les, wherever you are!!

Part III

Preflight

Pilot training begins with three months of "Pre-Flight Training" at Lackland AFB, Texas. The curriculum is essentially the same as Officer's Candidate School. It's a three month cram course on how to be an Officer and a gentleman. We spend all day in the classroom and spend the evenings studying.

Company grade Tactical Officers (Tac Officers) act as upper classmen for us and give us the dickens at every turn. We memorize a lot of "stuff" and are prepared to answer detailed questions any time we are approached by a Tac Officer. The conversation might begin: "Mr. Hughey, can you tell me the time of day?"

"Sir, since the inner workings and hidden mechanisms of my chronometer are not in accord with the great celestial movements by which time is commonly reckoned, I cannot state the exact time. However, without fear of being too far wrong, I can safely state the approximate time is sixteen minutes five ticks and four tocks past the hour of fourteen hundred, Sir."

Any deviation from the canned response results in a request for a demerit slip, which we carry in a properly buttoned pocket. Too many demerits result in having to walk "tours" of one hour each on the parade ground during our leisure time on weekends. Too many demerits could ruin one's entire weekend, and there were many ways to earn demerits.

The academic material seems appropriate for future officers. We are exposed to world geography; ideologies, especially Communism; efficiency engineering; military organizations; governments of major countries, etc. We also learn to prepare and deliver speeches.

The biggest single event our Pre-Flight class experiences is a trip to Washinton, D.C. to march in the Inaugural parade for President Eisenhower and Vice President Nixon.

Primary Flight Training

First Solo

From Lackland, I am assigned to Marana Air Base, Arizona for Primary Flight Training. I, along with several others, arrive at the Marana train stop in late January, 1953. We get off the train, and an Air Force blue bus transports us to our quarters. Marana, like all Primary training bases is run by a civilian contractor--in this case Hal Darr, owner of Darr Aero Tech, is the operator. The instructors are all civilians with Air Force oversight.

Our quarters are individual buildings arranged around a quadrangle with a Club at one end of the Headquarters building and Mess Hall at the other. The whole thing is new and very nice. Two Cadets share each room and a common bath area that is adequate for the number of occupants.

We spend half a day on the flight line and half a day in the classroom. Our academics includes, among other things, Meteorology, Engineering, Radio procedures, Morse code, and Navigation.

Each civilian flight instructor has a table in the flight line ready room that accommodates four students. We treat our instructors with the same military courtesy as commissioned officers. On the half days that we fly, we gather in the ready room and sit at our instructors table. When our instructor comes to our table we stand at attention until he bids us "at ease," and then we sit. Our flying day always begins and ends at the instructor's table with a discussion of the day's flight activities. My instructor is Mr. Don Dolan.

Mr. Dolan has four students, the usual complement. Two are French, one is a Commissioned Officer, and I am the fourth. (Photo 1)

Photo 2

Left to right: Jean Pierre Berdeaux; Edmond G. Carnez; Kenneth R. Hughey (sitting on the wing); Donald J. Dolan, Instructor; Lt. Bob Wells.

By February 16, we understand our flying training schedule. We know that the first airplane that we will fly is a Piper PA-18--a piper cub on steroids. It has a 235 Cubic Inch four cylinder Lycoming engine that develops 108 horsepower. Our class is the first class to begin pilot training in this airplane. Prior to our class, Pilot trainees began their flying careers in a North American T-6--a much bigger airplane with a Pratt and Whitney R-1385 radial engine that develops 550 horsepower. The T-6 is a handful for a beginner and requires at least twenty hours of training before first solo. The Air Force decided that it would be more efficient for future pilots to begin in a less complex airplane--solo flight would require a lot less time, and beginners could actually progress faster. Today I take my first flight as a Pilot trainee.

During our meetings with the flying squadron last week, we spent a lot of time with our instructors, and by now we know what to expect during this phase of our training. We would spend twenty hours flying the PA-18 and then move on to the T-6. We were expected to solo the PA-18 after no more than ten hours of dual instruction.

Today's flight is short. Mr. Dolan helps me taxi the airplane and get it off the ground. We work on fundamentals and I have an opportunity to begin to get the feel of the airplane; to use pressure on the controls, not movement; to be smooth and not to over control; to trim the airplane, to control attitude, air speed and direction; and become accustomed to a three dimensional environment. This airplane does not have a radio, so we have learned to understand light signals.

With Mr. Dolan's tutelage, I soon can do air work with precision and with a comfortable feeling that I can fly an airplane, but soon discover that I have a major problem to overcome if I am ever to become a pilot--I get air sick near the end of each flight, and I'm sure it's just plain fear of landing the airplane. I take Mr. Dolan's advice to talk to our flight surgeon. The flight surgeon advises me to stop drinking any alcoholic beverages, to get plenty of rest, and to observe a bland diet. The air sickness stops, but I'm still having a struggle making myself land the airplane.

At the end of flight number six on February 27, 1953, I ask Mr. Dolan to complete the landing. After we park the airplane, Mr. Dolan takes me aside on the ramp for a private conversation. He always speaks quietly and politely, and today he is extra quiet and extra polite. He explains to me that I cannot continue flight training, unless I have a turnaround regarding landing the airplane. He reiterates the obvious--if you can't land the airplane, you can't fly. Period. Today is Friday. Our next flight is scheduled for March 2--the coming Monday. Mr. Dolan lets me know, in his own gentlemanly way, that unless I make some considerable headway on our next flight, that I will soon become history as an Air Force Pilot. I listen carefully, and my insides are churning. My morale, already low, plummets into an abyss and bounces off the bottom.

When he finishes, it's my turn to speak: "The next time we fly, I will land this airplane, even if it winds up in pieces."

Mr. Dolan senses danger in my response and continues his counsel. "Why do you think I'm here? You have to have confidence in me. I'm not about to let you hurt this airplane, or me, or yourself. Maybe that's your problem. Think about it this week end and we'll see what happens on Monday." He heads off across the flight line walking briskly, and holding the seat pack up high enough that it doesn't bump him in the butt as he walks. I do the same, but my spirits are dragging out my tracks as I follow him from about ten steps behind.

Inside, we do the customary get together at Mr. Dolan's table. He wishes us all a nice week end, smiles, and we stand at attention as he rises and leaves the room. I look forward to a dismal week end.

Monday comes. It's comfortable in the desert. We are flying out of the Picacho Peak Auxiliary field today. Some of us will begin with a flight from Marana and land at Picacho. The rest of us board the bus on the flight line at Marana and ride for about 30 minutes to Picacho. Mr. Dolan flies the first flight of the morning with one of the other students--I am next. We arrive at Picacho and watch as students shoot landings with their instructors. Some of my classmates have soloed and shoot landings alone. In a while, Mr. Dolan arrives and goes around the circuit with one of his other students. I watch as they make three landings and then park the airplane. They take a short break and Mr. Dolan talks to his other student briefly and motions to me "Let's go."

We crawl in the airplane, crank up and, per our morning briefing, taxi out and take off to do a brief session of air work. After a bit of loosening up, Mr. Dolan tells me to enter the pattern for a touch and go landing.

I've had all week-end to stew and have decided that if this is my last flight with Mr. Dolan, I will make it a memorable one for both of us, one way or the other.

Air work is easy for me now. I cruise onto the entry leg to the traffic pattern for Runway 36 at Picacho at 2200 feet, turn downwind and hold my airspeed at 80 miles per hour (mph). As I pass the numbers on the runway, I turn on the carburetor heat, retard the throttle to idle, and trim the airplane for a 70 mph glide. As the airplane glides, I keep the touch down point on the runway in my cross check. When it looks like it's time, I make a gliding turn to base leg and hold 70 mph. On the base leg I advance the throttle briefly to clear the engine and then continue the 70 mph glide until it's time to turn final. I make the final turn and trim the airplane for 60 mph. I'm looking at the touchdown point from 300 feet in the air, and I'm lined up with the runway. At the moment there's nothing to do but keep things just like they are.

The Numbers on the runway remain in about the same place in the front wind screen as the 60 mph glide continues, and then they begin a slow movement upward. I am close to the ground; it's time to break the glide and let the airplane settle toward the numbers. I keep increasing the pitch to keep the airplane from touching the ground. The wheels touch and the airplane skips into the air. I keep the nose straight down the runway with rudder and increase pitch to a three point attitude. The airplane touches down again, and I concentrate on keeping it heading straight down the runway with the stick all the way aft. We roll about 200 feet and I hear Mr. Dolan's voice in my headset: "Take it around."

I push the carburetor heat in, open the throttle, let the tail of the airplane lift off the ground, and concentrate on making a normal take-off. We are quickly airborne and I trim the airplane for an 80 mph climb. This is the seventh landing that I have ridden through with Mr. Dolan, and the first one that Mr. Dolan didn't make. It was not a perfect landing, but it wasn't far from it. I learned a lot by doing it. On the next approach, I hold the airplane off a little longer and it settles onto the runway in a three point attitude.

We shoot six more landings and I make all of them. A couple of them are close to perfect. I now know that the ball game is over, and that I have won!!

I don't fly on Tuesday. On Wednesday March 4, we make a much shorter flight. Monday's flight was an hour and fifteen minutes. Today we fly 45 minutes and I make four landings. On Friday March 6, we fly 55 minutes and I make three landings. On Monday March 9, we do more air work and Mr. Dolan shows me how to loop the airplane-- strictly extra-curricular in that we aren't supposed to do acrobatics in this airplane.

On Wednesday March 11, we do just a little air work and return to Picacho to shoot landings. I make five touch and go landings and as we drift on downwind for number six, I hear: "Make this one a full stop." That's the way the last landing has occurred on the past three flights, so I do what I'm told. When we land and clear the runway, Mr. Dolan tells me to taxi over to the run up area and stop. When we stop, Mr. Dolan gets out of the airplane and secures the rear seat. He stands just outside the cockpit and looks me in the face as the engine ticks over quietly. "Remember, that without me in the back, the airplane will seem a little tail light. You'll need a little different trim, and the airplane will sail a little further down the runway before it touches down. Just keep it straight and don't worry about it. Make three full stop landings."

He steps away from the airplane toward the instructor who is sitting in a lawn chair with an Aldis Lamp controlling traffic. Mr. Dolan stands behind him as the Instructor aims the Aldis Lamp at me and flashes it Green. I move onto the runway and look his way again. Here comes the steady Green light. I release the brakes and open the throttle. The tail rises immediately and I'm soon airborne. This is Heaven. My world will never be the same again.

After the second landing I taxi to the hold position. There is another airplane on final, and I stop well short of the runway. The airplane on final is a solo student, and I watch his approach with great interest. He touches down wheels first quite a ways before he reaches the numbers. He just didn't round out soon enough. The airplane bounces. A little power and a new round out would cure this problem, but the cure doesn't come. The airplane hits the ground wheels first and bounds into the air again and I see the propeller speed up. The airplane stalls about ten feet in the air and drops off to the right. The right wing tip and the right main gear strike the ground simultaneously, and the right main gear collapses.

The airplane is stopped dead with the propeller turning at what I would guess to be about 1200 rpm with the tips just barely clearing the ground. The Instructor, who is directing traffic, and Mr. Dolan run to the airplane, and the other Instructor reaches into the airplane through the left window. The engine quits. Mr. Dolan motions me to taxi to the tie down area. (See Photo 2 for the results of the accident I just observed. The perpetrator was a classmate who successfully completed pilot training. Note Picacho Peak is the shadow in the background.)

Photo 3 March 11, 1953

*The low contrast shape in the background behind the right wing
of the airplane is Pichaco Peak. I had just watched one of my
classmates break this airplane on his first solo flight.*

I make three solo landings on each of my next two flights and then
fly totally alone for some long and fun flights just practicing air work,
and on one flight I fly for an hour and a half and make seven landings.
On my last flight, I have an hour and twenty five minutes remaining to
make exactly 20 hours in the PA-18, so I go sight-seeing all over the
place and come in and land.

*Retrospective: Forty years later, one of my high school classmates, Sam
Bradshaw, buys a PA-18 to tow his glider. I "borrow" it from him from time to
time when I am visiting Dyersburg. It's great fun.*

A "REAL" AIRPLANE

Now, it's on to a "real" airplane. Up until now, every chance we've had,
we have spent time on the flight line with upper classmen as they prepare
for solo flight in the T-6. It's a big boost for our morale to be around
those who are preceding us through the regimen of becoming Air Force

Pilots. Just a week or so ago, three of us walked through pre-flight and start up with one of our upper classmen--Aviation Cadet Deerenberg, from The Netherlands.

Mr. Deerenberg was very happy to have us and we learned a lot as he explained the preflight to us, and then, when he went through the starting procedures, we were standing on the wing roots listening and watching every move he made. I was standing on the right side of the cockpit as he went through the final items on the check list. The pitch control set to "full increase;" throttle open about 1/2 inch; mixture control full rich; three primer strokes; Call to the fire guard, "clear;" engage the starter for two blades; Magneto switch to "Both;" the engine fires and a puff of blue smoke bursts from the exhaust stack as Deerenberg adjusts the throttle to idle. The deep throated roll of a 1,340 cubic inch Pratt & Whitney radial engine rattles our rib cages and results in an immediate acceleration of our pulse rates.

We step down to the ramp and remain clear as Deerenberg adds a few RPM and lets the airplane roll forward. We see his right shoulder drop as he pushes the control stick forward to unlock the tail wheel. He taps the right main wheel brake to bring the airplane around 90 degrees to exit the parking area. He taps the left brake, and the tail wheel locks into sync with the rudder pedals. The airplane rolls out to the taxiway and makes a smooth left turn and taxis out to the runway for run-up and take-off.

We three fledglings stand in total awe of Mr. Deerenberg.

On March 25, 1953, I crawl into the front seat of T-6-G #876 and do my best to emulate Mr. Deerenberg's cool demeanor on my first flight in the T-6. Mr. Dolan is in the back seat. I go through the pre-start check list and call "Clear" to the crew chief, who is standing about ten feet in front of the airplane to my right. The crew chief raises his right hand above his head for a couple of turns as he calls back: "Clear." I depress the starter switch and hold it down and the prop starts to move. I see two blades flip by over the top of the cowling and move the magneto switch to "Both." The engine immediately chuffs a couple of time and bursts into life. I reduce the throttle a bit to keep the RPM at about 600. I've got the stick all the way back and I move both feet to depress and hold the brakes on both rudder pedals. The crew chief moves the chocks out of the way and positions himself to my left front, waiting for me to decide to taxi.

This, of course, is my first flight in an airplane with a radio. I call Marana Tower: "Marana, Air Force 876 for taxi." Marana responds: "876 cleared to taxi to Runway 30, current altimeter 29.96." I recheck the altimeter and adjust it to 29.96. Field elevation is 1220 feet. I set the altimeter to read 1220 feet, and take note of the slight difference in the altimeter setting and the field elevation for future reference. Mr. Dolan takes the controls and I follow him through as we taxi out. When we are on the taxiway, I take the controls and "S" turn down the taxiway to the run-up area. We could get away with taxi-ing straight ahead in the PA-18, but not in this airplane. We have to keep S-ing to clear ahead. The engine up front totally obscures the view straight ahead.

I like this airplane immediately and immensely. It's big, heavy, and solid. The nine cylinder radial engine speaks with authority that vibrates through your body. I am anxious to get on the runway and open up the throttle.

We go through the pre take-off check list, and Marana Tower clears us for take-off. I let the airplane roll a few feet to line up precisely and then smoothly advance the throttle forward to the stop. The cowling vibrates as the roar of the engine pulls us down the runway at an astonishing rate. I let the stick float to a neutral position, no pressure either forward of back, and the tail rises from the ground as the nose drops and the horizon cuts across the cowling until the center of the cowling appears to be about three inches above the horizon.

The airplane rolls straight down the runway as I stand on the right rudder to keep the nose from drifting to the left and hold enough back pressure to keep the nose right where it is. The airplane lifts off the ground and we're soon doing over 100 miles per hour. I raise the gear, trim the airplane for a 110 mph climb, adjust the throttle to thirty inches of mercury, and retard the propeller control to 2,000 Revolutions per Minute (RPM). At 2,200 feet, I make a 45 degree left turn to exit traffic and continue climbing. As we climb, I adjust the throttle to hold 30 Inches of mercury and at 4500 feet, I close my canopy and adjust the mixture. All this time Mr. Dolan is coaching me through these maneuvers, and my cup is running over with pleasure.

We climb out to 6,000 feet to do some fundamental air-work. At level off, I reduce the throttle to 25 inches of mercury and decrease propeller speed to 1,850 RPM. Our airspeed is 140 miles per hour. Mr. Dolan spends a few minutes discussing power settings, along with how to properly control the mixture and cowl flaps in flight. As we climb, the mixture becomes richer as a natural consequence of the air pressure dropping. One of the most important items to consider during climbs and descents is how to properly control the mixture of air and gasoline that is delivered to the engine. The cowl flaps regulate the airflow around the air cooled engine, and we use them to regulate the engine temperature.

The throttle quadrant controls three items: the throttle itself controls the manifold pressure; the Propeller lever controls propeller speed; the mixture control controls the mixture of air and gasoline delivered to the engine via the carburetor. A big part of today's lesson is to make these adjustments to keep the engine running smoothly no matter what we're doing.

We fly through a simulated traffic pattern and return to Marana and land. Mr. Dolan does the landing today and makes it look easy. I am anxious to try a landing.

We fly several flights concentrating on air work, and I only try one landing per flight. I have no anxiety about any aspect of flying this airplane, and am happy with my progress. If given the opportunity, I would gladly fly alone.

Soon, I am making more than one landing per flight, and then, as required by the curriculum, I ride with another instructor as a "pre-solo" check. The other instructor is a bit older than Mr. Dolan, flew combat in P-51s, and shot down three German fighters over Europe. His name is Gillette, and is fun to be around and to fly with. His conversation while flying is interesting and fun, as well as profitable. I would give a lot to have a recording of his colloquy as I demonstrated a rudder controlled power stall for him. Here is an attempt.

A power on stall can be a daunting experience. The sequence begins by clearing the area and then pitching up into a 45 degree climb with the power set for climb--30 inches of mercury and 2,000 RPM. The airplane slows down rapidly. As the airspeed diminishes, the idea is to keep increasing back pressure to hold the 45 degree attitude. Ultimately, the stick is full aft and the nose starts to drop as the airplane stalls. As the nose drops, the airplane tries to fall off on one wing or the other. The exercise is to hold a constant heading by using the rudder. We call this "walking the rudder." The airplane acts like a bucking bronco as it pitches downward. When the nose drops, the heavy front of the airplane pulls the nose down, breaking the stall, and the airplane, for a moment is flying. But, with the stick full aft, the nose rises and the airplane stalls again. This situation keeps repeating itself until the airplane is in a near vertical dive. The idea is to learn the feel of the airplane in this situation and how to cope with it.

We terminate the stall when the airplane arrives at a 45 degree nose-low position by releasing the back pressure on the stick allowing the airplane to regain flying speed. Since the airplane is in a steep dive, it will gain speed quickly and it's time to control the throttle and pitch to keep from gaining too much airspeed in the recovery.

I pitch up to begin the maneuver, and Mr. Gillette's calm voice describes the maneuver as I do my best to do it correctly: "As the airplane pitches up the propeller is up there in front, turning and turning; it is a gyroscope and is desperately attempting to remain stable in space. You, however, have the control surfaces of the airplane in your hands and feet and will do all you can to keep this beast behaving properly as it seems to wish to defeat your every attempt to do so." This speech continues throughout the maneuver with Mr. Gillette enunciating every word much like Ink Spots Tenor, Bill Kenny, as he so carefully articulates his feelings when he sings "If I didn't care."

I fight the beast for what seems like an hour, but is really just a few seconds, as Mr. Gillette enjoys the ride. He asks for other demonstrations of my proficiency, and then to return to Marana. I make two touch and go landings, and then, seemingly tired and bored, he asks me to do a full stop landing. He never once touched the controls during this one hour and ten minute ride.

Two days later I solo the T-6.

Soon we do cross country training that includes two solo "round robins" that begin at Marana and fly various routes such as Marana to Grapevine to Phoenix to Marana or Marana to Willcox to Safford to Marana. We are doing acrobatics on a lot of our flights and are assigned to practice acrobatics before landing after each of our solo cross county flights.

Acrobatic training includes slow roll, barrel roll, loop, Immelman, snap roll, half roll and reverse, clover leaf, Cuban Eight, and precision spins. The toughest of these maneuvers to do well is the slow roll. I'm not sure I ever get the airplane to execute a perfect slow roll.

A "Blown" Landing Stage

A part of our training involves "Landing Stages"--a system of scoring the pilot's ability to perform accurate landings. The stage is a series of six full stop landings. Instructors at the side of the runway grade each approach and landing. The idea is to score as low as possible. A perfect approach and three point landing on the target spot that is about the length of the airplane would be scored a 1. If the landing is short or long by the size of the touchdown spot, the grader will add 1, making the score for such a landing a 2. If the landing is short or long by twice the size of the spot, the grader will add 2, making that landing a 3, and so forth. If the contestant exceeds 18, he will have failed. The graders add points for bounced landings or other things that are outside the limits of a perfect approach. For example, if one adds power on the final glide in order to make the spot, the grader can add points, depending on how much power and how long applied. The lowest possible score for a stage is 6. An 18 is a bust.

It's May 22, 1953, and I am scheduled to fly the last of three Landing Stages that we must pass to qualify to continue in training. I have done well on the first two, and today is my birthday, so I expect (or at least hope) to give myself a nice birthday present. I am scheduled to shoot the stage at Red Rocks Auxiliary--about a ten minute flight to the north west of Marana. I will take off from Marana, do the stage, and ride the bus back to Marana later in the morning.

I pre-flight T-6 Number 836 and am very uncomfortable as the desert sun tries to fry my hide. All I can think about is to get in the airplane and climb out with the canopy open and getting high enough to cool off a little before flying the stage. I'm soon airborne and headed for Red Rocks. I climb with the canopy open and finally reach some cool air just in time to descend into Red Rocks. The instructor on the ground clears me into the pattern for the first full stop.

This is a "power on approach" that is designed to exhibit the pilot's ability to use a slower approach speed with full flaps and power; the kind of approach that one would use to land on a short field. I set up on final and the approach looks pretty good to me, but it is awfully hot in the cockpit. As I approach the spot, I am a little high, but since a go around is an automatic 6, I have to try for it. I chop the throttle to idle and make a lousy landing way past the spot. No matter, I'll shoot five one's and everything will be o.k.

I taxi back to the take-off end of the runway and the instructor clears me for take-off. On the second approach, I just can't tell where I am. What is wrong? I'm way long again and the touchdown wasn't a perfect three point either.

I taxi back and go for the third try. This time on final, I am in a hopelessly long situation and abort the landing. As I take it around, the Instructor who is controlling traffic tells me that I have blown the stage and to return to Marana and land. I head for Marana.

Just after I exit the traffic pattern, I get instructions to return and land at Red Rocks. I don't want to overshoot this approach, so I deliberately come in lower than normal and get on the ground in good order, taxi to the parking line, and shut down. I get out of the airplane and walk toward the open shed in the middle of the field where there is shade and cold water. My classmates take one look at me and shy away. I have broken out with measles, and none of them want to be near me.

What a day! I have blown the stage and have measles. All I can think about is how long I will be grounded, and how am I going to make up failing the stage. I ride back to Marana in the extreme rear of the bus with my classmates bunched as far forward as possible and check into the dispensary as soon as I can get there. It is not a hospital, but it has a couple of hospital rooms and the flight surgeon puts me into one of them, and I am quarantined. I get ice water to drink and a cool room. The doctor says that I have German measles that are sometimes referred to as "three day measles." At least the three day part is good news.

On Sunday, my buddies are allowed to visit me but must stand at the door and not enter the room. Jim (better known as Willy, the Actor) Sutton tells me that Mr. Dolan is a very unhappy camper. All instructors want their students to do well and I am the only one of his that has blown a stage. Willy says that when the troops assembled on Friday, Mr. Dolan asked where I was. Willy told him that I was in the Hospital, to which the reply was: "He'd better be!"

The measles popped out on Friday morning, and by noon I was in quarantine. The Flight Surgeon said that the best he could hope for would be a return to flying status on Tuesday May 26. The lucky part is timing. I will only miss one day of flying and will have plenty of time to make up for the blown stage. I now know why the runway kept moving around on me on those approaches at Red Rocks.

On May 26, I am back in the air with Mr. Dolan and we do some air work and three power on landings. The following day I do a solo cross country and then do three instrument flights followed by a solo practice session for the power on stage along with a thirty minute acrobatic workout. On June 3, I head for Red Rocks and shoot the stage--a very respectable 9. Mr. Dolan is happy, which means I am happy.

PRIMARY FINALE

The remainder of Primary training is a hoot. On July 15, I take the Instrument Final Examination with Lt. Huxman, the Air Force flight examiner, and it's over in thirty five minutes, the total opposite of what happened to me on the power on stage.

I fly two more flights with Lt. Huxman. One has no other purpose than that Lt. Huxman flew routine instructional flights and has never flown with me except on the instrument check. We share some stick time and both of us enjoy the flight. This was more of a camaraderie flight, like flying with a big brother. Then on July 21, Lt. Huxman administers my final check ride, and I am finished with all requirements for graduation from Primary flight Training.

Several of us have been notified that we will go to Williams AFB, at Chandler Arizona, near Phoenix for Advanced Training.

On July 22, 1953, Brigadier General Wycliffe E. Steel, the father of our classmate, Wycliffe E. "Wick" Steel, Jr., comes to Marana as the guest speaker at our graduation from Primary Training and sends us off to our Advanced Training with a dynamite speech. Wick took some ribbing about his old man coming over from Lackland AFB where he presides over the Pilot Training program, but it all went up in smoke after we heard the General's speech.

I could never recount the entirety of General Steele's speech, but his pride in the Air Force and in his son and in all of us was conspicuously comforting and pleasant. His concluding remarks deserve better treatment than I can provide, but I have to try.

General Steele trained in the Stearman PT-17, a bi-wing airplane that was for years a primary trainer. During discussions and briefings in flight training, General Steele's instructor passed on some philosophy about flying, including some sage advice on dealing with emergencies. His philosophy was that if you find yourself in a hopeless situation that you have never discussed, rehearsed, or expected, and have no real solution remaining, shove the throttle to the firewall!! If you're going in anyway, make as big a splash as you can.

The General reiterated that not long after hearing this bit of advice, he found himself on a solo flight on final approach in a Stearman. He was lined up with the runway with the power at idle and everything looking good. As the airplane continued gliding toward the touchdown point, Mr. Steele (then an Aviation Cadet) began his round out for landing and discovered that the control stick had somehow become separated from the elevator and he had no pitch control. The inevitable result was not going to be pretty, and he had no idea what to do.

At that point, he recalled his instructor's philosophy about this kind of situation, and advanced the throttle all the way forward. With full power on the engine, the nose of the airplane began to rise, and Mr. Steele kept the airplane straight down the runway with the rudder, kept the wings level with the ailerons, and, when the airplane arrived over the runway numbers in a three point attitude, he instinctively chopped the throttle to idle, and the airplane made a three point landing.

During his closing remarks, he told us that he hoped that the next time he felt the cold icy breath of the "old grim reaper" on the back of his neck would be the last time. Meantime, he advised us, along with himself, as to what to do with the throttle when that time came.

The entire Cadet Wing is present in the base theatre to hear General Steele's speech to our class and rise as one at the General's closing. The standing ovation is loud and long, and I'm absolutely certain that none of us will ever forget it.

(Retrospective: Fourteen years later, on July 6, 1967, I am over North Viet Nam in a battle damaged F-4. Two minutes ago, my fellow crewman 1/Lt. Mel Pollack and I pulled out of a 45 degree dive with both engines on fire. Like General Steele, we each have done all that we can. Mel is in the back seat attempting to keep enough circuit breakers in place to keep some of our systems going. All of our communications systems are gone. All that I can do now is to open the throttles and hope that the engines will continue to turn and burn long enough to propel us to an area that will permit our rescue before we are forced to eject.

It doesn't happen that way. The engine fires finally take their toll and, when the airplane goes out of control, we bail out. The throttles are positioned at 100% power when the airplane makes a big splash with a lot of black smoke and, no doubt, a lot of debris, striking the ground very nearly directly underneath us as we descend in our parachutes. Somewhere, General Steele is enjoying his retirement and will live until April, 2004.)

Advanced Training at Willie Air Patch

A T-28 AND A SHOESHINE

Those of us who are assigned to Williams arrive here in time to spend the last week of July in the classrooms and on the flight line in Advanced Pilot Training. The first subjects include Meteorology, Engineering and Navigation. Meteorology follows us everywhere we go and is my most difficult subject. Navigation will take us past the low frequency and low altitude issues we were exposed to in Primary. Engineering is the most interesting and vital subject to us at this moment.

All of us are excited about checking out in the T-28, our next hurdle. The T-28 is a single engine 800 horsepower, propeller driven airplane designed to be a lead-in to jet aircraft. It is not jet powered, but is designed to handle more like a jet than the T-6. It is a tricycle gear airplane, as are all our jets, and has a canopy that affords visibility much like a jet fighter. Right now, the Engineering course is all about the T-28.

We spend half a day each day on the flight line, just like in Primary. My new flight instructor is Captain Wayne Sarver. As in Primary, each instructor is assigned four students. Later on, some students will be reassigned to other instructors, but that doesn't happen to me--I will remain with "Jake" Sarver for the duration, and fly with him almost exclusively, except at the very beginning when he has a sinus issue that grounds him for about a week.

During the first week, before we get acquainted with our instructors, we are asked to write an autobiography. The purpose is to provide the flight training squadron a perspective on the demographics of the class, as well as to facilitate becoming better acquainted with each of us. A day or so after we turn in the autobiography, we assemble on the flight line. The procedure is that we, the students, arrive at the flight line by marching in formation and go to our instructors table and wait for the instructor to arrive. We all know who our instructors are, and their table locations, but we don't yet have name plates for our flying clothing, and our instructors don't yet know any of us by name.

The four of us who are assigned to Capt. Sarver are seated at his table when he arrives. As he approaches our table, we stand at attention. He asks us to be seated and takes his seat at the head of the table. His first remark is: "Which of you is Mr. Hughey?" I am seated next to him on his left. I answer: "Sir, I am Mr. Hughey." I don't like the tone of voice and like it even less when he continues: "Well, Mr. Hughey, we understand that you learned to shine your shoes in your Pre-Flight training, is that correct?"

CAPT. WAYNE D. SARVER
Bellingham, Washington

JAKE

"Yes, sir." Something is terribly wrong. I recall making a remark in my autobiography that I was a Staff Sergeant when I was selected for the Cadet Program, and that when I attended Pre-Flight Training I learned to shine my shoes there. I had not intended the remark to be cynical or disrespectful in any way, but now suddenly realized that I was in hot water because of it.

"Well, Mr. Hughey, let me tell you something--I expect to be able to shave every morning in my reflection from your shoes. Do you under-stand that?"

"Yes, sir.""Let me see your shoes." He leans to his left as I swivel to my right and place my feet so he can see them.

Jake makes no comment and I move my feet back under the table. Jake is not finished.

"Mr. Hughey, we don't appreciate your cynicism, and we don't appreciate your attitude about the training program. Captain Denny is our squadron Executive Officer and wishes to speak to you. He is in his office right now waiting for you to report to him. You're now excused. Report back here after your visit with Captain Denny."

Speechless, I rise and head off to meet Captain Denny. My heart is pounding. I am scared and angry. These two officers have totally misread my remarks, and I will be in their spotlight from now on, assuming there is a "now on." We all know something about all of our instructors and staff by the grapevine. Captain Denny is a hard-nosed West Point graduate. This audience with him may be my dying gasp as a Cadet.

The walk from Jake's table to Captain Denny's office is about forty feet. I position myself at attention in front of his desk. He looks up, and I salute and report: "Sir, Aviation Cadet Kenneth R. Hughey reporting as ordered." He returns my salute. He looks angry.

"Mr. Hughey, I take it that Captain Sarver has explained to you why I asked to see you."

"Yes, Sir."

"We take exception to your remarks that seem to us to denigrate the Pre-flight Program and indicate that you may have an unacceptable attitude in terms of your training and expectations of becoming an officer and a pilot. This concerns us. We are taking no action at the moment, but want you to understand that we expect a lot from you and all of your class mates. I hope that this is the end of this subject." He still looks angry. "That will be all."

We exchange salutes. I do the best left face that I can muster and march away to return to Jake's table. As I approach and sit down, Jake is talking and continues as though nothing has happened.

Monday following my meeting with Captain Denny is August 3, 1953, our first day to fly. Last week we spent a lot of time in briefings and are as prepared as we can be. I am scheduled to fly the first period with Captain Sarver. We have already covered flight training issues and curriculum and know the requirements for check out. We notice that in Advanced Training, our first flight alone is not referred to as "solo," but as "check out." It's a subtle recognition that we have been elevated to the final step.

Minimum check out requirements in the T-28 are:

1. Three patterns and landings.
2. Three simulated forced landings.
3. Three no flap landings.
4. Two complete stall series.
5. Acrobatics, including Loop, Immelman, Clover Leaf, Cuban Eight, Spins and Roll.
6. Radio compass operation.
7. A minimum of two flights with an Instructor.

Jake and I take off from Williams on my first flight, and we will land at the Rittenhouse auxiliary Field. The T-28s use Rittenhouse during the day to reduce traffic at Williams AFB, just as we used auxiliary fields during primary. It is a 3700 foot strip with an open shelter in the center. We are soon in the practice area for some air work. At about 7,000 feet, just south of Rittenhouse, Jake reduces the power and tells me that this is a forced landing and sets up the power and partial flaps that reproduce the glide conditions with a dead engine.

I am very confident about this situation. We have gone over forced landings in detail in our briefings and, as I look over and down at Rittenhouse, I know exactly what to do. I want to be over the approach end of Runway 30 at 5,000 feet. The runway elevation is 1500 feet. This means that I will have 3,500 feet to complete a 360 degree turn and touch down on the first third of the runway.

I head for Rittenhouse with one eye on the runway and continuously scan the area for traffic. The initial "trick" is to plan my turns and headings to make that first check point that we call "high key." It's always better to be too high than too low. There are some things that are useless to you in an airplane, and altitude above you is just about the first.

There's no rush here. The airplane is quiet with the engine at a very low power setting. I need to plan my turns to eliminate or at least minimize any steep turn. I keep the approach end of the runway on my "radar" and I will do everything I can to arrive over the end of the runway at exactly 5,000 feet on the altimeter. As we close in on the "target," I am more and more confident. In a few minutes I am exactly where I want to be--in a shallow bank heading 330 degrees with the end of runway 30 just ahead, and we are at 5,500 feet. I will hit the "high key" at 5,000 feet just by playing this turn. Given nothing unusual, if we are dead on at the high key, a blind man can arrive on the deck by simply making a 360 degree turn and controlling airspeed and configuration.

At 5,000 feet I begin the 360 degree spiral toward the touch down point. The next check point is the low key--3500 feet on the altimeter and opposite the touchdown point. We are there in a little over a minute. I put down the gear, half flaps, trim the airplane for 110 knots and ease off the turn. I soon see that I am a bit high and extend some more flaps and re-trim for 100 knots. We've got the first third of the runway made. I put down the remaining flaps and aim for the approach end of the runway. We cross the approach end and are on the ground just past the numbers. Where has this airplane been? We can see out of it no matter where are, including at all angles of attack on or near the ground! Even a monkey like me can chew gum and make a decent landing at the same time.

Jake is not feeling well. The big reason we terminated the flight early with a simulated forced landing was so he could clear his sinuses in a gradual let down and not suffer too much. Once on the ground, Jake re-schedules my upcoming flights with CAPTAIN DENNY. YAHOO, HOORAY!!

Two days later I ride the bus to Rittenhouse and meet Captain Denny to continue the process. If the shoe shine issue is on his mind, he doesn't show it. We go right by the book and do all the things we're supposed to do. The next day we have a really busy work out and land at Rittenhouse. I hang around the airplane and complete the flight record that stays with the airplane. As he walks away, I hear him say something like: "...take 490 next period." I complete the records for the flight we just made and note that Capt. Denny is about half way to the "shack." I grab my 'chute and follow him. He turns around, notices me and takes a few steps back toward me. "Where are you going?"

"To the shack to wait for you."

"Didn't you hear what I said? Take 490 and do some air work and come back and shoot two full stop landings."

I do what he says. I feel like an aviator. I may never shine my shoes again.

This solo is by far the best flight I've ever made. When I open the throttle and hurtle down the runway in this nearly new airplane, ecstasy is not the word!!

The Advanced Training schedule moves a lot faster than Primary. We are still trainees, but are treated as pilots. I soon take a routine proficiency flight check with Major Crewe, a Wing Staff Officer. We exit the pattern and he asks me to show him some acrobatics. I do a ten minute routine and he's seen enough. We return to the traffic pattern and I make three landings and we log Thirty minutes of flying time. This is the first, last, and only time that I fly with Major Crewe. As far as I know, we both enjoyed the ride.

We conclude our T-28 training with a mix of formation, night flying, instruments, and acrobatics. On September 11, 1953, I take my last flight in the T-28 as a student pilot.

JETS AT LAST

We have 69 hours of flight time remaining to graduate from pilot training-- all in our first jet powered airplane, the Lockheed T-33, affectionately known as the "T-Bird." The minimum requirements for check out are:

1. At least four dual rides.
2. Fifteen satisfactory traffic patterns.
3. Ten satisfactory landings.
4. Ten throttle manipulations.
5. Three stall series.
6. Five vertical recoveries.
7. Three simulated forced landings to touchdown.
8. Demonstrate proficiency in acrobatics, closed traffic patterns, and no-flap landings.

Jake is in the back seat for my first flight in the T-Bird. I do the start-up, taxi, climb out, and we are soon at 20,000 feet in the practice area. This airplane is quite different. First of all, it is quiet and totally free of vibration. Next, there is no torque--when I release the brakes and we begin the take-off roll, the airplane rolls straight down the runway with almost no need for directional correction. Once airborne, one could fly the airplane through almost any kind of maneuver with no rudder needed. Everything it does is smooth.

I'm getting used to it, and after just a few minutes of "play," Jake takes the controls. He rolls the airplane, and simultaneously allows the nose to drop into a fairly steep dive. We are soon doing nearly five hundred miles per hour, and he hauls the airplane through a six g pull out and we are in a vertical climb. He then lays the control stick against the left stop and we begin a series of rolls, and as the airplane rolls, it is arcing over and the nose cuts the horizon as the airplane continues rolling and soon we're diving and still rolling and old mother earth is switching positions faster than I can count. He pops the wings level and says: "O.K., you've got it." At this point the horizon is a bit unstable and I'm not real sure that I want it.

I level off and begin the real learning part of this first flight. Jake keeps his hands off the stick and calmly talks me through a mild acrobatic series, and then takes the stick and demonstrates a vertical recovery. This is the most critical and important maneuver that we must do correctly. The T-33 can exhibit some "undesirable" flight characteristics if allowed to enter an uncontrolled flight regime. If, for instance, one allows the airplane to remain in vertical flight too long, as might occur in a sloppy entry into a loop, and the airplane runs out of airspeed, the resulting gyrations can be exciting. Thus, taking the airplane into the slow flight in a vertical attitude and handling it properly and safely is a requirement for check out.

The vertical recovery maneuver is quite simple, but requires judicious manipulation of the flight controls to avoid some kind of scary gyrations. The idea is that, if you find yourself in a near vertical attitude with the air speed decreasing at a quantum rate, fix it now! The fix is to add full power and roll the airplane toward the nearest horizon until the bank angle is 90 degrees, as in knife edge. Stop the roll there and don't exert any control pressures, and the airplane will slice downward until the nose is well below the horizon, and will soon regain sufficient airspeed for "normal" flight.

We are soon finishing my fourth dual ride in the T-Bird. I roll out on the initial approach for landing at 250 knots. I feel good. From the back seat comes Jakes's growly voice: "You think you can handle this thing by yourself?" Without even thinking: "No sweat!!"

"No Sweat, huh? Well I reckon we'll see about that."

I'm confused by this response, but we're over the numbers and I have no time to cogitate--I snap into a sixty degree bank, put out the speed brakes and simultaneously reduce power to 60 percent RPM. I hold the airplane in the turn, and roll out on downwind. Everything is right--down goes the gear, down go the flaps, trim for 140 knots. Start the turn to final descending at 140 knots, roll out on final looking right down the runway, trim for 125 knots, the threshold approaches, click in some nose up trim, ease the nose up, ease off some throttle, the main wheels touch, throttle to idle, stick back, the nose slowly lowers and the nose wheel touches down on the centerline. Nothing from the back seat.

I taxi to the flight line and park. We finish the paperwork and head for the ready room. Jake's coterie gathers at his table for the usual end-of-the-flying-day debriefing. Jake comments on today's flights, we discuss tomorrow's schedule, and I learn that I have completed all the check-out requirements and that tomorrow I will fly by myself!!

The first solo flight in a jet powered airplane is a momentous occasion. There's a lot going on in my head, and I now know that I will finish the course in good order.

Thus far, pilot training has left a trail of wash outs. Several of our class washed during primary, and I remember that I was sorely afraid that I would join the also-rans early in the game. When we got to Williams, some of our classmates never checked out in the T-28, and all were surprises. Two in particular had done very well in Primary--had soloed ahead of me and seemed to breeze through, but then were eliminated when they failed to check-out in the T-28.

When we start the jet program, we lose others. One of Jake's students is having trouble with the T Bird. Jake's usual M.O. at the end of the day is to go around the table with his daily critique. He has a well-earned reputation as the meanest, most unforgiving, master of scathing critiques in the college of instructors. He is usually merciless in his remarks from the back seat and around the table, but we soon learn that Jake has a soft spot.

When we begin the jet program and one of us is having difficulty dealing with the T Bird, Jake goes around the table with his withering critiques of our collective sub-standard performance, and saves the struggler for last.

When he addresses Mr. X, he suddenly shows his Dr. Jekyll self by turning into a big brother or maybe a Sunday school teacher. He never once makes a scathing or derogatory remark to Mr. X. When it becomes clear that X is soon to be toast, Jake did his usual--turning the three of us into yard birds, but when he turns to X, it's: "Well Mr. X, we're past the threshold regarding the requirement to solo. You have made a valiant effort on all our flights, but your landings are just not getting there. I do not want to put you up for a check ride, but, as you know from the curriculum, I have to make a decision. We'll be starting formation flying right away, and our schedule just won't allow any more dual flights." Mr. X, and all of us, are fighting back tears. Mr. X is a good man. We would be more than pleased to see him succeed here, but, wherever he winds up, he's at least as good a man as any of us.

Mr. X, as are all of us, is guaranteed three check rides prior to elimination. He will ride with the squadron commander, Major Virgil Turgeau, tomorrow. If Major Turgeau passes him, he might have a shot at staying in the program, but it doesn't happen. His second check ride will be with a check pilot from wing headquarters--it's a no go. The Director of Flying, Major John Sollars will be the axe man. I would not like to deal with the emotional stress thrust upon these senior officers, who, themselves, are wonderful men. This is one of the saddest moments in my flying career, but we have to move on.

PHOTO 4

Jake, et al, late in the game. Mr. X is gone: L. to R.: Lt Dave Curtis; Jake; Lt. Nick Leontas; Aviation Cadet Ken Hughey.

Formation in the T Bird is more fun than ever. When we are flying close formation, there's no propeller out in front--in trail, we can virtually stick our nose up the leader's tail pipe, and the airplane is responsive and smooth.

Soon, the instrument flight check is the biggest hurdle left. I do well enough, but never have that "perfect" ride that everybody wants.

On December 16, 1953, we are commissioned as Second Lieutenants, even though we have until January 16, 1954 to complete our flight requirements. I leave Williams and go home to Finley, Tennessee to rescue my princess. The deal was that I would leave and return as a knight and sweep her away forever. Sue (later to be known as "Mimi") and I are married in an ante Bellum style home in Dyersburg, Tennessee on December 26, 1953.

We spend our honeymoon driving from Dyersburg, Tennessee to Chandler, Arizona where I have rented an apartment. I still have flying requirements to complete before graduation.

Toward the end of Pilot Training, our first assignment as Pilots is on our minds and, our squadron commander assures that we are well briefed on the possibilities. All of us want to be fighter pilots. There are two places to go next to proceed as fighter pilots.

Nellis AFB is the home of the Air Force Fighter Weapons School and is also the home of one of the two Gunnery schools. The primo fighter at this time is the F-86. All of the Air Force fighter aces in the Korean War flew the F-86. As far as I could tell, I, and all of my classmates wanted to go to Nellis AFB and fly the F-86.

Another choice for fighter pilots was to go to Luke AFB and train in the F-84. The F-84 is an older design than the F-86. It has "straight wings." and has a speed limit of Mach .82--82% of the speed of sound, while the F-86 has no speed limit. The F-84 is thought of as mainly an air-to-ground airplane.

Another option is to fly All Weather Interceptors. The only training available is in the All Weather version of the F-86, the F-86D, commonly referred to as "The Dog." Two bases conduct All Weather Interceptor training--Tyndall AFB, Florida and Perrin AFB, Texas. Some of our class, including me, are interested in the All Weather business.

Jake talks to us in detail about the prospects and he also has some one-on-one consultations with us. In one of these sessions, Jake asks me to consider becoming an instructor right here at Williams AFB. He tells me that soon after our graduation date, a training program for instructors will begin. He says that he believes that he can convince the selection committee to choose me to be an instructor and to join the program. At the moment the exact agenda and length of the program is unknown, but Jake thinks it will be about six weeks.

He points out some advantages: I am newly married and, if selected to be an instructor, would be eligible to apply for base housing. I note that Jake rides a scooter to work--a five minute ride--and we have all visited with Jake in his place on base, which is very nice. Jake also points out that, as an instructor, I will build flying time and experience far faster than my contemporaries, and that after this assignment, I will have a large choice for my next assignment. I am persuaded, and give Jake the "green light" to lobby for me.

When the assignments come in, I have orders to remain here and become an instructor.

Our official graduation date is Saturday January 16, 1954. There is a graduation ceremony, and Don Dolan is here. I believe that he is at least as pleased as I am. We don't need to verbalize our mutual respect and our experiences during the six months we spent together at Marana. I recall in my mind the Friday afternoon that he laid it on the line to me--get it together or pack my bags. I also recall his quiet, gentle, and patient approach to teaching flying and am not sure I would have been able to overcome the initial hurdle with anyone else. It's an awesome moment having him here. We are issued sterling silver pilot's wings, and Sue wrestles through pinning them over the left breast pocket of my jacket.

Gunnery

All of my classmates pack their bags and head for Nellis or Luke. On Monday January 18, I join the training class for future instructors. There are only six of us. Four of the other five are Service Academy graduates who have fighter experience--three West Point grads, one Naval Academy. The fifth is a product of the Aviation Cadet program, who has just completed a tour of duty in F-80s in Korea. I am the only class member with no fighter experience.

January 18 begins with a briefing by Captain Nick Patakos, one of the most experienced instructors in the business, on the nuances of instructing and the outline of the course. Later in the day I begin the flying program by checking out in the T-28. For the next two weeks, we are busy with ground school and proficiency flying.

During the second week, the Director of Flying Training at Air Training Command Headquarters directs that as of now, one of the requirements for becoming an instructor in the Advanced Pilot Training program is graduation from one of the gunnery schools. I am toast. I fly my last flight with this class on February 3, 1954, and on Friday February 5, I have orders to report to Laughlin AFB, Texas for phase 1 of the F-84 gunnery school.

One might think this would be a big disappointment--it isn't. First of all, whatever happens to me includes Sue. We are together, I have enough income for food and shelter, and life is a big adventure. We pack our bags and the few things we have collected in the few weeks we have been a couple and put them in the back seat of our car and head for

Texas. Housing in Del Rio is scarce. We spend a few days in a motel before finding a place to live. It is not an apartment.

Our new digs consist of an upstairs sitting room and bed room that joins a hallway. At the opposite end of the hallway from the entrance to our sitting room is a bathroom that we share with the couple who live at the other end of the hall. In the middle of the hallway there is a refrigerator that we also share. We never see the other two. Somehow we manage to look and listen and avoid any contact with them during the six weeks we are in Del Rio.

On March 1, 1954, I check into the 3645th Training Squadron (Fighter). The week is spent in briefings and checking out equipment, and on Friday I check out in the T-33. During Phase I of the F-84 gunnery program, we will fly T-33s equipped with a lead computing gyroscopic gun sight, two .50 caliber machine guns, and bomb racks that allow the use of ten pound practice bombs.

All of our work in Phase I is air-to-ground. The Air Force has the use of an enormous amount of land in West Texas so there is plenty of room to do whatever we need to do. We strafe and drop bombs form every conceivable angle and simulate napalm delivery using practice bombs.

The first gunnery practice is strafing. The Targets are ten foot high and twenty foot long panels that we also use for skip bombing and simulated napalm drops.

The dive bombing targets are one hundred and fifty foot diameter circles with a marker in the center. When we are practicing dive bombing, there are two towers on the range that are manned by instructors. They control entry and exit on the range and, by using sighting instruments and triangulation, they can score our hits in real time.

Gunnery is serious business, but is also a lot of fun.

I fly my last flight on April 6 and on April 12 we complete Phase I and depart for Luke AFB to do Phase II.

We find a nice apartment in Glendale, Arizona, and it's a real pleasure to have our own bath and refrigerator in the same enclosure with us.

I check in to the 3600th Flight Training Wing on April 19 and begin ground training for Phase II. On April 26, I check out in the T-33, and on April 27, I take my first ride in the F-84. This is a different beast. It's bigger than a T-33 and is a bit sluggish getting underway. When I release the brakes for take-off with 100% power, it doesn't really leap away from the starting blocks, but starts rolling at a gentle pace and the airspeed increases gradually as it rolls down the runway. I have the take-off data and know that everything is O.K. As we (the airplane and I) roll down the runway, the faster it goes, the faster it seems to want to go, and we finally lift off after more than a mile run. I pick up the gear and flaps and stay on the deck as we continue to accelerate toward an initial climb speed of 425 mile per hour (mph), which is 370 Knots (Nautical Miles per Hour)--considerably faster than a T-33. This is an airplane you don't want to slow down.

I am soon at 20,000 feet and pull off some throttle and maintain 350 mph. Note that these airplanes were designed, manufactured, and purchased before the Nautical Mile became the standard, and the airspeed indicator is in mph rather than Knots. 350 mph is about 300K (300 knots), a good bit faster than I would be flitting about in a T-33. The airplane handles very nicely. It is smooth and feels heftier than the T-33. I do some turns and some acrobatics and it all feels good. In the traffic pattern it is not much different than a T-33 and is very easy to fly--just remember to keep it moving.

Phase II gunnery is just like phase I as far as air-to-ground goes. The big difference is the addition of air-to-air. We learn to use the lead computing gun sight by shooting at a banner towed by a B-25 on a 5,000 foot long cable. To practice lead, we come along-side the B-25 1500 feet above the banner. At that point, we roll in to a diving turn toward the banner, and, as it passes in front of us we reverse the turn and start tracking it in the gun sight in an attempt to position the little dot in our gun sight that we refer to as the "pipper" onto the two foot diameter circle in the middle of the banner while that little pipper bounces around like a rubber ball with every motion we make in the cockpit, every change in pitch, roll or yaw, and every time you blink. It's an impossible situation. If this is the way things are in air-to-air combat, how did any of our guys ever shoot down a Mig?

We keep at it, and, once in a while I get smooth enough and lucky enough to see the pipper somewhere on the rag and get off a short burst. A few times the rag comes back with some of the colors from my guns.

The most fun and the worst tongue lashings I ever enjoy at once occurs during Aerial Combat Tactics (ACT), sometimes referred to as Aerial Combat Maneuvering (ACM). We do this training one-on-one with an instructor who is a master at it. The whole idea is to learn how to outmaneuver an adversary and get into a position to shoot him down. You learn the best tactics to employ regardless of where the adversary is when the fight starts. If you are slightly low and directly behind the enemy, just lift the nose and pull the trigger and hold it down until he explodes or comes apart. Otherwise, you have a problem--how do I get from where I am to a position right behind him such that by pulling just a little harder on the stick, the pipper will move out in front of him about a foot? Or maybe worse, how do I prevent him from getting in the same position relative to me?

Talk about a workout! Every time I come out of one of these sessions I am drenched and exhausted.

Before long mid-May is here, the desert is hot, and we use an awful lot of the nearly two mile long runway at Luke to get off the ground. We fly our last few missions with less fuel to improve take-off performance. Since our gunnery missions are short, there is no problem with endurance. On May 27, 1954, I fly my last mission in the F-84, and soon after set sail for our next assignment at Tyndall AFB, Florida.

We take a month off and drive to Tennessee to visit our families. All of our travels thus far have been in my mother's car that she loaned us due to our limited time and money when we married. Only a Mother would make such a sacrifice, and only a spoiled brat would accept it. My mother "made do" with local families of her brood of school children furnishing her transportation needs. The first thing we do is to purchase a car of our own and return my mother's car. Our first car is a 1951 Pontiac Sedan.

Part IV

Tyndall AFB and Moody AFB

Interceptors

I report to Tyndall AFB in early July, not knowing exactly what I will be doing, but hoping to enter the All Weather Interceptor program and fly the F-86-D. No such luck. I am assigned to an organization gloriously named "Fighter Operations" flying T-33s as radar targets for the interceptor students. This is a good way to build up flying time, but, as flying assignments go, not very exciting. The best part is that at the end of some of our missions we can sometimes meet up with one another for ACM practice, or, in the alternative, practice acrobatics. There are some experienced fighter pilots in the mix that are formidable adversaries in a dog fight, and I learn from them.

As soon as I get my feet on the ground, I begin agitating the system for a transfer to the Interceptor program, and, in October 1954, I am assigned to the Instrument School that precedes check out in the F-86. This is Phase I of the All Weather Interceptor program. Before checking out in the F-86D, one must be more than merely proficient in an all-weather environment, and the instrument phase is very intense.

I take my first flight under the hood in the back seat of a T-33 on October 25, 1954. The first two flights under the hood are purely basic instruments. The hood in the back blocks out any sight of the outside--very good simulation of weather conditions. Each of these first two flights begins with an Instrument take-off and terminates with a Ground Controlled Approach. In the intervening two hours, I do whatever the instructor asks me to do, beginning with various standard rate turns, steep turns, descending and climbing turns, airspeed changes in straight and level fligh and during maneuvering, and acrobatics such as loops, Cuban eights, Immelmans, and vertical recoveries. We practice these maneuvers until I can fly the airplane on instruments in any situation.

When we've finished these two flights, we begin including navigation procedures. We practice every conceivable type of radio navigation and low ceiling approaches in Visual Flight Rules (VFR) conditions. And then, we look for actual weather--the more severe the better. We file clearances into the worst thunderstorms we can find, as well as flying approaches during low ceilings and precipitation.

I graduate from Phase I in November, 1954 and am immediately appointed as an Instructor Pilot and begin instructing in the Instrument School on December 6. This year has been a whirlwind, and I have learned a lot about flying. The Instrument School instructors were first rate and very demanding. We practiced every nuance of instrument flying and overall proficiency until we got it right. Now, is up to me to be as disciplined as my mentors have been, and to hold my students to the same standards that my mentors held me. As a Second Lieutenant, I will be the junior instructor in the squadron--all of my students will be senior to me--some will be field grade officers. I hope I can carry the load.

My career as an instrument instructor is short. In a few weeks I am assigned to a class in phase II and begin training in the F-86D. We do ten hours in a very realistic simulator and then fly the airplane. I now fly simulated intercepts against my erstwhile comrades in Fighter Operations. When I am finished with the program, I am immediately assigned as an instructor--the best of all possible worlds for the moment.

By the time I become an instructor in the All Weather Interceptor program, Sue and I have established what will become a lifetime relationship with another couple who are our contemporaries--Bud and Sue Flesher. Bud was a few weeks behind me in pilot training, and he and his Sue moved into a neighboring apartment in Parker, Florida not long after my Sue and I arrived at Tyndall AFB. Bud and I have exactly the same goals--we want to become Regular Officers in the Air force, and want an education.

Soon after we met, we began attending night classes on the base that were conducted by Professors from Florida State University. We enrolled as History majors, but took all the math classes that were available in order to become eligible for the AFIT sponsored engineering programs.

We also fly together often, and "party" just as hard as we fly and work on our academics. We wind up spending five years together--three years at Tyndall AFB and two years at Moody AFB at Valdosta, Georgia. Bud was an only child, and since all of my siblings were essentially adults when I was born, I grew up as an only child. Maybe we both needed a contemporary brother, and that's essentially what we become--brothers. We help each other through the process of applying for Regular Commissions and are both sworn into the Regular Air force in 1957.

When the Army Air Corps became the United States Air Force in 1947, all regular officers were given new serial numbers by rank followed by the letter "A." Since General Carl Spaatz was the first Air force Chief of Staff, his serial number was 1A. The remainder was numbered 2A and following; for example, General Hoyt Vandenberg's serial number was 4A.

My serial number became 31352A and Bud's became 32199A. We were the 31,352nd and 32,199th officers to be sworn into the Regular air Force. In the sixties, the Air force modified the format of the numbering system by deleting the A as a suffix and adding the prefix "FR," and our serial numbers became FR31352 and FR32199. Later on, this system was replaced by using our Social Security Numbers. Just for clarity, if you were not a regular officer, you were a reserve officer. When Bud and I were commissioned at the end of Pilot Training, we were reserve officers, and the format for reservists was "AO" followed by a big number--My Serial Number as a Reserve Officer was AO3024574.

When Bud arrived at Tyndall AFB, he was assigned to Fighter Operations, and I was in the process of transferring to the Instrument School. Since Bud had the same ambitions that I had, he began the same process that I had followed, and from then on until we separated when I left Moody AFB, our careers were very similar. Not long after I became an instructor in the F-86D program, Bud joined the program as a student.

Bud Takes One In

On September 7, 1955, Bud is scheduled for his second flight in the F-86, and I am assigned to fly his wing as his instructor. The training program requires an instructor to accompany the fledgling Interceptor student on some of their early flights. The student's second flight is called an "engineering" flight. Bud will spend about an hour doing what Jimmy Doolittle referred to as "playing" with the airplane. I will fly his wing to observe what he does and to chat with him when he has questions. His learning objective is to improve his "feel" for the airplane so that when he flies intercept missions the actual handling of the airplane will be "second nature" to him. One can learn to fly this airplane by practice in the flight simulator--which he has done--but there is no substitute for the real thing to hone psychomotor skills to a fighting edge.

The training squadron building sits on the edge of the flight line. There are more than 100 airplanes on the ramp parked in neat rows with lines and parking space numbers arranged in perfect order. We step out of the squadron building and wait a bit for the flight line taxi. The taxi is an open trailer, towed by a tractor. There are no individual seats.--just two benches arranged back to back such that the passengers sit facing outward. The driver stops when needed and delivers us to the row where our airplanes are parked next to each other. We are wearing back pack parachutes and are carrying our helmet bags in one hand, and life rafts in the other.

The taxi stops and we walk a few steps to our airplanes. We pre-flight the airplanes and are soon strapped in with helmets on signaling the crew chief that we're cranking the engines. The starter motor in the F-86 is electric and requires an external source of power to turn the turbine fast enough to accept the injection of JP-4 fuel and the subsequent ignition without exceeding the temperature limits of the engine.

After signaling the crew chief that we're about to start engines, I hit the starter switch. The electric starter motor engages and the engine begins to "spool up." At 10 percent engine speed, I move the throttle from stop cocked to idle, and feel and hear the flames start coursing through the burners and the turbine blades and watch the exhaust gas temperature (EGT) and RPM gauges for deviations in the start sequence. The (EGT) climbs to about 700 degrees and then begins to decrease as the engine RPM increases. Soon the engine is singing at 45% RPM and a much lower EGT. I signal the crew chief to unplug the power cart and then turn on the radios and place the radar system in stand-by.

I look over at Bud's airplane. He soon glances my way and we nod. In between other transmissions Bud Calls: "Tyndall Ground, 867 to taxi with two F-86s." Tower comes back: "867 cleared to Runway Three-One with two." Bud: "867 to Three-One with two." Bud's airplane moves forward turns left to move out to the parallel taxiway. I space myself in trail as he turns right to parallel the runway. We taxi about two miles to the end of runway 31.

Bud parks in the run-up area, and I swivel into position on his left wing. We are out of the way of all other traffic and have a clear view of the runway and all other traffic. This space is ours for as long as we need to check out our airplanes. The checklist we carry on our knee boards is turned to "Pre Take-Off." Our clam shell canopies are open as we walk through each step, including an engine run-up to 100% RPM with a check of all the "vitals." We can't check the Afterburner during the run up because the brakes won't keep the airplane from moving with the AB running--the bird will scoot forward on the locked wheels and tires like pushing a pencil eraser along dry paper.

We finish our Preflight check, and Bud calls for a frequency change from ground control to tower frequency. I acknowledge the change and we switch frequencies. Bud calls the tower: "Tyndall tower, 897 for take-off with 2 F-86s." A short delay and Tower responds. "897 cleared for takeoff with 2." Bud: "Roger, tower, 897 taking Three One for takeoff."

Bud taxies on to the runway and stops just to the right of the center line, and I take a position on his left wing. We run up our engines, and when I am ready, I look at Bud. He tilts his head back to let me know that he is about to roll. His head tilts forward, and we simultaneously re-lease brakes and advance the throttles to the Afterburner range and roll together down the runway. My airplane is just a few inches from his, and we stay that way as we rotate to a lift off attitude and are flying. We raise our gear and flaps in unison. It's a smooth day--no turbulence--and we are as one as we climb out with a slight turn to the right to avoid flying over the base housing area that sits on a peninsula that juts out into the bay and extends under our take-off flight path. Bud heads for the Bay Bridge as we climb, but we never get there.

As we pass through 1,000 feet, I suddenly start moving forward and have to move out and reduce power to stay with Bud who has just started to slow down dramatically as he begins a turn to the right. I suddenly find myself stacked high with the throttle in idle and the speed brakes fully extended. I note a wisp of what appears to be fuel vapor escape from Bud's tail pipe as I stack high to the outside of his right turn, and with the speed brakes fully extended. I can maintain formation with him, but I loosen up a bit to see what he's up to and call him: "Bud, are you o.k.?" No response. I now know that his engine has flamed out. I call the tower to tell them what I think, as he maintains a gliding turn to the right. Tyndall tower immediately closes the Field. I try to talk to Bud, but no response.

All I can do is to keep the tower posted as to what is happening. It is soon apparent that Bud's engine has flamed out and he is attempting to continue the gliding turn so as to land on runway 17, a closed but usable runway. I cross over to his right wing and stack a bit high as he descends. Being close to him and looking at the ground track and the ground underneath us, I don't believe he can make it. I want to yell "Bail Out!" but hold my tongue. I believe that he's trying to air start the engine as wisps of fuel continue to exit the tailpipe. I also know that, if he is trying for an air start, which is virtually certain, the instant he engaged the air start switch, every electrical system in the airplane, including the radio, is shut down to assure enough electrical power to fire the air start ignition. We are not going to hear a peep out of Bud!

Bud has nailed the glide speed for best range--185 knots, 213 miles per hour-- and holds it steady as our descent continues. There are some really tall pine trees just off the end of Runway 17, and I am convinced that he can't clear them. He's now awfully low for a safe bail out, but it might beat the alternative.

Still stacked high, I watch him clear the trees with a little margin, but I don't believe that he will make the runway. He keeps right on truckin', and is just skimming the ground as he approaches the tarmac overrun. He clears the end of the runway, and sets down on the two full fuel tanks--one under each wing--120 gallons each. They explode like two napalm bombs. What runs through my head? I didn't think he would clear the trees, but he did: I didn't think he would make the runway, but he did--now he's gonna burn up right there before everybody's eyes.

I open the throttle, smoke by him, pull up into a left 360 degree turn, and keep him in sight through the side and top of my canopy. He slides out of the two napalm bursts and keeps sliding down the runway straight as an arrow--the fire from the tanks quickly subsides to nothing but smoke, and he's at least a 1,000 feet away. I continue my turn to let down for a low pass as his canopy opens, and he steps out on the wing. Shortest flight he ever made.

I pull up into a climb, take a deep breath, and circle the scene as fire trucks and an ambulance speed down the taxiways onto Runway 17 heading for Bud's airplane. By the time they park, he has crawled out of the airplane and steps off the left wing. The field remains closed for a while, and I lollygag out to the east until all the fire trucks, ambulance, and rescue crew are off the scene. As soon as the field reopens, I land on Runway 31 and go looking for Bud.

The standard practice following an aircraft accident is to take care of the crew, including a physical examination. When Bud stepped out of that airplane, he appeared to be in no different physical condition than he was when we took off. The touch down on the tanks and belly looked smooth to me; the slide down the runway was no different than a landing roll with the drag chute and brakes. So what? He gets a physical anyway. Also, accidents cause accident investigations. So, Bud gets quizzed from now 'til Sunday next. I have to make a report and answer questions all over the place. Big inconvenience for both of us. Almost made us late for happy hour at the club.

Later on I learn from Bud that the touch down was rather hard. From my overhead perspective I couldn't detect the real nature of the impact. I didn't know until Bud told me that he was slowing down as he rounded out and at the last minute he put the gear handle down and tried to hold the airplane off long enough and high enough for the landing gear to extend. Nice try, but he was running out of airspeed and the airplane paid off and dropped in a bit hard. His back was sore, but he never said anything about it to the medics.

C. O. Stull

I stay on as a Flight Instructor in the All Weather Interceptor program until August, 1956. During that time, I meet and fly with the best known F-86D instructor on the base. His name is Captain Clarence O. (C.O.) Stull, and he is the senior engineering academic instructor in the All Weather Interceptor Ground School. Anytime anyone has a knotty question about the F-86D, the mantra is: "Ask C.O." He knows every nut and bolt in the airplane and the location of every rivet.

I sometimes fly C.O.s wing on live rocket firing missions. On one of those missions, we take off and fly visually (VFR) under an overcast. We requested an Instrument Flight Rules (IFR) clearance before we took off, with the proviso that we would head for the rocket Range in VFR conditions and then climb up through the overcast after being cleared for IFR flight. I expected that we would take off in formation, and at 1,000 feet we would kill our afterburners and cruise at a comfortable level below the overcast and head for the gunnery range until cleared to climb. When cleared to climb, I thought we might or might not use afterburners, depending on how the mission was going. It didn't work out quite like that.

C.O. levels off at 800 feet and leaves the airplane in afterburner as we cross the Bay Bridge and make a loose 180 degree turn to parallel the coast line eastward. We switch frequencies, and C.O. asks for our IFR clearance. We are now flying at the highest indicated airspeed that I have ever seen--nearly 600 knots. It's also by far the fastest that I have ever flown formation. The control stick is very sensitive as I work hard to stay in position.

We get our clearance, and C.O. looks over at me and points upward, letting me know that we are about to ascend through this stuff above us. The target tow ship--a T-33 with a target banner trailing on a 5,000 foot cable--is waiting for us at 25,000 feet and the tops of the overcast are at about 20,000 feet. C.O. eases back on the stick and we are in the fastest climb I have ever been in. C.O. is smooth. I have no problem staying in position, and in a minute or so we pop out on top, kill our afterburners, and follow the ground controller's direction as he positions us to attack the target.

We are shortly on a heading that will put us in position for a 90 degree angle off shot at the target. C.O. locks his radar onto the target, and I loosen up on his left wing as he makes his attack. I see the target ship approaching about 500 feet above us with the banner trailing 5,000 feet at our altitude. The rockets will fire automatically when C.O.'s ship is in proper position for the "kill." As we close in on the banner, the rocket pod under the nose of C.O.'s airplane extends, and six Mighty Mouse practice rockets are on their way. I watch as they streak by the banner. It is impossible to see if any hit the banner, but if, they did, the banner will show damage when it's recovered after the mission.

C.0. now moves to my wing and the ground controller vectors us for another attack. It is my turn, and, in a few minutes I'm locked up on the banner and repeat what C.O. just did. We leave the range and switch frequencies to recover and land via a Ground Controlled Approach (GCA). The rest of the mission is uneventful and we are soon on the ground and back in the squadron ready room critiquing the mission. Nobody mentions the rather spectacular initial take-off and climb out.

Not long after this mission, C.O. approaches me and asks if I am interested in joining him as an academic instructor. I am flattered that this Guru is inviting me to join him, and I soon decide to accept, knowing that C.O. will never turn me loose in a classroom until he is absolutely certain that I can "hack" it.

I transfer to the Academic Section, and soon have a desk in a large room with the other instructors. My job is to learn everything there is to know about the F-86D and how to present it effectively. I have excellent mentoring. William S. "Bill" O'Leary is my direct mentor, and of course, we all have unlimited access to C.O., who is the best there is. We have a congenial environment, and soon I take on my first engineering class--the J-47 engine and its unique fuel control and afterburner system. I am a nervous wreck before the class begins, but once I begin, and the dozen or so students are listening, I am relaxed and enjoying the interplay. Maybe this is like the dealings I had not so long ago with Mr. Dolan.

After a while, there is a vacancy in the Academic Department, and I talk to C.O. about Bud. Pretty soon Bud joins us, and we have enough liberty in our work environment to prepare our applications for Regular Commissions. C.O. and all of the Academic staff are senior to us and are a big help in providing their own recommendations as well as steering us to other senior officers who are aware of our work. Each of us soon ship off about ten pounds of paper work that we hope makes it to the Air Staff for favorable action.

Along with instructing in the classroom, Bud and I spend as much time as we can on the flight line. We fly as much as we can and fly cross countries on week-ends. I have two sisters who live near Detroit and two who live in Washington, D.C., and I occasionally visit them. I go to Wright-Patterson AFB in Ohio when I can get there during the week to visit the Air Force Institute of Technology (AFIT) to let them know I am alive and well and to chat about my future as an undergraduate engineering.

On June 1, 1956 tragedy strikes the Academics organization and the entire wing at Tyndall AFB. C.O. Stull dies in an aircraft accident in Colorado. He was a passenger in a B-25 when the aircraft lost an engine shortly after departing Lowry AFB. C.O. had a lot more flying experience than the crew, and there was some evidence that he was attempting to prevent a disaster by coaching the crew through the emergency when the airplane crashed and killed all aboard. The memorial service for C.O. in the Base Chapel is packed. I shall never forget the walk from the chapel back to our office. Seven of us make the trip together and not a word is spoken. We file through the front door of our building and into our office and take our seats at our desks. This place and our lives will never be quite the same. It's trite to say that someone was special, but.....

By late 1956, I am itching for a change in scenery. Even though the Academic Staff is still well staffed with a group of marvelous men, the place has lost something that leaves all of us chilled.

Flight Test

For some time, I have been aware of the Flight Test organization that is a part of the Maintenance and Supply Group (M&S). The Group Commander is Colonel Harvey Liddon, by far the most interesting personage on the base. He was born in 1904 and joined the Army Air Corps sometime in the 1920s, became an aircraft mechanic, progressed through the enlisted ranks, and when WWII broke out, he was a Master Sergeant. Based on his experience and reputation, the Air Corps proffered a direct commission as an officer, and, by the end of the war he was a Colonel, and now he serves as the Commander of the M&S Group.

The flight Test Section Commander is Major Bill Disbrow, a well-known aviator and automobile expert, who, among other things, has designed and built a sports car with a fiberglass body and calls it the Disbrow Special. Major Disbrow is the most experienced Aviator on Tyndall Air force Base. He has flown dozens of types of airplanes and flew more than fifty combat missions in B-24s in WWII, several of which were to Ploesti.

In late 1956, the Flight Test Section consists of Major Disbrow, Captain Kennedy I. Bass (variously known as "K.I." or "Sam"), Captain Ed Powell, Captain Jerry Hattendorf, and 1/Lt Jack Harris. Sam Bass has more flying time in the F-86D than anyone else--something like 2,000 hours--and is due for a transfer that will leave a slot open in the Flight Test Section. Even though I have nothing like the experience of any of this group, ambition propels me to seek an audience with Captain Powell, who is now the senior member of the flight test pilots, and who will be instrumental in selecting any candidate(s) for a test pilot job. If Ed Powell will recommend me to Major Disbrow, I may have a chance.

My idea of an audience is a formal setting in uniform. In September, 1956 I'm mulling over how to gain an audience with Ed Powell, when I see him pre-flighting a T-33 that is parked near my next flight. I step over to him and introduce myself and tell him that I would like to get an appointment with him to discuss the possibility of joining his organization as a test pilot. His response: "Let's talk, right now." I tell him about my experience and emphasize my flying time and academic qualifications. Instructing in the classroom forced me to emulate C.O. Stull, and Captain Powell listens and asks a few questions. The conversation ends with his promise that he will contact me in a few days one way or the other. I salute and go about my business hopeful that I said all the right things in a convincing way.

In a few days, Captain Powell is in the F-86 Squadron ready room on a routine visit, and I happen to be there preparing for a flight. He approaches me and says that he is arranging for me to join him as a test pilot, and that unless I have changed my mind, I will soon be transferred to the M&S Group, and that I should start spending as much time as possible in the test pilot's office talking about the job. I am acquainted with Jerry Hattendorf and Jack Harris, and I visit them frequently during the next few weeks. By October 16, I have a desk in the Flight Test Section and fly my first test flight.

You won't be surprised to learn that this bunch loves to fly and there are sometimes dog fights between us. Even as the junior member, I am a part of the team.

One of the things that I want to do first is to check out in the C-45. All these guys fly the C-45 regularly, and Jerry Hattendorf gets the job of checking me out. We begin right away. I read the Pilot's Handbook and Jerry and I talk about the airplane when we have time, and soon go for my first flight. The C-45 is a classy machine built by Beechcraft. It has two 450 hp Pratt & Whitney nine cylinder radial engines, carries four passengers, and has leather seats for the pilot and co-pilot.

The first flight emphasizes fundamentals such as preflight inspection, how to start the engines, taxiing, run-up, take-off, and fundamental air work. At the end of our practice session, Jerry takes the controls, noses down to pick up some airspeed, eases the nose up to a few degrees above the horizon, and the next thing I know, we're inverted in the middle of a barrel roll. Back in straight and level flight, Jerry tells me to head for the traffic pattern to shoot a few landings and adds that we will practice rolls later.

The C-45 has conventional landing gear; i.e., it is a tail dragger, and takes some practice to make decent landings. Jerry is patient. He lets me beat up the runway and assists when needed as I struggle to get a good landing. I am not happy about the check- out process, even when Jerry laughs about it and points out that I am just as good as the next guy and will soon be making grease jobs without bouncing. He's right. I recall my travail in primary when I couldn't make myself try. Now I know how to try, and very soon it all comes together, and it's not long until I have the minimum flying time and other requirements to become an Instructor Pilot in the C-45.

I had several interesting flights as a Test Pilot, one in an F-86. Each test flight in an F-86 that had just gone through a 100 hour periodic inspection begins with an afterburner take-off and climb to 45,000 feet. During the entire flight the pilot is making notes on a knee pad strapped to the right leg. On this flight, everything is going normally. I have checked off all the performance parameters, including such things as take-off roll, time to climb, instrument readings, and level off at 45,000 feet. I complete my notes and for the flight thus far and go to the next item on the check list--an afterburner light at 45,000 feet.

I shut down the afterburner, check the engine throttle responses by changing power settings, and then I place the throttle in the afterburner range. The afterburner does not light. I recycle the throttle in and out of the afterburner range--no light. Then, as a matter of gathering data, I place the throttle in the full afterburner range, trim the airplane for a descent, complete my notes for the flight thus far, and wait to note the altitude the afterburner will light, or if it will re-light at all. I make some descending turns, and at 38,000 feet, I feel a disturbance in the aft section, and the engine flames out.

The instant the engine quits, the cockpit depressurizes and the inside of the canopy is covered with frost. I'm flying on instruments with a dead engine. The bad news is the flameout--the good news is the airplane seems to be flying normally, the engine is windmilling, and there are no fire warning lights. I have plenty of altitude to return to the base and make a dead stick landing, but would prefer to get a restart and have the comfort of an operational engine. Except for the disturbance, much like a mild explosion, I would not hesitate to try an air start.

I call Tyndall control tower and declare an emergency. All the flight instruments will work long enough to get me home, plus there is a small crescent of clear windshield that I can see through straight ahead--not enough for an approach and landing, but I can scrape away enough frost during descent to fly visually.

As it turns out, the head of the Flight Test section is on the air and hears what's going on. After a brief discussion, I ask his opinion about trying an air start. In his own inimitable style, Major Bill Disbrow responds: "Fire it up!!" I advise all that for the next few minutes, I will be incommunicado because when I hit the air start switch, my radios will be dead. With that, I begin the air start procedure by assuring that the throttle is in the stop-cocked position, turning on the air start switch, and moving the throttle gradually to control the Exhaust Gas Temperature when, and if, the engine lights. The engine lights promptly, and, in a very short time, all the airplane systems, including, radios, pressurization and defrost, are working fine. I fly a precautionary simulated forced landing pattern and make an otherwise normal landing.

The "explosion" in the tail section apparently resulted from fuel from the afterburner pump accumulating in the tail section outside the tail pipe. The airplane didn't sustain any structural damage, and after a thorough inspection and repair was back in business.

When the afterburner failed to light at 45,000 feet, I should not have left the throttle in the afterburner range--a common sense error. What I should have done was to recycle the throttle to afterburner at intervals during descent to discover the altitude that the AB would light.

In 1957, the F-86 All Weather Interceptor program transfers to Moody AFB, Georgia, and Bud and I transfer with it and remain in the Test Flight section. The others in Flight Test remain at Tyndall, and when we arrive at Moody we have a new boss--Captain William G., "Bill," or "Ker" Plunk. Other than the new location and new personnel, the job is the same.

Part V

Bud and I continue night school and in August, 1959 I leave Moody to register as an Aeronautical Engineering student at the University of Colorado in Boulder. Sue takes a job as cashier at the Harvest House Hotel in Boulder and I am buried with homework.

June 1, 1960 turns out to be the most painful day in our lives. Sue goes to the hospital in Boulder to deliver our first child, things are going well with her labor, and then, after a few hours, our obstetrician--Dr. Adrian Bodelson--comes out into the waiting room where I wait with Sue's mother. He takes me aside and tells me that he is concerned that our baby has died during Sue's labor. He doesn't close the door completely--maybe he's trying to let us down easy. Our baby is dead. After the delivery, it turns out that the umbilical cord was unusually long and probably got pinched off as she came through the birth canal.

The pain for me is horrible. I can't even begin to imagine how it is for Sue. For whatever reasons, we collectively thought it best for Sue not to see the baby--a perfectly formed little tyke with a head full of black hair. Sue and I have suffered a lot since and will mourn for her until we see her again. She is our guardian angel. Kelly Susan Hughey is buried in Boulder, Colorado. We visit her as often as we can.

After two years at CU, I join Air Force Space Systems Division (SSD) in Inglewood, California in September 1961. Sue takes a job with Interstate Hosts and soon becomes the manager of the restaurant, bar, and gift shop in Terminal Seven--the home of United Airlines. I am a project officer for various advanced technologies, including lasers and lifting body re-entry vehicles.

I was not able to complete the requirements in the two years allotted by AFIT and spent the 1962-63 academic year on temporary duty in School in Boulder. Sue works at her job with Interstate Hosts, and I commute a lot on week-ends by flying a T-33 from Lowry AFB to NAS Los Alamitos, near Seal Beach, to spend the week ends at home. Sometimes I ride a C-118 cargo plane that makes scheduled flights between Los Angeles and Cape Canaveral with a stop in Denver. I graduate in August 1963 with a B.S. in Aeronautical Engineering.

In April 1964, our son, Kenneth, is born. We can't wait to bring him home, and when we arrive with him, we take him to our bedroom to admire him by counting his toes and fingers, inspecting his ears, and generally enjoying this moment that stretches to several minutes. We finally regain enough composure to realize that we have rushed in through our front door and left it open. We are well prepared for his arrival. He has a room, furniture, high chair, bath apparatus, and everything he needs.

Viet Nam is heating up. Sue and I well remember the spring of 1954 when we went to the movies every week no matter what was playing. Short Subjects were always a part of the show and Movietone News had something about the siege at Dien Bien Phu every week for several weeks. Finally, in May, 1954, the Communist Army, known as the Viet

Minh, headed by General Vo Nguyen Giap, captured the garrison and ended French Colonial influence in Viet Nam.

As a result of the defeat of the French, the parties reached an agreement that divided Viet Nam into two parts, North and South, with the demarcation line at the 17th parallel. The agreement included a provision that after two years there would be a nationwide election to choose a government for all of a united Viet Nam. As the two year mark approached, the United States kept an eye on Viet Nam and when straw polls and other available data indicated that more than 80% of the Viet Namese people would vote for Ho Chi Minh and accept a Communist government, the U.S. decided to intervene.

We were then, in 1954, and still are, in 1964, in a cold war aimed at preventing the spread of Communism. We have "advisors" in Viet Nam flying various kinds of combat airplanes including B-26s, O-1s, and A-1s, and getting shot at. Sounds like a hot war to me, when some of my contemporaries are returning from Viet Nam with battle scars and chests full of medals, not to mention the few who are shipped home to their families "in a new nice pine box (collect. {sic}," to use an e e cummings description. If things don't change, there is no doubt that I will become a combatant in Viet Nam. Meanwhile, I have an exciting job as a project officer involving designing and testing a lifting reentry vehicle that can return from space and land like an airplane, but, like the grim reaper stalking in the shadows, the "hot" war in Viet Nam haunts me.

The vehicle that I am involved in is a Martin Company design in response to a request for proposal (RFP) form the Air Force Space Technology and Advanced Reentry Tests (START) program office where I am working. The Air force has an interest in developing a reentry vehicle that can maneuver during the reentry process and then glide like an airplane to a safe landing on an ordinary airstrip. Martin Company calls their design SV-5 (Space Vehicle number 5). The development concept we are pursuing is to fly a number of scale model tests through the reentry regime to prove (or disprove) the capability of the design. I participate in the process including such mundanities as testing a parachute designed to deploy at Mach 2 in the supersonic wind tunnel at Tullahoma Tennessee.

During the period from late 1963 through January, 1965, I work as hard as I can to contribute to the SV-5 program. The best thing I did for the program was putting together a briefing extolling the virtues of the SV-5 design; e.g., volumetric efficiency, and maneuvering capability. In February 1965, we were planning for the space flights using scale models mounted atop an Atlas launch vehicle, and I left the program for a tour of combat in Viet Nam as a Forward Air Controller (FAC) In Viet Nam.

My first stop on the way to Viet Nam is Eglin AFB, Florida to spend three weeks with the Air Commandos who have been engaged in the war for some time. The Commandos have put together a training program designed to familiarize new assignees with the situation in Viet Nam. The briefers are mostly combat veterans. The training includes a lot of material not directly related to combat operations, such as historical information and the presence of the relatively few French who reside there. Other than a thirty five minute "indoctrination" flight in the 0-1 airplane, there is no flying training--we will check out as FACs after we arrive in Viet Nam.

The most cogent parts of the training are the geographic, political, ethnic, governmental, and operational details of the conduct of military operations. We examine the theory of "Pacification" and a history of guerilla operations in Malaysia and other countries that we are using to make decisions as to how to root out the Communist forces and combat and disrupt the effectiveness of guerilla operations conducted by the "Viet Cong." It's three weeks on the receiving end of a fire hose.

Part VI

FORWARD AIR CONTROLLER

Initiation

After a short visit at home in Gardena, California, I say good-bye to my wife and ten month old son and fly via Commercial Airlines to Tan Son Nhut Airport in Sai Gon. After I check in to 7th Air Force Headquarters, I get a ride to downtown Sai Gon and check into the Brinks Hotel. The entire hotel is encircled by concertina wire and the entrance is secured by Military Police. The hotel sustained considerable damage a few months ago and still wears some of the scars.

It's March 4, 1965, and this evening I go to the roof top bar and restaurant at the Brinks Hotel for dinner and drinks. It soon becomes apparent why this city has long been referred to as "The Paris of the Orient." The view from here is spectacular and the night air is fresh and comfortable. There I meet some Army officers who live here and participate in the conversation with all the newbie attention I can muster.

One of those with whom I share drinks was in his room on the seventh floor using the bathroom on last Christmas Eve, the evening of the explosion. The plumbing in the Brinks is Paris 1893, just like in the song. The water closet for the commode was about six feet off the floor with the pull chain hanging down the side of the wall with an iron handle shaped like a short corn cob, or an elongated hand grenade. When my new found friend pulled the chain, the hotel exploded. At the moment he was dead certain that the V had somehow connected the trigger to his water closet. We all had a good laugh. The view of Saigon is spectacular—where's the war? I will soon learn.

After my night at the Brinks I check into the Bachelor Officer's Quarters (BOQ) on Tan Son Nhut for a few days of training and briefings on the situation in Viet Nam.

At Tan Son Nhut, I swim in the local swimming pool in spite of the presence of water bugs that resemble giant cockroaches and who swim around at all levels of the pool as if it were their private domain and the rest of us are intruders. These bugs love chlorinated water. I am surprised that I wasn't blond from chlorine exposure before I left. Among a lot of other things I am exposed to in the briefings, I learn that I will eventually wind up with the 20th Tactical Air Support Squadron (TASS) in Da Nang after a few days stay at Bien Hoa checking out in the 0-1 airplane and flying at least one mission with the Air Commandos.

On March 16, I take a 45 minute bus ride to Bien Hoa Air Base and check in to the Bien Hoa BOQ and spend the next day, March 17, visiting with the local FACs and Air Commandos. The Commandos fly AI-Es. One of them is an old friend and former boss, Major Bill Plunk, who is now a Commando Flight Commander. Bill helps me arrange to ride along on an air strike tomorrow as a "strap Hanger" with one of his best—Capt. William Henry "Bill" Campbell. I couldn't have picked a better ride.

We take off from Bien Hoa and head for the Delta southwest of Sai Gon, not far from a town called Can Tho. The VC are strong in the

Delta area and want to maintain control of it, largely because of the rich rice crops. The Me Kong Delta is a beautiful place to me, having grown up on the Mississippi River. The Me Kong divides into several lesser streams that complete the Delta as the fresh water flows lazily into the sea. The land is tropical rich and pleasant to look at.

As we approach the target zone we switch to our combat frequency to join up with the FAC that will be in control of this strike. Bill reports to the FAC as we approach the target area from about ten miles out: "Red Marker, this is Commando nearing Can Tho." The FAC responds: "Roger, Hoss, bring it on over to a little ways from the village on the river about ten miles west northwest."

Even if he hadn't called us "Hoss," I know instantly that our FAC is Capt. Harold Chaumont Flynn--a friend and fellow interceptor jockey from Tyndall Air Force Base, Florida. He is known far and wide as "Chaumont," and is one of the most unforgettable characters in a large circle. He has many claims to fame, but I believe his proudest, and also the most memorable is the source of his middle name, by which he is most widely known.

Chaumont's father was a Marine Corps officer. In 1927, he completed a tour of duty in China and shipped out to the States aboard the USS Chaumont. His wife was great with child when the young couple boarded the USS Chaumont in Shanghai harbor for a voyage that would take them to Pearl Harbor and then to the States. It was no surprise to the ship's doctor or to the Flynns when Mrs. Flynn went into labor in transit. Her labor terminated with the birth of a healthy baby boy. After the delivery, the ship's doctor noted the time of the birth and completed the official record of this momentous event.

The ship's doctor did a superlative job, as far as his professional medical responsibilities were concerned, but made a very natural and almost inevitable mistake in recording the time of the birth. You see, the ship was very near the International Date Line—a small detail in the record keeping process, but a major defect in the process of determining and recording the birthdate of this healthy young Marine. For the remainder of the voyage, Captain Flynn, the youngsters father, the doctor who attended the youngster's delivery, and the ship's navigator agonized over this issue, which never got resolved—the result—two birthdays for this future Marine and Air Force fighter pilot.

The youngster's mother, the calmest of the group which was trying to nail down this boy's birthday, ignored the issue that, to her, was trivial, and got on with naming her newborn son. She wisely chose Harold as his first name, and then, even wiser, chose the name of the ship, Chaumont, as his middle name. Thus Harold Chaumont Flynn began his illustrious career as a human being. And thus, for the next few minutes this Air Commando Flight will do Chaumont's bidding in his role as a Red Marker FAC.

We soon see Red Marker ahead of us. He is lower than we are and is turning from our right to left as we fly northwest from Can Tho. There are a lot of waterways here with heavy foliage covering the banks. As we approach, Bill converses with Red Marker. "Red marker, Commando here. We're closing in on your position with Two A-1s with bombs, napalm, and 20 mike mike."

"Roger, Hoss. We've got some VC activity down this little creek a ways. Just gimme a minute or two and we'll see what we can do about it."

Bill takes our flight of two out to the right of Red marker, and we weave around to keep him in sight as he follows the gentle bends in the bayou below us. Bill and Red Marker discuss details of our exact ordnance load. I am excited about the whole thing as the big 3,300 cubic inch eighteen cylinder radial engine voices its support of this mission with its deep throated rumble furnishing 2,000 plus horsepower to keep us airborne, and the telltale uncertainty of the tachometer readings that refuse to settle on a number and stay there--just one of the remarkable little details that characterize this fine airplane.

Red Marker is busy talking to ground troops and to the Tactical Operations Center (TOC) that controls air and ground operations in this area. This is a hot area and a major terminus of the Ho Chi Minh trail that is the pathway for logistics support from North Viet Nam to the Viet Cong operations all over South Viet Nam.

Our interest in all of Viet Nam is on a vertical rise, as we realize that this conflict we are in has a lot of uncertainty. We are facing a movement that totally defeated the French at a place called Dien Bien Phu and re-sulted in the end of French Colonial rule in Indo China, including not only Viet Nam, but Laos and Cambodia as well. For the first time since our interest in this area began in the mid-fifties, the United States is committing combat personnel to this effort, no longer as "advisers," but as active combatants.

I am riding along as a trainee on an active combat mission. Red Marker's role today is to provide the catalyst that will result in the death of VC soldiers, and in doing so, he and this commando flight are risking all we have to achieve that objective. I am carrying an M-16 rifle and a .38 caliber revolver with the full intent that if the worst comes to us, I have been a marksman since the age of seven and will do my best to con-tinue the fight on the ground.

Red Marker briefs us as we proceed to the target area. "Hoss, this is a hot area we're approaching. We can expect small arms fire from au-tomatic weapons. Our objective is to knock out some VC support facili-ties and to kill any VC that we can. The village that we're approaching is total VC territory. They are well dug in, and we probably won't see a soul. I will hear any ground fire, and you may see some. If we sustain any battle damage, head for Can Tho. As far as I know we still hold Can Tho, and you will be o.k."

Man, is this war, or what. The Commandos I'm flying with today have faced ground fire before--usually no big deal. These big airplanes with radial engines can sustain a lot of battle damage from small arms and make it to safety.

{As I write these words in retrospect, I re-live a discontinuity in the Force. Just three days after today's mission, Bill Campbell will be living out Red Marker's advice to try to make Can Tho if he sustains battle damage. In this same area the VC open up on the Commandos, and Bill's airplane with that big radial engine sustains battle damage and catches fire. Bill finds himself in an awkward position in terms of making a safe dead stick landing at Can Tho airport. He puts down on the paved runway, but there's not enough room to stop. The A-1 rolls off the runway into a bayou--the landing gear buries in the mud and the big airplane flips forward onto its back with Bill and Capt. Jerry Hawkins trapped in the cockpit. They do not survive. While Bill and Jerry are dead, the airplane has sustained very little damage and is returned to service. Later on, another valiant Commando will earn the Medal of Honor while pilot-ing the same airplane at a place called A Shau. Ken Hughey, October, 2013.}

We soon go to work. Chaumont puts out a red smoke and directs our attack. We, and our wingman, roll in for repeated attacks. We expend bombs and napalm, and end by strafing the periphery of the area with 20 millimeter cannon fire. Chaumont is pleased as he warns us that he expects to see us all in the Officer's Club at Bien Hoa this evening.

The Club at Bien Hoa is a rather open building--plenty of fresh air. The weather is nice, and open air is comfortable. I am about to take a quaff from my beer glass when a bugle blasts "Charge" through an open window about ten feet away. I hold my beer steadily and turn to the window to see Chaumont's smiling face as he peers inside, his bugle clearly visible in his left hand, spies me, and calls out: "Hey, Hoss, good work today. I'll be in in a few minutes and we can catch up on the war." I wave a "Roger," hang out 'til Chaumont shows up, and we spend the evening catching up.

The last time that I had seen Chaumont was on a Sunday afternoon about two years before at Andrews AFB, Maryland, just outside Washington, D.C. I had spent the previous night visiting my sisters, Catherine and Ruby, and was filing a flight plan to return to Los Angeles, where I was stationed at Space Systems Division. Chaumont had two children--Soupy and Boy. At that time, my only son was not here.

Chaumont was the Airdrome Officer that day. I completed my flight plan and passed it across the counter to him for filing. Chaumont dropped my flight plan on the floor behind the operations counter and picked it up. He perused it for a moment, looked over at me with my flight plan in hand as he critiqued it: "Hoss, " he says, "I've known you for a long time. Always thought you were a professional aviator, and here you are filing a flight plan purporting to depart from the same airdrome as the President of the United States. Hoss, I can't approve this flight plan as you propose to file it -- back to the drawing board, and bring me a flight plan worthy of a professional aviator." With that, he ripped my flight plan to shreds, tossed it into the trash can behind the operations counter, and gazed at my confused, and befuddled face.

I should have known immediately that Chaumont was up to something. In a moment, he stooped to the floor and recovered my "real' flight plan, and, of course he signed it, and I was soon on my way.

Tonight there are no jokes. We have a nice dinner and say farewell. Tonight I have no way of knowing that I will never see this wonderful man again in this world.

I spend the next few days learning how to fly an O-1, and flying a FAC mission with an instructor. We do our pattern work on a dirt strip in the middle of a rubber plantation near Vung Tau, more commonly known by its French name--Cape St. Jacque.

Hello Da Nang

The day after finishing checking out in the 0-1, I ride the regular courier bus to Tan Son Nhut and catch a ride to Da Nang on a C-130. This thing is loaded with a bunch of cartons that occupy the entire cargo space. After I stake out a space on top of the cargo, because the seats are all folded away, the crew invites me to move to the flight deck, and in less than two hours, I thank them for a pleasant ride as I disembark.

I nose around the operations building, and in a few minutes the transient crew gives me a ride to the 20th Tactical Air Support Squadron (TASS) headquarters where I find a warm welcome.

This evening I join some of the other FACs for dinner at The Grand Hotel in Da Nang and spend the night with them in their "villa." Several officers have gone together and rented an estate from a local Viet Namese family. The place is walled and gated, and there is a guard house just inside the front gate. The occupants have hired a group of Nung soldiers to provide security. As soon as we are inside, a Nung soldier closes the heavy iron gate behind us. We stop here and my hosts introduce me to the Nungs. The Nungs look me over and smile. They won't shoot me on sight. They understand that I now belong here, and they will open the gate and salute and smile the next time I approach the gate.

Until further notice, I will live here in the villa. It has lots of rooms and plenty of baths, and ceiling fans in every room. The beds don't have mattresses--just wooden frames (probably teak) and woven rattan mats. We have mosquito nets, but if the fan is running, we don't put them up--as it turns out, mosquitos have a problem landing in a cross wind. One of the denizens is the treasurer, and I pay him by the night until I decide if this is what I want to do. Right now I don't have any other options in mind.

March and April 1965

After my first night at the villa, I learn that I will be assigned to the Viet Namese Second Infantry Division. The senior ALO is Major Wilbur Stone. Because I am the next senior officer to Major Stone, I will be his deputy. Major Stone lives in a two bedroom house in Da Nang that he has been sharing with another officer who is in the process of clearing out. I meet Major Stone and, along with flying missions as a FAC, I begin the process of learning my duties with the Viet Namese Army. I meet the Division Commander, General Lam, and his staff, and begin spending time with the Division Headquarters.

The Division Headquarters is across the Da Nang River on the Beach side of Da Nang. When Major Stone and I are not flying missions, we go to the headquarters to keep track of current intelligence and to learn what we can about the Division, and to bond with the Viets.

Da Nang sits on the Da Nang River that separates the main part of the city from the beach. Every day I go to the pier on the west side of the river and ride a ferry across to the beach side. The headquarters is located on the peninsula that forms the eastern bank of the Da Nang River. The over-riding subject of staff meetings and planning exercises is the impending move to Quang Ngai.

The war here is escalating. The 3rd Marine Amphibuous Force (MAF) has just landed and is stationed in Da Nang to secure the area, particularly the airport. More Americans are joining the fight every day. Along with this increase of American support, the Viets are attempting to turn the war around by their own activities. Moving the 2nd Infantry Division to Quang Ngai is a small part of the overall effort to change the way things are going. Our successes on the ground with the VC have been worse than disappointing. The VC are in control of the war. They show up when least expected, carry out an operation that costs the lives of a hundred or so of "our" guys and disappear. The V believe that placing forces within those areas controlled by the maquis (known in current parlance as VC) will improve the situation. Maybe.

For the next few weeks, Major Stone and I spend time at the 2nd Infantry Headquarters every day. We have two FACs located on the airport at Quang Ngai airport who fly every day in support of the Battalions that are located at Quang Ngai. This whole area is in a state of transition. In the meantime, Major Stone's room-mate departs and I move into the small house with him.

The house we live in has two bedrooms, two bath rooms, a living room, and a combination dining room and kitchen. A Viet family lives in a small house in the back yard that has all the necessities. The man of the house is a Viet soldier who is seldom home. His wife, their eight year old niece, and an infant son live there and do our housekeeping.

We rent this house from Madam Nam, a refugee from the 1954 split when all the French sympathizers and non-communists moved South, and the Viet Minh, who supported Ho Chi Minh moved North. I soon learn that not all of the Viet Minh chose to move to the North. Many sided with Ho Chi and Vo Nguyen Giap to rid themselves of the French, but once the French left, they wanted no part of the Communist regime that Ho Chi wanted to impose. Some of these former Viet Minh soldiers became soldiers in the ARVN and now stand with "us."

Madam Nam is not a soldier, but she, like many others who lived in the North, wanted no part of a Communist government. In 1954

Madam Nam left Ha Noi with all the worldly possessions she could pack, and moved to Da Nang. She now owns a lot of real estate in Da Nang, and rents homes and villas and apartments to the newly assigned American members of Military Assistance Command Viet Nam) MACV.

RON STORZ

From March 26 until April 10, I fly combat missions, most of them dual flights with an experienced FAC. On April 11, I participate in a ground operation about thirty miles south of Da Nang. Airman First Class Borofsky and I load about a ton of radio gear into a jeep and convoy to the prospective battle zone. We spend three days in the field pretending to look for VC. Often, the VC are the ones that do the finding, and they do it when and where you least suspect them.

Given a day going, three days camping out, and one day returning to Da Nang, we are gone five days. The best result of the operation, from the ALO/FAC point of view, is the successful operation of our radio equipment. For us to be effective "in the field," we need to be able to use HF (High Frequency for long range communications), VHF (Very High Frequency) for talking to our Command Center, Ultra High Frequency (UHF) for talking to fighters, and Frequency Modulation (FM), for communications with ground troops.)

I am now completely averse to any attempts to control air strikes from the ground. If we had been pinned down, we couldn't have seen enough to give any directions to fighter cover. Conclusion: arrange for airborne FACs, which is what we routinely did, even on those occasions when we had FACs on the ground.

On April 28, 1965, I fly a FAC mission west of Da Nang. While we are flying our mission, Capt. Ron Storz is flying a mission in the northernmost part of I Corps. He departed one of our airports and was expected to land at another, but, as the day progressed, he never showed up. It soon became apparent that he wasn't going to show up.

For the next three days, our number one mission is to search for Ron's airplane, believing that he had to have been forced down somewhere in the northern part of I Corps. We organize the search by dividing the area that he "had" to be in into grids. We comb all the grids repeatedly—not a trace of Ron or his airplane.

Some of the grids include the hills to the west toward Laos. One of the searchers, flying low, looking at the sides of the hills, spots a discontinuity in the jungle canopy, and soon we have a rescue helicopter to investigate. They don't find an O-1 or Ron Storz, but what remains of two T-28s and their occupants that had flown into the hillside in formation, apparently in bad weather, about two years ago. They were on their way to Thailand and had disappeared. We don't find any trace of Ron, but maybe one day someone will locate the wreckage of his airplane and at least find his dog tags.

Ron is not the first, nor will he be the last, but he is the only one that I know of that just vanished into thin air.

(Two and a half years later, I am living in solitary confinement in prison in Ha Noi when I make contact with 1/Lt Loren Torkelson, another POW, by tapping through a foot thick masonry wall. We share this wall for about ten days during which Loren passes 170 names of our fellow POWs for me to memorize. The names are arranged by service and rank, and late on the list of Air Force Captains comes Ron Storz. I am nonplussed and can only surmise that he inadvertently crossed the DMZ and was shot down and captured. Years later, while still in prison, I learned that Ron Storz was one of the Alcatraz 12--the *toughest of the tough resistors, and that when the V vacated the Alcatraz Camp where the 12 were held, they left Ron behind. His body was returned after we were released. The V reported that he died on April 30, 1970. They omitted the*

fact that they had tortured him mercilessly and steadily for five years-- from April 1965 until April 1970.)

May & June 1965

In May and June 1965, the Second Infantry Division goes through a lot of changes. First of all, the ARVN high command has decided that the Second Division should move from Da Nang to Quang Ngai so as to be more closely located to the outlying areas that supported the *Maquis*, in that these areas were controlled by the VC. At the same time, the U.S. Army appoints a senior Colonel, Bruce B. Jones, as the senior advisor to the Second Corps. This move, combined with Colonel Jones' appointment, resulted from the increased VC activity throughout South Viet Nam and the generally poor performance of the Army of the Republic of Viet Nam (ARVN). In our first joint staff meeting with Colonel Jones, he makes it clear that he intends to have a heavy hand in training the Second Corps, and that he expects positive results.

After these changes, the Second Corps goes berserk with planning activity. The II Corps Commander, Major General Lam, the Civilian Province Chief of the Quang Ngai Province, along with Colonel Bruce B. Jones, and the entire combination of their respective staffs are anxious, not just for vindication of the Corps' mediocre prior performance, but to move out and be more proactive in operations to rid this area of VC. General Lam orders his battalion commanders to plan ground operations to that end. Colonel Jones is everywhere at once. My boss, Major Richard B. Davis, the Senior Air Liaison Officer (ALO) for the Second Corps, participates in the planning, and one or more of the FACs under his command are present at the planning exercises.

Soon two of General Lam's Battalions move out to the area northwest of Ba Gia in an effort to engage the VC in an open battle. This is hard to do. The VC's usual modus operandi is to carefully pick a target and plan a surprise attack, usually at night, execute the plan, and then blend into the local population, or simply retreat into the countryside. There have been occasions when men who work at local businesses, or even on military installations, turn up in the VC body count after such an engagement. The VC seldom fight in pitched battle conditions, but, when they do, they are formidable adversaries. At one time, Time Magazine published an article entitled "Their Lions; Our Rabbits" that discusses the difference in the vastly superior performance of the VC troops compared to the ARVN. There are very few ARVN units that have had much success against the VC, and General Lam wants to reverse that trend.

Colonel Jones and some of his advisors are salted into the command sections of the ARVN units. On the second day of this "sweep," the VC come out to play. A large contingent of VC engage the attacking units in a head on confrontation, and suddenly the attacking forces begin a retreat in the face of early losses. As the retreating troops move rearward, the VC assault their left flank, and things worsen rapidly. The ARVN withdraw completely, in mass disarray. Only the superior mobility of the ARVN forces prevents a total disaster. The VC are all on foot, and disappear just as rapidly as they showed up. Soon, the stench of the dead ARVN bodies becomes very noticeable. US Army helicopters along with ARVN trucks, evacuate the battlefield.

After the disengagement, I pull up to a group of jeeps loosely assembled at a safe distance from the fight. Colonel Jones and a group of senior ARVN officers are discussing the operation over a map spread across the hood of one of the jeeps. I creep in and stand at Colonel Jones' left as he queries the commanders about the situation. Colonel Jones is becoming increasingly agitated.

Whatever has happened is getting to Bruce B. Jones in a big way-- unusual in that his usual demeanor is very calm and measured. The

ARVN must have done something really bad. Suddenly, Bruce B. raises his right fist and pounds the map on the Jeep's hood with such force that I'm surprised he didn't injure his hand as well as the Jeep's hood, and says something like: "What were you thinking about? Why did you violate our plan? Where were you when...? "

In the aftermath of this engagement, all parties go back to the drawing board. This was Colonel Jones' first experience with ARVN forces, and he is determined to assist General Lam to get the Second Division shaped up for a better showing.

In the meantime, we, the FACs, fly every day in support of the outposts by doing visual reconnaissance (VR) and by calling in and controlling airstrikes in an attempt to keep track of VC activity and to locate and engage them when possible. Sometimes we land at our outposts and take the Army advisors on VR missions in their area. On one of those missions, I take a US Army Ranger Captain with me to look over the area surrounding the outpost that he advises. A segment of hilly jungle on the west side of the outpost troubles him. The VC have probed his outpost several times and the movements that the ARVN have been able to observe seems to come from the area we over fly today.

The area is heavily wooded--a tropical forest. We can't see much. I let down in an attempt to spot trails or other activity through the tree cover. We see nothing, but our lower presence may have made those who were concealed below believe that we had spotted them--the VC open fire with automatic weapons. They can see us, but we can't see them. Tracers are emerging from the tree canopy like hail going the wrong direction. I am terrified and turn hard toward the outpost, believing that our mission may soon be over. One of the rounds enters the airplane near the throttle quadrant and fragments rip through my flight suit near my left elbow. Another round shatters the rear window. I roll the wings level and pull my arms in so that shots fired from directly below will strike the armor plating that we sit on.

Soon the hail stops and we continue toward the outpost. I turn to take a look at my passenger. His visage is not appealing. His face is covered with blood, and blood is streaming down from cuts on his forehead. I don't feel anything, but blood is oozing through the rips in the left sleeve of my flight suit. I return to the 500 foot airstrip near the outpost and land.

We have a fix on the source of the gunfire, but we never saw a soul through the jungle canopy. Frustrating.

We have a pow-wow with the Army advisers and the V Commander. The US Army has a medic present who cleans up our wounds. The Ranger Captain's bloody face looked a lot worse than his injuries turn out to be. After a clean-up and some bandage cover on his forehead, he is good to go. Same for me. My flight suit is more damaged than I am. The medic cleans and dresses our injuries and submits a medical report. I get in my airplane and fly back to Quang Ngai. A short time later the Army awards us Purple Hearts.

We were lucky. For several of us, there was no flight back to any-place. The first blood they lost was all they had to give--their first Purple Heart was also their last.

The Paint Job
In April Major Stone departs for the states having finished his tour of combat duty. For a few days I live alone in our cottage, waiting for Major Stone's replacement. During the first week in May, Major Rick Davis arrives, and reports in to the 20th TASS. We maintain the precedent that

the 2nd Division ALO and his assistant lives in the house that Major Stone and I occupied, and my new boss moves in with me.

Rick Davis is a different breed of cat from most of us who are manning the FAC positions in the 20th TASS. He has spent his entire career in Tactical Air Command (TAC), and has considerable experience dealing with joint operations with the Army in different potential combat scenarios. I soon figure out that either he is the biggest liar in the world, or that he is one of the most talented officers I have ever met.

The day he joins me in his new digs as my new boss and room-mate is unseasonably hot. I am at home when one of our vehicles deposits him in the front yard. I am expecting him, but have no idea what he will look like or what kind of person he will be. I am hoping that he will be friendly and capable, and that he will be the kind of person I like.

As the jeep that brought him here pulls out of the yard, I see through the screen door a tall dude in fatigues, soaking wet with sweat, carrying a fully packed duffle bag, hustling across the yard. I step to the door and open it for him. He steps into the living room, plops the duffle on the floor, extends a long right arm with hand attached, and says: "Hi, I'm Rick Davis," with a detectable Texas tone. Whatever preconceived perceptions I had about my future boss, they were instantly forgotten. Whatever or whoever this man is, he is cut from a special mold. It only takes a few fractions of a second to figure this out.

After the usual greetings and initial process of getting acquainted, Rick says: "Look, a shower and a cold beer would really feel good right now. You must know your way around in this town, so what do you say I get a shower and some dry clothes and let's go to one of your favorite bistros here in the Orient and figure out where we're headed?" I say: "O. K."

I show Rick his room and wait for him to freshen up. In the meantime I reflect on where we should go for a cool one and a talk. I've only been here a few weeks myself and really am not the best choice for a tour guide, but in a minute I recall that the best known bistro in this part of the world is *The Forget-me-not Bar*, that has been immortalized by Bernard Fall in *Street Without Joy*. I happen to know where it is and instantly decide to show off my social acumen by taking my newly acquired boss to the most famous bistro in Southeast Asia--just a short drive in our jeep.

Rick quickly shows up in civvies--slacks and a short sleeved shirt-- and we take off in our jeep. I park in front of *The Forget Me Not* and soon we are sitting at a table with a couple of *Ba Mui Ba* beers. I can't help but show my awesome knowledge of the local language and culture by explaining to Rick the origin of the name of this famous beer.

First, I have to teach this Texan fighter jock how to count in Viet Namese: Mot, hai, ba, tam, tien,..., mui." Then I explain that *ba* means three and *mui* means ten, and that to express multiples of ten you just combine the two terms and that *ba mui* means three tens which is thirty and that *ba mui ba* literally translates into English as "three tens three" which means thirty three (33). The label on the bottle is "33." After a couple of these, we get on with more serious conversation.

It is soon clear that Rick has a clear understanding of the type of operations we are engaged in and has a plan to make us the best we can be, given the situation we're in.

Rick and I are soon fast friends. He is a "big brother." Not the kind that goes around out-smarting you and for whom you have a dislike for looking down on you, but the kind that bails you out when you are in over your head--the kind that calls you "dummy" when you do something dumb, and then takes you aside to share a coke, and tells you how not to be a dummy. By the time we get in our jeep to go to the most upscale restaurant in Da Nang--*The Grand Hotel*--for dinner, I have come to believe that Rick Davis is the "real article." The next ten months in combat will prove me right.

Perhaps the most important function a leader can perform is to do all those things to improve morale of those whom he leads. Rick understood this function as well as the greatest leaders. Right off the bat, he showed his respect for the people who made us a success. He made sure that the men who kept our airplanes in running order knew that we all understood that their efforts kept us alive. He let our administrative staff know that our schedules and mundane paperwork was really important to all of us in operating efficiently. He accomplished these things by being a "normal" human being, but, in the process, we all came to view him as a demi-god.

Not long after we became ensconced at Quang Ngai, Rick suggested that we do some kind of nose art on our airplanes. Rick fires off a missive to Walt Disney studios asking them for suggestions and for permission to use an appropriate cartoon character. The studio responds promptly, but the illustration they were going to allow us to use was not a Bird Dog, so we decided to design one of our own.

A day or two after we decided to do our own art work, I went to Da Nang, and, per Rick's orders, procured a gallon each of red, black, white, and gray paint. Rick then took a pencil and drew an outline of a Bird Dog image on the nose of one of our airplanes. We were all standing around as he finished the job. Then he noted the colors that each section of the outline needed to be painted. We set to painting each section by taking turns with the brush. While we were doing that, Rick marked up another airplane, and soon we had all six done.

We were all incredulous at Rick's imagination and skill. Soon he had constructed, with labor from all of us, a command post display in our corner of the 2nd Infantry Tactical Operations Center (TOC), and arranged our furniture to make the place look like a Command Post. We were learning fast how to do things like careful planning of flying time so that the six airplanes were staggered a few hours apart and we had one airplane at a time out for periodic inspection.

Rick's staff meetings were simple and effective in keeping us on track with details. We soon had a very close-knit and effective team, and our airplanes soon became well known.

Rick later retired from the Air Force and moved to Denver, Colorado. He took his final flight West way too soon. Thanks, Rick, for a lot of jobs well done!!

Photo 5

Glenn Jones, Bird Dog 42, in one of our Bird Dogs about fifteen miles east of Quang Ngai. Note the White Phosphorous warheads protruding from underneath the wings just outboard of the support struts.

One for the good guys

On 23 June, 1965, things are hopping around Quang Ngai. The VC are brazenly taking on the ARVN every chance they get. Today the Second Infantry Division (ARVN) is in the middle of an operation in the Quang Ngai Province about 30 miles from the city of Quang Ngai. I am alone in an 0-1-E as we work the battle zone in relays. I have the shift from 08:30 to 10:30 and have six flights of fighters at my disposal to support the troops on the ground. We are never certain how these operations will play out, but always hope for engagements with the VC that allow us to use air power. Clear weather and daylight make things easier, as well as terrain and location. This operation looks promising as to all these criteria.

I am overhead on the leading edge of the battle area. The Tactical Operations Center (TOC) in Quang Ngai relays targeting information to me, and there are also some Americans imbedded with the ARVN on the ground who can keep me informed of their situation. At about 08:25, the TOC relays a set of Universal Transverse Mercatror (UTM) coordinates to me and asks me to take out a segment of a village at BS 490 345. I am soon over this area at 2,000 feet. The weather is clear--great visibility and I have no trouble laying out an attack plan for the first flight of fighters, a flight of two F-100s from Da Nang, call sign Yogi 11. Just before 08:30 Yogi checks in.

"Bird Dog 41, Yogi 11, Flight of two Huns with four Mark 82s and 20 mike mike, each."

"Roger Yogi, let's start with the bombs and then get more specific with some 20 mm. Let me throw in a Willie Pete and we'll get started."

"Roger, Bird Dog, we'll hold."

I roll in, launch a rocket with a Willie Pete warhead to mark the area, and call Yogi:

"Yogi, my smoke is the eastern boundary or the target. I'll hang out to the east for your attack north to south. Lead, put one fifty feet to the west of my smoke and we'll work from there."

"Roger, Bird Dog, any ground fire?"

"Haven't seen or heard any yet."

"Roger Bird Dog, Yogi Lead in hot with a single."

Yogi Lead plants the 500 pound Mark 82 right where I asked him, and, as Yogi 2 rolls in, I ask him to put his first bomb just south of leads, and we begin a steady decimation of this target area. Yogi makes four nice bomb runs and we begin strafing the adjoining area. Four strafing passes and Yogi has expended his load and says good-bye.

At 08:55 Chain 1-1, Marines from Chu Lai, calls in overhead with 4 A-4s with four Mark 82s and 200 rounds of 20 mike mike each. We work systematically to complete the destruction at Bravo Sierra 490 345, then hold up and move a bit to the west to Bravo Sierra 488 333. Chain completes the job and heads home.

I circle about looking over the ARVN ground positions and talking to the TOC and to the troops on the ground. The TOC, who is also in contact with the ground troops, asks me to proceed to Bravo Sierra 520 720 about two miles north northwest of the area we just smoked. The attacking ground forces think that they will engage a large contingent of VC locals, along with some North Viet regulars in that area. I can't detect any indicators but that doesn't mean they aren't there. The VC are not going to run out into the open and wave greetings to me.

Our normal minimum altitude is 2,000 feet above the ground. When we are in VCville, we normally stay at or above 2,000 feet, unless something unusual entices us lower. I stay at 2,000 feet today since our intelligence indicates that if we encounter a large number of enemy, they will most likely be carrying at least one .50 caliber machine gun. An up close encounter between a low flying Bird Dog and a .50 is extremely dangerous for the Bird Dog.

Hatred 2-1, a flight of four Marine A-4s from Chu Lai shows up at 09:45. By this time, I have laid out a plan of attack to soften up the area around the BS 520 720 coordinates. This is a village that is believed to be well dug in and well-armed. Some of our ground forces are already near here to the west and others are on their way. Our ground forces are close enough to have a good view of Hatreds work, but far enough away not to worry about debris. Hatred expends their load and leaves. Chain 2-1, also Marines from Chu-Lai, continues the work that their team mates began. Hatred 4-1 is right behind Chain and puts on a good show.

Our last gasp this morning in our effort to soften the target battle ground, is another flight of two F-100s from Da Nang--Yogi 31. Yogi 31 is the parenthesis of this morning action. I circle directly over the target area and point out places that could stand a little more treatment. We wouldn't want to leave any VC neglected, not that any of the prior strikes left much to be done. At 10:40 I depart the area as one of my kin takes over and continues to work the periphery of the intended battle zone.

At 13:30 I am back in the area. Our ground forces have closed in on an area about one mile west and a half a mile north of the last area that Yogi 31 struck this morning. The ground troops are in shooting range of the VC, and I can hear the sporadic gunfire. Chain 5-1, another flight of Marines, is overhead waiting to get into the fight. I see movement too close to friendlies for bombs. I talk to the ground troops who are nearest the front of the engagement and tell them what I see, and then I launch a Willie Pete far enough to the west so as not to splash any of our friendlies, but close enough to direct an attack on the movers.

As Chain Lead rolls in to strafe, he can see my smoke and he also sees the movers. He is passing from north to south and knows where the friendlies are. I see the flame from his 20 mm cannons as he spots a long burst into the VC. I couldn't understand why they were moving in the open, but it was their last move. Chain hammers away at a couple of spots that I relay to him and then unload their bombs into the VC rear positions.

Apple 6-1 replaces Chain. The battlefield position is moving westward, and we have moved an armored car with a machine gun into a position slightly north and a bit west. As the ground troops move aggressively, the VC retreat toward the west. There is a lot of cover in the form of trees, but I can see individuals as they dart about. Apple Flight uses their 20 mm cannons and we make it hot for the other side. I can see several bodies and estimate that Apple took care of at least 25.

Mead 51, two F-100s from Da Nang, replaces Apple. Mead has a crazy mix of ordnance--two 750 pound bombs each and two napalms each, along with their 20 mm cannons. The VC are still showing up where I can detect their movement and I know where our guys are. I pop out a willy pete and Mead 51 comes in with napalm parallel to our guys and about 75 feet away. We hold up after the first pass to let some smoke clear and to talk to the ground troops. The front is moving steadily west--the first time I have seen the ARVN react aggressively in the face of fire. Mead 51 comes back in with their remaining napalm and then two long strafing runs out in front.

Mead 61 shows up with 4 F-100s with napalm and 20 mike mike. The VC have cleared the battle field and have retreated into a village of about 30 hooches. Our ground forces hold up and Mead 61 takes care of the village. As the village goes up in smoke, I note the remaining VC force retreating toward the trees to the west.

Hatred 7-1, Marine A-4s, arrives with bombs and 20mm. We paste the trees as the retreating force tries to move through them toward another small village a few hundred yards further west. We space the bombs throughout the trees and lace the area with cannon fire. I can see bodies lying about.

Chain 8-1, Marines again, finish the day. They are carrying four 250 pound bombs each along with 20 mm. We continue plastering the battle ground as the ground troops keep it close. We work the bombs to stay about 100 yards or so ahead of the ground troops. They are ok with that--just get low as they watch the fighters roll in. When we are through bombing, Chain loiters while I talk to the ground. The ground commanders are pleased with the air work that we have done. We talk about working the area in front of them (west), and say that they intend to move rapidly westward to occupy the entire battle zone before dark. It looks like a cake walk to them.

I search for movement in the frontal area and see none. I advise the ground and they move out as Chain holds overhead. Chain has about an hour of loiter time remaining and will stay with us until something else happens. The ground troops move out smartly. They have artillery positioned to cover as needed and will have Chain overhead for another hour.

I am in the max loiter mode, and we can get more air if we need it. The operation has all the earmarks of success. There can't be much resistance left, and I have counted a lot of VC bodies in the process. As Chain loiters, my relief shows up, and I say goodbye to all and head to Quang Ngai for food and rest.

The week after this operation was a hoot for the 2nd Infantry Division. There were very few casualties on our side and a huge body count on the other. The Division brought a bunch of recovered weapons to the Quang Ngai complex for display. There were more than a hundred AK-47s--many nearly brand new-- and a room full of 75mm recoilless rifles and grenade launchers--all very new. The 75mm rifles are exact replicas of our own, but with Chinese characters all over them. I make a big mistake by not helping myself to a new AK. Several of my Army buddies carried AKs from then on, and I know that there were ways to get them home.

The ARVN needed this success. Since I got here in March, this is the only time that II Corps has connected. General Lam and his staff are trying hard to "pacify" this area, but the job is difficult and success is hard come by against the *Maquis* all over the country. Our friendlies seem to be holed up in the more urban areas, but the VC pretty much own the Maquis. It is an astonishing piece of luck that the VC showed up in numbers in broad daylight to face off with the ARVN in daylight and perfect weather. *(I don't know it now, but this will be the first and last time that I will ever see this happen.)*

PHOTO 6

General Lam, Commander 2nd ARVN Division has just pinned a Viet Namese decoration (Cross of Gallantry) on my shirt. Lt. Terry Luke, Bird Dog 48, is to my immediate left, and will receive the same decoration next. The Viet Namese soldiers you see were also decorated. This formation occurred a few days after the previous events--these are some of the "good guys." These Viet soldiers went after the VC with a vengeance during the operation, and are lucky to be standing in this formation. Terry Luke and I took turns directing air strikes covering the ground troops during the aforementioned proceedings.

Snarks and Boojums

During the remainder of June, we continue to attack VC targets as they are identified by our combined intelligence. We have several flights of fighters nearly every day, and we get shot at sometimes. The idea is to keep the VC "on the run." The targets are outlying villages that are enclaves of VC activity. The operation we just finished was a surprise to me. I never expected to catch the VC in such numbers, or with so much equipment.

Our main targets are scattered small villages that make up the *maquis* that stymied the French, more like the typical guerilla activity that we came here expecting. In all the lectures regarding the French experience here and a review of the British experience in Malaysia, we thought we knew that pitched fights like the one we just finished would be rare, and that has been the case. Hunting VC is a little like hunting the Snark; they are very hard to find and when you think you've found one and have him by the scruff of the neck, you discover that he's really a Boojum.

We spend a lot of time hunting Snarks.

From June 27 through July 3, I fly seventeen sorties, in search of, and sometimes killing Snarks. We concentrate on areas in and around the outposts at Ba Gia and Ba To, hoping to eliminate any VC activity.

On 27 June, Lt Tu, a VNAF FAC and intelligence officer flies with me in my back seat. During the morning, we do visual reconnaissance (VR) and then lunch at the Hotel Viet Nam in Quang Ngai. During the lunch break, Lt Tu arranges for a flight of VNAF A-1s to join us in the afternoon.

Back in the Ba Gia area, Panther Pink flight shows up with four A-1s loaded for bear. Panther Pink 3 is a U.S. Air Force pilot. My final note on thi+s mission is "…had a little fun today." We did indeed have some fun. I had the privilege of watching VNAF A-1s on more than one occasion, and was always impressed. Panther Pink did not disappoint.

The VNAF never carries big bombs, but load down with small stuff, ranging from 50 pounds to 250 pounds. Their specialty is a lot of time on station delivering one bomb per run with pin-point accuracy. Some of their pilots have thousands of hours of A-1 time and it shows. These four airplanes stayed with us for nearly two hours picking off targets per Lt Tu's instructions.

The morning of June 28 is a briefing and planning session. In the afternoon, I meet a flight of Marine F-4s from Da Nang--Fly Train 45--loaded with Napalm, 1000 pound bombs, 500 pound bombs, and Zuni Rockets. I love watching F-4s do their stuff up close. They are beautiful, fast, noisy, leave a humongous trail of black smoke, and put their ordnance on the target. Today they level a good sized housing area in VCland.

29 June is a Marine day featuring sorties by Marine fighters. We spend the day around the Ba To area striking targets with UTM coordinates BT 9xx 2yy, destroy every building we can find, and leave the area smoking. The call signs are Fly Train, F-4s from Da Nang; and Hatred, Chain and Apple, A-4s from Chu Lai.

PHOTO 7

Hunting Snarks, June, 1965

30 June is a replay of 29.

1 July is another Marine Corps day--this time seven flights of four F-4s from Da Na+ng with 1,000 pound Bombs, 500 pound bombs, Napalm, and Zuni rockets, followed by an RF-4 reconnaissance bird to

photo the carnage. 1, 2, and 3 July are similar. We seem to be on a Holiday roll, and then there is...

Ba Gia July 5, 1965

The outpost at Ba Gia, a village and farm area about 30 miles to the north west of Quang Ngai, is the centroid of the intense Snark hunt during the last days of June and early July.

All of the outposts are similarly laid out. There is a central area mostly underground. This central area is protected by barbed wire and concertina wire and is surrounded by a mine field usually 30 or 40 yards deep. Inside the wire, there are machine guns and howitzers and grenade and rocket launchers. The VC are always eager to overrun these outposts and seize the armaments, beginning with the howitzers.

Just before midnight on July 5, the TOC sends a runner to waken Major Davis, and in turn, to roust out Capt. Glenn Jones and myself in our quarters. We congregate in the TOC in very short order to learn that the outpost at Ba Gia is under siege. VC are all over the place. Major Davis dispatches Glenn Jones and me to take off and get over Ba Gia ASAP and stand by for developments. Glenn and I, along with our ground crew and Viet Namese observers who will ride with us in our back seats, head for Quang Ngai airport. In about half an hour, we are over Ba Gia.

PHOTO 8

Bird Dog 40, Major Rick Davis and Bird Dog 42, Capt. Glenn Jones at the front door of the Tactical Operations Center, 2nd Division, ARVN, Summer 1965. Glenn Jones played a huge role in all 2nd Infantry operations described herein.

We have asked for flares, and a flare ship is on its way from Da Nang. The Marine fighter wing at Chu Lai is scrambling A-4s, and we know that we will soon hear A-4s overhead with call signs Apple, Hatred, or Chain—the three fighter squadrons from Chu Lai. All of our communications from the ground will come from contact with the outpost and/ or the TOC through our FM radios to the Viet Namese observers in our back seat. There are no Americans at Ba Gia.

Glenn and I set up with altitude separation and start trying to figure out what is going on. The half hour or so that it took us to get here has already added up to eternity for a lot of the troops inside Ba Gia. From the reports that our observers are relaying to us, our presence or absence may not matter to the rest. The VC are blowing holes in the barbed wire defenses and swarming into the compound, and there's nothing we can do but listen in. The outpost is dark. Our friendlies in there are either already dead or in hand-to-hand combat with the VC.

The first Marine flight checks in: "Bird Dog 41, Hatred 41 over your position with 2 A-4s. Four Napalms and 200 rounds of 20 mike mike each."

"Roger, Hatred, loud and clear. We're on hold trying to sort out what's going on down below. Can you hold while we work it out?'"

"Roger, Bird Dog, we'll hold."

My VHF receiver crackles to life: "Bird Dog 41, this is Panama, do you read."

"Roger, Panama 5 square, go ahead."

"Bird Dog 41, Flare ship call sign November November is headed your way. He's a VNAF C-47 that speaks English. He'll be at 8,000 feet on your UHF strike frequency."

"Roger, Panama, can't wait to hear from him."

I call Hatred: "Hatred 41, Bird Dog 41. We have a flare ship inbound at 8,000 feet, where are you?"

"Birddog, we'll stay below 6,000."

"Roger, Hatred. As soon as we get some information and some light we'll be in business."

My back seater tells me that the TOC tells him that we will be cleared to strike anything that moves in the vicinity of Ba Gia. He's telling me that there are no friendlies in the area, and any movement will be hostile. I'm Jake with that. Now if only November November would show. I call Panama. "Panama, Bird Dog 41, where is November November?"

"Bird Dog 41, we're painting November November about ten miles from you at 7,000 feet climbing, I'll have him call you now."

"Roger, Panama, we're switching to combat frequency, will monitor Guard."

"Roger, Bird Dog we'll listen on both."

I wait impatiently for November November. Why doesn't he put that Gooney Bird in After Burner?

"Birddog 41, November November heading your way. Will light up Ba Gia whenever you ready."

"November November light when you get here. We want to see whatever we can. Just let me know when you're dropping your first flare."

"Roger, Bird Dog. This may be long mission. We drop one flare at a time. Don't worry; we keep you lit. This is number one crew."

"Roger November November, we have fighters below you with lights. They will stay below 6,000 feet."

"Roger Bird Dog, I see the fighters. We are also lighted. No Sweat!"

I look around and spot the fighters, and keep searching for November November, then, there he is, right overhead. He'll call a drop any second.

"Bird Dog here is light." I see the ignition that looks like a one second burst from a blow torch, and then it's day light as the parachute pops about a second after November November's drop crew threw it out the door.

Glenn and I circle Ba Gia. There is nothing much to see from 1,500 feet. I drop down to 1,000 feet and circle tighter. I don't want to go any lower, in case the VC are still nearby and have a .50 Caliber. My back seater is talking to the TOC. He breaks off and tells me to look at a group of houses at BS 471 786. The settlement is about 500 yards from the Ba Gia compound. I tell him that I see it. His response: "Destroy it." That's easy.

I talk to all present: "Bird Dog 42, we're talking to TOC, they want us to level the settlement about 500 yards south west of the compound. I intend to mark it and turn it over to Hatred." Glenn comes back: "Roger 41, go for it."

I roll in on the settlement and launch a Willie Pete. The rocket exhaust wiggles a little, settles down, and the white phosphorous warhead bursts in the center of the village. "Hatred do you see my white smoke?"

"Roger, Bird Dog, we see it. "

"O.K. Hatred can you see the low hills to the east and the rise to the south? "

"Roger, Bird Dog it's pretty much like daylight. We can work from north to south, no sweat."

"Roger, Hatred, if we get a temporary dark, it won't last long; our flare ship is dropping one at a time. Meanwhile, you are cleared in on my smoke north to south with napalm."

"Roger, Bird Dog. Hatred two, set up for singles napalm"

"Hatred 2 setting up for napalm singles."

Seconds tick by and: "Hatred lead in hot." Here he comes. He's almost on the deck and descending as he approaches the village. His nose rises and the napalm tank is tumbling as Hatred Lead noses up and into a left turn to a downwind. The Napalm splashes past my smoke and streaks of flame rise from near the center of the group of houses and plays out at the edge of town—perfect delivery.

"Hatred two in hot." Same show. Perfect delivery. But then, that's why we send the Marines.

Four passes and the entire village is burning.

Chain 5-1 Calls inbound, and we exchange appropriate pleasantries and greetings. My back seater is in constant contact with the TOC. The TOC orders us to take out the village at BS 505 793. November November lights it up, and in about five minutes it is also in flames.

Apple 6-1 relieves Chain. The TOC puts the finger on two areas nearby—BS 474 786 and 500 790. Apple takes care of both with day light courtesy of November November.

Second Infantry Headquarters and the Province Chief are in constant discussions and review the situation in detail. The VC killed everybody at Ba Gia and walked away with two 85 millimeter howitzers. The ARVN team is determined to eliminate all parties who made the raid possible. This area has been a hot bed of VC support for a long time, and it is now apparent that we didn't scratch the surface with our recent raids. Snarks are surprising critters.

The next two days are a frenzied search for the howitzers. On July 6, the ARVN re-occupy the outpost and capture/kill the VC who decided to stay. Hatred, Chain, and Apple squadrons show up when needed, and we attempt to destroy every vestige of support for the VC in this corner of Quang Ngai Province. On 8 July the ARVN, with assistance from the U.S. Army, locates and recovers the howitzers. Apparently, the VC crew that annihilated Ba Gia abandoned the howitzers because the burden became too cumbersome, and the presence of the howitzers was like a beacon. Things slow down and we get some rain that impedes our air operations.

For the present, I take a rainy day off and sack out for about ten hours.

This raid on Ba Gia typifies VC operations. They strike with well planned ferocity and disappear. The VC left some bodies behind in Ba Gia, but the raid, in terms of losses, was very efficient on their part. This will not be the last time they take on an outpost at night. They will take losses, but we are losing this war. The VC, including erstwhile Viet Minh, have been doing this stuff for twenty years. They live here and can survive on very little and can appear and disappear, and turn into Boojums, seemingly at will. "Our" troops (the Army of the Republic of Viet Nam [ARVN]) are scared to death of these country bumpkins, who show up out of nowhere armed with AK-47s and fight with unheard of ferocity. The Americans who deal with the ARVN on a daily basis joke about the feckless ARVN.

Everybody in the Second Infantry Division, along with all the Americans involved are smarting from Ba Gia and anxious for revenge.

We have always known that air power alone cannot win a war, much less an effort against a determined force adept at guerilla tactics. We are dealing with a situation that has more than one prong. We not only must deal with the guerillas, but with the mind set of those who support them, along with the complicated intelligence issues--how do we locate the adversary before he locates us?

MARINES

Something needs to be done. The 2nd Infantry Division Staff, along with Colonel Jones and the U.S. Army Advisory Team, as well as the USAF ALO staff, begin a plan to repair the damage and to improve the situation in Quang Ngai province. The plan includes a large scale ground operation in the central part of Quang Ngai Province supported by a massive set of strikes to "prepare" the area and a special set of intense airstrikes to prepare a helicopter Landing Zone and provide air support for the boots on the ground.

Because of the density of the planned air traffic, I go to Chu Lai on July 14 to brief the Marine Air Group. All the pilots and the Group staff are present: The Air Group Commander is Colonel Noble. His Operations officer is LtCol Harris whose personal call sign is *Oxwood*. LtCol. O'keefe commands VMA Squadron 214—their call sign is *Apple*. LtCol. Stender commands VMA Squadron 311—call sign *Chain*. LtCol Baker commands VMA 225—call sign *Hatred*. (*A note: VMA 214 was Pappy Boyington's "Black Sheep" Squadron during part of WWII--they're still a bunch of bad dudes--as are their fellow Squadrons 311 and 225*)

Dealing with Marines is always fun. Marines never ask dumb questions; they listen carefully, make notes, and fill in any blanks with discussion and questions. When I leave Chu Lai, I know that the Marines will show up as planned and get it done.

The next day, July 15 begins at 09:00 with a strike by Oxwood 11, LtCol. Harris himself leading the parade. For the next eight days Hatred, Chain, Apple, Oxwood, Sorel, Condole, and High, a mix of Marines and Air Force are overhead every day. It's interesting to note that Oxwood

11 opens the show on July 15 and Oxwood 12-1 closes the show on July 21--The Marine Air Group Operations Officer personally providing the parentheses. Those #%^&* Marines!!

THREE ON A MATCH

One of my favorite ARVN officers is Captain Cuc. Dai Uy (pronounced "die we" and means Captain) Cuc works in the TOC where his desk is across the room from mine. He has considerable combat experience including fighting the Viet Minh prior to 1954. During that conflict he commanded an armored car and was seriously wounded. His right ear was burned off almost flush with his skull and the left side of his back was burned, including his left hand. He is a member of General Lam's staff and is a player in the intelligence world.

One of Dai Uy Cuc's best friends is a young Artillery observer, a Second Lieutenant named Hiep. Cuc is a full time staffer who spends all of his time in the TOC. Hiep visits the TOC sometimes, but spends most of his time with the ARVN Artillery unit where a part of his routine duties include flying with us as an artillery observer and an intelligence gatherer. Sometimes we hang out together by visiting the local restaurants and knocking around the one main street in Quang Ngai.

During the middle of the planning activity and the intense preparation for a big operation, the three of us--Cuc, Hiep, and I, decide to have dinner at the Hotel Viet Nam on the main drag of Quang Ngai. The dining room at Hotel Viet Nam seats about fifteen people. There is one big round table that will accommodate about eight and there are three booths and one other square table. The head chef is "Mommy-San" who prepares the meals in the back of the room squatting on the floor cooking over an open fire that vents into a chimney like a fireplace. Mommy-San is a skinny little runt who wears a lot of years, chews Beetle Nuts, and squats for hours over the open fire preparing delicious food.

The six VNAF officers assigned to Quang Ngai have an account here paid by the VNAF that makes this place a combination Officer's Mess and Officer's Club for them. I am a frequent lunch guest. Our lunch always begins with some warm beer that we pour over tall glasses of ice. There is no refrigeration in Quang Ngai, but there is an ice plant that furnishes ice to those who can afford it. The only full scale restaurant in Quang Ngai is known as "The Chinaman's," and puts out some great meals. There are other smaller establishments, but the Viet Nam Hotel meals are great.

As soon as the beer is on the table, one of Mommy-San's elves brings several garlic cloves and several bunches of Nim--raw pork crushed, seasoned, and wrapped with mint leaves in bite-sized packets and then over-wrapped in banana leaves cut to enclose each bite. The banana leafed bites are then tied in clusters like grapes hanging in bunches. We each pick some bites of Nim and separate a few garlic cloves as hors d'oeuvres. Next, the elf returns with a round bottomed woven basket, about eighteen inches in diameter and eight inches deep, filled with freshly steamed rice, along with a stack of plates and "dua;" i.e., chop sticks. We tear into the beer, raw garlic, and Nim while we wait for whatever comes next.

There is no menu here. We eat whatever Mommy-San sends to the table, and Mommy-San keeps sending food to the table until we stop eating. Her elves keep an eye on the proceedings, making sure that there is plenty of everything to keep us busy. Sometimes the VNAF troops will ask her to prepare something special, but unless I am with them, I, like everybody else, just take what comes.

Tonight, Cuc, Hiep, and I occupy a small table. We have a delicious meal with lots of talk and camaraderie. Our limousine tonight is the FAC jeep with no muffler, no top, flames streaking from under the hood, the windshield tied down out of the way. After our meal, we leave it parked near the front door of the Hotel and stroll around town, poking our heads into the shopping kiosks along Main Street. We have some sweets as we stroll, and then we find ourselves in front of a photography shop. Cuc suggests that we order a photo of ourselves to commemorate and memorialize a great little get-together. We step into the shop and pose for a snapshot of the three of us.

PHOTO 9

After dinner at Mommy-San's: Left to right: Captain Cuc; Capt Hughey; Lt. Hiep. Note that Capt. Cuc is carefully hiding the left side of his face from the camera. His left ear is burned off level with third degree scars on the side of his neck and down his back as a result of taking a direct hit in the cockpit of an Armored Personnel Carrier (APC) near Hue.

With that, we retire for the evening, and I pick up the photos the next day and distribute them. I send Sue photos that I take on a regular basis, and I include one of these with a note on the back.

On July 22, we continue our routine operations in the province by flying reconnaissance missions and air strikes on intelligence targets. Bird Dog 47--Captain Ed Geiger--has Lt. Hiep with him today, and I am flying alone, as we work in the northern part of the province. The

Fighters are fragged to report to me as they approach the target. As they call in, I funnel alternating flights to Ed and Hiep, who are working target areas that are five to ten miles from me. The flight lead that I had handed off to Ed about ten minutes ago calls me: "Bird Dog 41, this is Hatred 41."

"Hatred 41, go ahead."

"Bird Dog 41, Bird Dog 47 has just crashed. His airplane is on the ground, inverted and burning."

"Roger, Hatred. We'll be there ASAP."

I head for Bird Dog 47 and bring a flight of A-4's with me. Ed and Hiep are about four minutes away. I feel a disturbance in my heart as I call Panama on VHF to give them a position and to report the loss and request an Air Rescue effort. As I approach I can see the smoke from the crash. The countryside here is beautiful—gently rolling, mostly green with scattered trees and grass. There's not a cloud in the sky, except the few that God sometimes scatters around to suit His own whimsy. There are two flights in the area—Hatred 41 who was working with Ed, and one other. As others show up, I will stack them overhead until we figure out what's happening.

I near the scene and see Ed's airplane flat on its back on top of a ridge just down-hill from a large hooch. There is no movement anywhere. The cockpit area of the airplane is gone—it's as if the nose, wings, and empennage were placed there with nothing to hold them together but a black spot that's still smoldering. Panama lets me know that a rescue team has been dispatched. I stay in the area and pass the incoming fighters to Panama, except for keeping one flight overhead, just in case.

It takes a little more than an hour for the Jolly Green to show up and land. Three men exit the helicopter and make their way to the wreckage. I don't need to hear the report. I stick around for a few minutes while they do what they need to do, and then head home. I call Panama and tell them that the rest of our day is scrubbed. Panama diverts the remainder of our planned strike force to other parts of I Corps.

Francis Edward Geiger was not the only FAC we lost. It's a wonder any of us survived, looking back on those times when bullets whistled through the skin and sometimes through the cockpit and sometimes through one of us. But that's for another day, and FACs were not the only casualties of this war--there are over 58,000 names on a smooth black-surfaced wall that sits halfway between the Lincoln Memorial and the Washington Monument on the Mall in Washington, D.C. Because we were small in number compared to the ground forces, we are small in number there.

The day after the loss was a gloomy day in the TOC and everywhere else. I guess that no matter which ones of us were lost, we would all agree that we had lost two of our best. In this case that's what happened. Captain Geiger and Lieutenant Hiep had a lot in common. Both were quiet, serious, and mature--a good match for the mission they were flying. Both were young and handsome--too "pretty" to be lost.

During the afternoon of July 23, I am sitting in the TOC, busy with some paper work. From my desk, Captain Cuc is at my 2 o'clock position about fifteen feet away. I look up to see him rise from his desk and head for me. He crosses the room, tears streaming down his face, places his hands on my desk, and leans forward: "Now, I know why Hiep is dead," he chokes out between sobs. "Three in a picture." He doesn't have to say more. All my life I have heard "three on a match." Never allow the third person to take a light from the same match. The Viets have the same superstition: "Never appear in a picture as the third person."

151

LEADERSHIP AND LEADERS

We occasionally visit various outposts and sometimes hang out with Marines and Army troops in the countryside. On some of those occasions we bump into Marine Corps Brigadier General Jonas Platt, Vice Commander of the 3rd Marine Amphibious Force (MAF). General Platt is a fighter pilot, but is also, like all Marines, a ground combatant. He is uncommonly tall for a fighter pilot--easily recognizable from a distance. He always travels alone, driving a jeep, and busies himself in every detail of whatever is going on. One doesn't need to see much of General Platt to discern that he is in vernacular terms: "The Real Article." He is a General, but also a friend--more like a big brother. It's always a pleasure to deal with him. He and Colonel Bruce Jones, the Senior army advisor to the ARVN 2nd Division are fast friends and accomplices in working to improve all aspects of the situation we are in--a very frustrating job most of the time.

The ARVN continues to plan a ground operation to attempt to draw out the VC into a fight similar to the failed engagement in May. As part of the plan, I will accompany the ground forces in a U.S. Army jeep along with Army Majors Brown and Schnibben.

During this time I meet frequently with General Platt and Colonel Bruce Jones. Both are familiar figures in all the combat activities in this part of Viet Nam and are capable, experienced, and dedicated.

A part of the planning for the upcoming operation will involve the ALO/FAC team on the ground. A ground team of one FAC and one Radio Operator will accompany the upcoming ground operation. Airman First Class (A/1C) Melvin Borofsky and I make preparations to participate.

The Quang Ngai Air Laison Office has only one jeep--a relic from WWII that has no muffler and the ragged remains of the top is stored in one of our maintenance containers. Our ground crew has painted it with a beautiful hot-rod motif including flames streaking from under the hood and down the sides. The crew chiefs on our airplanes spend more time keeping the jeep running than they do on all six of our airplanes. Because we don't have a reliable piece of ground transportation, we are forced to cadge a ride with the Army. Two Army Majors, Borofsky and I, along with what feels like a ton of Radio equipment, cram into the Army Jeep and join the convoy to what we hope will develop into a battle area with the VC.

The ARVN Second Infantry Division commits its entire force to this operation. It's a wonder that the VC don't just walk around us and take out a lot of facilities--but they don't. Instead, they decided to engage our force just as we occupy our "jumping off" position. They chose a perfect day for themselves. The weather is overcast with ragged drizzly ceilings that make the use of fighter cover impossible.

Shortly after noon on the third day, the VC assault the leading edge of our infantry with everything they have. The battle "front" is about one statute mile from where Mel Borofsky and I are holed up with the Division Headquarters staff on a low rise with enough height to visibly survey the countryside in all directions. In about an hour, everybody realizes that the situation is degrading rapidly and that our front line troops are retreating toward us while taking casualties from small mortars and infantry fire. As the battle front recedes towards us we see .50 caliber tracers crisscrossing the horizon. We start packing up.

An Armored Personnel Carrier is parked nearby. Suddenly, General Lam sprints the twenty or so yards from his field desk and climbs up to the opening just behind the machine gun turret on the front and grabs the microphone from the operator's hand. We can hear him shouting into the mike in Viet Namese, but none of the Americans present speak Viet. Our struggle to pack our gear into the jeep picks up some velocity.

In a few minutes we are mobile ready and the .50 caliber tracers look closer. The ARVN staff tells us that the troops are retreating and that it is time to go--facts that we already know. We load up. Major Brown drives, and Major Schnibben is riding "shot-gun" in the right front passenger seat. Mel and I sit at the two rear corners of the jeep with our radio gear stacked and secured wherever we could get it done in a hurry. Major Schnibben is carrying an M-14, and Mel and I have side arms and M-16s.

The rain has muddied the trail that we intend to follow to a village near the beach where an infantry battalion has secured the area. Major Schnibben, Mel, and I have one job for the duration of this drive--keep the retreating ARVN troops off the jeep.

We head east in a light rain and soon discover that a large contingent of the ARVN Infantry troops have somehow flowed around the Division Headquarters and we are passing them as they walk toward the beach. As they try to climb aboard, the three of us use our rifle butts and voices to keep the would-be hitch hikers off our jeep. Major Brown is operating the jeep as best he can through the axle deep mud and we move steadily through the crowd. The trail improves some as we proceed, and, as the sky darkens with heavier clouds and impending sunset, we leave the "retreating" troops behind and keep driving toward the secure village.

A little after dark, we are in the village and locate a large tent, park our jeep outside, and barge in on a party. Three Battalion Commanders are present with their staffs--about thirty people in the middle of a feast--and invite us to join the celebration. Majors Brown and Schnibben are carrying their M-14s, and Mel and I have our M-16s. For a moment, I fear that Major Brown is about to select the automatic mode on his M-14 and mow down all the Viet occupants, including three ARVN Brigadier Generals. Major Brown contains himself as to physical violence, but screams out at the gathering. I have to admire the Viet officer's composure. When Major Brown stops to catch his breath and to listen to a response, the senior commander stands, motions toward the table, and repeats his invitation for the four of us to join him. I am a foodie, as is Mel, and I would love to partake of the sumptuous meal these guys are enjoying, but it is unthinkable, considering the situation.

We leave, return to our vehicle, and wait for the Division staff to arrive. This is just another ARVN fiasco in a war that we cannot win.

During the next few weeks, we plan and conduct airstrikes wherever we can locate the Snarks. Every day we have a steady stream of fighter/bomber sorties overhead and we are all over the lower half of I Corps attempting to disrupt, destroy, confuse the VC, and to kill as many of them as we can find.

As a part of the planning and execution of all of our operations I sometimes bump into General Platt. He is always the same--alone in his jeep, driving himself wherever he thinks it's most important for him to be. Our conversations always include significant happenings and analyses of current situations as well as conversational pleasantries. It is always a pleasure to see him unfold his tall frame from under the jeep steering wheel and follow our salute with an extended hand for a handshake. I will always remember the heroes who surround me daily, and this Marine fighter pilot who cares so deeply for all who serve with him will always occupy a special place in my heart.

Dai Uy Si

During the planning phase, I visit one of our outposts where Mel Borofsky is living with the ARVN. Mel has a complete communications set up and we can talk to him at any time. I will stay about three days.

I am assigned to an underground bunker room with Dai Uy (Captain, pronounced "Die We") Si, a very senior ARVN soldier who fought with the Viet Minh until they ran the French out of the country. While he was fighting the French, he and his wife owned and operated the "Forget Me Not Bar" in Da Nang. When the fracas with Ho Chi Minh and his bunch began, Si signed up to fight with the ARVN. He and his wife still own and operate the Forget-Me-Not, and his wife runs the business while Si is away from home.

Bernard Fall made the Forget-Me Not famous in his book *Street Without Joy,* and then Richard Tregaskis added to the PR in his work *Viet Nam Diary.* Mel has known Captain Si for a while and has a letter of introduction from Si to Si's wife that reads in part: "Ma Cher, this will introduce the Borofsky...," and continues a request to treat Borofsky well. Whether or not Mel used this valuable piece of paper, I do not know.

We reach the underground quarters by taking a very steep stairway down. The earth floor is covered with raised board walkways so we don't walk in the damp red clay soil. The outpost has a gasoline power generator for lights and refrigeration. Si is the mess officer and sees to it that we all eat well. The outpost proper is elevated and surrounded by concertina wire with a mine field laid out like a donut protecting the approach. There is a safe path through the field for entry and exit. Sometimes an unsuspecting dog wanders into the field and winds up dead. If there is enough left, Dai Uy Si uses a long fishing pole to salvage the remains for dinner.

Each morning that I am here begins with a wake up from Dai Uy Si's alarm. Our bunks are on opposite walls so that when each of us sits on the side of our bed we are facing each other from about five feet away. Si clicks on the light and reaches for an apparatus sitting next to his alarm clock. It looks like the classical opium water pipe seen in movies depicting opium dens in the Orient. It is a can with a long stem and a bowl on top of the can that he fills with something that looks like a funny colored tobacco. He then uses his cigarette lighter to light a long stick that burns with a big flame. He puts the end of the pipe stem in his mouth and holds the flaming stick over the bowl and takes about three really deep inhalations. With that, he leans back against the wall and relaxes for a few seconds, after which he gradually exhales a large volume of dense blue smoke. The expression on his face reminds me of Buddha, except that Si is skinny, and the pleasant smile that he wears lasts most of the day.

Dai Uy Si may be a junkie, but he does a good job of taking care of the troops. I don't think any dogs wandered into the mine field during my stay, but we ate well.

August 11, 1965

I begin the day with a FAC mission south of Quang Ngai where the VC are actively recruiting from villages that are openly friendly to them. Presumptively, if the village allows this they are all VC. The area today is not very populous. I have Fighter flights scheduled and expect that's enough to do all the damage there is to be done.

Oxwood 7-1, four Marine A-4s from Chu Lai, show up on time and make short work of a small group of hooches in seven minutes; from 10:23 to 10:30. At 10:35 Fly Train 1-1, two Marine F-4s from Da Nang loaded with 250 pound bombs, 500 pound bombs and Zuni rockets, are overhead. They depart at 10:50 having leveled another small settlement.

Pal 3, two F-104s from Da Nang shows up at 11:00 with two Napalm cans each plus a load of 20 mike mike. The F-104 wasn't designed for air-to-ground work, but these guys put on a very good show. The Napalm cans replace the usual fuel tanks that fit on the tips of the Seven foot long wings--all the droppable ordnance they carry. The best news is their 20 millimeter cannon. They smear the Napalm in all the right places, make multiple strafing passes, level the 22 hooch village, and depart for Da Nang.

I return to Quang Ngai, take a break from combat, and fly to Da Nang to pick up some parts and a case of White Phosphorous ("Willie Pete") grenades for marking targets. One of our radio operators, Airman Ernie Yahn comes with me. We gather the items we came for and load up to return to Quang Ngai.

It's a beautiful day to fly. We take off and head for the beach, looking forward to enjoying the scenery on the one hour flight down the beach from Da Nang to the mouth of the Quang Ngai River. The Beaches all along this area are spectacular. As we head south east down the coast, we pass Hoi An and fly at about 300 feet watching the coast line wander from a hundred yards or so to a mile or so from us. The water surface is nearly perfectly smooth.

Fishing boats are a common sight from as close in as a quarter of a mile to about a mile from the beach. Some are setting nets in the shallow water. Their shadows flutter about on the white sand bottom as the boats bob gently on the surface and the crews tend their nets. At a half mile from the shore, the water appears to be about 30 feet deep.

Inside the cockpit, my M-16 hangs from the ultra violet instrument spotlight on the right side of the instrument panel. I have fired up a 45 minute cigar. The two rear hinged windows are latched to the open position to the bottom of the wings. Ernie is sitting in the rear seat with a Thompson Sub-machine gun lying across his lap as we chat about the scenery and enjoy the flight.

South of Hoi An, we close in tight to the beach and drop down to about 50 feet. The smooth sand beach rises from the shore and then, about 300 or so yards from the water's edge, tumbles into dunes, a combination of bare sand, shrubs, and grass. At the top of the dunes, a tree line parallels the beach. Occasionally we pass a fishing village with boats pulled up on the sand facing thatched roof houses nestled in the tree line. It is siesta time and we haven't seen any people on the beach.

We meander along a deserted stretch, and I look ahead and see four or five fishing boats pulled up on the sand facing a settlement of houses in the tree line, but don't see any people. As we are adjacent to the boats, a gunshot rings in my ears as if the shooter is firing from a few feet away from our right wingtip. My head jerks involuntarily to the right, and I'm looking down the barrel of an AK-47 as the shooter unshoulders his piece, and he and his three companions crouch in the sand behind one of the boats. These four are obviously North Viet Namese regulars. They are wearing combat boots, full fatigue dress with back packs and crossed ammo belts hanging around their shoulders. We were no more than 75 feet from the muzzle of the gun when I heard the shot.

I simultaneously open the throttle, start a right climbing turn, fling both front windows open, and toss my lighted cigar out the window. My eyes are glued to the four soldiers as they leave the cover of the boat and run across the beach toward the sand dunes. My immediate goal is to get around the turn in a position to drop the nose and launch a Willie Pete rocket. I soon realize that I started my climbing turn way too early and won't be able to aim a rocket. I loosen up the turn to fly by them as they cross the beach so I can keep them in sight. We're less than a hundred feet in the air as we approach them, and they are soon about to pass under our right wing, running as hard as they can in the loose beach sand.

As we pass them in a 45 degree bank, Ernie's Thompson bursts into a basso profundo rumble. I have never fired a Thompson, have never heard one before, and am impressed with the authority of its speech. The 45 slugs spew from the muzzle and hit the sand about four or five feet apart as we pass. The soldiers hit the dirt as Ernie's bullets kick sand on them while they lay spread eagled on the beach.

I ease off the turn, leave the throttle open, set up a max rate of climb, and keep the VC in sight as they scramble to their feet and continue to move toward the dunes. At the 180 degree point, I roll in for a rocket shot. As the airplane turns facing them, they dive for the sand, and I toggle off one rocket. These rockets are the famous two and a quarter inch "Mighty Mouse" variety and are not noted for pin-point accuracy. The rocket leaves the launcher under our left wing, wobbles a bit, and impacts between them and the dunes, close enough that some Willie Pete particles leaves one of them with a burning and smoking uniform.

The four of them get up and continue across the beach as I continue a right hand pattern. One of them is limping noticeably. I see two Army Cobras headed north on the inland side of the tree line, and, a voice comes through my headset: "Air Force Bird Dog over the beach south of Hoi An, this is Cobra flight of two, are you o.k.?"

"Cobra, Bird Dog 41 here. You're just in time for some fun. Did you see the four NVN regulars run into the tree line?"

"Negative, Bird Dog, but we've got rockets and machine guns, if you can use them."

With that, the Cobras start a left hand holding pattern. By this time I have tracked the pedestrians into the dunes and then into one of the hooches in the tree line. I loosen my pattern seaward and roll in and launch a Willie Pete in an attempt to hit the hooch in question. It's close enough. "Cobra, the four NVN entered the hooch nearest my smoke. How about taking it out first and then let's smoke the rest."

"Roger that, Bird Dog, it's a done deal."

With that, I stay on the ocean side and watch the U.S. Army take care of business. In a few minutes this fishing village is history. When we're done, we exchange some small talk with the Cobras who tell us that they're headed for Da Nang. All of us will turn in intelligence reports.

The news that NVN regulars are infiltrating South Viet Nam is not a big surprise. Four is not exactly a division, but then I remember sitting in a movie theatre in 1954 watching movie newsreels of the stunning results at Dien Bien Phu, and later in the aftermath, how the French were totally shocked to learn that their opposition, like a determined and innumerable nest of ants on the move, had placed artillery and supplies in and around the hills surrounding them, and that they were trapped. This war we're in now should have ended right then.

The worst of the whole thing is that, when we go any place where French Colonials show up, the French treat Viets like dirt. I think to myself: "How long will it take to put enough of these VC soldiers here to repeat Dien Bien Phu." I don't believe that the VC can ever do that to us, but then in the short time I've been here, we haven't done much to them, and they seem to becoming more plentiful as we go along.

Retrospective: My passenger and I are lucky to have survived this incident. All the VC soldiers had to do was stand up and open up with their AKs on automatic when we were close to them. I unwittingly gave them the perfect shot at very close range when I made the firing pass. No lead required—just put their sights on my nose and hold down the trigger, and Ernie and I would have been toast. We lost more than one FAC in shoot outs with VC ground troops—my name just wasn't yet up on God's Rolodex. Or, maybe He chose to give me a 'bye in the divine hope that I would someday come around.

I was to recall this moment five years later when, as a POW in a camp near Ha Noi, I learned from a senior State Department employee, Phil Manhard, that North Viet Namese regulars had walked into his quarters in Hue and taken him prisoner..

WHERE IS SQUARE ONE?
For the next few months, we seem to spend a lot of time on square one as to how to slow the VC expansion and produce some success for the ARVN.

{By now, I have had little complimentary to say about the South Viet Namese fighting men. Let me apologize to the thousands of Viet Namese who were courageous and patriotic to their country's cause to keep the inept governments that were largely imposed on them indirectly by the United States. I don't have the time and space in this missive to even begin to layout the pieces of U.S. ineptitude in our attempt to run things in South East Asia, particularly in Viet Nam. If you are interested, start by reading Dr. Arthur Schlesinger's The Bitter Heritage.

Having said that, there were many people, men and women, like Dai Uy Cuc, Thieu Uy Hiep, Major Nguyen Ngoc Sao, Dai Uy Si, and a number of others who fought courageously in the Viet Nam War, even though they believed that Ho Chi Minh was a good man. Their closing remark about him in any conversation was inevitably "He's a good man, too bad he's a Communist." I served with a number of Viet Namese that I hope made it to America.

My disparaging remarks regarding the ineptitude of the Viet Namese fighting forces and the inept and corrupt top leadership are not meant for those who might be living here now and reading these words--that group exhibited amazing courage in their quest for a free government during the war and in going through great tribulation to come to our country.}

It is becoming clear that Lyndon Johnson's declaration that he will not "...send American boys to do what Viet Namese boys should do" is a hollow promise if we are to succeed. In the meantime, we own the skies over all of Viet Nam, especially the South, and will continue to do with air what can be done, but it is clear that Ho Chi Minh and Vo Nguyen Giap are not going to show up on the north end of the bridge that connects North and South Viet Nam with their hands in the air in response to our air strikes.

After another shellacking, we fall back to planning and continuing to do what we can in the air, while hoping that the ARVN can pull itself together and mount some kind of effective resistance to the VC.

For the remainder of August through September 3, 1965, we do everything we can from the air. Weather is sometimes a problem, and our intelligence is always weak. It's the same old story--we're hunting the Snark--Snarks are hard to find--a lot of the time the Snarks turn out to be Boojums.

From September 3 through September 9, we plan an air operation in the II Corps area that will involve carpet bombing of certain areas by B-52s, with a ground search and destroy mission by 50 U.S. Army Rangers and 200 ARVN Rangers to follow the air strikes closely enough to take on any remaining VC.

The morning of September 10, 1965, B-52s saturate the area from 08:05 until 09:05. From 09:05 until 09:33, A-1 Air Commandos and Helicopter Gunships comb the operations area, further softening the selected Landing Zones (LZ). At 09:33 the 250 ground troops land in the selected LZ and spend the day searching for Snarks. While the ground troops are doing their search, we have flights of B-57s from Da Nang and Marine A-4s from Chu Lai overhead at all times.

All the events occur exactly as planned, to the split second. The ground troops fan out and spend the day covering the area and find

NOTHING. Late in the day, the lead troop carrier, Dragon 6, makes the first extraction and soon the 250 ground troops are back at home plate.

We spend the remainder of September, all of October, and most of November planning future operations and pecking away at intelligence targets. We occasionally run into a .50 caliber position, and that's always troubling. We can avoid most small arms fire by staying above 2,000 feet, but a .50 Caliber machine gun can hit us at that altitude and we are lower than 2,000 feet most of the time. One day, Rick Davis (Bird Dog 40--our boss) sees a .50 open up on him too late to get away. He takes a hit that enters the airplane from just behind the engine and ruptures the battery sitting between the rudder pedals in the cockpit.

The battery breaks up and Rick is suddenly without a radio and is splashed with battery acid. He leaves the scene as fast as he can and heads home. Battery acid eats holes in his flight suit and starts to eat holes on Rick's face. He uses his canteen to rinse away all the acid that he can and arrives home with holes in his clothes and some burned spots on his face and arms.

NOVEMBER 21, 1965
In November, planning continues for future operations to purge the province of VC influence. The plan includes a lot of air cover and close air support for troop lifts into selected areas.

On November 21, I fly into Chu Lai in a drizzle under a 200 foot ragged ceiling to meet the Fighter Wing Commander and his Fighter Group Commander along with the squadrons: VMA-214, Apple; VMA-311, Chain; and VMA-225, Hatred. The group Commander's personal call sign is Oxwood. I brief a roomful of Marine fighter jocks on all the details that I know, and for the next few days we will be a team. Our game is to gain (or regain) control of a big section of this area in two Provinces for the RVN.

After our meeting, I step out from the Marines Operations Room into the drizzle and jog across their PSP ramp to get under a wing and preflight the airplane. Since I landed only a short time ago, and the airplane has been in USMC custody, and I don't want to get wet, I skip most of the preflight.

As I'm preparing to step in the airplane, a Jeep pulls up under the shelter of my right wing, and a Marine Corps Brigadier General steps out. He is about 6 feet 4 inches tall and is wearing a steel helmet and poncho over combat fatigues. I recognize him at once. It is General Platt, the Marine Corps fighter jock who commands a big chunk of USMC support in I Corps. We have a cordial relationship from our prior dealings, and I am always glad to see him.

His height will not allow him to stand erect under the O-1 wing, so he stoops and extends his hand for a hand shake in response to my salute. He asks what I'm up to, and I give him the short version of the briefing that I just gave to the Marine Air Wing. He nods his approval, and then asks what I'm about to do. I tell him that I'm just getting into my airplane and going back to Quang Ngai. He leans out under the leading edge of the wing, peers at the low overcast with drizzle, then turns to me and laughs as we shake hands and he says: "Well, try not to hit a tree." He slides into his jeep, we exchange salutes, and he drives away.

I don't think about it now, but this turns out to be the last time I will see General Platt on this planet. We both finish our tours and go on to other things. General Platt completes a fine career as a Marine Hero and lives a long, interesting, and successful life. General Jonas Platt, Semper Fi!!

I crank up and head for Quang Ngai. The flight is easy. I have enough ceiling to fly comfortably at about a 100 feet and can see a half a mile or so. I fly south down the beach to the mouth of the Quang Ngai River and turn right and follow the River until I see the airport on my left. I pass the airport a little ways and make a 180 degree turn and land.

Scud Run?

November 22 brings some improvement in the weather, but it's still blustery with cumulus clouds all around. We believe that it might be possible to get some air strikes into an area about 30 miles to the west where there is an outpost in the southern end of a valley just over a low range of hills. I take off well before the first fighter sortie is due and head for the outpost to see what happens.

As I approach the south end of the valley, solid overcast ceiling obscures the tops of the low range of hills. I skirt the south end in the clear and enter the valley between the low hills that bound the east side of the valley and a higher range on the west side. The outpost is about five miles ahead as I turn north to fly the length of the valley. As I approach the north end of the valley, about ten miles north of the outpost, rain and zero visibility closes the route out of the north end. I make a 180 degree turn and head for the south end, hoping to get there before the rain blocks the exit from the valley. As I pass the outpost heading south, it is beginning to rain in the valley. I soon see that I can't escape to the south and am trapped, as far as a visual escape is concerned.

I make another 180 degree turn and am now flying in increasing precipitation and decreasing visibility. I don't have much of a choice. As soon as I reach the outpost, I open the throttle and begin a left spiraling climb. I plan to climb to 6,000 feet and then head due east toward the coast. I am not happy with this situation. I haven't flown instruments in this airplane and it's been a while since I have been on instruments at all.

As I ascend into this winter monsoon cloud layer, the rain increases and there is turbulence. Soon water is coming into the cockpit from all directions and the turbulence increases to "moderate." Note that the next step in the severity of turbulence is "severe" and includes loss of control of the airplane. I have total control of the airplane, in that when the airplane changes attitude, airspeed, or rate of descent, I can correct for it, but only with large movements of the controls. If it weren't for the accepted definition of severe turbulence requiring "loss of control," I would call this situation severe turbulence, and I am scared.

The fight for control of the airplane continues, and at 6,000 feet, I am well above the hills and head east, continuing to climb. The turbulence abates, but water is still coming into the cockpit around the side windows and my maps are wet--a minor inconvenience, considering some alternatives. After about 30 minutes, I am in relatively smooth air, and then I pop out into an opening and can see the South China Sea.

The rest is easy. I fly past some of the scud below me and start letting down in the clear. I know that I am close to the coast and am no longer concerned about recovering. As I descend, I get below the scuddy clouds and pick up the coast. Soon, I am in familiar territory over the coastal plain and return to Quang Ngai much like yesterday.

The remainder of November and most of December is more of the same. The operation we were planning when I visited Chu Lai and met General Platt doesn't produce what we hoped. The VC are tightening their grip on Quang Ngai and surrounding provinces little by little, like a patient Python. We continue to attack areas of known VC sympathy and activity. The VC only play when they want to--at night or in inclement weather, or both.

12th Wedding Anniversary

December 25, 1965 is the eve of our twelfth wedding anniversary. As I turn in tonight, I think about Sue and the day we married. We were married in the home of Mrs. Rebecca Moss, a widow and a role model for Sue. She helped Sue plan our wedding and then very generously furnished her home for the ceremony.

A successful business man, who was also an inveterate gambler, built this house in the late 1800's. The house is modeled after the classic antebellum homes in the South, complete with the winding stair case and high ceilings with a walk-in fire place in the living room. Just before the turn of the century, the builder lost the house to a local Doctor in a poker game. Since that time, the house had been occupied by Doctors until it wound up in the last Doctor's estate, and Rebecca bought it.

I relive our wedding day. I did not see Sue at all that day, and as the wedding party gathered at the Moss residence, Sue's sister, Elizabeth played an appropriate selection of nuptial piano music, and, then Glenda Pritchett, the daughter of the Pritchetts who lived in Finley, sang "Oh, Promise Me." Glenda sang in a soft soprano voice that moved the guests, along with me, to tears. Then, to the bridal march, Sue descends the stairs with her matron of honor, Mrs. Maxine Pate, as her brother, Titus, waits to accompany her to the alter and give her away. Sue's father, Reverend J. H. Austin; my best man, Neely Pritchett; ushers, Sue's brothers Joel and William; and I watch in awe.

Titus approaches the alter with Sue, and Sue's Dad has a problem speaking as he attempts to ask the question: "Who is here to give the bride away?" He finally gets it out and Titus responds.

Sue is her parent's first child to marry. Her mother and father are happy for her, and her father granted his consent to me when I asked him for her a long time ago, but that does not quell their emotions.

The room I share with Glenn Jones where I sleep in the upper bunk, is about seven feet wide and maybe twelve feet long. A desk sits against the back wall, opposite the front door. Glenn and I share the desk that includes photos of our families. Glenn manages our Officer's Club and is in his office when I turn in. Under my mosquito net I continue the reverie about our wedding day and am soon sound asleep.

It's a cold dark, rainy night between midnight and dawn on December 26 when one of our troops wakes us up to tell us that Major Davis and others are in the TOC and that our presence is requested post haste, if not sooner. We scramble out from under our mosquito nets and into our flight suits, boots, pistol belts, and flight jackets, and grab our "ditty" bags that we cram under the seat of our airplanes, and step out into a steady drizzle with an occasional gust accompanied by inscrutable dark.

We don't talk much. First of all, Glenn Jones does not produce much idle chatter under most circumstances, and second, we both know something is terribly wrong or we wouldn't be stepping quickly through the compound toward the lights of the TOC, and speculating would only slow us down.

We hop up the half a dozen steps onto the veranda and into the central office of the TOC. Several Viet Namese Army officers are present, along with Rick Davis, our boss. Rick is sitting at his desk. He doesn't mince any words of greeting, but points to the map on the wall near him to an outpost near the village of Bong Son and tells us that it is under siege by a large VC force, and that the VC are attempting to breach the concertina wire and mine field that forms the outer perimeter. Our guys have their 85mm howitzers firing grape shot at point blank range and VC bodies are hung up in the wire. He tells us to take off and get over the outpost ASAP. He points out that the adjunct to the main outpost on a little hog-back rise about a mile to the north-west is also under attack, and at least one American is there. The only firepower we have available is a US Navy Destroyer about ten miles out to sea.

We jot down call-signs and coordinates and head for the airport in our private limo--a WWIl vintage jeep with no muffler, no top, but with a hot rod paint job that includes flames coursing from under the hood and down over what paint is left since it entered the US Army inventory in WWII.

We are wearing ponchos with our .38 Smith & Wesson revolvers with waist holsters and are carrying M-16s with as much ammo as will fit into a helmet bag alongside a few .38 rounds, a canteen of water, a pound of chocolate, a few pencil flares, and a hand held radio. The drizzle is light, so we won't get too wet on the five minute drive to the airport. Our ground crews are at the field waiting for us.

In a few minutes we are on our way in formation. I am in the lead airplane. Glenn stays close to me as we trundle down the coast at about .12 Mach. We haven't had any time to talk or to speculate about what we will find, but both of us have been involved in these things before, and the only good news is that we couldn't see or hear the incumbents as they gave up the last few minutes they had on this planet. I don't expect that this soiree will turn out any differently.

The ceiling is low with maybe a mile visibility. The drizzle varies a bit from time to time, but it looks like we will be able to see well enough to find the place. The weather is too bad for flares and for any kind of air support, except for the air commandos and their A-1s at Qui Nhon, about 70 miles south of us. Major Davis was working on letting them know what's happening as we ran out the door. The A-1s can operate in this stuff. They are faster than we are, but still slow enough to follow the ground action. With guns and napalm they don't have to dive and can get the job done. My fingers are crossed.

It's still not day-light as we approach the outpost, but there is some pre sunrise light as the sun is approaching the horizon somewhere east of us. The dim light is enough to get us there, but it would be nice to see a bit more detail on the ground. I use this time to establish contact with the Navy destroyer standing by to assist us. The destroyer is positioning itself to be at the best location to support us.

I see the outpost. We approach on the coast side and I make a loose 180 degree turn to the right around the south side. I concentrate on the ground--trying to see if there are any clues. As I'm heading north peering down to my right at the outpost, we are suddenly flying through a hailstorm that's going the wrong direction. We can't see the shooters, but the upside down precipitation is clearly visible, even when they're not firing tracers. Crazy!! Then one of those streaks passes through my left window and out the top forward windshield plexiglass. I am stung by the little fireflies that disappear as fast as they showed up. I roll my wings level and pull as much of me as I can into a position that will place the armor plate I sit on between me and the ground.

I look out the left window and Glenn is in close. It's light enough that I can see his face clearly. He calls: "Are you o.k.?" I pull out a pen from my flight suit pocket and stick it through the nearest jagged breach in the plexiglass windshield. Glenn laughs. I'm flying as high as I can with my vertical stabilizer cutting into the ceiling at about 600 feet above the ground.

We don't hear anything from the outpost as we move northward and out of range of the AKs that were firing at us. I move over to the hogback and contact the American. He is an army Sergeant and the only English speaker in either of these compounds. I can't see any activity in or around this little outpost. The hogback has very nearly vertical approaches on all sides. I will never know how they manned this little piece of real estate, but there is a flat spot for a helicopter at the end nearest the coast. The Sergeant's voice is calm as he responds to my questions.

"Are there VC near you?"

"They're scaling the south slope."

"We are in contact with a Navy destroyer just a few miles from here who can support us with Navy gunfire. I'll set him up to lay some gunfire on the south face. OK?"

"Roger."

"I'll take a break now and talk to the Navy. Call me if you need to."
"Roger."

I strike up a conversation with the Navy by briefing them on the situation and the terrain. I give them the UTM coordinates of the center of the outpost and explain where they need to lay in some assistance. The Destroyer will be firing such that their projectiles are coming in almost parallel to the nearly vertical south face. The height of the face is about 100 feet. It's a difficult shot, but we have no choice but to try. With no support, the little hog back is in grave danger.

The Navy isn't shy. They come back with the line of flight and we agree on a target for a marker round from which I can ask for adjustments. They give me the max altitude of the projectile and time of flight and an "on the way" signal. In a few seconds (about half a minute) their White Phosphorous (Willie Pete in common combat jargon) impacts the level ground about 100 meters past the center of the cliff face. I ask for a reduction in range of 100 meters and fire for effect. The shells start dropping. The range is right on, but we need to move the impact point a bit to the north. Navy ceases fire for a few seconds to adjust and opens up again. In spite of the irregularity of the terrain and the bends in the face, the rounds pound the south face.

Suddenly, there is black smoke in the eastern end of the compound. My first reaction is that we have "slung" one, and ask the Navy to cease fire. I switch frequencies and ask my Army Buddy if we have "short rounded" him by putting a round in the west end. I am already puzzled, because the explosions keep up, and they are smaller and different than the Naval ordnance. The mystery ends with The Sergeant's response.

"No sir, those aren't short rounds, the VC have breached our west end. You're looking at hand grenades."

I don't know what to do. We could continue to shell the outpost with Naval gunfire, but I have hopes that with daylight and the difficulty the VC will have holding the place when and if the Air Commandos arrive in this miserable weather that somehow the troops can hold on. It doesn't work out that way.

In a few minutes the Air Commandos report in. They are well on their way. It is now as daylight as it's going to be today. The A-1s are soon here. The TOC relays to us that the occupants in the main outpost have taken some casualties, but that the VC never breached their inner perimeter. The outpost also reports that the VC are disengaging and that any movement we see to the west are enemy. I keep trying to reach the Sergeant on the hogback, but he is silent.

The VC are departing the area. Some are slogging through the flooded rice paddies and some are moving as fast as they can by staying on the paddy dikes. The Air Commandos don't need much help from us. They can see the movements just as well as we can. At one point I call their attention to a group of about six running west on a paddy dike. The Lead commando rolls in for a napalm drop. As he approaches, the VC dive off the dike and into the flooded field. The napalm hits the dike and spreads over the water. Napalm burns on the water surface just the same as on land. Sayonara.

Glenn and I and the Commandos scour the hogback as closely as we can. It is quiet. Not much to see. The way it is laid out we can't see any bodies, but we know that some are there. We don't see any movement of any kind. Helicopter gunships and airlift are preparing to come here and clean up. The commandos will stay around with their guns as long as they can. We scour the area for VC, but those who survived have disappeared.

As the day progresses, the ARVN and the US Army move in together to airlift casualties and reestablish these two outposts. The only U.S. casualty is the Army Sergeant who died on the hogback along with the entire complement of ARVN soldiers.

I never learn the Sergeant's name, but I will meet him somewhere in eternity, and I will know him immediately by his calm, almost nonchalant, voice as he spent his last few moments on this planet. Sometimes I wake up in the middle of the night with the vision of a young Army Sergeant squatting on top of that little hog back as he drops his hand held FM radio and raises his rifle, Grenades exploding in front of him, having spoken his last words to Bird Dog 41 whose name he didn't know.

Four hours after take-off, Glenn and I are back on the ground at Quang Ngai. My airplane will get a new windscreen. I hope Sue had a nice day today.

FEBRUARY 2, 1966

It's early morning in the TOC on a rainy February day. We are essentially grounded because of the poor weather and several of us are sitting around chewing the fat when we get a message that the Army Special Forces outpost at Hay Tan has lost contact with a Squad on patrol in the hills south of Hat Tan. We discuss the problem for a few minutes and decide to send two airplanes to Hat Tan to participate in a search and attempt to locate the incommunicado squad. Buck Loggins (Bird Dog 46) and I volunteer and are soon riding in our topless hot rod to the airport.

Hat Tan is south of Quang Ngai. The outpost sits on the south side of a stream that empties into the Sea about fifteen miles south of Quang Ngai. We are very familiar with the topography and can fly there by "scud running--" staying low and following land marks. If the weather closes in, we will climb into it and fly east on instruments and get radar vectors to Chu Lai or Da Nang. This scheme is not nearly as hairy as it sounds--if we have a little ceiling and a quarter or half mile visibility we can do it easily.

We are soon airborne and Buck flies formation with me as I follow the coast line south and then follow the stream to Hat Tan with more than a 100 foot ceiling and about a half a mile visibility--piece of cake. We land at the improvised dirt, stone, and mud airstrip on the south side of the river. The Special Forces Camp Commander and some of his troops meet us, and we walk up the gentle slope to their outpost.

The commander briefs us on the situation. Yesterday, a dozen men set out on a reconnaissance mission southeast of the Outpost. Just after sunset they reported their position and made camp for the night. Since then, there have been no communications from them. The Commander and all of us fear the worst. Buck and I have come to attempt to search for them, but the weather is zero zero in the hills, and we are stuck here in the valley. We decide to stick around and hope the weather improves enough that we can conduct an aerial search, but the day goes by and it doesn't happen. Staying here overnight is unthinkable for several reasons, not the least of which the Special Forces guys don't want us there to attract unwanted attention from any VC who might have some sapper capability.

At mid-afternoon, one of the look-outs lets us know that he has spotted a single soldier approaching from the east walking along the stream bank. We all fall out outside to watch him approach. Soon he is close and angles up the slope toward us. From the waist down, he is stark naked! He has his firearms and pack, but no boots or pants. We all go inside, and someone grabs a pair of pants for him as he unloads his gear. He calmly gives us a de-briefing.

The squad made camp in the jungle area after dark last night. They ate and soon set up to spend the night. About mid-night, grenades started landing around their encampment, and tracer fire was flying through the trees. It was pitch black. They yelled at each other and, in the total darkness, they grabbed their essential gear--guns, ammo, etc.-- and moved away from the camp site in all directions. Since then this soldier moved as far as he could in the dark and hunkered down for the night, having left his pants and boots hanging on a near-by bush in the campsite. Since daylight, he has been walking home, and now, here he is. He has had no contact with any of the other members of the squad.

The weather remains too sour for us to do any aerial search. The area covered by the squad is all covered by the low hanging clouds with no visibility. The day continues with no word from any other members of the missing squad.

Late in the afternoon, Buck and I prepare to leave. I will take off first and lead the way out. I take off and then, as Buck leaves the ground, we both realize that it's much more convenient for him to head up the stream and for me to follow. Buck heads home and I fall in behind him about a quarter of a mile. I can see him o.k., and we have enough ceiling to make it. As we follow the gentle bends in the stream, Buck passes a narrow point in the stream bank that forces us to fly near one bank or the other. Buck is close to the right and I am a few seconds behind. As I pass, a single shot rings out in my right ear. I don't see a muzzle flash and in a second or so, I have passed out of sight of the shooter. He had to have been less than a hundred feet from us as we passed.

Last FAC Mission

February becomes a transition planning month. It looks more and more like the Second ARVN Division will move to Tam Ky--a little north of Quang Ngai and closer to the coast. Tam Ky should be a safer venue with more consolidated defenses. We fly every day. On days when we have no planned FAC missions (i.e., no targets), we fly visual reconnaissance (VR). A lot of our hot targets are closer to Quang Ngai than before.

On February 25, I fly my last mission as a Forward Air Controller. It's a beautiful day--a perfect day to fly. I look around Quang Ngai Province to the northwest and don't see much. The VC are very clever about staying out of sight and I don't note any observables that might be giveaways.

When I return to Quang Ngai airport a C-123 is parked on the east end of the runway unloading cargo. I see a man standing in the shade of the wing with a German Shepherd on a leash, and can see the crew and others milling about the airplane. Without even thinking about it, I roll in for a pass down the runway as low and as fast as an 0-1 can fly. I pass the C-123, pull up on a downwind, make a short field landing, and taxi to our ramp. I exit the airplane and stand just aft of the cockpit using the fuselage as a desk to complete the flight record.

As I am writing I become aware that there is a person standing directly across from me with a German Shepherd on a leash. I look up and into the face of the 366th Tactical fighter Wing Vice Commander who is wearing fatigues and a flight cap with his rank--Colonel. I salute him.

He speaks quietly: "Were you flying this airplane just now?"

"Yes, sir"

"What were you doing? Why did you pull that buzz job?

"Sir, I just flew my last mission!"

He is very quiet. I can tell that he is angry.

"Are you sure that this was your last mission?"

"Yes, Sir."

"Well, I'm going to think about that. You should be more responsible than to take risks with one of our airplanes."

We exchange salutes as he turns to leave.

I will hear about this later from Major Rick Davis. Rick corners me in the bar at the DOOM (Da Nang Officers Open Mess) at Da Nang. We order something to drink, and Rick tells me how lucky I am that the Wing Vice Commander is not taking any action re my buzz job. This particular Colonel is one the hardest-nosed uncompromising seniors that Rick has ever known. I'm not particularly happy about being forgiven for what we all think is our due.

Into our talk, this same Colonel walks into the bar and joins us for a drink. He is cordial and wishes me well on my next assignment.

This will be the last time I see Rick Davis on this planet. Rick was the best boss I ever had. I learned more from Rick Davis in the ten months we spent together in combat than I learned in any other ten month segment of my life. If the measure of those we have known is measured by the emotions we feel--grief, laughter, respect, and love--when we think of them, Rick is one of a handful at the top of my list.

Rick was a friend to all who served with him, and all of us, from our newly hatched maintenance men, our senior experienced maintenance team, radio operators, clerks, and FACs loved him and respected him. He was a very talented man. He designed the unique paint job for our six airplanes, and laid out the outlines on each airplane with a pencil. All the rest of us painted the colors into the outlines like children completing their paint books. The activity itself, the pleasure of seeing our handiwork, and enjoying the reactions of everybody who admired our airplanes were great morale boosters. Everything that Rick did had the same effect.

Any departure from the Force causes a disturbance. There was a giant rift in the curtain when Rick made his final exit.

I depart Da Nang the next day and arrive home in Gardena, California on March 4, 1966 to continue my career at Space Systems Division.

Part VII

FIGHTERS IN VIET NAM

Transition

I first came to Viet Nam in March 1965, spent a tour as a Forward Air Controller, and returned to my job at Air Force Space Systems Division dealing with designing and flying lifting bodies for returning from space. I soon felt strongly that I needed to return to Viet Nam and fly a tour in fighters. By June 1966, my little family and I were living in Tampa, Florida, and I spent the summer at McDill AFB checking out in the F-4.

The F-4 requires a crew of two--an Aircraft Commander (AC), and a Pilot, Systems Operator (PSO). (*At this point in time, these were the crew designations. Both crew members were pilots. Later on, the Air Force deleted the requirement for a second pilot in the rear seat and changed the crew designators to Pilot (the front seat occupant) and Weapons Systems Operator (the rear seat occupant).* Young fighter pilots were not happy with enduring a tour in the back seat of any kind of airplane, not even the hottest thing around.

The fighter pilots, who were senior enough to fly in the front seat as ACs, were sometime disdainful of their back seaters, referring to them as

"Pesos," a take-off on PSO, or as GIBs (the Guy in the Back). The really "old hand," dyed-in-the-wool fighter jocks sometimes had an attitude about the situation and essentially informed their GIBs to strap themselves in the back and "sit down and shut up." As a matter of policy, we formed into crews and flew as crews throughout our training. My PSO was 1/Lt Harold Monlux. We flew all but one or two of our training missions together.

At the end of our training, we were assigned as individuals, not as crews. I was assigned to Da Nang and Harry was assigned to Cam Ranh Bay. Harry and I were a good crew, and both of us knew it. I thought I had enough "connections" to have Harry's orders changed to Da Nang, and asked Harry if he was interested in switching to Da Nang so we could remain a crew. Harry didn't want to. His reasoning was valid. The Wing at Cam Ranh Bay flew most of its missions in South Viet Nam and Da Nang flew a lot of missions into North Viet Nam. Harry wanted the best odds to stay alive and return home to his wife and daughter. I couldn't fault him for that, and, in fact should have been placing my own family first.

Sue, our son, Kent, and I return to our apartment in Gardena, California to wait for my transportation orders to Viet Nam. As soon as we get settled, I contact the Ferry Command and ask to ferry an F-4 to Da Nang. Right away, I get a response that a flight of six F-4's is scheduled to depart for Viet Nam, and I need to be at George AFB, Victorville, California on October 17, 1966 for preparations to depart the following day.

On October 17, I leave home in the morning and arrive at George AFB shortly after noon. Six airplanes will leave here tomorrow for Viet Nam. I draw personal equipment for the flight that includes a helmet, flight harness, and a "Poopy Suit." The Poopy Suit is a dry suit that fits over all your clothing and seals your body from the neck down so that, in case of bail out in cold water the wearer will not get wet and can stay in cold water a lot longer than otherwise. If the water temperature in the Ocean we fly over is 60 degrees Fahrenheit or less, we will wear them.

Six airplanes are leaving George AFB tomorrow. We will fly to McClellan AFB rendezvous with three KC-135 tankers. Two F-4s will fly formation with each of the tankers, and we will take fuel during each leg of the flight such that we can always make an airport without the next refueling. I am crewed with Major Richard Housum. Major Housum and I will take turns as Aircraft Commanders. Two of the birds are going to Da Nang and the other four to Cam Ranh Bay.

We fly to McClellan AFB on October 18 and spend the next day briefing for the trip and visiting with friends. The flight plan is for three legs. We will fly to Hawaii tomorrow and spend the night. The next day, we will fly to Guam and spend the night, and then fly to Da Nang.

Ferrying is not terribly exciting, but beats flying with the airlines and is practice flying. The rules for ferrying are very strict. To assure that we can always reach a base from wherever we are during the flight, we refuel at pre-planned intervals that means we always have a lot of fuel aboard during mid-flight.

We take off from McClellan on October 20 and rendezvous with our tanker. About 100 miles off the coast we refuel as a check to see that there are no system problems in any of the airplanes. This refueling goes routinely and we continue toward Hawaii. To assure that the fighters will have ample fuel, either to return to McClellan or make Hawaii without another refueling, we refuel three times during mid-course. We fly formation with the tanker until we are near Honolulu, and separate until tomorrow, and spend the night at Hickam AFB and dine at the Pearl Harbor Officer's Club.

On October 21 we takeoff and join our tanker on the way to Andersen AFB, Guam. The refueling procedures are the same. During the mid-phase of the flight, Midway Island is nearest landfall and we stay topped up. The flight to Guam is Seven Hours and twenty five minutes, and since we crossed the international date line, it is October 22 when we land. The weather at Guam is miserable. We complete the flight in a tropical rainstorm via a GCA. My First approach is terrible. I am not smooth with airplane and wind up too fast and too high to make a safe landing. We go around and my second attempt is much better, but not perfect--just good enough for a comfortably safe landing. I need to get some rust off my instrument flying in this airplane.

On October 23, we repeat everything, except for the destination, which is Da Nang. As we approach Da Nang the weather is below minimums, and we divert and land at Cam Ranh Bay. The flight was five hours and forty five minutes with three hours in the soup.

On October 24, we fly to Da Nang. I check in to the 480th Tactical Fighter Squadron(TFS) and am reunited with my oldest and best buddy, Bud Flesher, who has been here just a short time and has flown two combat missions--an "old hand" by my standards.

First Fighter Missions

I am soon squared away in a room with two bunks. I take the upper bunk and leave the lower blank until someone joins me. Our quarters are shaped like a big "H." The shower and toilet facilities are located in the crossbar of the H. The areas at each end of the crossbar are common areas with refrigerators, table, chairs, and cooking facilities like hot plates and coffee makers. The vertical stems of the H are hallways with divided areas enclosed with screens. The foundation all around the base of the H is poured concrete that supports the wooden framework that holds up the roof and the screening structure of the outer walls--rather primitive.

New, fully enclosed structures with air conditioning and private rooms are under construction. Field Grade Officers (Major and above) live in air conditioned trailers.

About a week after I arrive, I am sound asleep in my upper bunk, when loud and nearby explosions jar me to full consciousness, and I am instantly head first in mid-air heading for a position under the lower bunk squeezing against the two foot high reinforced concrete lower wall. The VC are launching rockets. We wind up with a damaged roof over the middle bar of the "H," but suffer no casualties. The dive from the upper bunk to a smooth landing and snuggle against the safety of the concrete is an acrobatic feat that I could never duplicate.

The 480th is part of the 366th Tactical Fighter Wing(TFW) that consists of three fighter Squadrons: the 480th, 390th, and 389th. The Wing flies every kind of mission flown over North Viet Nam Packages I, II, V, VIA, and VIB, with an occasional mission in Packages III, and IV. We also fly missions "in country," mostly over I Corps and Southern Laos.

I deliberately chose to open up *in medias res* with the night mission to the Bridge not far from Ha Noi, to preview what was coming. You have now been exposed to one of 106 missions over North Viet Nam and to enough samplings of FAC missions in South Viet Nam to have some feel for the war.

On October 26, I fly my first combat sortie in the F-4, carrying 500 pound bombs to southern Laos to strike an area where supplies for the VC are stored.

We are in and out quickly and don't draw any enemy fire. We go back the next day with six bombs and 1,000 rounds of 20mm. We make multiple passes to damage and destroy materiel headed for South Viet Nam. Back to Laos on the 29th with Napalm.

On 30 October, I fly my first mission to Package V as number two in a flight of four escorting a B-66. The B-66 is converted from bomber configuration to jamming enemy gun laying systems during air raids in Packages V, VI, and VI-A. Our job is to intercept any Migs that might try to interfere.

We depart Da Nang and proceed due west to join a tanker over northern Thailand. Lead and I refuel and head north to join the B-66 at 35,000 feet and escort it into Pack 5. Number 3 and 4 remain with the tanker and thirty minutes later will refuel and relieve us. We will then return to the tanker, refuel and relieve our 3 and 4 who will then return to the tanker, refuel and relieve us. We will continue this cycle until the B-66 completes its mission. The idea is to have two fighters with full internal fuel loads with the B-66 until the mission is over and we are all safe out of North Viet Nam.

While we are with the B-66, we stack high and about half a mile out line abreast on each side of the B-66. When we are in position, each of us is looking down at the B-66 from our perches on each wing. A Mig attack will come from low and behind the B-66. If we see a Mig, one of us will call the B-66 to break and will advise him which direction to break. The exact position of the Mig will determine the direction of the break. The B-66 will break into a hard diving turn into the Mig. There will usually be two Migs. One of us will go for the attacking Mig while the other F-4 takes care of any wingman.

When the B-66 completes its mission we escort it out of North Viet Nam and accompany it into northern Thailand until it is well on its way home to TaKhli Royal Thai Air force Base in south-central Thailand.

This is the most usual denouement to these escort missions. This is not an air-to-air war. North Viet Nam does not have a big air force--just a few fighters--and they use them with care, much like the guerilla style of warfare they practice on the ground.

When we are not flying into Laos and North Viet Nam, we fly support missions "in country." On 31 October and 1 November, 1966, I fly missions into the southern part of I Corps in support of the same style of operations I experienced as a FAC and soon learn that my FAC experience is a big advantage.

31 October begins with a four hour stint in Mobile Control from 05:00 to 09:00. The Mobile Control Officer sits near the approach end of the active main runway in a small mobile trailer unit whose outside walls are glass and provide 360 degree visibility. An Auxiliary Power Unit (APU)--a gasoline powered generator--provides electrical power for air conditioning and communications. We have Very Pistols that fire flares if we need to. The principal purpose of Mobile Control is to increase safety. Mobile has a clear view of the traffic pattern and observes every approach and landing. If the Mobile Officer observes deviations that might affect safety, he can interrupt the control tower and give suggestions to help correct whatever is unsafe. In the case that Mobile can't interrupt tower communications, a red flare from the Very Pistol is a direct order for an approaching airplane to abort the approach.

A secondary duty of the Mobile Control unit is to keep records of operations as observed during their watch. These observations can be helpful to improve overall operations.

After Mobile duty, I have a snack and take a load of Napalm to a target near Quang Ngai--very familiar territory. It's a lot more fun scraping a can of napalm off on the heads of the bad guys than watching someone else do it.

November 1 is a repeat--same ordnance in another VC enclave about twenty miles from yesterday.

2 November is a rotten weather day. My flight is in the soup under radar control to drop a load of bombs in Package I. This mission is called "Sky Spot," and we do it when the weather is bad or the target too difficult to spot visually. Today the radar controller is having some technical problems with his equipment and we discontinue the mission. We let down break out into visual conditions and head for the target. Lead locates the target, we maneuver around some clouds and stay with it until we find a way to hit a roll-in point and put our ordnance on the target. My entry in today's diary reads in part: "...I was particularly proud of today's work--right on target in ripple."

November 3 is an armed reconnaissance mission into Tally-Ho, the southernmost part of Package I in North Viet. The weather is marginal. We are carrying four 500 pound bombs each, and lead has a gun with 1,000 rounds of 20 mike-mike. We dodge clouds, climb, descend, and maneuver continuously and finally find some small boats that had beached and managed to get our bombs all around them, and then lead got in a good run with his cannon. My notes for this mission in part: "Lead ...probably did more damage with his gun than all the rest of our bombs."

We leave Tally-Ho and come home amongst scattered clouds and varying conditions a la winter monsoon. Corky Prahler is the other half of our crew and he flies a practice GCA to low approach. As we go around, Da Nang GCA directs us to maintain VFR and contact Panama. In seconds Panama tells us that an RF-101 driver has abandoned his battle damaged airplane 26 miles east southeast of Da Nang and asks if we have sufficient fuel to relieve a Marine RF-4 who is running low.

We head for the downed aviator who is now paddling his dinghy around in the South China Sea. We don't have voice communications with the pilot, but we can steer to him on his homing radio signal. As we approach his position, the Marine heads home and we start making figure eights over the downed airman's position. We are at 1,000 feet and can't see him, but can stay over him as long his radio lasts. A Jolly Green helicopter rescue crew is on their way, and we soon pick them up as they have us in sight and are steering on us until they get closer. Since we now see the Jolly Green, we start letting down in an attempt to get a visual on the dinghy.

We circle lower. We know exactly where he is, but still can't see him. Then the Jolly hovers and we can see his prop wash on the water, but never see the rescuee until he shows up on the end of the recovery boom. The Jolly soon tells us that they've got him aboard, that he's ok, and they are heading for Da Nang.

Corky and I are a bit low on fuel, so we say sayonara to Panama, et al, report in to the Wing command Post, and head for the traffic pattern. The command post knows we've been airborne for a while and immediately asks for our fuel state. When I tell them we have 1,200 pounds in our main fuselage tank, the response is: "Hell, baby, you'd better RTB." We let them know we're heading for the pattern and will be on the ground post haste. 1,200 pounds is not much fuel for a hungry F-4. At full military power it would be gone in about five minutes. We will burn at a little less than half that rate, but we don't waste any time letting the Da Nang tower know where we are and asking for priority. We make it with no sweat.

USAF Captain D. J. Haney had taken battle damage at about 7,000 feet over Package I. He made it out to sea and was headed south when he ran out of options. I feel privileged to have had a role in his pick-up, even though there's no doubt the Jolly Green crew would have found him without us.

4 November is another B-66 escort. We keep our eye on a single engine contrail coming out of China as we circle over the Gulf of Tonkin just east of Hai Phong. Had we not been escorting the B-66, we would have tried to close in. Air-to-air combat is always on a fighter jock's mind.

I sat out 5 November. One of our flights did the B-66 escort duty. Well into the flight, Captain James "Friar" Tuck and Lt John "Rabbit" Rabini were on the left side of the B-66 about 2,000 feet higher than the B-66 and line abreast looking low and behind the B-66 while 1/Lt Joe Latham and 1/Lt Klaus Klause were in the same position on the right wing. As Friar Tuck searched the area low and behind the B-66, he spotted a Mig-21 closing rapidly from below heading for the B-66. At this point, the Mig would be in position to launch an Atoll radar guided missile in a few seconds. Friar yelled at the B-66 to "Break Right." The B-66 breaks hard right into a steep diving turn and Friar breaks with him. At that moment, the Atoll separates from the Mig and flies past the rapidly turning B-66.

The Mig follows the B-66 attempting to get another shot and seems unaware that Friar is turning in behind him. Latham and Klause now see a second Mig who is attempting to get behind Tuck and Rabini, and they maneuver to position themselves behind the second Mig for a shot.

Now we have this flight of five airplanes in a right hand descending spiral: B-66, Mig-21, F-4, Mig-21, F-4. The lead Mig-21 is trying for another shot at the B-66; Tuck and Rabini are trying to get a shot at the lead Mig; The second Mig is trying to line up on Tuck and Rabini; and Latham and Klause are after the second Mig.

Tuck and Rabini lockup and launch a Sparrow that blows the lead Mig out of the sky.

With that, the second Mig pulls into a steep climb with Latham and Klause looking up at him from below--a hot tailpipe with the cool blue sky as a background. Latham puts his pipper on the Mig and when one of his sidewinders whistles the "I'm locked on" signal, Latham pulls the trigger. The pilot of this second Mig is luckier than his leader. He bails out of his damaged airplane and Latham and Klause join up to observe the missing canopy and the empty cockpit.

It's easy to see why the VC didn't try that trick again. It's also easy to see why their mission could have turned out differently. The Mig-21 is a fast airplane with a rate of climb very similar to an F-4. Had they planned their mission a bit differently they could have nailed the B-66 and, with a little luck, taken to the deck and gone home.

On 6 November, I go on another B-66 escort mission. No joy.

On 7 November I carry a load of 500 pound "snake-eye" bombs on a VC hunt in my old stomping ground. The Snake Eye is a standard bomb fitted with a set of four speed brakes that open like an umbrella on release. The big speed brakes slow the bomb abruptly allowing the airplane to separate to a safe distance from the explosion. An ordinary bomb delivered at low level would go off right underneath us and take us with it. We carry Snake Eyes because we can deliver them at low level in bad weather. If we can get under a ceiling with a little visibility, we can use the bombs that would otherwise be undeliverable. Low level work is always more fun.

On 8 November, Bud Flesher and I are assigned to alert duty. We move into a trailer parked on the flight line, preflight our airplanes and lay out our flight gear so that we can be taxiing for take-off in five minutes. The alert airplanes are always loaded with ordnance that can be delivered at low level, in low ceilings and visibility because, if you recall the outpost where I spoke to our man on the ground just seconds before he died, the need for close support for ground troops is the most likely source of need.

Our airplanes today are carrying Napalm, Snake-Eyes, and 20 mike-mike. If we have any kind of ceiling or visibility, we can get the job done.

Soon as we are settled in our trailer, we make ourselves comfortable and see what's for chow. We have stacks of C rations and soft drinks and snacks. We also have some reading material. We get into the C's and coffee, and get a scramble. We dash out to the airplanes, strap in and hit the starters. In five minutes or so we are moving into take-off position. The command post has informed us that we are heading for Package I to look for a "SAM" convoy. Package I has been getting steadily hotter and since the VC are intent on getting supplies and personnel into the south, they want to interrupt our air activity.

Since we're carrying all low level ordnance, we don't climb out, we just level off at 1,000 feet and streak for Pack I. In minutes we are in the target area. The central coordinates we're looking for are near an area that is always "hot"--Bat Lake. Pretty soon we're seeing sporadic gunfire--some .50 tracers and some 37 mm bursts. We can't find any trucks, but that's no great surprise. These guys are good at camouflage and are never gonna wave at you from the middle of the highway.

We have a description of the target area and the target coordinates, but when Bud gets a fix on muzzle flashes, he turns in and unloads his napalm. From then on we violate what eventually becomes a rule no matter where you are over North Viet Nam, it's a one-pass situation--deliver all your ordnance on one pass and LEAVE. Well, today, we make several passes, delivering ordnance each time, until we run out. I thought the VC were gonna hit us both, but we were lucky.

RANCH HANDS
On 9 November I lead a three ship raid into Tally-Ho. We work with a FAC and the thing he most wants is to cut a small bridge on the main north-south roadway. We manage to do that.

Later in the day, I am scheduled to lead a Ranch Hand escort mission. The Ranch Hands fly C-123s and spray crops and jungle with poison that kills vegetation. When it kills trees, we can see the roads, and when it kills crops, it starves the VC. We escort them because they get shot at a lot--as in every time they fly. We take this escort duty very seriously because we love and respect the Ranch Hands and will do all we can to assist them in staying alive.

The major qualification for being a Ranch Hand is certifiable insanity.

Once a month they have a full-blown Dining In, except it's Ranch Hand style, meaning Mess Dress is "Formal" fatigues. They always have an honored guest who must address this bunch from Bedlam. Their most recent "Dining In" was last week. The guest speaker was our Wing Vice Commander. Ranch Hands like to invite their favorites--the best mannered and most straight laced. Academy graduates are preferred. Innocence is a preferred quality as well.

The party began with several toasts, especially to the guest of honor. Then dinner and more toasts. Then the guest of honor speaks. Our Wing Vice rises to speak. The room becomes ghostly quiet--an almost unheard of situation when there are more than two Ranch Hands present. The Guest speaker takes the podium--the Ranch Hands exhibit reverential awe--staring in radiant worship as the Speaker takes his moment of silence. Then the guest utters his first words: "Good Evening." The place goes mad; the Ranch Hands are on their feet as one, screaming "Bravo! Bravo! Well Said Fearless leader!" and whistling and clapping and cheering, then just as suddenly, as one, all the Ranch Hands are seated--staring, in absolute silence and awe at the Speaker standing at the podium--waiting with bated breaths for his next words.

The speaker takes a deep breath and with only a smidgen of trepidation: "I came here…" --but no further. As one the ranch Hands are on their feet, screaming, applauding, gesticulating. "Bravo! Amazing! How Courageous! How Daring!" And then--you may have guessed it--the Ranch Hands take their seats, silently staring at their hero of the evening, obviously awed by his presence.

The speaker is onto the rules now, but he's in a trap--he's in Ranch Hand Land now, the land where all the rules are twisted. The speaker takes his speech, tears it to pieces and sits down. The ranch hands go Berzerk. As one they are standing and cheering. The head "Hand" picks up a piece of bread, soaks it with wine, and tosses it into one of the overhead fans. His underlings, following the fearless example of their leader, grab the nearest bread, soak it thoroughly with wine and toss it into the overhead fans. Wine soaked bread is soon oozing down the walls and covering all within fan-shot of this wild bunch.

Somewhere in the world, if a Ranch Hand is reading this, he is probably pronouncing a curse upon me for failing to adequately capture the Ranch Hand spirit. Sobeit.

My wingman today is Fran Vyzral. We fly a lot together and are friends as well as fellow Flight members. Fran's fellow crewman today is 1/LT Jim White. We have a scheduled rendezvous time and do our flight briefing and preparation to be punctual. We taxi out to the arming area for runway 35 Right, park, and extend our hands outside the cockpit, where they will remain until the armorers give us a signal that they are finished arming our ordnance and are clear of our airplane. The armorers finish my airplane first and Corky and I can do things in the cockpit. They are about to begin with Fran's bird when Da Nang Tower calls and informs me that the wing command Post wants to talk to me. Since Fran and Jim and are indisposed with their hands outside, we nod to let them know we're leaving the Ground frequency to talk to the CP.

The CP tells me that the Ranch Hands have been delayed for one hour. Rather than going through disarming, taxiing back to revetments, shutting down, etc., we are to take off, refuel on Brown Anchor over the South China Sea, and time our refueling to the adjusted rendezvous time. I acknowledge all these instructions and return to Ground frequency. In a short time, we are cleared for take-off, with Fran and company totally unaware of the refueling, etc.

We are soon airborne, and instead of leveling off and turning west to proceed to the target, I turn slightly to the right and keep climbing to join our tanker on Brown Anchor and call Fran to ask him to switch to Brown 22's frequency. He checks in on Brown 22's channel and I call Brown 22 as we close in on the south end of his track. We are soon in formation with Brown 22, refuel, and, at the appropriate moment, we depart and head for our rendezvous with the Ranch Hands.

The mission today is a crop killer southwest of Hue. We join up with the two Ranch Hands who are 100 feet above the ground at about 150 miles per hour in formation with about 100 yards of separation for maximum coverage. We stay with them by circling overhead, separated such that as one of us passes to their right at grass top level, the other is traveling in the opposite direction on the opposite side at 1,000 feet. We are flying at about 450 miles per hour as we circle and this 180 degree offset allows for optimum coverage in case of ground fire.

Things are going swimmingly when, just as I am approaching the lead Ranch Hand on his right, and Fran is at 1,000 feet on the opposite side going the opposite direction, I see what appears to be a stream from a fire hose coming from the ground and terminating in Ranch Hand Leader's left engine nacelle. The left engine bursts into flames, and the engine is suddenly trailing black smoke. In the next two seconds, the crew activates the left engine fire extinguisher, feathers the left engine, and salvos the remaining load of agent orange in a big globule that slides out of the open loading doors in the tail of the airplane. I pull up and turn ninety degrees to the left and ask Fran to stay with the Ranch Hands as they head for home.

I have a fix on the source of the ground fire. It's a .50 caliber camouflaged in a hole in the middle of the rice field that would have remained invisible if it hadn't fired at Ranch Hand Lead. I don't take my eyes off the gun position, roll in for a Napalm run. approach the gun, and scrape a can of Napalm off on the gunner's head.

By this time, Fran and Jim are circling the Ranch Hands as they turn for home, and I rejoin. As we exit the area, Fran and I stay at crop top level for about a quarter of a mile after each pass with the Ranch Hands now flying at about 100 feet. Ranch Hand Lead and his wingman recover at Da Nang without further incident.

After we land and park, I wait for Fran and his fellow crewman, Jim White, and we stroll across the flight line toward the squadron headquarters. I ask Fran if he thought we were headed for downtown Ha Noi with that load of low level ordnance. I know that Fran is a cool dude and good at what he does, but his response is still a pleasant surprise: "No, but wherever you were going, we were going with you! "

Later in the day, the Ranch Hand crews visit our Squadron Commander, Lt. Col. Bob Tanguy, to pass on their appreciation for taking out the VC .50, and for leading them home safely with low passes.

Colonel Tanguy always has substantive things to say at our morning staff meetings. The next morning, he passes on the Ranch Hands thanks and then elaborates on how dangerous it is to associate with Ranch Hands--not in the air, but at their "Dinings In." Colonel Tanguy is a West Pointer and sometimes it shows. This morning he is particularly concerned that some members of the 480th will wind up at the next Ranch Hand party standing in the middle of one of the tables throwing wine soaked bread into the ceiling fans.

MORE IN THE NORTH

On 10 November I'm scheduled for a B-66 escort, but we're weathered out. My regular fellow crewman, Corky Prahler, stopped by the veterinarian's place a few days ago to visit the stray dog collection. One of the puppies bit Corky, and the vet quarantined the dog that turned out to be rabid. Corky is now grounded until he finishes the three week ordeal of taking rabies shots in his belly.

On 11 November I fly the B-66 escort mission with Lt. Don Newell. Our own surveillance radar reported Bogeys in our area, but they never approached us close enough for a reaction. It's within the realm of speculation that the North V were baiting us to leave the B-66 to attack the baiters, while a flight of Mig-21s tried to pull off what they failed to do six days ago. We stayed with the B-66 hoping for a repeat. No joy.

Later in the day, we learn that that Cam Ranh Bay has lost two F-4s in Package I today. Both airplanes were at very low level on napalm runs when they were hit. Speculation is that the lead crew is dead and that the other crew is a "maybe." I hope Harry Monlux wasn't in either airplane.

13 November is a go for a highly classified C-130 escort mission into packages V and VI. Yesterday I noticed an acquaintance from Tyndall AFB

at breakfast in the DOOM Club. The day before, we all took note of a C-130 as it taxied in and parked near the control tower. As soon as it parked, several Air Policemen wearing berets and armed with M-16s, exited the airplane and roped off the perimeter around it and posted two guards to keep anyone from getting closer than about fifty feet of the airplane.

As my acquaintance and I were rehashing old times, I asked him what brought him to Da Nang. His response: "Have you noticed the C-130 parked on the ramp with armed guards protecting it?" I said that I had. His response: "I'm flying it. Don't ask me any more questions."

Today he will fly that same C-130 over North Viet Nam, and I will lead the flight of four escorting him. Four of us depart Da Nang and refuel over northern Thailand and Laos. Two of us then join up with the C-130 over northern Laos at 25,000 feet and circle him from above as he wends his way into North Viet Nam. By shuttling to and from the tanker in a timely way, two of us will be with him with at least full internal fuel during his entire mission. Our job: to take care of any Migs that might want to try their luck, and to see that he comes home without a scratch. After about four hours, he heads for northern Laos and we stay with him until we are all in Thai air space. The C-130 goes his way, perhaps to Shangri La, and we recover at Da Nang having been airborne for a little over six hours. Any Questions?

When I get home, the Command Post has the latest on the two F-4s from Cam Ranh who were shot down in Pack I day before yesterday. Harry Monlux was in the lead aircraft. It's almost certain that they didn't make it. No chutes, no beepers. No joy. My diary today reads in part: "To think I tried to get him to come up here, and he didn't want to, because he didn't want to 'tempt fate.' His little girl, Tammy, is the same age as Kent. I don't really mind going that much, but I'd hate to be killed here and…leave Sue with Kent to raise all alone."

Flew another B-66 escort on 14 November. No Migs. My diary entry in part: "I think about Sue and MacFergus an awful lot, and I really miss them. I think about them when I'm flying sometimes, and I plan to be very careful. I don't want to leave Sue and the boy, and I have every intention of going home to them."

Two days later I'm in the middle of a fight with Jake 44 as the FAC. We were carrying low level ordnance and take out a few VC.

The days go by. Some bad weather scrubs, some close air support here in South Viet Nam, and then on 22 November, I fly a B-66 escort, and we send other flights on Mig combat Air Patrol (MIGCAP) to cover F-105s on their strike missions. We lose one of our MIGCAP to a SAM--Scotty Wilson and Joe Crecca--too deep in Pack VI for any rescue attempt. There were two chutes, but one of the chute's occupants was hanging limp as though he was unconscious--not good news, not clear which one it was. I wonder where Scotty and Joe are now.

I spend the remainder of November fighting a cold and getting in a couple of close air support missions. Then...

BUD'S DEMISE
December 1, 1966 is a coolish day in Da Nang. The leading edge of the winter monsoon season has issued its pre-season warning with some modest rain, including a bit of bluster and lower temperatures. I am barely comfortable in a summer flight suit and jacket. There has been enough rain to keep me on the improvised board sidewalk to avoid the mud.

I sleep in this morning because today promises to be a casual, relaxed day. The better half of our two man F-4 crew—Corky Prahler—and I are scheduled to take an F-4 to Clark Air Base in the Philippines today to fire a Sparrow missile at a drone target. The purpose is to proof test the entire Sparrow launch system in the airplane. These exercises are conducted periodically on each airplane to assure operational readiness.

We will fly to Clark today, fly the exercise tomorrow, and return the day after on December 3. These trips are considered a mini Rest and Relaxation (R&R) and are assigned in rotation so that all crews have a chance to participate. We do it out of Clark because a large gunnery range is located over the Pacific Ocean, and the equipment for launching the drones, tracking the operation, and gathering data is all in place. Its three days away from the bustle associated with daily combat flying, and is a relaxed pace that allows leisure time to sleep, eat, drink, play tennis, socialize with other crews, etc.

It's about 8:00 AM, and I am walking alone from my quarters to the Da Nang Officer's Open Mess—more commonly known as the DOOM Club, where I plan to meet Corky for breakfast. Ahead of me I see Bud Flesher leaving the club alone walking toward me.

Bud and I meet and stop to chat. He asks me about my mission today, and I explain that Cork and I are taking a plane to Clark for Sparrow Proof Testing. I also tell him that I'm pretty sure that another plane is scheduled to go today, and that he might think about looking into the flight schedule and maybe come along for the fun. He refuses the opportunity. His explanation: He is heading for the Wing Command Post to check into a rumor that there are some Package Six strikes scheduled for tomorrow, and, if so, he wants to go.

Package Six is certainly a more exciting place to be than Clark. Package Six, right now, is the most dangerous place on the face of the planet. If you want to dodge SAMs and AAA while hoping to bump into the very occasional Mig for a little more fun and the opportunity for air-to-air engagement, Package Six is the place, and Bud Flesher doesn't want to miss out on the fun. I've got no problem with an occasional trip up to Package Six, but today I feel more like a steak dinner and martini or two at the Officer's Club at Clark.

I try to persuade Bud to come along. We can go to Pack Six almost anytime we want to, but at a later date. Bud wants to stay and win the war. We leave it at that. Bud heads for the flight line, and I continue to the DOOM Club.

Corky and I breakfast among the usual crowd who constitute the 366th Tactical Fighter Wing (TFW) and occasional visitors. There is the usual banter and conversation--particularly among the fighter crews who constitute the majority of the constituency at the DOOM Club. As soon as we finish our breakfast, Corky and I, along with an assortment of flight crews, head for the flight line where our respective squadrons are located, along with the Wing Headquarters Building and the Wing Command Post. We plan our two hour flight to Clark, and late in the day we are there. It's a beautiful day. The flight is very smooth and uneventful--a day over the perfectly blue and beautiful South China Sea.

On December 2 Corky and I breakfast at the Clark Air Base Officer's Club. After breakfast we go to the flight line operations building and prepare for the days exercise. After briefing and lunch, we meet at the flight line, spend an hour suiting up and doing our preflight inspection of the airplane. Our next stop is the gunnery range about a hundred miles from Clark, out over the Pacific Ocean.

We takeoff and climb out following the directions of the intercept controller who sits in front of a radar screen in a dark, air conditioned room at Clark Air Base as he watches tiny blips move about on his radar screen. We are one of those tiny blips as we follow the controller's directions. The controller positions us to attack a drone target head on, as if the drone were an inbound enemy aircraft. Our job is to locate the drone on our radar and shoot it down with a Sparrow missile.

The F-4 carries four Sparrow missiles tucked into four nooks in the belly of the fuselage. Each sparrow fits into a cavity that is shaped to accept the upper half of the missile such that when the missile is properly stowed, only the lower half is visible. We call this "nook" a bay. When the missile is stowed in its cavity, it is a part of the airplane. During the attack process, when the crew passes the "launch" order to missile, it drops out of its bay, the rocket motor lights up, and the Sparrow rides our radar beam to the target.

The controller positions us at 30,000 feet a hundred or so miles from the incoming aircraft that will launch the drone. The "mother' aircraft is an F-89 Scorpion, obsolete in the combat inventory, but is now in service here to carry the target drones and launch them for our practice. Corky is soon tracking the F-89 on his radar screen in the back seat, while I observe on my radar screen in the front. After a short time, while the F-89 and our target are still one blip, the single blip splits into two targets. The F-89 turns to its right (our left) and dives away, off our screen. The drone, just released, continues toward us on a collision course.

When the drone is about 50 miles away, Corky locks up on it, and our radar is in the automatic track mode, stopping our radar from scanning and ordering it to hold on to the drone and track it. As the drone moves down our tracking beam, it soon moves into range of our Sparrow. Corky tells me that we are well within the "kill" parameters of the sparrow we are carrying and advises me to launch.

I pass the launch command to the sparrow through a switch on my control stick. There is a commotion under the belly of our airplane much like a steam locomotive clawing for traction as it pulls away from Grand Central Station in 1939, and the Sparrow screams out ahead of us leaving a white trail of exhaust. The Sparrow soon disappears from view, and in a few seconds, we see a burst of debris as the Sparrow destroys the drone. Our mission is over. We make a lazy 180 degree turn and return to Clark Air Base and land.

After the mission debriefing, we loll about and eventually wind up at the Officer's Club for the usual round of drinks and a steak dinner.

On December 3, we sleep in, have a late breakfast, prepare a flight plan, load up and head for Da Nang. The weather is CAVU [Clear and Visibility Unlimited] all over the Pacific and the South China Sea. Corky flew the front seat over and takes the front seat back. If we got "caught" switching seats, something bad would happen to both of us, especially me. The reason that I am willing to take this risk is that Corky has done a great job when flying with me, and this is a small reward for his diligence.

After landing at Da Nang and gathering our gear, we walk to the 480th Headquarters building. Routinely, we would enter the headquarters building via the personal equipment room where we would stow our helmets, G-suits, and harness and then walk in through the back door of the main part of the building where the squadron commander, operations officer, and support personnel offices are. Today, because there's not much traffic, and for no other good reason, we saunter in through the front door. The squadron Operations Officer has an office very near the front entrance which we have to pass to get to the personal equipment room.

As we walk by the Ops Officer's office, I can see the Ops Officer--Major Ruben McClure--sitting at his desk. When he sees me walk by he calls out to me and asks me to come in for a minute. I stand near his desk and he asks me to be "...the summary courts officer." I know immediately that something is wrong. The only reason that Ruben would ask me to perform as summary courts officer would be that we had lost someone. When we lose a crew, the Uniform Code of Military Justice requires an officer to be appointed to administer their estate. I know that we have lost another crew, and that part of Ruben's job is to appoint a "Summary Courts Officer" I just didn't know whose. So I ask: "Who for?" Ruben stands up and says: "Oh, I'm sorry. I didn't know that you didn't know that Bud and Jim Berger were shot down yesterday. I forgot that you were over at Clark."

I am stunned. Bud went to Package Six yesterday, just as he wanted to, and he's still there.

I go on in to the personal equipment room, stow my equipment, and come back to Ruben's office to get details. The story is not pretty. Bud and Jim took what appeared to be a direct hit by a Surface to Air Missile (SAM) at 14,000 feet. Their airplane emerged from the dirty cloud of the exploding SAM inverted and in a flat spin. The nose cone, tail section, and wing tips were separating from the fuselage as it spun toward the earth. No parachutes--no beepers. Bad news.

I arrange to talk to the three flight crews who were with Bud and Jim. Another of my squadron mates has been appointed to take care of Jim Berger's affairs, and I concentrate on Bud. It's no fun. The crews who were with Bud corroborate what Major McClure told me. We all believe that Bud and Jim are most likely dead. One crew said that they saw what appeared to be the drogue chute deploy from the separated tail section--a natural result of the violent separation from the main fuselage. I want to weep for two good men, but somehow manage to exit the interview and slink away.

I soon get orders appointing me to duty as Bud's Summary Courts Officer. The Staff Judge Advocate General (JAG) briefs me on the legal details and explains that I have access to legal advice any time I need it. I go to Bud's quarters and start rounding up his "stuff." He has a little

Honda 90cc motorcycle that a B-57 crew had delivered to Da Nang from Clark Air Base a few days before he was shot down. It's parked near his quarters with the steering fork lock engaged. I look everywhere for the key, but can't find it. I recover all of his stuff from his lock box where he stowed it before the flight. The key is not there either. I finally give up and find a professional from a dealer in Da Nang to remove and replace the lock and put the bike up for sale.

Bud has a gallon of Bombay gin, a full box of Tabacalera cigars from the Philippines, along with two sticks of dry salami and a lot of crackers. I immediately invite our flight, and other "dignitaries" to a farewell blast. We do justice to the entirety of these consumables and have a lot of laughs.

So long Bud and Jim: hope our surmises about your fate are all wrong, and that we will see both of you as soon as we finish this business--whenever that may be.

The Beat Goes On

From 3 December to 9 December we are weathered out of North Viet Nam and fly only a couple of in country air support missions. Not a lot of excitement. Then on 9 December we lose an airplane and recover the crew in the South China Sea just off the coast of Package I. John Young is the Aircraft Commander and winds up in the hospital with a fractured tail bone. Fred Porter, the other crewmember, is uninjured.

On 11 December we lose another airplane. Jerry Woodcock and Jerry Alford were the crew. Both bailed out over the South China Sea, but we never heard from Alford, other than a short response from his SAR beeper that works automatically after ejection.

Jerry Woodcock's rescue may be instructive as to surmising what happened to Jerry Alford. When their airplane was hit, Woodcock and Alford headed east. They made it out to sea and were forced to eject about

15 miles from the coast. Woodcock descended through a solid overcast and landed in the South China Sea not far from the USS Keppler, a Navy Destroyer. The dark was overwhelming--Jerry could see nothing--he did everything by Braille.

The flotation vest was inflated and Jerry was afloat, but just barely. He fished his two way radio out of its storage pocket and managed to turn it on. To his great relief, it was working. As he was attempting to make a call to let any listeners know that he was alive, he kept hearing an occasional "psst, psst" sound--like air escaping from his life vest--not comforting. He felt around and found the inflation tube to discover that the mouthpiece for oral inflation was in the "inflate" mode allowing air to escape when he moved about and depressed the lock. He quickly added air to the vest orally and locked the tube so it wouldn't leak.

Having done that, he made a call on the Radio. The destroyer answered him immediately and told him that they were "cutting" his radio and steering toward him. It was still totally dark. As the conversation continued, Jerry saw a bright light on the surface heading for him. His first thought: "These Navy dudes are gonna run me over with their Destroyer." The light came closer, and in a minute or so, a boat, much smaller than a destroyer, pulled near him, and the crew pulled him to safety. In another few minutes, he was drying out aboard the destroyer, and the Navy returned him to us the next day.

We never heard from Jerry Alford.

Let's close the Airdrome for a While

We continue to fly armed reconnaissance in Laos and North Viet Nam and Ground Support missions "in Country," as weather permits. Our night schedule and bad weather are holding us up. One of our operations rules is that when we're returning to Da Nang in bad weather, unless we're on the ground with at least 5,000 pounds of fuel, we must divert to

Thailand. The reasoning is that if we find ourselves in a low ceiling situation with much less than 5,000 pounds of fuel, we won't have enough to make an alternate, unless we go there now.

On 22 December, 1/Lt John Rabini and I are leading a flight of two on a Sky Spot mission in Tally-Ho. The weather is terrible. When we complete our bomb run, we return to Da Nang and separate to fly individual GCAs. Our wingman is in trail with us about seven miles as I fly GCA final. Just before we break out, I can hear background chatter in the GCA trailer. We break out into a light drizzle at about 200 feet, and I'm looking right down the runway and see two flashing beacons sitting on the numbers of Runway 35 Right. Simultaneously, the GCA controller stops steering us and says: "Abort the approach and go around." As I add power to climb back into the soup, I make out the silhouettes of two Marine A-6s loaded with twenty-six 500 pound bombs each holding for take-off. As we clean up the airplane, our fuel gage shows 5,200 pounds. There's no way we can get on the ground with 5,000 pounds of fuel. We call for a flight clearance to Ubon Royal Thai Air Force Base in Thailand.

Lt. Rabini and I arrive at Ubon and check into the 8th Tactical Fighter Wing Command Post. We get a cordial welcome and a telephone call from the 366th TFW Command Post. I take the call and find the Deputy Commander for Operations, Colonel Skip Stanfield, on the other end. He asks me if we are okay. I am bit puzzled that he has called, but he soon clears it up. He tells me that right after we went around and headed for Ubon, the two Marine A-6s took off, and then my wingman landed with a hung bomb. When he touched down, the bomb came off the airplane and followed him down the runway for about 2000 feet and then veered off the side of the runway and sank in the mud. Da Nang Airdrome is closed indefinitely pending locating and disposing of the M-117 bomb. His good night advice: "Have a steak at the club, get some good rest, and we'll see you sometime tomorrow."

The remainder of December is pretty ordinary. Lots of bad weather. Christmas day was rain all day, and I spent the day and night inventorying and packing Bud's "stuff." We had canned turkey for dinner at the DOOM Club. I flew as an Instructor Pilot (IP) on two in country missions with two new Aircraft Commanders on 30 December. All of these in country missions are just like the FAC missions I flew for a year, except I'm on the other end.

OPERATION BOLO

I flew 564 total sorties in Southeast Asia (SEA)--106 over North Viet Nam, the rest in South Viet Nam and Laos. Many of them could be described in a few words, and were "strictly routine." On Monday January 2, 1967, I was a participant in one of the most noticeable and important missions flown by fighters during the Viet Nam War.

In late December, our Deputy Wing Commander for Operations (DO) scheduled a briefing for all fighter crews to assemble in the Wing Command Post. The subject of the briefing was "Operation Bolo." Colonel Robin Olds, Commander of the 8th Tactical fighter Wing (TFW) at Ubon Royal Thai Air Force Base, Thailand had prepared a plan to lure the North Viet Namese to commit their fighters to come up and join us in a real air-to-air confrontation.

The genesis of this plan has to do with the way North Viet Nam use their fighters against us. By late 1966, our air operations over the heavily defended areas of North Viet Nam had become routine enough that the North could essentially extend the philosophy of guerilla warfare they had used against the French and with which they were now making monkeys out of us in South Viet Nam, to the air war. The NVN Air Force was an extension of their Army. Their organizational structure bore army nomenclatures and their goals were as defined by the Communist Party to achieve the goal of "liberating" the Viet Namese people from the ravages of foreigners--namely us--by the same tactics.

Until now, there was no air-to-air war. The V avoided air-to-air confrontations by employing what were essentially guerilla tactics.

A significant part of these tactics consisted of making passes at the heavily loaded fighter bombers, especially the most vulnerable F-105s, and sticking around just long enough to force them to jettison their bomb load to defend themselves. Once the bomb load was gone, the Migs headed for the deck and home and it was difficult to chase them down, although it did happen occasionally. Meanwhile, the airfields from which the V air force operated were off limits as targets; i.e. we weren't allowed to attack their airplanes when they were on the ground. We routinely sent F-4s on Mig Combat Air Patrol (MIGCAP) missions in an attempt to cut off the attacking Migs and protect the strike forces. Just as routinely, the Migs avoided F-4s like the plague. There were some air-to-air shootdowns, but they were few and far between a lot of missions.

Every time we went to the hot spots in the far north of Viet Nam-- Packages V, VIA, and VIB--we were on the lookout for Migs. I never saw a Mig in my life until I was a POW in a Camp called the Plantation. I just happened to be outside my cell during the allotted ten minutes to bathe, when two Mig-21s made a low pass.

Colonel Olds observed all these factors and came up with a plan to lure the V into a trap. We would frag a set of missions to be flown with F-105 call signs, but to be flown by F-4s loaded for air-to-air combat. There would be seven flights from Ubon and seven from Da Nang. The flights from Ubon would refuel over Northern Thailand and proceed as though to bomb targets in North Viet Nam. The flights from Da Nang would refuel off the east coast of Viet Nam and do the same. We know that the V monitor our radio conversations, and that they will be convinced that all these flights are F-105s and will scramble a large number of fighters. They will discover too late, that the sky is full of F-4s, not F-105s, and we will have a turkey shoot.

The attack force from Ubon uses names of automobiles as call signs. Colonel Olds would lead the first flight as *Olds*. Colonel Daniel "Chappie" James would lead the second flight from Ubon as *Ford*. The next four flights would be other cars. Colonel Stanfield will lead the Da Nang force as Omaha.

A part of the plan includes what to do in case the weather is too bad to fly the mission. The rule is that if there is an abort, we abort before we get into North Viet Nam, hoping that we can repeat the drill at a later date. Thus, if the weather is bad, discontinue and go home before we get anywhere close to area that any of us would be spotted.

I am Omaha 4--the number four airplane in the lead flight. We refuel over the South China Sea off the east coast of Viet Nam and continue north at 20,000 feet to a point off the coast east of Hai Phong. The weather is terrible. We are able to remain VFR by threading our way north surrounded by towering cumulus. There are solid clouds below and to our left. North Viet Nam is socked in solid. As arranged beforehand, Colonel Stanfield attempts to contact Colonel Olds. We get no response.

The clock is ticking away, and the decision to abort from our side depends on what Colonel Olds sees from his side. Olds is leading the parade and, by the plan, they have by now refueled over Northern Thailand and Laos and are approaching the Ha Noi area from near Dien Bien Phu in North Viet Nam. The mission plan calls for precise timing for our arrivals. No response could mean that Olds has turned back, because the weather is similar to what we see. If that is the case, we do not want to proceed inland and blow the cover for a repeat. If we knew that the weather on the inland side was good enough for Olds to proceed, we could let down and go in to close the pincers as planned.

The time for us to either go in or abort the mission arrives, and with no contact with Olds and a solid cloud cover over all of North Viet Nam that we can see, Colonel Stanfield decides to abort. We turn and head for home.

As we approach Da Nang the weather has deteriorated to below minimums, and our strike force diverts to Ubon. The weather at Ubon is clear and we are soon on the ground to discover that the weather over the north was good from the inland side, that Olds had proceeded with the mission, that the Migs fell for the trap, and that the 8th TFW had nailed seven Mig-21s with no losses.

We joined the mission de-briefing in the 8th TFW Command Post. Each of the victorious warriors participated in the de-briefing--a glorious moment for all of the 8th. The 56 members of the Da Nang force sat through the celebration with the best faces we could put on, and left quietly later in the day when the weather at Da Nang had improved--hugely disappointed, recognizing that circumstances had robbed us of a moment of glory.

Winter monsoon weather continues to plague us. When we can see, we go to Laos and Package I on armed reconnaissance missions. Then in the night of 19 January, I flew the mission that I opened with on page 4--"The Bridge." It was a fun mission and also satisfying in that we got away with a visit to North Viet Nam without being detected until we were in the act of delivering ordnance. Then it's...

FLYING THE AIRWAYS
Today, January 20, 1967, Corky and I lead an element of two F-4s on a MIG-CAP (Mig Combat Air Patrol) to Package VI-A. Our job is to protect the attack force as it goes after a JCS (Joint Chiefs of Staff) target.

The "frag" order specifies the route, times and altitudes that we are to fly in order to best position ourselves to protect the attacking fleet. One of our best and most respected crews will fly our wing today--Capt. Bill Baugh and 1/Lt Don Spoon.

Our route into North Viet Nam calls for refueling on the Brown Anchor at 22,000 feet over the South China Sea about 50 miles off the coast of Viet Nam. We will then head for a point near Ha Long Bay and turn west to enter Package VI-B north of Hai Phong, head so as to pass north of Kep air field and position ourselves to spot any Migs that come up to attack the bombing operation. We have flown this route so often that the V don't even have to aim; they just point their guns skyward and wait for us to arrive.

Kep is easy to spot--just look for the black cloud of flack as you turn inland. We are tracking our planned route at the fragged altitude, when number 2, Baugh and Spoon, start drifting toward us from their position on our left wing. As they close into a near trail position, I know that something is wrong. They continue their turn to the North and call to tell me that they are battle damaged and have lost an engine. Corky and I now become their wing, and we head North East to get out of range of AAA and SAMs. Corky works out the best route home and generates a flight plan, based on single engine performance, that will get us home safely.

We close in on their airplane and inspect it for visible battle damage. There is very little. All we can see is a few almost unnoticeable holes in the airplane's skin. There is no smoke or fuel leaks. They are doing their check list and ask us to verify our position and give them a steer. We are very close to the China border, nothing but wild, undeveloped land--a safe place to be, so we stay there and steer toward a position over water so that we can turn south as soon as possible.

On the way home, we have almost no conversation. We contact Panama, our mission control center, and tell them that we plan to make a straight in approach to Runway 17 at Da Nang.

As we near Da Nang, we have plenty of altitude and are a bit high to make a straight in approach. Bill continues on a high downwind leg for Runway 35 and makes a loose 180 degree turn to land on Runway 35 right. The crash crews are in position as a precaution. Bill makes a nice approach, lands and after braking to a stop, shuts down as the crash crew approaches.

Back in the squadron, we all voice our mutual concern about the airline style routing the mission planners have choked down our throats. Baugh, in particular, is very unhappy about it all. Later in the evening we congregate for dinner and drinks at the DOOM club. There are a few laughs as we banter about Baugh and Spoon having dodged an opportunity to visit with some of our squadron mates who are now lounging in the Ha Noi Hilton. There are also some laughs about the fact that "Big Eye," our airborne Radar surveillance aircraft, had reported us for violating Chinese airspace during our exit. We will respond to that accusation in due time. But now, some rest.

The next day, January 21, Corky and I lead a flight of four F-4s on another MIGCAP to Package VI-A. The target is Northeast of Ha Noi. SAMs and AAA are always present. We position ourselves so that we will be between the MIG base and the bomber stream and decide to stay relatively low. The Mig-21 has a pretty good zoom capability and can attack fast from below. Our hope today is that, should the Migs try that low-high tactic, we can be near enough to cut them off. We maneuver at fairly high speed so as to be able to climb with the Migs if they try a "zoom" style attack. The Migs stay on the ground today, as they usually do.

This war is not an air-to-air war. The V use their limited air capability with wisdom and caution--much like the guerrilla tactics they employ on the ground. We have shot down a few of them, but the score is pretty close to even. Something is wrong with this picture.

That something has almost everything to do with the way the war is run from a remote position somewhere in an ivory tower in Washington, D.C. One or two well-planned strikes could destroy the V air component on the ground. Why don't we do it? Their airfields are off limits. We fly daily strikes in packages VI-A and VI-B, sometimes with a clear view of Migs parked safely on their off-limit airdromes. One quick swoop with a long burst from a SUU-16 firing at the rate of 100 rounds per second could easily take out half a dozen per pass. Certainly we would sustain some losses from ground fire, but the kill ratio would be very high--at least an order of magnitude better than it is now, not to mention the fact that we would have completely eliminated that portion of the threat.

We did manage to engineer one big success and down seven Mig-21s on Operation Bolo earlier this month, but on a day-day-basis, we are largely frustrated. Bolo should never have had to happen. How absurd to be forced to trickery to get them airborne so we could shoot them. This ain't a duck hunt!

Some pundits say that if we attacked the V Air Forces on the ground, they would deploy to China. One concentrated set of surprise raids on a clear day and there would be nothing left to deploy to China or anywhere else. The V might restock and deploy a replacement set somewhere in China. What then? A daily combat Air Patrol (CAP) could easily keep them essentially hemmed in. Yes, there would be engagements and losses, but with a lot better leverage.

Baugh and Spoon are in another MigCAP flight today that is a replica of yesterday--same mission, same target, same ingress route, same ingress altitude, same result--they take a hit in the same place we were yesterday, but are not so lucky today. They eject from their battle damaged airplane while attempting to make the same turn to safety they made yesterday, and join our comrades in the Hilton. How many times will this scenario play out?

ETHAN ALPHA

7th Air Force laid on a photo mission to highlight our airborne early warning mission. The objective--take an Air Force photographer in the back seat of an F-4 to photo the C-121 radar ship on an actual mission off the coast of North Viet Nam. I am hired for the job, and we fly it on January 26.

I will fly an F-4 fully armed for an air-to-air mission with four each Sidewinders and Sparrows, just in case, but under orders to use them only in a dire emergency. The photographer is a qualified air crew member and we spend time together such that, if necessary, he can complete certain tasks in the back seat. Otherwise, I will position our airplane as he requests for getting a good set of photos.

We depart Da Nang, climb out to 20,000 feet and head for where we expect to find "Big Eye" as he flies a race track pattern somewhere over the Gulf of Tonkin. His call sign today is *Ethan Alpha*. We soon contact Ethan Alpha to let him know we're looking for him. We know about where he will be, but not his altitude. We never reveal our actual altitude on the air, but each day, a classified "base altitude" is sent through classified channels to all air crews. The base altitude today is 20,000 feet. I never bothered to ask about Big Eye's altitude, so I ask him now. His response: "Base minus 19,850 feet." This dude is flying at 150 feet!

My buddy in the back seat knows how to run the radar system, so while we're letting down, he positions the radar antenna angle to look down. In a minute or so we're locked on to Ethan Alpha. We descend through a solid overcast, break out under a 500 foot ceiling, and catch sight of a beautiful four engine Lockheed Constellation, with a big saucer on top, cruising at 180 knots 150 feet above the water. I slow down and drop full flaps to join Ethan Alpha's right wing. The photographer directs me into various positions as he uses his camera equipment. In a few minutes, he's through and we wave good-bye.

That's the mission. All we have to do now is to go home and land. I ask my fellow crewman if he has ever flown supersonic and he hasn't, so I add some power and we are soon supersonic at 30,000 feet. I ask him if he would like to photo an aerial refueling and he says he would appreciate it. I call up Brown 24 and ask if we can join him for a practice contact and he says o.k. In a few minutes we join up with Brown 24 and do a hook up for a couple of minutes. We say good bye to Brown 24, and go home and land. My diary entry in part: "Flew a photo mission. 'Big Eye' --alias Ethan Alpha--150 ft. off the water--much fun 2+15 boondoggle."

The weather is getting warmer. Maybe the winter monsoon will expire soon.

MEANDERING

On 27 January, Corky and I go into Package I on an armed reconnaissance mission, but the weather was too stinky to find a target. We exit toward Laos and there are some clouds but much better visibility. We call our Airborne Command Post and get a clearance to strike a target in Laos.

On 28 January we fly a Mig-CAP in Package V, just north of "Thud Ridge" No Migs. No AAA. No SAMs. Milk run.

For the next few days, weather permitting, we go to Package I or Laos for some fixed targets and armed reconnaissance. On February 7, Larry Peterson and I are in the lead airplane with Fran Vyzral and Jim White on the wing for an air support mission in I Corps. When we approach the area, we check in with the local FAC who tells us he has no targets at the moment. We excuse ourselves and check in with Panama to see if there are any hot targets happening. Panama sends us to Jake 47, a FAC from the southern part of I Corps, my old stomping ground. Jake 47 is right in the middle of a VC nest just east of Mo Duc and asks us to join him. In minutes we are overhead and make six runs each dropping bombs in singles. We then go to work with our 20 mm guns. The weather is good and all of our ordnance is right on target. We decimate the target--a VC controlled village. My diary entry for the day includes: "Best mission I've had since coming over here...a good FAC--Jake 47."

During my entire assignment with the 480th TFS, the 366th TFW was assigned every type of sortie flown at the time--from close air support in South Viet Nam to the most fearsome mission of all, the Package VI strike. For the record here is a partial list of the types of sorties we flew:

1. Close air support in South Viet Nam.
2. Bombing raids against intelligence targets in Viet Nam and Laos.
3. Armed Reconnaissance in the lower packages in North Viet Nam.
4. Escort for B-66 intelligence gathering missions over Pack North Viet Nam.
5. "Ranch Hand" escort--the only times I was hit by ground fire in an F-4 in South Viet Nam was .50 Caliber hits while escorting Ranch Hands.
6. Night Armed Reconnaissance in the lower packages.
7. C-130 escort over North Viet Nam.
8. Package VI Strikes and/or Armed Reconnaissance in Pack VI.

The words *Package six Strike* have a special meaning. When you go to Pack VIA or VIB, you will see a lot of flak and it will be close. Keep going back, and the flak will get closer. Mig CAP can be dangerous too--we have lost several crews on Mig CAP missions.

On April 3, 1967, I fly number 500 total in SEA. It's unusual for news people to fly with us--practically unheard of--but for this flight ABC news has wrangled approval for a David Snell, a reporter, to fly with me. The rules are that it has to be "in country." We are to remain over South Viet Nam. Period. The mission is a trail dust crop killer escorting Ranch Hands. Our load is six 500 pound bombs and 1000 rounds of 20 millimeter, commonly referred to as "20 mike-mike."

We join the Ranch Hands--two C-123s--near Hue City, and they proceed to the rice growing countryside that feeds the maquis--better known to us as VC. The Ranch hands complete their mission and we follow them until they reach a safe altitude and a safe area outside the range of any VC gunfire.

As we separate from the Ranch Hands, Panama calls to let us know that a FAC located a few miles south west of Hue has cornered a group of VC and is requesting an air strike. We switch to an air strike frequency and head for the action--we are there in about three minutes, and the FAC throws out a Willy Pete rocket marker and talks us into the target. We make six passes with our bombs and a couple of strafing runs, and the fight is over. Whoever was there are no more.

The "action" changed a rather routine escort mission into a bit of excitement for Mr. Snell and for the folks back home watching the war news. Here's what we looked like after the mission:

David Snell, ABC News   *Ken Hughey, 480thTFS*

PHOTO 10

On April 3, 1967, Mr. Snell flew with me on my 500th mission over Southeast Asia (SEA). Here, we are discussing the mission after we landed.

On 18 April, Colonel Jones E. (Jonesy) Bolt and I go to Tally Ho just before dark to try and destroy some trucks that an earlier flight had stopped on Highway 1. That whole thing is a fluke in that the V never move anything on their roads during daylight, unless the weather is too sour for air activity. Very occasionally, during marginal weather, we were present during a break and caught traffic in the open road before they could hide. This was one of those occasions.

We are loaded with the wrong kind of ordnance to go after trucks. The two airplanes that were ready were loaded with ten 500 pound bombs each. If they had been loaded with CBUs and/or guns, we could have destroyed most, if not all, but with the trucks parked several hundred feet apart, even if we could get individual hits with all our bombs, we wouldn't get very many. But, we don't have time to reload. We spot the trucks strung out for a mile or so and go to work. I drop six bombs on my first pass and pull off to set up to drop the other four on a second pass.

As I maneuver for the second run, a big gun--probably 57mm--opens up on us, and the flak is coming too close for comfort. In my turn, I can see the muzzle flashes and, without even thinking about it, I roll in on the flashing barrel. Into the run, with the gun in my gun sight, I can see the concentric rings as each round comes out of the barrel--there is no way I can miss this target. I salvo the remaining four bombs in a 45 degree dive and load down with Gs. We are headed south on this run, and as soon as I can start a turn, I break left (east) for the coast. I know that Colonel Bolt was in on the trucks and will be off right behind me. As soon as I am safely over the water, I turn south, and can see where my bombs hit. There are secondary explosions all over the place, and debris and smoke pile up over the target. In a very short time, Colonel Bolt joins up on my left wing, and we head for home. We can see the smoke and fire from miles away as we depart.

Earlier in his career, Colonel Bolt helped to form the "Aerojets," the first Air force demonstration team and flew with the team until it was temporarily disbanded due to the Korean War. When the team was re-formed, it was named "The Thunderbirds." Colonel bolt also flew combat in WWII and wound up as a POW in Germany. He flew my wing more than once during my tour when he Commanded the 366th TFW. He was a great wingman!! He was a great pilot and enjoyed flying combat. His personal style was to fly wing with as many of us as he could.

April 28, 1967

Today I am Venom Lead, a flight of two F-4s, with Lt. Corky Prahler as PSO. Capt. Homer Lee and Lt. Art Sabosky crew the number 2 airplane. Our mission is armed reconnaissance in the lower packages of North Viet Nam. We are carrying low level ordnance--CBU, rockets, and pistols (20 mm cannons). Our job is to visually reconnoiter the roadways and waterways to interdict supply lines. Our mission preparation includes reviews of any current intelligence that might help us in our search. If we can't find visual moving targets such as trucks or boats, we are prepared to strike preselected fixed targets that are known staging areas. There are a couple of hot areas that we will hit if we don't spot movers.

We leave Da Nang and follow the coastline north until we are past the 17th parallel. We turn left into North Viet Nam and proceed at low level in a series of S turns across Highway 1, the "Street Without Joy." This patrol also allows us to search for boat traffic on the inland water ways as we weave our way north. This entire area can get really hot with ground fire ranging from hand held weapons, to .50 caliber machine guns, .37mm and .57mm flak. This stuff is not as deadly as the bigger and more concentrated defenses in packages V and VI, but like the old saying about the Piper Cub being the safest airplane around because "it will just barely kill you," you're no less dead when you die from smaller stuff. The fact is that, because we fly low and not real fast in this recce mode, we're really vulnerable, and we've lost several airplanes messing about down here in the lower packages.

We continue S'ing northward. A lot of the time, the V will stay under cover and never fire a shot until we drop something. Our enemy is not dumb, but once in a while a "Nervous Nellie" VC will cut down on us. In case we don't spot any "movers," such as trucks or barges, we have back-up targets that are pre-approved based on intelligence. These targets can be staging areas where ammo and supplies are stored, bridges, especially underwater bridges that the V think we can't spot because they are submerged, or places where their troops bivouac. It's clear today and the VC are laying low.

On the northern leg we see nothing out of the ordinary--just peace and quiet. Our major pre-planned target of the day is a small bridge on a segment of the main north/south highway we call the "Black Route." We are carrying bombs as well as rockets and use the bombs to knock out the bridge. We try to keep all bridges in a state of disrepair to disrupt the north to south supply traffic. These bridges never stay out of commission for very long. In a few days or weeks, we may hit it again.

After the bridge, we don't see anything that would make a suitable rocket target, so we move off the coast and head south for home. As we approach Dong Hoi, we note an area where some of our prior missions have reported heavy ground fire. Guns are always very well hidden--we almost never spot them on our visual recce runs. The area that our predecessors reported heavy ground fire is coming up on our right as we cruise south. The area looks very innocent. It is a typical village area with lots of trees and foliage and could contain a lot of guns that we just can't detect with the naked eye.

We roll in on the centroid of the area in a shallow dive. As we descend I place my gun sight on the middle of a grove of trees that could very well contain AAA. The target gets bigger in my gun sight and I fire both packages of 2.75 inch "Mighty Mouse" rockets. As the rockets depart, my gun sight is filled with 37 mm muzzle flashes as the VC open up on us. I stop worrying about watching our rockets and load up with g's and roll into a jinking left turn to get back out to sea as quickly as possible, in case the V get lucky.

We are over Dong Hoi in the turn when Corky yells: "Break Right, Break Right." Cork and I work as a team. I don't question his request for a right break and immediately reverse our turn with the g's still on. As I start the roll, I note the sky full of flak that we were just about to fly through. We can hear the pops as the AAA rounds either pass near us or burst--can't tell which. I just get into the right break when a large crowd

221

of Cambridge gray AAA bursts to our right and Corky yells: "Break Left, Break Left." This time the bursts, my stick movement, and Cork's request for a left break are virtually simultaneous. We're climbing now, and I want to get out of here and over water ASAP. I can still hear it going by and it's breaking outside our turn. The Cambridge blue, and the size of the bursts verify 37mm. I hold the turn until we are at least closing with the coastline, and continue jinking turn reversals, as we rapidly pull out of range of the shooters.

I just made a dumb move. I should have approached this target from the inland side NOT the seaward side. If we had taken a hit heading seaward, we would have been over safe water airspace coming off the target, as opposed to having to maneuver through some pretty fierce 37mm fire while hoping to survive long enough to complete a 180 degree turn to relative safety. We were lucky today.

CORKY'S LAST MISSION

On May 12, 1967, Corky and I wind up on Jay Hargrove's wing in a two ship Mig-Cap Mission. The mission was scheduled as a four ship, but airplane availability somehow left us as a two ship element.

Our briefing details the targets we are after in Package VI-A and the units that will bomb each of them. As usual, the brunt of the attack on these targets will be borne by the F-105 fighter wings that fly from Takhli and Korat in Thailand. Our job today is to intercept any Migs that might come up to interfere with their mission. There is nothing much we can do to interfere with or to protect them from AAA and SAMs, but since the Migs will usually avoid any confrontation with F-4s, we offer protection from Migs just by being there.

The air war in Viet Nam was never an Air-to-Air War, particularly in 1967. When we are challenged by Migs, we usually win. We had shot down some Migs by this time, but confrontations were rare. As time progressed, the Migs chose their engagements carefully and the score wasn't much better than even. "Smart" bombing technique, which had not emerged by May 1967, because we weren't yet using smart bombs, cost us some losses later on. We lost some fighter crews that could easily have killed their Mig adversaries in a dogfight, but for the fact that there was never a dogfight.

Smart bombs were very impressive in their capability to fly through the window of a designated target. The problem was that the fighter that carried the Smart bomb had to maintain a steady straight and level course in order to show the Smart bomb its target. A few seconds in straight and level flight in enemy territory protected by competent fighter jocks, who are in your radius of operations, is an eternity. An enemy aircraft with guns or missiles, can zoom from the deck to your six o'clock position and blow you to smithereens in a very small fraction of eternity.

Of the 106 combat sorties over North Viet Nam, several were Mig-Cap missions. Ironically, the only time I ever saw a Mig over North Viet Nam was from the ground on a sunny day in September 1967 when two Mig-21s buzzed the Plantation as I was returning from the bath. Since the V were absolutely paranoid about Americans seeing each other, all the other Americans in the Camp were locked up in their cells, I was quite likely the only American in the camp who saw them. They were low and fast and beautiful, with Delta wings and a gorgeous sparkling aluminum fuselage profile. The rolling thunder of a healthy turbo-jet engine followed them out of sight. I stopped and watched as the Turnkey and AK bearing assistant screamed at me to return to my room. The show was over by the time I heard their screams.

Migs or not, our mission is to be there to protect the strike force, just in case.

We depart Da Nang and turn east to join up with our tankers. Refueling goes as usual, and we move into Package VI-B from the east coast of North Viet Nam just north of Hai Phong. There is always a polite greeting from the NVN troops by way of large black pop-corn bursts that are sometimes thick enough to walk on like cobblestones.

The F-105s never pick easy targets. Today they have more than one objective--one is at a place called Ha Dong--we know it as "Ha Dong Barracks." If the place is just a barracks, it has to house the most important VIPs in NVN. The occasional bursts we move through to stay close to the raiders are a small deterrent compared to the steady stream of bursts that form a wall in mid-air between the strike force and the target. The "Thuds" don't have to worry about Migs where they're going--the Migs will hang around outside this sea of flak. Sometimes they feint into the attack force and may fire an atoll of two in an attempt to coerce the Thuds to jettison their bomb loads before reaching the target. The Migs then skedaddle as soon as they can, unless there's some easy pickins. None of the Thuds fall for this trick today--they all get to the target and unload.

Jay keeps us near enough to the fight to be useful if any Migs show up. It doesn't happen, and we wind up on the west side of main target low on fuel as the strike force exits.

A lot of stuff is going on in all this melee. The 366th TFW Deputy for Operations (D.O.), Colonel "Boots" Blesse is leading a flight of four doing the same thing we are doing--looking for Migs. Like us, all he's finding is a lot of flak. Colonel Blesse's number two man is the D.O. from the 12th TFW at Cam Rahn Bay, Colonel Norman "Snap" Gaddis. Colonel Gaddis joined the mission today as a participant in an exchange program to allow senior members of the fighter organizations to mix it up and work better as a team.

Colonel Gaddis took a hit from the AAA barrage that slowed him down. As he exited the immediate area of the target zone, a Mig 17 snuck in and hit his airplane with cannon fire. The rest of the F-4s were busy with Migs and Colonel Gaddis and his PSO bailed out.

Colonel Gaddis was the first O-6 to wind up in the Hilton. His PSO, 1/Lt James Milton Jefferson did not survive.

The fight is over for us. The strike force is wending its way to safety by jinking through flak patterns. Colonel Gaddis is the only F-4 loss today. He and Lt Jefferson had the misfortune of colliding with one of those black cobble stones that pop up like magic. The NVN used what air power they had very wisely. Until late in the game, years after Colonel Gaddis and Lt Jefferson were blown out of the sky by cannon fire from a Mig-17, Migs almost never allowed themselves into a real dogfight. All they had to do to dodge a fight was to head for the deck and head home. Most of the time that was a safe exit, but not always. Just eleven days ago not far from the area we are in today, Bob Dilger and Mack Theis from our sister squadron, spotted a Mig-17 as it tried to run for home. Dilger and Theis gave chase, and in the resulting dogfight the Mig ran into old mother earth. Dilger never had a chance to fire a shot.

Bob Dilger is a primo fighter jock. We flew our 100th over North Viet Nam together On 21 June, 1967. I describe these proceedings elsewhere.

As everybody is leaving we learn that an F-105 is in trouble and is probably on the ground out to the west somewhere. As we head that way our drop tanks run dry. We can't afford to carry a few pounds of empty tin along with the drag when we may need all the longevity we can find. Sayonara to empty tanks. Jay reiterates that their Radar Warning (RAW) gear is not working. Corky immediately takes the job of keeping track of any SAM sites that might be after us. I concentrate on staying with Jay and looking out for any sneaky Migs lest they all haven't headed home.

We overfly the area where we think the Thud driver ought to be and get a brief cut on a radio emergency squawk signal from a downed airman. We're west southwest of Ha Noi far enough that a rescue force could make it. We contact the Airborne Command and Control Center (ABCCC) and learn that a Search and Rescue (SAR) operation has been ordered up and that we should head for the nearest tanker over northern Laos to stay full and lead the parade while the ABCCC scrapes up some more F-4s to fly top cover.

Here's the situation. One of us is on the ground out here in the hilly jungle. The SAR will begin soon, or probably has already started, which means that a Flight of A-1s will head our way from a base in northern Thailand. At the same time, a flight of Jolly Greens, the best Helicopter ever built so far, will be right behind. Our job right now is to head for the tanker, refuel ASAP, and get back to where we heard the squawk to keep any Migs that show up away from the A-1s, who will fly low and slow and try to gun down any locals who might show up and shoot at the Rescue Helicopters.

The Thud driver on the ground has to have seen us heading west and is now hoping that we will come back with the rescue squad.

The tanker is waiting for us over northern Laos, just a few minutes away. The Tanker dudes are just as aware of what we're up to as we are and cheat a bit on the north end of their track. We fill up and head back from whence we just came. Jay leads us back at a modest cruise to minimize fuel consumption and we are soon over the same shallow hills and valley where we hope to find a live Thud driver.

We're talking to ABCCC. Two Sandys (A-1s) are headed our way. There is a jolly green behind them. The Sandy's are about 20 minutes away, and the ABCCC has ordered up more F-4s to cover the rest of the day. The weather is not getting any better. Jay has added some power so we have a little excess airspeed. We maneuver around the hills and we're getting lower as the clouds force us down. Corky has told me that we are very close to a SAM site--Lead 54. So far we haven't heard a peep out of Lead 54, but that could change in a hurry.

Suddenly I hear a funny noise in my headset. It ain't a downed airman's radio--its Lead 54 making initial contact with us. The vector beam on the 2 inch RAW oscilloscope shoots out toward the edge of the scope showing us the direction to Lead 54--right where Cork said it was. If we're high enough for him to paint us, we're high enough for him to launch a SAM.

I call Jay: "Jay, take it down, Lead 54 is up."

With that, Jay racks into a tight right turn, and I cross over and take his left wing as he heads for the deck. We don't have much room to dive so are instantly at tree top level headed down hill in a shallow valley opening in exactly the right direction--southwest. Lead 54 goes off our RAW screen. We're supersonic. This is the first time I've gone supersonic on the deck. I tell Jay that we're clear of Lead 54. He takes off some throttle, and we slow down.

The weather is getting worse. Back toward Lead 54, it's looking pretty socked in. We circle toward the north, and Cork keeps one eye on the RAW scope. The Sandys close in and probe the area for ways to get to our buddy on the ground. It's hopeless. We've run out of ceiling in the hills. After a conversation with the Sandys, ABCCC scrubs the mission and begins a plan for weather watch and a rescue tomorrow. The setting sun and the rain are more than we can cope with.

We are not happy to leave one of ours on the ground in North Viet Nam.

The downed airman we were looking for was Capt. Earl Wilfred Grinzebach. His remains were identified after we left Viet Nam. His name is on "The Wall" at 19E 95.

Colonel Gaddis' PSO was 1/Lt James Milton Jefferson. His remains were also identified after the war. His name is on "The Wall" at 19E 96.

"The Wall" is the Vietnam Memorial Wall, *in case you want to find it on line. Also note that the names on the wall are in the order of their loss, with the exception of those we didn't know about until the initial engraving was complete. Thus, the proximity of the coordinates of these two heroes who died on the same day.*

Col. Gaddis spent the rest of the war in the Ha Noi Hilton, one of the four O-6 officers there--all USAF Colonels. You will meet him later in Camp Unity late in the game. He was one of the three who became General Officers after our release.)

Tooling around at low altitude has taken its toll on the 2,000 gallons of internal we took on nearly an hour ago. We depart the area and head for a tanker rendezvous over Northern Laos.

Corky Prahler completed his tour and went home soon after this mission. He is very proficient with the airplane, and on three occasions we swapped seats--a violation of rules--and he did a great job in the front seat. We share the flying load whenever we can. He makes every other landing, every other instrument approach, nearly all the aerial refuelings, and flies formation when he's not busy with his unique tasks such as running the radar, radios, and Inertial Navigator. He is personally responsible for getting us out of several dangerous situations by his professional approach to flying combat.

(In my original manuscript I included the following remark about losing Corky as my steady fellow crewman: "The saddest part is that I may never

see this heroic fellow warrior again." *The fact is that we may never* **see** *each other again, but we are now in contact with each other. I feel good that Corky is living well and is enjoying a successful career.)*

The Last Few Weeks

On June 4, I lead a typical night high/low armed reconnaissance mission looking for trucks. Joe Fitzgerald is the AC in number 2 airplane. I am loaded with CBU, and Joe is carrying six 500 pound bombs. We take off from Da Nang, join up and head for Pack I. As we approach the south end of the section of roadway, we turn off our running lights, Joe stays at 9,000, and I drop down to 300 feet to start the mission. I begin flying an S pattern crossing the road in continuous turns, while Joe does the same thing above me. I give him a brief position report every few minutes so he knows where I am. We have a quarter moon, and can see the ground well enough to spot trucks that are not carefully camouflaged. We complete our run and spot no movers.

Plan B is to do a recon by fire on a fixed target near Quang Khe. I let Joe know where we are and make a level run across the area sifting out CBU's. I pass the target, continue straight and level for a few seconds, and the skyline lights up like daylight in my rearview mirrors. We have hit pay-dirt. Joe holds high while I turn and crisscross the area dropping CBU's from different attack headings. When I finish with CBU's, I move out of the way and watch the target as Joe places his bombs. Several V gun positions fire aimlessly, putting on an aerial fireworks display in our honor. When Joe expends his bombs, I turn on my running lights and he joins up, and we head home. We can see the conflagration from forty miles away as we return to Da Nang.

On June 22, Nolan Voight and I lead a two ship element with Wendy Schuler and Doug Rotman in the number two airplane against a "Special" intelligence target just west of Dong Hoi. Bob Dilger has spent several days reviewing photo intelligence and watching an area that has all the markings of being large collection point for materiel headed into South Viet Nam. This is also Bob Dilger's 100th mission as he leads another two-ship element on the first strike just ahead of us. We are all carrying snake-eyes and rockets and will attack at low altitude for maximum accuracy.

As Dilger's flight complete their work, we come in at the highest speed I have ever attacked a ground target--just sub-sonic. Speed and jinking are our defense, as we make multiple runs to take out as much of the complex as possible. We leave behind a lot of smoke, fire, and secondary explosions.

When we land, a welcoming committee meets our airplanes and Bob and I each get a bottle of champagne for our immediate and personal use. We are then doused thoroughly by the fire control crews and taken for a tour of the flight line with a fire truck escort. We debrief and head for the DOOM club for further celebration.

The next night, June 23, Wes Featherston and I lead another high/low raid into the same part of the country where we hit pay dirt on June 14. Joe Fitzgerald and Lt. Mills are the high flight. Tonight was a good mission, but not as spectacular as Jun 14.

To illustrate the diversity in results on our armed reconnaissance missions, on Jun 24 I ride in the back seat as an Instructor Pilot with Lt Colonel Flagg, a "new guy," on a check ride on an in-country mission with Joe Fitzgerald and Jim White crewing the number two airplane. We cruise around the I Corps country and find no action, so we divert into Tally-Ho in an attempt to find one truck that has been spotted by our radar surveillance airplane flying just off the coast. We search for the truck with no luck and then drop our bombs on a fixed target. Here is a part of my diary entry for this mission: "We couldn't pick up any targets in I Corps so we went to Hillstone and got a divert into Tally-Ho to try for one truck--no luck..., so we just scattered bombs all over the place." (*Hillstone* is the call sign of the Command Center for Package I missions.)

The next day, June 25, I fly with LtCol Flagg again as wingman with Scotty MacKeller and Jim White leading. We work with a FAC in I Corps and then practice Air Combat Maneuvering (ACM). Scotty MacKeller is the 480th Operations Officer and is a "good stick." We begin the ACM session by flying a "fighting wing" session. Col. Flagg is a real Tiger and plays the game like a pro. All this stuff is great fun when you're flying the airplane yourself, but can get a bit torturous riding in the back. In spite of that, it was a fun mission for me. My diary entry for today reads in part: "This guy (i.e., Lt Col John B. Flagg) is a real Tiger--His ordnance delivery was outstanding. Real pleasure to fly with a Tiger."

On July 3, Mel and I fly number three in a flight of four on a Package VI strike against a railroad yard not far from Kep. This is number 104 over North Viet Nam for me. Not long ago, Lt Colonel Bob Tanguy, the 480th Squadron Commander and I have a conversation regarding the fact that I have flown 100 over North Viet Nam and have no obligation to go North, much less to Package VI. Colonel Tanguy reminds me that every time I go north, the odds are better that I won't make it back. I pooh-pooh his argument by telling him that the odds are the same every time you go there, no matter how many times you've already been. Col Tanguy lets it go with something like: "You are an idiot."

If I wrote enough to do justice to all the wonderful men that I served with, this book would be a tome, assuming I lived long enough to come close to finishing it. Col. Tanguy is one of those men. Our staff meetings were always useful, and always conducted in a gentile, professional, and sometimes humorous atmosphere. Several months before this conversation, he brought up the issue of proper wearing of our hats per regulation. Here is a paraphrase of his opening remarks:

"Regarding the wearing of hats, there are four kinds of people in the 480th. One kind wear their hats all the time, both indoors and outdoors. Some others never wear hats, indoors or out. Some wear their hats indoors, but never outdoors. Then there is a very small group that wear their hats properly--that is, they wear their hats outdoors and remove their hats when they come indoors. Wouldn't it be nice if we could all be like that?" By the time he finishes his remarks, the squadron is in an uproar. All present are participating in identifying the four groups the "old man" has just described. The Old Man listens politely as the audience gradually calms down, and the meeting resumes. The careful observer would note that from then on, nearly everybody had joined group four.

On July 4, I lead a flight of four on an Armed Reconnaissance flight into Package VI loaded with six M-117 bombs on each airplane, plus two sidewinders and four Sparrows. We have a back-up JCS target in case we can't locate movers, such as a truck convoy or a train. In good weather, finding a moving target is a long shot--the V will know we're coming and will be holed up in camouflaged areas.

The weather is good today, no cloud cover and excellent visibility. The only problem is high winds--surface winds over Package VI are predicted to be 30 to 40 knots. We won't have any problem finding movers, if there are any, but the big offset and some uncertainty in the exact wind velocity will degrade our accuracy. We decide to offset our aiming point using the higher wind value and hope for the best. We can come up with fairly accurate flight level wind by comparing our CAS with ground speed and will use this comparison to validate the predicted winds.

We refuel over the South China Sea, head inland and enter Package VI from the South East at 12,000 feet. We move about in fluid four formation, searching for movers. We don't search very long. As we come into Pack VI, we spot a long train moving slowly toward the North West. No need to waste any more time, I set up and we make our individual runs parallel to the track, off-setting our aim points for the 40 knot direct cross-wind. If this were a bridge, we would take a 30 degree cut, but with this train, if we miss, we miss completely, but if the wind is close, by dropping parallel, all of our bombs will hit the train, We come off to our right and break hard for the coast. Coming off a target, I always try to plan my first turn to get a visual as our bombs strike the ground. My view today is disappointing. The brief look I get over my right shoulder through the top part of the canopy is a snapshot of the entire train with the smoke and debris from our exploding bombs leaning very steeply away. I am convinced that the wind was much stronger than predicted by the drift angle of the smoke and the fact that I can see the entire length of the train. We exit the area and head home.

When we recover, I report what I saw and leave the de-briefing disappointed.

The next day, July 5, I learned that a Recce bird was in Pack VI after our raid and took photos showing that we were right on target and the train was heavily damaged. The smoke and debris was, in fact, leaning steeply westward carried by the high surface winds leaving the damaged train exposed to view.

Before proceeding any further, I would like to note that I served under three remarkable Squadron Commanders while with the 480th.

LtCol. George Sylvester was the first. LtColonel Sylvester was on such a fast track that he was promoted to Colonel early, and this was the only time I've ever heard of an 0-6 commanding a fighter squadron. Colonel Sylvester was fun to fly with, a pleasure to be around, a good leader, a good commander, and a good wingman. He retired as a Lieutenant General.

As soon as it could be arranged, Col Sylvester was transferred to an 0-6 position as Base Commander, and LtCol Bob Tanguy became the 480th Commander. You have already heard my "evaluation" of Bob Tanguy. He went on to become a Major General.

When Colonel Tanguy completed his tour, Lt Colonel John Armstrong took his place. Colonel Armstrong, like Colonels Sylvester and Tanguy, was a West Point grad. He was the 480th Commander when I was shot down, and on 9 November 1967 he died on a raid in Laos. His name is on "The Wall" at 29E 55. His name says it all: "Jack" Armstrong, the All-American boy- One of the best of the best.

OUTLAW LEAD'S DEMISE
July 5, 1967 21:00.

It's been seven months since I tried to persuade Bud Flesher to abandon his opportunity for a Package Six mission. In the meantime I have been to Package six a number of times and will go again tomorrow, God willing. Every time I go there I think of Bud and the number of others who went there before me and are still there, and wonder if they hear the thunder of our engines and the inevitable explosions of our bombs and the sounds of the defense ordinance when we are overhead.

I think particularly of Bud because he is my best buddy and is most contemporaneous to me. We began our flying careers early on and bonded, not only by flying together, but by partying and socializing. Our wives are both named Sue, and we were a foursome for a long time. We both love airplanes, sports, fast cars, airplanes, good food and drink, and our country--not necessarily in that order. In fact, if you asked either of us in an interview about the order of things, we would both very likely quote Commodore Stephen Decatur's toast from 1816: "...I give you my country. In Her intercourse with foreign nations, may She always be in the right, but my country, right or wrong." I'm convinced that Bud thought that he was a combination of Stephen Decatur and John Wayne and had come to Viet Nam to win the war --singlehandedly, if it came to that.

It's been a long day. I did not fly today, but the routine duties required of all of us to keep a fighter squadron running smoothly have consumed me. I am in my trailer and am tired. My usual habit is to write Sue a note at the end of each day. I take a shower and am planning to skip today, but quickly change my mind and sit down to pen a note. I write a short paragraph with the usual mushy stuff and close out. I am about to put this very short missive into the envelope which I have just addressed when, almost in a dream I pen: *"P.S. There's (sic) two things I want you to remember: (1) If something should happen to me, you must live for Kent, and (2) if I should become missing, remember that this thing will be over, and I'll be home soon. I love you, Sue, and I know we'll have many (100 or so) years together. All my love kh"*

Why did I break with my fundamental attitude and include any allusion to the possibility of danger in this business? As I begin to slip into the oblivion of a good night's rest, I have a strong premonition that tomorrow's mission will be my last combat sortie. I am not bothered by this feeling of virtual certainty of impending doom, but rather a surprising peace washes over me as if something very important has just been settled—just hope it will be quick.

July 6, 1967

Today I wake up as Outlaw Lead. My assignment today is to lead a flight of four to strike a railroad yard in Package VI.

In spite of last night's premonition, I do not suspect what awaits me before I sleep again. Little do I know that before I sleep again, I will be contemplating the "sleep of death" from whose grasp "dreams may come" chilling one's mortal soul to the point of horror. Nor do I know that contemplating the relief of martyrdom could seem like a respite, or that the prospect of the flaying knife might seem, in retrospect, despite the horror, a relief for the tortured soul of the would-be warrior. These thoughts are placed on hold for more than forty years—only to be re-vived by a piercing view of Tiepolo's *Martyrdom of Saint Bartholomew*—the demise of the one who questioned Jesus' origin with "Did anything worthwhile ever come out of Galilee?"

Galilee is far from my view of things. Galilee might as well be on the fringe of the currently measured edge of the universe. My need for spiritual strength and any notion of secular or spiritual character will be on hold for several decades. I have no notion that I am travel-ing suspended in the gondola of a balloon inflated with whatever the substance of ego consists. The happenings in and around Galilee two thousand years ago would wait for nearly four decades to penetrate my spiritual environs. I am a soul wandering about on the imagin-ings of childhood dreams of glory—misplaced, immature, and virtu-ally worthless.

Our intelligence efforts have learned of a railroad yard north and west of Ha Noi. Our job: destroy it--a prospect that I relish.

First Lieutenant Mel Pollack will soon join me for breakfast and will ride in the back seat with me today. But for age and experience, he would be riding in the front seat, and I would be in the back. We have been a "regular" crew for a few weeks and work well together.

Mel and I will not breakfast alone. The six other crewmembers—Outlaws 2, 3, and 4--will join us. We meet at 04:30 at the Da Nang Mess Hall. Service is standard military chow line. I grab a tray—metal with indented compartments to separate the various portions so that they don't mix-- and ask for an order of SOS—"Something" On a Shingle. The "Something" is creamed beef—the Shingle is toast. It's about the best breakfast available in the mess hall at Da Nang Air Base. I have some orange juice and milk to wash it down—along with an order of scrambled eggs.

After we finish and turn in our mess trays, we walk about a quarter of a mile to the 480th Tactical fighter Squadron (TFS) headquarters, retrieve our kneeboards, and proceed to the 366th Tactical Fighter Wing Command Post briefing room. For any feather merchants who might be listening in, the Command Post briefing room is the nerve center of a Fighter wing. The maps, intelligence data, aircraft status, and anything else you need to know to make a fighter wing function are here.

Last night I came here to preview our mission and to review current intelligence information about guys we have lost. We knew, as of last night, that about thirty of those who had been shot down over North Viet Nam were Prisoners of War (POWs). There were some disturbing reports that these guys are not being treated in accord with the 1949 Geneva Accords regarding treatment of Prisoners of War, but are being brutally tortured. Just something to think about as we prepare for today's soiree.

Other important information is either on display or available for review in the Command Post. In the main briefing room there are sufficient seats for any size strike we may mount. A map of the theatre of operations covers the back wall. The map includes all of Viet Nam, Cambodia, and Laos, and that part of China contiguous to Viet Nam and depicts targeting divisions of North Viet Nam, officially known as "Route Packages."-- the seven "Route Packages," commonly referred to as "Packages" or "Packs" you have heard about before--packages are I, II, III, IV, V, VI-A and VI-B. (Figure 1)

There is a circle on the map whose center is the geographical centroid of Ha Noi. The circle is ten miles in radius, and is a "no-fly" zone. The only time we are allowed into the no-fly zone is when specifically ordered. Ha Noi is the "hottest" part of Package VI-A. We won't be far from there today.

It's 05:30. The briefing officer enters the room, along with some senior staff and some snivelers who hope that some of us may be grounded for some reason (usually a cold too severe to take aloft). If that is the case, there might be an opportunity to substitute in for a Package VI strike. It's a game we sometimes play, and I have picked up a couple of good missions playing the sniveler.

The briefing officer is experienced in the theatre. He goes over every detail of the mission: radio frequencies; start times; tanker tracks; entry and exit routes for the target; rules of engagement, including no fly zones, such as the ten mile radius of Ha Noi, and remaining clear of the China border; review of Selected Areas For Evasion (SAFE), in case we suffer battle damage we will know how to reach the nearest SAFE areas at various positions during the mission; expected enemy reaction; minimum fuel levels for various situations, etc.

The briefing is over. We don't have to rush, but we must keep moving along to make all the coming events happen on time. As a flight, the eight of us return to the 480th conference room to meet together and complete the detailed planning. We go over every aspect of the mission as we intend for it to play out from the time we leave this room—from take-off, join up, and flight to rendezvous with tankers over northern Thailand, ingress route to the target, delivering ordnance, egress from the target, refueling on the way home, to landing back at Da Nang.

Next move—we go by the 480th ready desk and divest ourselves of personal belongings that we don't want to fall into enemy hands.... Just in case. We put pretty much everything we have in our pockets into lock boxes. If we return we will empty those boxes back into our pockets. If we don't return, the Wing Commander will appoint a Summary Courts Officer to take care of our estate, as I did for Bud Flesher last December, and our next of kin will take possession of whatever we have left behind.

We also pick up a Geneva Convention card and a "Blood Chit." The Geneva Convention Card is a laminated document, much like a driver's license, prepared as directed by the terms of the 1949 Geneva Accords. It states that the bearer is a member of the United States military, who is subject to treatment in accordance with the 1949 Geneva Accords—i.e., that as military personnel we are Prisoners of War and must be humanely treated. Part of the humane treatment that we are supposedly guaranteed is that we cannot be mistreated in any way to extort any information other than name, rank, serial number, and date of birth. We place this card and some ready cash in a plastic packet and zip it into a flight suit pocket. The cash will come in handy in case we have to divert to a base other than Da Nang—the Geneva card and the cash, we all recognize, will be worthless anywhere else we wind up, other than back home.

The Blood Chit is a square of plastic cloth-like water proof material, much like the plastic material in some plastic rain gear, only thinner and foldable into a small packet about 4 or 5 inches square. A map of south East Asia is printed on one side. The other side has a message in several languages, informing the reader that the bearer is an American and the reader should be nice to us. Unfolded, the blood chit is about two feet square and could be used to protect one from rain, etc. in a survival situation.

It's time to suit up. The eight of us move to our personal equipment room, about 50 feet from the front desk. Our helmets, flight suits, G-suits, personal firearms, and any other items of personal equipment are stored in this room. Personal equipment specialists are experts at assisting air crews to assure the proper fit and good repair of any of our gear, e.g., helmets, G-suits, etc. We zip into our G-suits and put on our parachute harness much like putting on a standard back-pack parachute. The harness is an integral part of a vest that includes a Life Preserver Unit (LPU), sometimes still referred to as a *"Mae West"* flotation vest, several compartments which hold our emergency radio, flares, a .38 Smith and Wesson revolver, ammunition, and emergency food rations.

We're now dressed to fly. G-suits are zipped; the harness is re-checked for proper fit. We stow our helmets in a protective bag, and head for the door. Last stop—the refrigerator where each of us pick up at least two 8-ounce baby bottles filled with frozen water. We stow these frozen water bottles in the lower pockets of our G-suits—just above our ankles.

There is no discernible excitement in this group of eight fighter pilots—just a quiet aura of competence. Words cannot express my pride in this group of aviators and support personnel. We are a team. Not the "A" team, but the "Super" team. I make eye contact with the personnel specialists who have just made sure that we are all suited up and ready to go. Each of them wishes us well as we file out to head for our airplanes.

I have lived this ritual a few times before. This is to be my 106th combat sortie over North Viet Nam—number 564 total. During these moments I savor the prospect of another successful mission.

Time slows, and I look at Mel Pollack. He's a man of stature—not bulky like a professional football player, but a husky six-foot plus. He is Jewish. He is an American. He is a fighter jock. He is my right hand today. I am so proud of him. Proud to know him. Proud that he is my friend, and prouder yet that we are a team. In our private talks, we have shared our outrageous ideas about leading a flight (illegally, of course) into the "no-fly zone--that area defined by politicians who have no idea how to conduct this war." A fleeting moment, and those thoughts are stored away for a later time when, hopefully, Mel and I will be in another place, and the memory of today and other days we have shared will lift us to our toes, and this pride will swell within us again just as it did for Henry V and his courageous entourage long after their miraculous victory at Agincourt on Saint Crispin's Day in October 1415. I love you, Mel.

We jump into the van that serves us as a flight line taxi. It deposits us where we need to be—just in front of our airplane. We climb the ladder up the side of the airplane and place our personal equipment inside the cockpits. Our pre-flight has begun, and it will end when we are satisfied that this airplane is airworthy.

Included in the preflight is the combat load of external stores--items that are attached to pylons, which are a part of the aircraft. External stores today include two external fuel tanks--380 gallons of Jet fuel (JP-4) in each, one set of electronic equipment which is designed to jam enemy gun laying radars, six 750 pound Mark-117 bombs, four Sparrow missiles, and two heat seeking missiles (Sidewinders). If the mission goes as planned, when we return home, we will bring back all of these external stores, with the exception of the Mark-117 bombs whose purpose is to destroy an enemy railroad yard.

As we pre-flight, we exchange small talk with flight line personnel, including the crew chief for this airplane. And then, it's time to climb up the ladder, seat ourselves in the cockpit, and strap that wonderful piece of machinery to our posteriors. The airplane becomes a part of us.

The crew chief, wearing a communication headset, plugs a long communication cable into a receptacle in the nose wheel well of our airplane. He stands in front of our airplane in clear view of Mel and me and positions himself to have a clear view of his airplane. Sometimes he slinks about much like Mack the Knife patrolling an alley somewhere in London looking for Louie Miller. By this time we are strapped in, and our helmets are snugly in place with chin straps fastened and oxygen masks mimicking an extra layer of skin about our face. I can hear Mel breathing into his oxygen mask, as he can hear me. I hear a click, and the crew chief's voice comes through my earphones. We exchange greetings to assure that we can hear each other.

I ask the crew chief to initiate the start by turning on compressed air from the starting cart. This high-pressure air flows through a hose connected to the left engine starter turbine that is in turn geared to the rotor spool of the engine, and the engine begins to rotate. When the engine rotation speed reaches 10%, I move the left throttle forward to start fuel flowing to the engine and simultaneously depress the ignition switch imbedded in the throttle grip. I feel the flame coursing through the burners as the left engine comes to life. When the engine turbine speed reaches 45% (100 % being maximum allowable), I ask the crew chief to stop the air flow. The left engine turbine continues to accelerate and stabilizes at normal idle--65% RPM. Soon, both engines are running at idle and the crew chief disconnects the starting cart. We run through our pre-taxi checklist. Mel is setting up the various systems he controls from the back seat, and soon we are ready to taxi out to the runway.

When taxi time comes, Mel and I assure that our radio is set on the Da Nang ground control frequency. Until now, the other three crews have been doing exactly what we have been doing, and, if all is going to plan, they are expecting to hear my voice on their radios when I call:

"Outlaw Flight, Check in." I hear a crisp response in order:
"Two,"
"Three,"
"Four."
"Da Nang ground, Outlaw Flight to taxi with 4 F-4's."
"Outlaw, cleared to taxi to Runway 35 Right."
"Roger, Outlaw taxiing to 35 Right."

We roll out to the taxiway toward 35 Right, and the other three members of the flight join in behind us in order. We taxi to the end of Runway 35 Right and park in echelon in the arming area near the end of the runway. As we park, each crewmember extends his hands outside the cockpit so that the leader of the arming team can see them. The arming crew is about to crawl underneath each of our airplanes and arm each piece of ordnance so that it is ready to be expended. Up until now, safety wires have been in place to prevent any accidental mishaps. The armorers are assuring that all of our combat stores are ready for use. This is the final step in our preflight activities.

As soon as the armorers are finished with us, we are free to move our hands and switch radio frequencies to Da Nang Tower. My call:"Da Nang, Outlaw, flight of four F-4's holding for 35 right." A few seconds later Da Nang tower responds: "Outlaw flight cleared into position on 35 Right." Response: "Roger, Da Nang, Outlaw taking 35 Right."

We taxi onto the runway. I take the right side of the centerline. Outlaw 2 takes the left side. Outlaws 2 and I are positioned so that Outlaw 3 has space to line up behind and to the left of Outlaw 2, and Outlaw 4 can line up behind and between myself and Outlaw 2. (Figure 2-A)

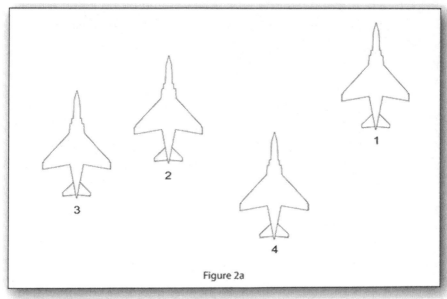

Figure 2a

Figure 2 A

As soon as we are all parked in position on the runway, we perform our pre take off run up checks. We throttle burst each engine individually to 100% power and let the engine stabilize for a moment, then rapidly retard the throttle to the idle position, checking engine instruments for proper indications and performance. When all four of us are ready, I notify Da Nang tower: "Da Nang, Outlaw ready to roll." Immediate response: "Outlaw, cleared for take-off."

When we are loaded, as we are today, we take off singly and roll at ten second intervals. During our flight briefing, one of the major items we covered was aircraft loading and gross weight as it affects performance. At the top of the list was how we determine if the airplane is performing as it should. In automobile parlance, a car might be designed to accelerate from zero to 60 miles per hour (mph) in, say 4.3 seconds and to reach 100 mph in 10 seconds on a standard day, on a level track with no turns, given that the operator is a typical, well trained, experienced driver. Today we have calculated a parallel set of performance figures for the F-4. Each crew has these figures at hand in the cockpit. As each of us begins the take-off roll, we note the time and very carefully take note of the expected performance parameters as they occur.

Today we expect to be at various airspeeds and distances down the runway as we accelerate toward lift-off. We are all at the maximum gross weight permitted for the F-4--56,000 pounds. At this weight, our air speed at lift-off will be 179 knots—206 miles per hour. If we have a head wind, our ground speed (the speed that the airplane is rolling down the runway) will be slower by the amount of head wind present. For example, if we have a 20 knot head wind, our lift-off airspeed will be 179 knots, but our rolling speed down the runway (our ground speed) will be 159 knots. I sometimes like to think of our velocity as miles per hour rather than knots because that's the way we think when we drive or calculate trip times, etc. when we are not flying, and also because most of us think in terms of miles per hour in our everyday lives.

Having been cleared for take-off, I hold the brakes to keep the airplane motionless, and move the two throttles forward until each engine stabilizes at 85 % of maximum RPM. At that point, I simultaneously release the brakes, shift the throttles outboard, and place both throttles against their forward stops calling for 100% engine RPM with full afterburner. The airplane, even though fully loaded, leaves the starting position and begins to accelerate rapidly. In full afterburner, each engine is producing 17,000 pounds of thrust, and we now have 34,000 pounds of thrust pushing this 56,000 pound airplane forward.

Until our airspeed reaches 60 knots, I steer the airplane using nose wheel steering that allows me to steer using the rudder pedals to position the nose wheel--like steering a car with your feet. The airplane passes 60 knots quickly, and I release the nose wheel steering button and now rely on aerodynamic forces produced by the rudders to maintain our heading down the runway.

When the air speed indicator moves past 70 knots, I firmly pull the stick full back against the aft stop and hold it there. At about 170 knots, the nose of the airplane begins to rise, and as the airspeed needle crosses the 179 knot marker, the airplane leaves the ground. I release some back pressure on the stick, raise the landing gear and flaps, and the airplane accelerates rapidly as we begin to climb. The airspeed indicator soon reads 325 Knots (360 mph). I move the throttles out of the after-burner range to maintain 100% engine RPM without the afterburners for about 21000 pounds of thrust--plenty to keep us in a comfortable cruise/climb.

We reach 1,000 feet altitude and begin a shallow left turn and our wingmen close up with us. Soon, we are on course on a westerly heading toward central Thailand, and Outlaw Flight is assembling in "normal" formation.

I look around as the flight closes in. Today Outlaw 3 Aircraft Commander (AC) is our Squadron Commander, Lieutenant Colonel John Armstrong. If something happens to Mel and me, Colonel Armstrong and his Pilot Systems Operator (PSO), 1/Lt. Roger Lundberg, will assume the lead. The Outlaw 2 Crew is Captain John Tietjens (AC) and 1/Lt Tommy Lane (PSO). Outlaw 4 crew is Captain Paul Bauman (AC) and 1/Lt Tommy Almquist (PSO). This is sometimes referred to as a "Finger 4" formation. Look at the fingers of your right hand and you will see that the middle finger represents the lead airplane, the forefinger is Outlaw 2, the ring finger is Outlaw 3, and the little finger is Outlaw 4. (Figure 3)

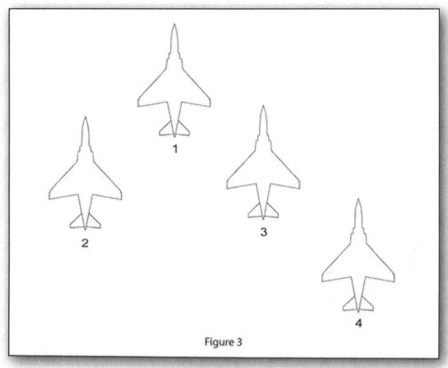

Figure 3

Figure 3

Our westerly heading soon places us over the jungles of Laos, and we are across Laos and entering Thai airspace in a few minutes. Our tanker today is Red 24. There are three tanker tracks over North Thailand—Red, White, and Blue, representing the geographic position of each track. The number represents the altitude of the tracks; thus, Red 24 tanker is on the Red track at 24,000 feet. The tracks are also referred to as "Anchors." We level off at 23,500 feet and head for the south end of Red Anchor.

When we arrive at the south end of the Red Anchor, we turn north and switch to Red 24's assigned radio frequency. "Red 24, Outlaw with four F-4's." Red 24: "Roger Outlaw, Red 24 turning south." We turn north to fly up the Red track. Mel is operating our radar in search mode and, in a few seconds, we have Red 24 on our radar about 60 miles north of us, and we notify Red 24 that we will "call the turn." We slide north on the Red Anchor track at 23,500 feet, and watch Red 24's blip on our radar screen as Red 24 moves toward us on a head-on collision course.

When Red 24 is 21 miles away, I call: "Red 24, start your turn." We continue north and watch Red 24 on our radar as he turns. In less than two minutes, Red 24, a big, beautiful C-135, the tanker version of the Boeing 707, hoves into view at 12 o'clock, slightly high, as he completes his 180 degree turn from south to north. I call: "Outlaw, noses cold." The response: "Two." "Three." "Four." Our radars are now on stand-by for the re-fueling operation--a safety precaution. The energy in our radar beams could ignite any fuel vapors in and around the tanker, not to mention jamming the stuffin' out of all their electronic equipment.

PHOTO 11

A flight of four F-4s approaching the Tanker over Northern Thailand in early 1967. Note the large two-letter identifiers on each vertical stabilizer bearing letters identifying them as 480th Tactical Fighter Squadron. Charlie Zulu (CZ) is the lead airplane. Number 2 in the flight is Charlie Victor CV), the Aircraft nearest us. Number 3 is flying Charlie Sierra (CS), and the far left airplane Number 4 is Charlie Golf (CG). This flight is armed for a MIGCAP (Mig Combat Air Patrol) in Package Six. The tail markers are there so that the flight can more easily spot each other in case of a dog-fight.

We ease up closer to Red 24 and move into the pre-fueling position, just behind and just below the extended fuel boom (Figure 4). As we park in the pre-fueling position, I open the refueling receptacle door located just behind Mel's cockpit on the top center of the fuselage, and look up at the face of the boom operator looking back at me from about twenty feet away.

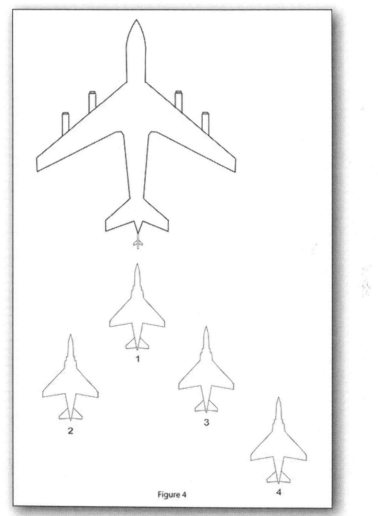

Figure 4

Figure 4

When they see my fuel receptacle door open, Outlaw three and four move up and right to assume a wing position on Red 24. Outlaw two moves left and up to assume a wing position on Red 24's left wing. (Figure 4a)

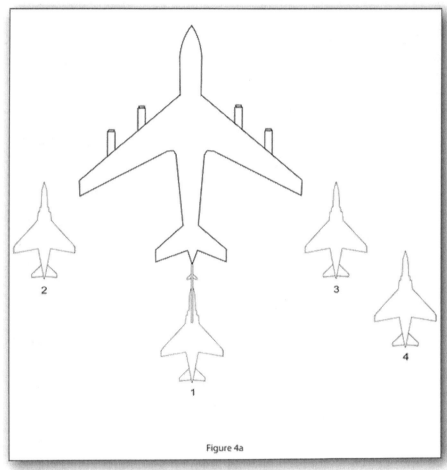

Figure 4a

Figure 4a

I close the space between our airplane and Red 24. The boom operator's face is now about twelve feet away as he maneuvers the refueling boom. I hear the tip of the fuel nozzle tap gently against the top of our fuselage as the operator positions the nozzle to plug into our fuel receptacle. Then there is a click, and the operator starts pumping JP-4 into our fuel tanks. He is dispensing at the rate of nearly 200 gallons per minute. In about six minutes we have taken on over a thousand gallons of JP-4 and are topped up.

The boom operator disconnects from our airplane and maneuvers the boom upward and retracts the nozzle to wait for the next customer.

We move back, down, then left, and up to join Outlaw 2's left wing. As we move down and left, Outlaw 3 eases back, down, and left into the pre-fueling position. In seconds, Outlaw 3 is directly behind the refueling boom, and soon is connected to the tanker and taking fuel. (Figure 4 b).

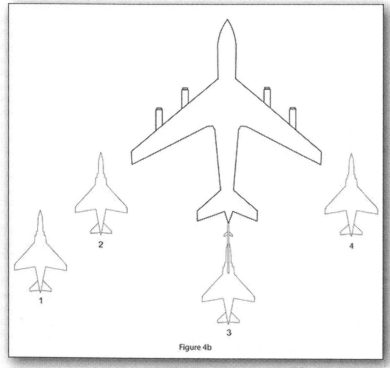

Figure 4b

Figure 4b

About six minutes later, Outlaw 3 is full; drops back slightly, and moves up and right to take a position on the right wing of Outlaw four. As Outlaw 3 moves right, Outlaw 2 drops down and back and moves right into the pre-fueling position, and then moves forward to fuel. (Figure 4 c).

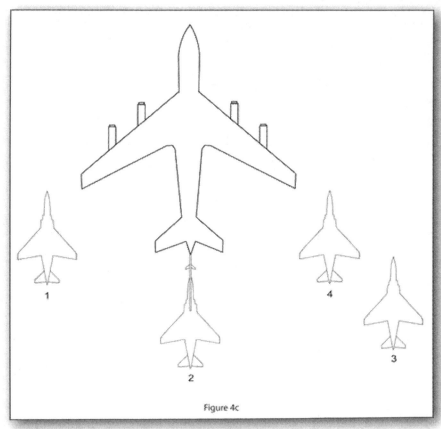

Figure 4c

Figure 4c

In seconds Outlaw two is hooked up with the tanker, and in a little over six minutes, is filled to the brim.

Outlaw two then moves back, down, left, up, and joins Outlaw Lead's left wing as Outlaw four moves back, down, left and takes fuel. (Figure 4 d).

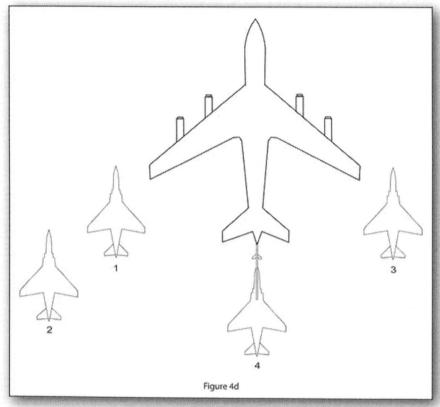

Figure 4d

Figure 4d

When Outlaw 4 is full, he moves right and up to join 3's right wing. The first half of the refueling choreograph is complete. (Figure 4 e)

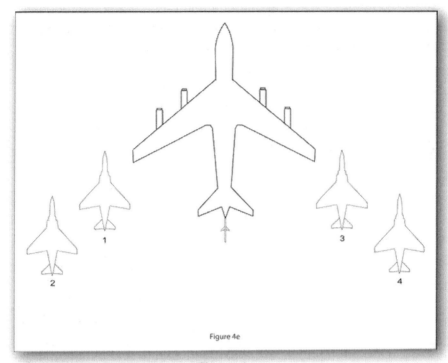

Figure 4e

Figure 4e

The second half of the refueling choreograph order is the same-- 1,3,2 4. (Figures 4 a, b, c, d, e). The order of refueling is the reverse order of rate of fuel consumption each member typically needs to complete the mission. Lead (Number 1) will burn less fuel than the others; 3 will burn second less; and 4 will burn the most. This is so because the leader sets his/her power and makes very few throttle adjustments. #3 is the "element lead," and burns less than his wingman, #4. # 4 gets "slung around" more than the others and burns fuel faster than the rest.

The tankers are more than a purveyor of fuel. Red 24 must plan his movement along the Red 24 track such that we can complete another refueling cycle and be topped up when we drop off at 19 degrees North. Red 24 does a perfect job, just as the tankers always do. As Outlaw 4 drops off after the second refueling cycle, we are at the extreme north end of Red Anchor over Laos at 19 degrees North latitude at exactly the right moment, and Red 24 begins a left turn as we drop down about 500 feet and continue north.

As we leave the tanker, we move into a combat spread formation and set our ground speed at seven nautical miles per minute. Combat spread is a loose formation allowing us to look around and protect each other. Now is the time to sip some water, take a fresh chew of gum, and settle down to concentrate on the mission. We are headed northerly to pass just to the west of Dien Bien Phu in Package V. This is a relatively quiet relaxing time.

PHOTO 12

Over Northern Laos a Flight of four, an earlier Mig-CAP mission, has completed their second refueling cycle and the Tanker has turned to the South as the fighters move into a "Combat Spread" and continue North. The Wing element--Charlie Sierra (CS) and Charlie Golf (CG) have moved out of view to the left of this frame. In the frame shown, Charlie Victor (CV) is in the process of moving away from the leader, Charlie Zulu (CZ), to assume a position about 1500 feet to the right of the Leader. These airplanes are carrying only air-to-air ordnance--Sparrows and Sidewinders. Note the jamming pod hanging under CVs right outer wing in lieu of a Sidewinder missile. Between the jamming POD and nose just aft of the right engine intake, you can see the nose of a Sidewinder protruding forward. I photographed this flight while flying spare. We nearly always took a fifth airplane (a "spare") to accompany the flight of four to until refueling was complete to assure an intact flight of four in case one of the four had to abort.

We pass Dien Bien Phu and turn right toward the target, located north and west of Ha Noi, and increase our ground speed to eight nautical miles per minute. Soon we are above a stratus layer and climb to stay 5,000 feet above it. Surface to Air Missiles (SAMs) are our biggest fear in this situation. If we can see a SAM in time, we can out maneuver it, but a cloud layer between us and a SAM launch site on the ground gives the SAM a big advantage. If we are attacked by SAMs, we won't be able to see them until they emerge from the cloud cover beneath us, as opposed to the possibility of seeing them from the ground up. This means that even if we spot them the very instant that they join us in the clear airspace above the clouds, we have precious little time to outmaneuver them—potentially a very dangerous situation.

We increase our ground speed to nine nautical miles per minute.

Soon we overfly the cloud deck into a virtually cloudless sky and move onto Package VI-A. We look ahead and spot the target area. Mel and I scan the photos of the target spread across our knees, locate the target on the ground, and put the photos away. At about the same time, slightly low and to our right, the sky comes alive with bursts of anti-aircraft fire.

The Flak bursts like magic cobblestones, suddenly appearing from nowhere-- closely spaced, and black. Our jamming equipment hanging on a bomb rack on each of our airplanes has disabled their radar targeting system, and the enemy is using a back-up visual system. It's not as accurate as radar, but is still effective, as they fill the sky with flak. We move down and right as this first burst appears, anticipating the flak crews making a correction--playing a brief game of cat and mouse--the next burst appears where we would have been—but soon we have to abandon the game to start our attack. By now Flak is all over the place. We are near the heartland of North Viet Nam.

I steer the airplane toward a position to begin our attack on the target. We roll in on a 45-degree dive and when our altitude, dive angle, airspeed, and sight picture are properly synchronized, I release our bomb load, which, if I have done my job right, will follow their trajectory to the target. We feel the slight reaction as the bombs separate from the airplane and, at very nearly the same time, there is another jolt that I scarcely notice. I haul back on the stick to pull six or so Gs. Along with the buildup of g force, the nose of the airplane rises toward the horizon. We keep the wings level until the nose cuts the horizon and then we begin jinking maneuvers to try and spoil the enemy gunner's aim.

A retrospective from the future. During the attack on the target from the time we start our roll in until we release our bombs and our nose cuts the horizon as we pull out of the 45 degree dive, I am totally occupied with our relationship to the target. The accuracy of our bomb pattern (Circular Error Probability [CEP]) depends on how accurately we set up our dive angle and how accurately and smoothly we track the target with the gun sight such that when we arrive at the release altitude, dive angle, air speed, altitude, and sight picture are in perfect harmony. I have done this a lot of times and know that during the attack phase, my flying job must be letter perfect. I cannot be concerned with AAA, Migs, or SAMs, or anything else for these few moments.

Mel has to endure this ordeal and watch the action, while I remain unaware of all else but the target, the target, and the target. The bottom line is that Mel had a better perspective of what was happening during the attack phase than I did. I saw no flak during the attack phase, which would be normal, even if we were moving through a wall of bursts, unless the bursts were very close and perhaps ahead of us. I can say this, as we rolled in, the sky was literally alive with flak bursts, and we had no choice but to head for the target. I did not have an opportunity to talk to Mel about this mission until years after the fact. His observations confirm that the intensity of the AAA did not subside until we had finished our run. Mel believes that the jolt that I didn't notice was the fatal blow to our airplane. I can't argue with his assessment.

Years later I learn that two of my wingmen, Outlaw 3 and Outlaw 4, had taken significant battle damage, but recovered successfully. Outlaw 3 suffered a badly damaged flap on one wing, among other things. Outlaw 4 took a hit that passed through the fuselage and luckily did no mortal damage. The fatal blow to our airplane was the damage to our engines--a difficult situation to survive.

I learned later in Prison that Outlaw 3, Lieutenant Colonel John Armstrong, was presumed dead after a very unfortunate accident. On November 9, 1967, Col. Armstrong and 1/Lt Lance Sijan were on a night interdiction mission over Laos when his wingman saw an explosion near their airplane as they were attacking the target. They were carrying bombs with proximity fuses, and there is a likelihood that their loss was a result of a premature detonation.

Col. Armstrong's crew mate survived, but was seriously injured. Lance Sijan's ordeal led to his death in Ha Noi about three months later. Lance Sijan is quite likely the only POW who never answered the fifth question. The V tortured him severely, even though he was virtually helpless from his injuries. After we came home, he was awarded the Medal of Honor (MOH)--the first Air Force Academy recipient. Sijan Hall at the Air Force Academy now bears his name.

There are 58,272 names engraved on a stark, black, marble wall on the Mall between the George Washington Spire and the Lincoln Memorial in Washington, D.C. Armstrong and Sijan are two of them.

Soon after our release from Ha Noi, we learned that the Bomb Damage Assessment (BDA) photos showed that we did our job--we obliterated the putative railroad yard. I was not surprised. I thought we made a good run, and we had never had any problem putting our ordnance on any assigned target.

Please note, that there were four of us in my flight who had the same problem--to dive through a wall of flak in order to put their ordnance on the target. Nearly every day for a long period of time, a lot of fighter jocks from a number of Aircraft Carriers and from our bases in Thailand and Viet Nam, were faced with this problem, and can make the same claim--we did our job in the face of whatever defense the enemy could mount. The Ha Noi Hilton was filled with those who drove every kind of fighter in the DOD inventory and were doing just what Outlaw Flight was doing when their doom finally tracked them down.

As our nose cuts the horizon, I bank to the right and keep some g's on and keep the nose coming up. At about twenty degrees pitch up I crank the airplane back to the left and keep pulling and look back over my left shoulder through the top of the canopy to spot the target and see explosions as the bombs impact the target. Roll back to the right and keep pulling g's to avoid AAA hits as there are plenty of giant black cobblestones visible between us and the target. Don't see any of my wingmen. Where are they?

As we move away from the target, we have more time to pay attention to ourselves and the wonderful machine that brought us here. I'm sure that Mel is doing whatever he needs to be doing to assure our survival—I do the same. As we continue our jinking maneuvers, I now have time to look around the inside of the cockpit. Right in front of me, attached to the bottom and both sides of the glare shield that keeps ambient outside light from over lighting the instrument panel, I see two red "FIRE" lights glaring at me, telling us that both engines are on fire. A part of a fighter pilot's nature is never to believe bad news. The FIRE warning light is no doubt wrong. Soon, however, material evidence begins to pile up in favor of the FIRE light.

I look around outside and still can't find any of my wingmen. My missing them as we come off the target bothers me some. I very much want to lead all of us safely away from the target and home. I have been here before, and pride myself in having led a number of raids into North Viet Nam without leaving anyone behind. As we are increasing our separation from the target, I feel my responsibility to take care, as best I can, of the three other crews who came here with me today. I search the sky around and behind me –no joy.

My radio is strangely silent, until Outlaw two's voice breaks through to let us know that our external fuel tanks had jettisoned along with our bombs. I try to explain to Outlaw 2 that we didn't deliberately drop anything but bombs on the target, but soon realize that I'm not talking to anybody--our communication equipment is failing. I can't talk to Mel and his breathing is intermittent. We're incommunicado. We're outrunning our wingmen because we're flying a "clean" airplane, having lost our external tanks over the target.

I check our telepanel lights just outside my right armrest below the canopy rail. These lights come on as problems occur. At a glance, nearly all are lighted—every system in the airplane is failing. No need for any sophisticated troubleshooting. Our immediate future with this airplane depends on two things—how long the engines will burn and turn, and how long we have hydraulic pressure in at least one of our flight control systems. I don't even consider other possibilities, such as some kind of structural failure resulting from battle damage.

Mel's voice crackles through my helmet earphones sounding like he's talking from the bottom of a barrel: "We're hit." "Mel, I know we're hit." No response, as he hangs forward in his harness--I can only see the top of his helmet and the straps supporting his shoulders. My heart sinks. I now know that some of the stuff that was bursting around us has not only penetrated our engines but has penetrated the fuselage and rear cockpit, and now Mel is hanging helplessly drooping forward in his harness bleeding to death, and there is absolutely nothing I can do for him. He might as well be in the cockpit of another F-4 in another theatre. For the remaining seconds in our ride, Mel sporadically repeats "We're hit," and I respond "I know we're hit," and it's obvious that Mel either doesn't hear me, or that if he does hear he's so physically debilitated from his injuries that he's unable to act.

We're moving right along. Except for the warning lights and Mel's situation, one could be perfectly serene about the situation. That old saw about the man who jumped off the top of the Empire State Building reporting to the world as he passes the 50th floor: "So far, so good!" might well apply to us now. Things can't stay like this very long.

I check the hydraulic pressures. Bad news. One control system pressure is zero and the other is half what it should be and dropping. Life is getting shorter in a hurry. We're at 22,000 feet at Mach .94. Suddenly Thor or, some other god of doom, hits the side of our airplane with a big sledgehammer. I feel the jolt and hear the blow as the control stick rips itself from my grip and slams all the way forward. The stick is now rooted in concrete in the Northeast corner of the cockpit, and we are out of control. I reach for the ejection loop extending upward from underneath the front of the seat between my knees, grab it with both hands, and pull it out by the roots.

I'm on my way to a place I don't want to be. There is nothing on my mind—no ideas of survival—nothing about Mel—no thoughts of home and the most precious things in my life—my wife and my little boy who are far away in Gardena, California. I am only reacting to my environment via pure animal instincts with no thoughts of anything other than myself.

The next few milliseconds are slow motion—a series of stills--not even a blur. The seat rises from its position in the cockpit and stops as my knees are about level with the canopy bow. Even though I'm in a 620 mile per hour slip stream, the air seems calm. I am suspended here for a moment and then continue the ejection trajectory into calm space—the airplane is someplace else—I am someplace else—no view of anything—might as well be in orbit around a strange planet. Then, as if this had always been the way it was, I am sitting comfortably in the seat, with a beautiful view of the world around me. I can see, with a turn of my head and the extension of my peripheral vision, nearly 360 degrees of the horizon. No clouds. Just landscape below and the beautiful countryside from four miles above. My left glove is missing and I have a clear view of my watch on my left wrist. Time: 0905 Da Nang local—0805 Ha Noi time.

The seat is stabilized by a small ribbon drogue parachute attached to a hard point just behind the pilot's head rest via a steel cable. Without this drogue chute, the 620 mph breeze could have placed the seat in a tumble and my limbs might have been thrust into the high velocity wind resulting in serious injury. The designers of this system had tried to think of everything. So far, they have done a good job. I am alive, in one piece, with no injuries, four miles above the earth. As I descend in the seat, I now have two miles to go before we (the seat and I) reach 10,000 feet where the automatic sequence will do some magic things, and I will suddenly find myself hanging in the parachute as the seat falls away.

The downward descent continues, and I must concern myself with where I am and what needs to be done. My thoughts quickly turn to the fact that I'm in free fall somewhere between 22,000 and 10,000 feet about 40 or 50 miles north west of Ha Noi over North Viet Nam, still strapped in the seat of an F-4 fighter which has by now been reduced essentially to atoms, having collided with old mother earth at some supersonic speed off to my right where I can see some of those atoms rising from the scene of the collision in the form of a thick, black smoke. So much for U.S Air Force F-4-C # 797.

As we (the seat and I) continue to drift earthward, I survey the horizon and the countryside below. The automatic system designed to pull the parachute canopy out of its enclosure in the top of my seat so that it can deploy and allow the seat to fall away is set to do its job at 10,000 feet. If, for some reason it fails, it's up to me to go through the manual procedure—separate myself from the seat and pull the ripcord to open the chute manually.

I'm reviewing this procedure, when it occurs all by itself. I hear a .22 rifle shot, the seat falls away, and then I hear the slight pop as the canopy inflates, and I'm hanging in the parachute harness. There is a little cloud of dust under the canopy, much like shaking the sand out of your beach towel or popping the dust out of a dust cloth. Surprise! Surprise! The packing procedure is not as sterile as I had imagined. No matter—it worked—and I am alive because of the conscientious efforts of the riggers who left the dust inside so that it could comfort me in this precarious time.

Straight ahead at twelve O'clock, slightly high, a mile or more away, Mel's parachute blossoms. He has to be o.k.

I now hang in the parachute harness. My mind allows itself to ruminate. My first thoughts run in a burst of just a few seconds. I go back a few months to the beginning of my previous combat tour as a Forward Air Controller (FAC) in South Viet Na--a lot of exciting missions as a FAC--going home from that tour unrequited in terms of my participation in this war--a fighter pilot flitting about in a light airplane, when I should have been thundering through the sky in a supersonic fighter. I volunteered to go back to Viet Nam, under the condition that it would be as a fighter pilot.

The most important person in my life--my life's companion--my wife--asked me to do something else. I came anyway. This very selfish and wrong decision has plagued me ever since I said good-bye to her for this assignment. My mask is disconnected on one side and dangles below my left cheek. My heart wants to stop. I look up at the canopy and shout out: "Sue, forgive me!"

Nearly 10,000 feet separates the ground and me. It's very quiet. I now have little to do, or that I can do. The parachute in a fighter airplane is not a sport chute—it is strictly for use in an emergency. It is designed for simplicity and for reliability, not for sport or maneuverability, and the user cannot steer it. The only maneuver this chute can do is to allow the user to change the direction the user faces. I can "spin" the parachute by grabbing the two risers above my head in a cross-armed fashion and rotate my view. I have absolute total control of the direction I want to face, but nothing else. I take advantage of this limited capability to scan the horizon and to view the earth as it rises to meet me.

I have lost sight of Mel's parachute. He is some distance ahead of me over an area of Karst. When will I see him again?

The descent seems very slow. Soon I'm in an area of turbulence, at what I perceive to be about 7,000 feet. The parachute feels like it's jumping around, and I begin to oscillate below the canopy. The pendulum swings become steeper. The one pound steel cylinder that fired from the seat to deploy the canopy is hanging over the edge of the canopy by its long lanyard and swings inward toward me as the canopy oscillates. During some of these oscillations, the parachute canopy begins to collapse on the downward side, the metal cylinder swings in close to me, and I fear the canopy might totally collapse. An experienced paratrooper would laugh at this prospect, but to me, it's more than a bit uncomfortable.

I recall the intelligence reports I have read over the past few weeks in the Command Post regarding our limited knowledge of my predecessors who survived and became POWs and contemplate my immediate future and consider pulling the .38 Smith & Wesson revolver from under my left shoulder to "terminate my command," but soon discover that I am an abject coward. I had only thought of myself as a coward once before. This part of my psyche has been buried within me since I was a little boy, and didn't surface until an encounter with a man with a knife who intended to use it on me. I was petrified with fear, and only the primal instinct for survival saved me from serious harm. This incident occurred a year or so before. I had not wanted to admit my cowardice before, but had to face it now. The coward wins. I don't pull the gun.

Our (my parachute's and my) descent continues. Mother Earth nears. At about 1,000 feet above the ground, I see ant-sized figures moving about on the ground. They are running and converging on a spot where, it appears, I will collide with the ground.

As I descend toward a clear area in a dry rice paddy, I can hear the ants' voices as they zero in on my position. The landing is very soft compared to what I expected. I drop to one knee in preparation for the "roll" that we were conditioned to expect. Next step—reach up on each side of the harness and release the clips that hold the parachute to the harness. The left clip separates, but the right clip refuses to let the right riser line disconnect from the harness.

A shot rings out not far away; sounds like a shot gun. In microseconds, I decide to ditch the harness along with the survival vest attached to it, and run into a nearby thicket and attempt to evade the ants who by now are closing in on me.

GOOD MORNING, NORTH VIET NAM

The thicket is a little smaller than a football field. It is made up of thick underbrush among small trees—fairly good shelter to hide in, but far too small and insignificant to offer much hope of evasion. I squat down near the center of the thicket and pull out one of the baby bottles from the lower pocket of my G-suit, empty it in one swig, and toss it aside. I grab the second and drink all I can hold and toss it away. By this time the ants surround the little thicket and are making a lot of noise that I don't understand. My minutes of "freedom" are counting down rapidly. My pistol, radios, food, and flares are in the discarded vest, which, by now, is in the hands of the ants surrounding me--about 50 ants and one of me.

When I dashed into this thicket, I hoped that it connected to a near-by karst. Now I see that it connects to nothing, and that the ants have completely surrounded the periphery of this little island of small trees and underbrush. I am trapped. The Code of Conduct states, in part, "...I will never surrender as long as I have the means..." I now have no means. Now is the moment of truth.

I stand up and walk toward the closest point on the periphery of the thicket. For a few steps none of the ants notice me. Then, as I near them, there is a lot of excitement. I emerge in the dry rice paddy to an excited group of Viet Namese peasants. This group of five or six soon expands to more than a dozen and others are approaching. This is a village, and every adult male villager must be here, and all are armed with something. Some are carrying hand implements like hoes and rakes and machetes. Others are carrying sticks. One old man is carrying an antique shotgun--looks like a 16 or 20 gauge. The shot I heard as I hit the deck must have come from his gun.

The leaders approach me nervously. They appear to be much more afraid of me than I am of them. They want me out of my clothes. It immediately becomes apparent that none of them have ever seen a zipper. They want to cut my G-suit waistband with a machete. I push their hands away and unzip the leg zippers and then the waist zipper and the G-suit falls loose. The leaders toss it to by-standers and then try to unzip my flight suit. They don't seem to realize that you can't unzip someone else's zipper. I gently move their hands aside, and unzip the front of my flight suit and stoop and unzip the enclosures at the bottom of the legs. They stand aside and, as I zip out of the flight suit, they peel it away and roll it up in a ball.

Next, the eager beaver with the machete goes after my flight boots. I move him gently out of the way and untie and unlace my flight boots and step out of them. The boots disappear. They want my sox. I remove them one at a time and hand them over. Another eager beaver has already grabbed my dog tags, and, after ripping them from my neck and breaking the chain, he is recovering the chain and the separated dog tags from the dry earth where they have fallen.

I stand in this crowd of about fifty in my jockey shorts, and I'm not the least bit embarrassed. Soon I am wearing a blindfold, quickly constructed by taking the handkerchief from my flying suit pocket and tying each end to a twig so that it would reach around my head. It is far from the perfect blindfolds used in the grade "D" detective movies we saw for a dime at the Ritz Theatre in Dyersburg on Saturday afternoons. I can see my feet, and I can see the upper torsos and some of the faces around me. Those who are near me are draft age males. The older folks and women are excluded to the periphery of the crowd.

We move from the edge of the thicket toward the nearby village. In the center of the village, in the shade of a grove of tall trees, there is a big smooth boulder; just right for an adult of my size to sit on in relative comfort. I sit down. An old man looms into view from the periphery of the crowd. The crowd seems to have grown somewhat from my original estimate of fifty. I'm not sure how many are present, just more than fifty. The old man has a stick in his hand. He swings the stick and hits me across the belly. Just a whack—not painful.

I am the only one here that has even the semblance of a belly. These are peasants who live off the land—no different than those I saw in South Viet Nam. They are bone thin—no extra fat—hard workers who survive by their hard labor in a subsistence environment--little different than the environment I tried to escape when my mother signed me over to the Air Force in 1949.

Just as quickly as the old man moves from the crowd and swings the stick, several younger men grab him and move him away from me. He is screaming and trying to free himself for another whack at my belly. The younger men speak to him, and move him out of my view as he continues to scream. I can't help but think of how this situation would have played out had the situation been reversed. If a Viet had somehow been able to drop a bomb on Dyersburg Tennessee, my home town, and then bailed out somewhere in the Dyer county countryside, he might or might not have gotten the protection that I am getting now. After having read the intelligence reports with their rendition of treatment of POWs, I am relieved to still be alive.

It is still early in the day. When I checked my watch right after I hit the ground, it was 09:27. By that reckoning, it took about 22 minutes to travel the 22,000 feet from the out of control airplane to the ground. Given conventional aerodynamics, this is far too long to be believed. I believe that the turbulence we encountered on the descent included up-drafts that slowed our progress earthward. However that may be, some-how I don't feel like taking any more time right now to consider the aerodynamics of descending parachutes. Maybe later. The villager who stripped my watch from my wrist has disappeared, along with my para-chute bundle and my clothes. I wonder where he is now.

I tilt my head back and see many of the faces looking back at me. With the exception of the old man with the stick, they are not unfriendly. Many are smiling. The smiles are mostly those of the curious who are not totally aware of the situation—much like country bumpkins, who go to a carnival and are amused by the oddities they see there, like the tat-tooed lady, the contortionist, or the two headed dog. I'm not sure which of those categories I might most resemble, but just feel like...

This place seems to be the village meeting place—the village square. The only structures around are rather open thatched roof huts made largely of bamboo poles and grass thatching. How long will we be here? After an hour or so, there is some movement among the spectators, and those who seem to be in charge of me, push, shove, and otherwise motivate me to get up and walk. We walk out of the village square, and I can't really tell which direction, but we move steadily for an hour or so.

It's nearing noon when we come to a shallow stream of water, ranging from ankle to knee deep. We wade across and continue to walk until we come to a larger stream and stop. The crowd increases. Some see me tilt my head to look at them and look back at me with amusement, and some seem rather friendly. We are in an area of deep shade. The banks of the stream are rocks of various sizes ranging from footballs to small boulders, arranged by nature such that the crowd can make itself comfortable. They sit, stand, meander, gawk, and sometimes smile and wave.

We hang out here for a while. My keepers offer me a drink of water from a gourd. It's cool and welcome.

After a rest we continue our march. In mid-afternoon, three young soldiers join us at a rendezvous point, and we all stop for a chat. The soldiers appear to be militia men. I have called them soldiers because they have some military gear, ammo belts, pouches, and bolt action Mauser style rifles.

We move away from this rendezvous shelter into a clearing, like an unplanted field. The land has been tilled, but is between crops. My escorts place me on one side of this small clearing and everybody moves about fifty feet away, and when I tilt my head to see what's happening, my knees get a little weak. The three militiamen are loading their Mausers by first rotating the bolt upward and then pulling the firing mechanism rearward until it stops. Then they push each round downward into a permanently installed clip. I watch in horror as each of the men push rounds into their guns. They catch me looking, smile at me, and point each round at me as they continue to load up. I notice that, to my right about ten feet from where I am standing, there are shovels and other digging tools. I am horrified. Then, I tilt my head further back to view the sky. It's a beautiful day. I say to myself: "Hughey, at least you picked a nice day." I look at the ground and wait.

After an eternity or two, I tilt my head back, and see the militiamen slinging their Mausers on their shoulders. I internalize a huge sigh of relief, as the villagers close in on me, and we set off in a new direction.

We walk across dry rice paddies, cross another stream, and rest occasionally. My escorts offer me food and water. I drink, but somehow, I'm not interested in eating. I'm not thinking about much of anything, just living in wonderment at my new surroundings, and wondering what may happen next.

So the day goes, until the sun gets low near the horizon, and we reach a motorable road. It's not much of a road--just dirt--rutted from vehicle traffic.

We walk along the road to a group of hooches. The road follows a ridge line and the hooches sit above the road as it makes its way in front of them. We sit down on the side of the road. A strange man approaches me and my escorts step aside in deference. This man removes my blindfold, orders my escorts, who are obviously more than a little subservient to him, to remove the ropes from my arms, and sits down at my side. He offers me a cigarette. I have not smoked for several months. I quit cigarettes and alcohol to concentrate on the business at hand. I take the cigarette. It's a Dien Bien—same brand that Ho Chi Minh and his cohorts smoke. The Stranger offers me a light. I light up and he joins me in a smoke. Not a bad smoke. We finish the smoke and begin to communicate as best we can.

With a combination of gestures and a few words of English, I gradually learn from this man, who is probably the local Commissar, that Ho Chi Minh has ordered all Viet Namese people to make sure that all captured Americans be safely transported to Ha Noi and am relieved to get this news. In spite of the rather gentle treatment afforded by the Viet Namese peasants and militia, I still think about the intelligence reports I read as recently as last night and wonder just when the next shoe will fall. At least it won't fall until I reach Ha Noi. I feel a bit of dread, but am grateful for what is, at least, a momentary reprieve from any violent acts. The Commissar goes on to tell me that but for Ho Chi Minh's orders, the local gentry would cut off my nose, cut out my tongue, gouge out my eyes and force me to eat them. Given that he's not kidding, I am very grateful for Ho Chi.

As we sit by the side of the road conversing and smoking, a young man walks out of the hooch across the road from where we sit. He approaches with a metal tray containing what appears to me to be medical tools. As he approaches, he lifts a pair of forceps from the tray, deftly picks up a cotton ball and dips the cotton ball in what appears to be iodine or mercurochrome. He then reaches toward my genitals with the swab. I feel a wave of panic. This guy is about to swab me down and castrate me right here in front of God and everybody!

I am nearly paralyzed with fear and watch as he motions with the swab. He wants me to look in the direction he is moving the swab. I look down to discover that apparently the parachute straps had left cuts and abrasions on the inside of my legs and these abrasions had been bleeding all along and I just hadn't noticed. All he wants to do is to swab down these injuries with the disinfectant. He is motioning me to spread my legs so he can see the entire area of concern and do the job. I am hugely relieved to learn the real purpose of his visit.

After a few minutes, a jeep-like vehicle comes down the trail and stops near us. From out of somewhere nearby, a group of our captors show up with Mel. The people in charge of us keep us separated and reapply our blind folds. They help me into the right rear bench seat, and then load Mel into the left side. Our arms are tied loosely behind our backs, and our parachutes and clothing are piled on the floor board in front of our feet. Our captors make it clear that we are not to talk to each other. Mel manages to move his right hand and squeeze my arm. I manage to move my left arm so that we can hold hands briefly. That's all the direct communication we are going to manage for the next five years.

We move out as the sun disappears below the horizon and bounce along this barely motorable trail until sometime in the middle of the night when we stop at what seems to be a way station. I can't see much because we are blindfolded, and only get glimpses by tilting my head. The people at the way station appear to be soldiers—most are in uniform and some are wearing side arms. They are courteous enough and offer us food and water. The food is something like oatmeal cookies. Mel is nearby, and I hear him ask for water, and know that he's speaking so that I can hear his voice. He sounds o.k.

I want to talk to him about his perceptions of what happened to us. At this point, I don't believe we took any direct damage from flak, but that we were victims of FOD (Foreign Object Damage) by way of having ingested some of the debris from the AAA explosions. We will never know for sure, unless Mel observed something that I didn't. During the dive, when my attention was totally focused on the gun sight picture and the other parameters involved in visual dive bombing, such as airspeed, altitude, dive angle, etc., Mel would have been scanning the airspace all around us and would have seen a lot of what was going on that I would have necessarily missed. Having an extra pair of very capable eyes along is a huge advantage, and I would very much like to hear Mel's report.

We sit around the way station for a few minutes—maybe half an hour—and then load into the bed of a large flatbed truck, much like a U.S. military truck called a "six-by-six." (This designation means six wheels on the ground and all six can be driving wheels at the driver's option.) The truck bed is high and we step up into it with some help and with a step platform, like a small portable stair.

I can't judge how much time we spend riding in this truck—I am tired and I doze, even though the floor is hard and we bounce around a bit. Eventually, I am aware that we are stopped. The truck motor is running. I hear voices and a sound like a metal gate opening. The truck backs up a few feet and stops. The guards, who have accompanied us, assist in getting us out of the back end of the truck. As I step down onto the ground, an English speaking voice whispers in my ear: "What is your rank?" I reply: "Major." With that, some hands steer me and lead me as I walk away. I want to say something to Mel, but I don't. I am soon sorry that I didn't. When will I see him again?

Part VII

ETERNITY IN THE VIET PRISON SYSTEM

The Ha Noi Hilton

I have no way to be sure what time it is, but it must about midnight. July 6/7, 1967

Hands guide me as I walk in this new and strange place. I am vaguely aware that we are in some kind of building compound. We are walking on hard surface, like pavement, or stones. We come to an open door. My hands are tied behind my back just above the elbows. I am still in jockey shorts and am blindfolded. The hands suddenly become hostile hands as they grip harder and thrust me through the door, and someone behind me kicks my legs out from under me, and I fall on my knees face forward onto a stone floor. I now realize that I am about to discover, on a personal basis, the truth of the intelligence reports regarding " inhumane treatment" of our POWs.

This place must be the infamous "Ha Noi Hilton." (Figure 5)

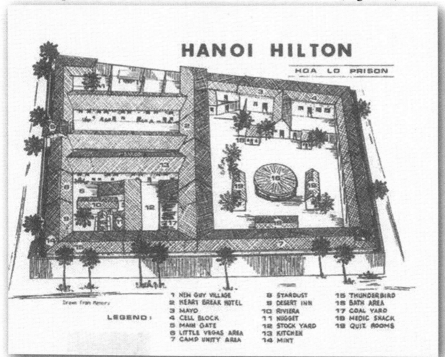

Figure 5

Someone removes the blindfold and ropes, and I stand. I am in a small room, about ten or twelve feet square. My back is to a wall. The door is to my right and is not centered on the wall to my right, but is set near the corner of the room. There are no windows. All the walls are covered with a very rough concrete plaster, much like the acoustic surface of a soundproof room. A single light bulb hangs from the ceiling, along with an iron hook, much like a meat hook. The walls are painted a bilious green—the ugliest shade of green imaginable.

Across the room, with his back to the opposite wall, a uniformed Viet Namese man stands facing me from behind a small table covered with a blue cloth. He leans forward and picks up a pair of red and gray cotton pajamas lying on the table, tosses them at my feet, and rudely orders: "Put them on!" I put them on. They are cotton and tailored much like my Brooks Brothers pajamas back home, except there are no buttons. The pants are draw string—the jacket has strips of cloth sewn to each side, which tie, much like tying one's shoes. It's hot. The pajamas are newly dyed raw cotton. They don't help the heat. I am sweating, and I am afraid. I don't like the looks of the Viet dude standing across the room from me. My back is beginning to stiffen up, I hurt. I am suddenly very miserable.

The Viet sits down in a chair behind the table. I notice that there is a low stool in front of the table—my side of the table. He starts to talk. He explains that I am a criminal, but will be well treated by the people of Viet Nam, provided I obey all the "rules of the camp." I listen to his briefing about the rules. One must eat all of one's food. One mustn't tap on the walls, or talk to other criminals. One must obey all instructions of the guards. In particular, one must answer all the Viet Namese people's questions completely and truthfully. One must keep silent at all times in one's room, etc., etc. After this recitation, he sits down behind the table. There is a yellow legal pad on the table and my friend has a pen.

"Now I will ask you some questions. What is your name?"
"Kenneth Raymond Hughey."
"Spell it for me."
I spell it for him.
"What is your rank?"
"Major"
"What is your serial number?"
"FR 31352."
"What is your date of birth?"

"May 22, 1932."
"What is your base?"

I now have a problem. My conduct as a POW is strictly governed by the Code of Conduct. The code consists of six "Articles." I am now facing Article 5, which states: "When questioned, should I become a Prisoner of War, I am required to give only my name, rank, serial number and date of birth..." and continues by stating that I must resist going any further. The simple fact is that I can't answer the 5th question, whatever it may be. Our code of conduct is consistent with the 1949 Geneva Convention regarding treatment of POWs. Ho Chi Minh signed the terms of that convention after asserting a caveat of some kind. Our position on this is that he is a signatory, regardless of the caveat, and NVN is bound to treat us accordingly. I know only one course of action for the moment; therefore, my response is: "In accordance with the 1949 Geneva Convention, I am a Prisoner of War, and I am not required to answer any further questions."

I know this answer won't fly, but I have no recourse at the moment. My buddy across the room practically has a heart attack. He leaps to his feet, clinches his fists and raises them above his head; his right eye disconnects its self from any synchronization with the left, and focuses randomly on whatever it chooses. He screams at the top of his lungs: "HERE IS NOT GENEVA, HERE IS VIET NAM. YOU ARE NOT A PRISONER OF WAR; YOU ARE A CRIMINAL, GUILTY OF THE BLACKEST CRIMES."

He's only about eight feet away from me, and this performance is very impressive. To say that he has my attention would be a gross understatement. I am terrified at the prospects of my immediate future. This dude is acting like an insane man. The out of focus eyeball and his overall appearance, along with the fact that his hair flops over one eye, similar to Adolph Hitler when Adolph had just completed one of his tirades, is worse than disconcerting.

After this abbreviated tirade, he takes one hand to spread his fingers and brush back in place the Hitler-like mop of hair that covered his forehead. He calms down, and, in a few seconds, it's as though nothing unusual has happened. He tells me that it is obvious that I didn't understand his explanation of the rules, and therefore that he will now review them for my benefit. And so he does.

After the review, he seats himself again, places the legal pad in place and says, just as though we're starting all over: "Now I will ask you some questions." The same conversation begins again with: "What is your name?" and soon we're through the first four questions and here comes question number five: "What is your base?" I only know one thing to do. "In accordance with the 1949 Geneva…" and get no further. My friend again leaps to his feet and screams, but not in English. The room fills with Viet soldiers who bury my face in the stone floor; my hands are behind my back; ropes encircle my arms just above the elbow and tighten until they seem to be parallel and touching from shoulder to elbow—an impossible position. For a moment the pain is excruciating, but subsides gradually from a crescendo to mere fortissimo. Uncomfortable, nevertheless.

The soldiers move away. I can't see where they are, but am aware that they are nearby.

The V leave me in this awkward position. I soon realize that I can't take a lot of this situation, but what is the choice? The interrogator has departed. Two or three guards loll about somewhere outside the open doorway. I am one miserable creature.

After a while, the interrogator returns and speaks to the guards. They untie me and help me to my feet. I am beginning to have some real difficulty moving about. I crawl to the wall and by somehow using the wall, I am able to turn and assume a sitting position. The guards step outside and a V man, dressed in V peasant clothes, comes into the room with two metal porcelinized dishes—one is a bowl, one a plate. He places them on the floor near me. The bowl contains a soup with mostly liquid and some greens that I have seen and eaten when I was with the South Vietnamese 2nd Infantry Division as an Air Liaison Officer/Forward air Controller (ALO/FAC). I have seen these greens growing in ponds, much like water lilies, and have eaten them in the Viet Namese Officer's Mess. The 2nd Infantry cook knew how to fix them into a tasty dish.

Whoever fixed this dish before me now either didn't have a clue or didn't have the wherewithal as to seasoning and meat to prepare a tasty dish as Esau had fixed for his old man. This "soup" is not terrible; it's just not much of anything. At this moment, however, I'm not really interested in a gourmet meal—but am greatly interested in the watery broth, which I swig down in great gulps by holding the bowl in both hands and tipping it toward me until there is nothing left but the greens. The rice, and whatever else is in the plate, I ignore. I could use something more to drink.

After a while, maybe an hour, an English speaker arrives and takes a look at the dishes on the floor near me. He asks me why I did not eat my food. I tell him that I am not hungry, only thirsty. He shrugs, and leaves. A little later one of the guards picks up the dishes and leaves.

It's getting more and more difficult to move. I am not in a lot of pain, but, for some reason, I can't get my body to respond to do what I want it to. I want to move about, to stand and take some steps, but it's really too hard to do, so I give up and sit on the floor, leaning against the wall. It's not clear to me what time it is, but I know that it is the 7th of July and that I was shot down yesterday. I determine that I must work hard to keep track of time—that somehow it is imperative to keep a calendar in my head—that the passage and accurate reckoning of time is somehow so important that I must keep track, no matter what. It is Friday, July 7, 1967 and I was shot down on Thursday July 6, 1967. There is some daylight left today.

As my overall discomfort increases and my ability to move decreases, I flash-back to May 30, 1967, just a few weeks ago, when two of my squadron mates, Walt Schrupp and Tom MacDougall, were battle damaged in Package I. They managed to nurse their airplane eastward over the South China Sea where the airplane went out of control, and they bailed out. After their rescue from the Sea, they wound up in the hospital at Da Nang. I, along with a number of our squadron mates, was able to visit them before they were evacuated to the Philippines.

Walt was lying on a board mounted across the top of a hospital bed. About twenty four hours had elapsed since the ejection. He was in some discomfort, and it was difficult for him to move. The medics had diagnosed his injury as a com-pression fracture. He was in good spirits, but it was obvious that any movement caused him a good bit of pain. I hated to see his combat tour ended this way.

I met Walt in 1964 when we were both assigned to Space Systems Division (SSD) in El Segundo, California. At that time, Walt was checked out as Pilot in the T-39, a twin engine executive jet, requiring a crew of two. The first time I met him, we were the crew for a flight from LAX to Washington, D.C. I was in the process of checking out in the airplane and flew as co-pilot. Walt flew the left seat on the trip east, and I occupied the right seat. On the return trip, I asked Walt to allow me to sit in the Pilot's seat. He didn't have to do that; in fact, he probably shouldn't have—but Walt Shrupp was more than a nice guy—he was on the "fast track" and had just been selected for promotion to Major below the zone. He was tall, dark, handsome, very mature, and exhibited a pleasant demeanor. It was obvious to all who knew him that he would be a general some-day. He thought for a few seconds and said: "O.K.," and we traded seats for the return trip. Walt played the perfect co-pilot, just as he always played the game.

As we were doing our flight plan, the Airdrome Officer (AO) approached us and informed us that we needed to plan our flight plan so we could deliver a General officer to Edwards AFB, CA. The passenger was Major General Osmond J. "Ozzie" Ritland, former commander of SSD. It was a privilege and a pleasure to have him aboard. General Ritland had more flying time than both Walt and I had totaled. He had a very distinguished and unusual career, having been a military pilot since 1932, having flown the air mail as a military pilot, and having had a break in service in the 1930's to fly with United Airlines. He had flown more than 200 types of aircraft, including the first jet proto-types—the P-59 and the P-80. On top of that, he was just about the nicest person you could ever meet.

After we landed at Edwards, I taxied the airplane to a position directly in front of base operations where a staff car was waiting for the General. I shut down the left engine, and the ground crew opened the combination door/stairway so the General could exit. Before he left us, General Ritland came forward and thanked us heartily for a nice ride from Washington to Edwards. That was the last time I saw him, and I'm grateful to have taken that one flight with such a marvelous man.

Tom MacDougall was in a lot of pain. His left arm had a severe compound fracture. He was flat on his back. I wanted to comfort him in some way, but didn't know what to do. I tried to be light hearted, but it didn't work too well. Tom is a big Scotsman, with dark hair and a visage that could easily portray a Scottish Prince—even Macbeth. His bulging muscles would fit well in a suit of medieval armor. I was pained to see this magnificent man flat on his back in a hospital bed with injuries that would take him away from us and back to the States.

After dark, the interrogator returns and orders me to stand. It is difficult, but I claw my way up the wall to my feet and move toward the center of the room while he watches patiently. He explains to me in more detail the "Rules of the Camp." I listen as intently as I can. At times he appears on the verge of losing his temper as he had done before, but he remains relatively self-controlled. He explains to me that he has total authority over me. He explains that if I insist on violating the rules of the camp by refusing to answer all of his questions, completely and in detail, that he will exercise that authority, and will punish me severely, including, if necessary, taking my life. He tells me that I will not leave this room alive unless I answer his questions. I believe him. I am very frightened. I have just come face to face with the fact that I am a coward—the most despicable name a man can wear. It hurts. It's what I am, and I can't help it, but it hurts.

He soon brings up the subject of the questioning process, and another man joins him. This newcomer seems to be the senior of the two. His English is more fluent, and he is more articulate. The two confer in Viet Namese, obviously talking about me. The first begins the questioning process again, and I politely tell him that I cannot answer any further questions. Without raising his voice, he speaks to the guards who are waiting just outside the door.

Two or three of the guards enter the room and force me toward the corner of the room to my left and position me facing the corner. They tie my arms behind my back—not extremely tight, but secure. Someone brings in a low stool and places it behind me. Then someone brings an electric lamp with a high wattage bulb and sets it on the stool and turns it on. The bulb has a bright reflector behind it, and I immediately feel the heat.

I am now in some pain in my lower back. It's difficult to stand, but I comply with the rather stern orders coming from the interrogator to remain standing. Soon I am standing in a puddle of my own sweat as the heat wrings my body dry. It's not long until I am having trouble standing, and gradually, I sink to my knees and then somewhere on the floor. It's hard to tell where I am. This is not the first time in my life that I have encountered this "sinking spell."

Summer, 1941

I am nine years old and wishing that I was "grown" so I could drive the tractor, sharpen plow points, change mower blades, repair things that needed straightening, and other black smith work requiring the heat of our forge and the hardening by immersion into the tub near the forge inside our shop, and strike mighty blows with the big shop hammer applied to a nearly white hot plow point held in place with one strong hand wielding a set of tongs whose length was more than half my height.

My brother, Jack, is wielding the tongs with his left hand that holds a damaged plow point in the heat of the forge fire. The muscles in his left forearm bulge with uncommon strength. Sweat streams down his face, and drips from the tip of his nose and chin. He holds a shop hammer in his right hand while he watches the glow of the plow point as it heats to the proper color to maleate to the blows that he will soon inflict as he holds the hot metal and positions it exactly on the anvil standing nearby. Even though I would rather be grown, I am proud and pleased that I have a part in this work. I am standing near the forge turning the blower fan that forces air through the bottom of the forge resulting in the heat necessary for smithing.

Ordinarily, we would not be doing smithy work on an unusually hot day like today, but plow points don't necessarily wait for cool weather to fail, and the plow that we are repairing is essential to the cultivating job that needs to be completed as soon as it can be done. Thus, Jack and I are forced to complete a job in this excruciating heat when we would have ordinarily picked a cool time, like very early in the morning.

I watch the plow point as the glow begins with a deep red and then slowly lightens as I keep up the RPM of the blower. The light of the glowing plow point is fascinating. My knees start to fail me as I hang on to the blower and try to keep it turning. I am on my knees, sinking toward the hard packed floor of the shop. My knees touch the dirt floor and the shop disappears into distance.

My eyes open, and I am supine under the shade of the cottonwood tree that stands between the shop and our house. I look up into Jack's face, wondering why I am here and what is going on. My mother is soon there beside Jack, and they are talking. My mother kneels beside me and, as only a mother can, she strokes my forehead and wipes my face with a damp towel, and offers me a drink of cool water freshly pumped. It is cool in the shade. In a few minutes, I am fully awake and recall the peculiar whine of the blower and the glow of the plow point as it heated just before my legs failed me and the world went blank. Jack lifts me gently to my feet and assists me to our front porch.

From someplace, hands grip my arms and lift me to my feet. The guards assist me to a seating position on a low stool. Interrogator # 2, the polished dude that speaks English with a slight Oxford accent, does the talking. There is a porcelain finished metal cup on the table brim full of water. He explains to me that all I have to do in return for that cup of water is to answer one question—what is my base.

The rules I am bound by have not changed. This is still question 5, and I am bound by the Code of Conduct to refuse to answer question number 5, no matter what it is. Will I sell my soul for a cup of water? The answer is yes—after all, the V have my parachute and its record packet with Da Nang written all over it—so what matter, other than principles and my honor?

I respond: "Da Nang," and join Jabez Stone, wrapped in a pocket handkerchief, and tucked inside the Devil's jacket pocket. Congratulations, Outlaw Lead, you just bought yourself a lifetime of shame and disgrace. You know, in your heart of hearts, that some of your compatriots have died in this room, and you would be better off if you had followed suit.

Question five, of course, will not be the last. I drain the cup and most of a refill, and other questions follow. The V want to know future targets. I don't know any future targets. Air crews were sheltered from any involvement in planning future operations which would expose us to exploitation if we should find ourselves in the position I am now in. I try to avoid any response. The V reiterate my choices—I can die here in this room, or I can answer ALL their questions. I decide to answer with lies.

The V produce a map of North Viet Nam and ask me to identify future targets. I point out random places on the map that I believe that there is no chance we would ever strike. They query me as to why I think the locations I identify will be target. I make up the lamest of explanations, but they seem to fly.

This exercise doesn't last long. The next subject is the name of my squadron mates. I am not about to give these people any real names, so I give them names of some of my childhood playmates and schoolmates, including the name of my imaginary companion, Jesse, who drove an old red truck. In my cloudy mental state, I believe that I can remember these names if I'm ever queried in the future. I hope this ends the subject. It ends that subject, but there are others.

Eventually they turn to my experience in the war. They want to know about targets I have struck in their country--when, where, and how many. My response: the past two years; everywhere; and 564 missions. They are incredulous. Both interrogators stare at me in stunned disbelief. The Bug asks me to repeat what I just said. I repeat my answer. When he asks me to tell them where, I respond: "I have seen every square inch of your country from the air and have struck targets in all but a few provinces in North and South Viet Nam." Silence. My heart starts to pound. Have I just committed suicide?

The Bug and his glib English speaking companion turn toward each other and have a long conversation in Viet Namese. They turn to look at me from time to time. Eventually they recognize my presence. They begin again, but our discourse becomes more of a conversation than an interrogation.

"Have you been over Ha Noi?"

"Near, but not directly over."

"What kinds of targets did you strike?"

"All kinds."

"What were some of your targets in the DRVN?"

"Targets of opportunity, railroad trains, boats, trucks, bridges, AAA positions, ammunition storage depots, fuel storage facilities."

"What about towns and people?"

"Didn't see people at any of the places I struck."

"Don't you know that you must have killed innocent people?"

"Probably."

"Are you sorry that you killed innocent people?"

"If any innocent people died as a result of what I did, of course I am sorry. I am also sorry that a large number of women and children in South Viet Nam have died as a result of the DRVN's activities there."

"But the DRVN has not invaded the South."

"Not true--I have encountered DRVN regulars in South Viet Nam."

Silence.

"Where?"

"Everywhere."

"You are mistaken."

"Don't think so."

I wait for the next shoe to fall.

The Bug and his Oxford associate pick up their notes and depart.

I struggle to a position as near vertical as I can manage and move toward the left rear corner of the room. Using the cornice of the walls, I ease toward the floor and gradually arrive in a prone position with my feet toward the back wall. As long as I am still, the pain is bearable. I stretch out on the stone floor and sleep better than you might imagine, in spite of my totally demoralized state. I do not dream.

July 10, 1967

I wake up in the Interrogation Room. (See Figure 5.) The Interrogation Room is almost directly under the number 2. I have only left this room to relieve myself since showing up here. The first time I left, I was allowed to urinate a few steps from the door. Later, I used a standard V outside toilet. Too bad to describe, now. I'm having a hard time moving, but when I'm still, it's relatively o.k.

Someone brings food about mid-morning. The someone is the same male dressed like a V peasant from the country. He places a bowl and a plate on the floor near me. This has happened twice a day since the second day here. Two meals a day—one in mid-morning and one in mid-afternoon.

The haggling by the interrogators over targets and names of squadron mates and trivia questions such as the number of bathrooms in my home continued through most of yesterday. They have assiduously avoided my combat experience. Sleep is a relief. I do not dream. When I am awake, I think about what I have done here, how I have flunked the course and try to numb my mind to it all. The day goes by.

The guards have locked the door and have left it locked except when the V peasant, or one of his friends, brings the plate and the bowl. The bowl always has some kind of soup in it. It has been different each day. The first day it was the alfalfa-like greens. I don't recall the other days, but today it looks like cabbage. I mostly just drink the liquid part of the soup. The plate always has some rice in it along with a vegetable. Today

I don't recognize the vegetable. Other times it has been the same alfalfa that has appeared in the soup. The civilian V picks up empty dishes.

I spend the day lolling on the stone floor. I am dirty, sweaty, and smelly, as well as very uncomfortable. I require what assistance I can manage from the wall to get to my feet, so I spend most of my time prone on the stone floor and squirm about frequently in an attempt to find some comfort. No position is pain free—some are just less painful than others. Little happens as the day progresses. The heat is stifling. I have a terrible taste in my mouth and need a bath.

It's soon late in the day. I have had my afternoon meal and the sun is setting. I lie still on the stone floor. The stone is awfully hard, but it is slightly cool to the touch–helps to make the heat a little more bearable. I wonder what's next and doze to the drone of the flies which light on various parts of whatever of my exposed smelly skin they can find.

Three of Ha Noi's finest prison guards rouse me from my position on the floor. As I regain consciousness and attempt to stand, I realize that my body is very reluctant to assume any new position. I squirm closer to the nearest wall and feel my way into a relationship with the corner nearest me and creep up the wall to something near vertical.

The guards direct my movements with grunts and points. We leave what I later will learn that my fellow POW's have dubbed "Room 18," "The Knobby Room," or "The Green Room." Room 18 because, at least at one time, the number 18 was stenciled above the door. I never saw the door from the outside well enough to see if there was a number above it. The Knobby Room because the inside walls were finished with what appeared to be globs of cement which were applied much like the randomly rough and uneven finish used to produce sound proof rooms. Green Room because of the bilious green paint job.(Figure 2, Under the Number 2 in Heartbreak Hotel)

We wander about outside for what seems like about fifty yards on a sandy surfaced hard dirt—not uncomfortable to my bare feet—and, eventually, after passing through a maze made up of one building with a connected ell of what appeared to be a row of very low ceilinged cells and a row of small enclosures with about six foot high walls with no ceilings (The Bath Area, Number 16 in Figure 2), we enter a building through a wide opening, like a large doorway from which the door has been removed. We are in Thunderbird, Number 15 in Figure 5.

The cell doors are made of heavy wood, reinforced with iron strips, and equipped with a square window cut out of the upper center and covered with a steel plate attached to a swivel arm and a lever handle that the guards can swivel open to look inside the cells. As we pass down the corridor, a soft cough or grunt or a sound like a man clearing his throat comes from some of the cells—my predecessors are welcoming me to this cell block. I am very depressed, and am grateful for the welcoming signals.

We stop at the last cell on the right side of the hall. One of the guards opens the door and motions me inside. The door clangs shut behind me. The cell that I am in is about seven feet wide and maybe nine feet long. There are two bunks made of heavy timber—one attached to each side wall. Each bunk is a little more than two feet off the floor, and each is equipped with leg irons attached to the end nearest the door.

[It will be some time before I learn that I have just departed *Heartbreak Hotel* and have wandered into *The Thunderbird* and that I am now in Thunderbird 5. (See Figure 6.)

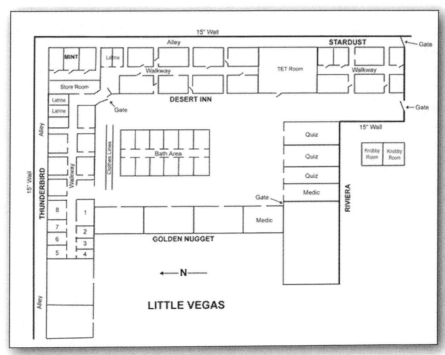

Figure 6

*Note the numbering of Cells 1 through 8 in the Thunderbird
area. Lt. Ron Mastin was in Cell 6. "Jim" was in Cell 3.*

The ceiling is about ten feet up with a single small light bulb hanging from the dead center by about three feet of insulated wire. The bulb looks to be about twenty watts. The floor is concrete. There are no windows. Being here is like being inside a cubic shell. The room seems to have been recently used. There is no dust on either of the bunks, and I notice that the leg irons seem to be in good working order.

I spend a few minutes contemplating my future and wondering about who might be in the neighboring rooms. It's possible that some of the noises I heard from the cells as I passed down the corridor were made by one or more of my compatriots who had preceded me here. I wonder if Joe Crecca, Scotty Wilson, Ed Mechenbier, Kevin McManus, Bill Baugh,

Don Spoon, or any of the others might not be right down the hall, or even in the cell next door. Just a few days ago I was in the intelligence room in the Wing Command Post reviewing the latest files on our POWs and saw a photo of Joe Crecca wearing the same prison garb I'm now wearing.

After a few minutes a guard opens my door. He is accompanied by another V who places a round can with a lid in the front right front corner of the room. The guard points to the can and says "bo." The purpose of this "bo" is obvious. The other V then hands me two 15 inch squares of what appears to be unfinished wrapping paper.

July 11, 1967

I have learned to use the "bo." In my current state of repair it is hard to move about—to get up from the wooden bunk, or to bend. Using the bo is a chore requiring a monumental effort. But, given that the dirty jockey shorts and the dirty pajamas comprise my entire wardrobe, I am motivated not to dirty them any further—thus, success with the bo.

About midmorning, I hear noises in the hall—footsteps and the sound of metal plates being deposited just outside my door. I also hear the rattle of keys and the sense the scraping noises as the doors up the hall open and close in succession. I hear the key operating the lock on my door, and the door opens. The V point to a metal plate and bowl on the floor just outside my cell. The bowl contains soup, and the plate has some rice and some kind of vegetable in it--the same stuff I got in the interrogation room. With grunts and hand motions the guard lets me know that I am to pick up the dishes and take them into my room. After I set the plate and bowl on my bunk, the guard grunts again and his helper produces a crockery pot with a spout and a lid, along with a metal cup with a mug-like handle. The pot is brimming full of hot water; the cup is empty. I take them and set them on my bunk. The V lock my door and depart.

There is a metal spoon in the plate. I eat as much as I can from the plate and drink all the liquid in the soup. I pour some water from the pot into the cup and sip some of the water. I have a huge case of B.O. and a horrible taste in my mouth.

Later in the morning, a guard opens my door. A part of the "indoctrination" process in room 18 was a lesson on how to bow politely along with an explanation that failure to bow politely to all Viet Namese would result in "severe punishment." I bow politely. The guard motions me to precede him down the hall to the exit.

I make a right turn and step out into the sunlight. He directs me straight ahead to a very small room in which a young man in military uniform is sitting behind a desk. The young man asks me to sit down on the low stool in front of his desk. I sit. He delivers a lecture on the wrongness of the U.S. Intervention into the internal affairs of Viet Nam. His lecture includes the fact that the Viet Namese people regard me as a criminal, but in spite of that, they insist on humane and lenient treatment for me with one big however--such treatment will, naturally be predicated on my strict compliance with the rules of the camp, etc., etc., etc. Eventually, he asks if I have understood all that he has said. I say "yes." Then he asks if I have any requests. I say that I would like to write a letter to my wife.

He waffles, and, suddenly the anguish and guilt I am feeling about having volunteered to return to combat after completing a combat tour as a Forward Air Controller (FAC), and then voluntarily extending my tour in fighters, overwhelms me. I fall apart and start to cry. Pretty soon he calls the guard who escorts me back to my cell. I'm not having a good day.

I continue having day mares about my impending Courts Martial. Because of the nature of the charges dictated by the Uniform Code of Military Justice (UCMJ), it will be a General Courts Martial—the court that tries the most serious violations of the UCMJ. The "Court" in a General Courts Martial consists of nine military officers. The grades (ranks) of the nine members can vary depending on the level of the charges and the rank of the defendant. In my day mare, the president of the court is a Major General, and the other eight members are field grade offices; i.e., Major through Colonel.

The trial is over. The court has reached its decision, and the General is reading the results to me. I am standing at attention and listening carefully.

"Major Hughey, this court finds you guilty of all charges brought against you. You have disgraced your Country, the USAF, and yourself by your behavior as a Prisoner of War. You violated every aspect of the Code of conduct. You betrayed your fellow POWS, by your virtual total failure to resist the enemy's interrogation by caving in to their demands without resistance. Some of your compatriots died rather than answer the fifth question. Others were physically abused and crippled and brought home with them the scars to prove it. A thorough physical examination of you has revealed that you suffered little or no physical abuse before revealing to the enemy the identity of your home base and other information. Even though we grant you the premise that such information was inaccurate or lies, you divulged it basically to save your hide. Sir, you are a coward and are unfit for military service. Therefore this court sentences you as follows: 1. You are stripped of your rank. 2. You will be dishonorably discharged from the Air Force, immediately, without benefit of any pay or privilege...."

I relive this day mare repeatedly, and anguish over my selfish decisions to gain personal glory through extended tours of combat to the detriment of my family. I have betrayed my best friend and the person to whom I am most responsible and the one I love the most--my wife. My personal predicament here in this prison pales in comparison to the pain of these thoughts.

In spite of all that, I have to remain alert to my situation. I am now aware of some of the goings on around me. I know that there are several of "us" in this building, and am certain that one of us is just on the other side of the masonry wall that separates our cells. I know there is some kind of routine. We are fed twice each day, and I was allowed to empty my bo earlier this morning. There are other routines that I must learn by being alert. In the quiet of my cell I try to concentrate on any signals, any intelligence, any noises or occurrences that might prove of any value or comfort in this environment.

Soon after my return from this first encounter with an English speaker other than the interrogators, a guard opens my door. He has with him a mosquito net, an extra change of pajamas, and two sets of red and gray shorts with matching short sleeve shirts. He motions me to precede him back to the exit and then guides me to the group of bath stalls not far from the building my cell is in. I go in the stall and he closes and locks the door behind me. There is a vat filled with water and a cup. I remove my clothes and use the cup to "shower." I rinse out my white jockey shorts and put on a pair of the new shorts under the pajamas. Soon, the guard opens the door and motions me to return to my cell. As we near the entrance to the cell block, the guard points out a clothes line and indicates that I should hang my newly rinsed clothing. I hang my clothes and return to my room and am soon locked safely away.

Midafternoon comes and I hear footsteps and the noise of doors opening and closing and the noise of the metal plates being placed on the floor outside the cells. Soon my door opens and the plates are there on the floor waiting for me. I pick them up and place them on my bunk. This time the guard asks for my pitcher. I hand it to him and he takes it away and refills it with hot water. I am not sure of the source of the hot water, but am grateful for a full pitcher. I finish my meal and soon the door opens again and I set my dirty dishes out in the hall. After a little delay, I hear footsteps in the hallway and hear the rattle of the metal dishes as someone collects them from the front of each cell.

After a while I hear voices whispering. I can't tell what they are saying, but I'm sure they are American and that my fellows are talking to each other. I listen, and then there is the sound of the person in the cell next to mine tapping "shave and a hair-cut" on my wall. I know in an instant that the tapper is one of us and that the next thing that comes through that wall will be in Morse code. We all have learned International Morse, but I know that I have forgotten most of it through disuse. In the millisecond before I respond "six bits" I am hurriedly trying to recall the letters I remember. It's precious few. E is dit. A is either dot dash or dash dot and N is the reverse of A. X is dash dot dot dash and H is dot dot dot dot, That's about it, but here goes—six bits.

The person on the other side starts to tap. He taps rapidly and softly and meaninglessly. I don't recognize any sort of pattern. He stops tapping. I then try to tap a message using just the numerical relationship of the letters to numbers; i.e., one tap for A, two taps for B, etc., He responds with a series of rapid taps and gives up.

I am frustrated. I know that there is a fellow fighter jock just inches away from me on the other side of about a foot thick brick and mortar wall. If I could stick my hand through that wall, I could shake hands with one of my own. If I could talk to him, what tales could he tell? Just to learn his name, his rank, what he was flying, and his base would be the equivalent of a Tolstoy moment!!! And then to give him two short sentences about me….This frustration ends my day. I relive my day mare with all its refinements—are firing squads still the preferred doom for traitors?

July 12, 1967

My day begins with a really bad taste in my mouth, and a realization that I have to move very carefully. I use the wall and my hands on the edge of my bunk to achieve a sitting position. Sometime in the morning, I hear a whispering voice. I can't make out what the voice is saying, but I know that it is an American voice. Hope swells in my chest and I listen with all the intensity I can muster. The whispering voice goes away. The cell block becomes silent. The same sequence as the day before reenacts itself.

Then, in the afternoon, before the last meal of the day is served, I sense that something is happening and am not sure what it is. The cell block is eerily quiet. I stand near the door to my cell and listen with all my might. Then, I clearly hear an American voice whispering from the cell next to mine: "Hey, Jim, I'm going to try to talk to the guy in the last cell." I know instantly that the "guy" in the last cell has to be me. My ears suddenly develop the equivalent capability of the listening posts we have established to intercept any potential radio frequency signals from interstellar space.

The next words I heard are: "American in the last cell, can you hear me?" I immediately respond with a whispered "Yes."
"Do you know the tap code?"
"No."

"Listen carefully. Here is the Tap code. Take the alphabet, throw out the letter K, form a five letter box—A B C D E across the top, A F L Q V down the left side. To tap a letter, tap down and then across. For example, the letter M is tap, tap, tap—tap, tap. Use the letter C for K. Do you understand? "

"Yes."

With that, the whispering stops. I now know that the gibberish I heard the day before was the tap code I have just received. In a few seconds, I hear the "shave and a haircut" sequence through my wall and immediately respond with "six bits." Slowly and laboriously and with great patience by the tapper on the other side of the wall from me, we begin a conversation. I keep the matrix just given to me in my mind's eye:

A	B	C	D	E
F	G	H	I	J
L	M	N	O	P
Q	R	S	T	U
V	W	X	Y	Z

The tapper takes charge by asking questions. He wants to know my name, rank, base, and shoot down date. Then he tells me to "tap twice after each word if you understand" and to "tap many times" if I don't. I am beginning to get the hang of communicating with the tap code. I learn that he is 1/Lt Ron Mastin and was shot down on January 16, 1967 on a mission from Udorn, Thailand. I am jubilant to know that the system, whatever it is, has reached out to me, and from now on, I can be a part of it. I can't wait to talk to Ron again, and wonder what he looks like. I do not suspect that it will be more than five years before I will see him, and that we will see each other face to face about 150 feet from where we are now in this same prison complex.

July 13, 1967

I slept better last night and am beginning to understand the routine of life in this prison. Early in the morning a guard makes the rounds opening the peep holes in each cell with a grunt. He pokes a cigarette through the hole. As soon as I take the cigarette, the glowing end of a punk stick comes through. I light up. I quit smoking and drinking a few months before I was shot down, but gladly smoke the three cigarettes per day that are offered. About midmorning the V come around with the morning meal. The two meals each day consist of one plate, one bowl, and a metal spoon. The plate always consists of rice with some kind of vegetable. The bowl is soup made with vegetables. Thus far I have seen no meat. The second meal comes in mid-afternoon.

I am excited about yesterday's initial contact with Ron Mastin and can't wait to learn more about who's here and what is going on. Not long after the first meal, the building becomes peculiarly quiet. I stand near the door to my cell and listen intently as Ron Mastin opens a conversation with Jim in the cell across the hall. "Hey, Jim, The guy in the last cell is Major Ken Hughey—spells his name H-U-G-H-E-Y. Shot down 6 July. Says the war is about the same—guess we won't be home much before Christmas."

Neither of us has any way of knowing today that Christmases of 1967, 1968, 1969, 1970, 1971, and 1972 will come and go, and we will still be here.

Ron is soon up on our common wall with shave and a haircut. I ask him how many of us are here. He says he knows of about 50. I ask him if he knows if Bud Flesher is here. He does not know. He explains, among other things, that the danger signal is to hit the wall hard, and the all clear is two raps.

After our second meal, Ron comes up again. This time, he gets serious. His transmission begins with: "The senior officer in this camp is Colonel Robinson Risner." My backbone stiffens. I have never met Robbie Risner, but know a lot about him. His reputation and overall career credentials are unimpeachable. He is one of the great fighter pilots and shot down eight Migs during the Korean War. He is a family man who lives the life of a Christian. He is a role model for all who know him or know of him. I know we are in good hands for leadership.

Ron continues: "Here are Risner's Rules:

1. Don't bow in public.
2. If forced to write, write sixth grade.
3. The next two rules are the evening ceremony.

4. In the evening, face the east, present arms, and pledge allegiance to the Flag of the United States.
5. Before you go to bed at night, repeat the 23rd psalm."

We don't have time for much else and soon sign off.

I spend a lot of the rest of the day thinking about Risner's rules and trying to dredge up the 23rd Psalm: "The Lord is my shepherd, I shall not want...."

Just about the time for the V equivalent of Taps, the V unlock my door. A guard gives me hand signals to roll up my belongings and prepare to move. As I pack up, there is a conversation between the guards who are at my door and those at the other end of the hall. The two at my door push my door closed and move away toward the entrance to this hallway. I, for the first time, tap shave and a haircut on Ron's wall. He responds immediately with six bits. I tap: "I am moving." He responds: "Where R U going?" "Don't know." "I pray U."

The V are back in a trice and motion me to follow them out. They direct me to toward the main entrance where a jeep-like vehicle is parked. At their direction, I get in the jeep. I estimate that we motor about a mile or so through the streets of Ha Noi to my next prison venue.

WELCOME TO THE PLANTATION
We pull up to a large barred steel gate with hinges that that allow it to swing open. Three or four people are waiting. One advances toward us as the five of us exit from the vehicle. He speaks to the group briefly in Viet Namese, then turns and addresses me. He directs me to follow one of the guards just a few feet to the right as I stand with my back to the barred gate that has now swung closed. I do as I'm told, and we approach a door to the room whose wall is adjacent to the entryway we just drove through. (Figure 6)

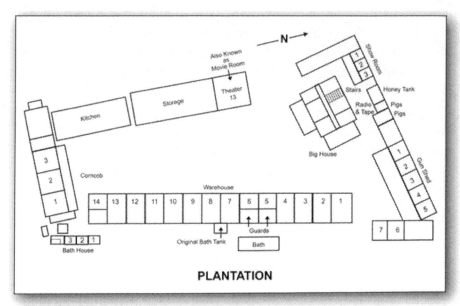

Figure 7

The room is huge, maybe four times the size of the cell I just left. While the cell I just left was a prison room, this room is just a big room that has been converted to take prisoners. There are three windows with wooden shutters on the outside and steel bars imbedded in the masonry walls--one window on the side wall, and one window on each side of the double doors. The shutters, steel bars, and heavy wooden double doors are "after-market" additions aimed at converting a big empty room into a cell. The doors can be barred shut by a long 2 x 4 plank that was removed from the brackets fastened to the outside walls on either side of the door opening, and now stands vertical, leaning against the wall adjacent to the door on the left side as we enter. There is a bunk in the far left corner made of boards nailed together like a wooden door and supported about 2 feet off the floor by two saw horses—one at each end. I note with some sense of relief that the ankle pillories are missing.

The Viets motion me to take my belongings and place them on the bed. I don't have much in the way of belongings--just the mosquito net, a change of clothes, a pot, and a cup. I place my things on the bunk, bow politely and watch them leave. As soon as the doors are closed and locked and barred, I move around the room. I look at the boards that block my view from the inside to the outside. A light bulb hangs from the ceiling just like in the cell I just left. The only difference is that this room is much bigger, the ceiling is higher, and the bulb is a little bit brighter most likely because of the size of the room. Soon I give up wandering about and roll up my mosquito net. I use it for a pillow and I sleep the best I can on the bare boards.

July 14

I hear a noise at my left front window and pull myself out of a fairly deep sleep. With great difficulty and very slowly I move so that I can see the window clearly. The shutters on the outside are open, and a guard stands just outside the window. He grunts and it's obvious that he wants me to come over to the window. I struggle to get out of the bunk--it's very difficult to move. The guard waits with some impatience. I move as quickly as I can but it's not really quick enough for him. He keeps growling and motioning to me to rush, but rushing is out of the question for me. I finally make it to the open window, and he passes a cigarette through the bars. I take the cigarette and then he pushes the glowing end of the punk stick through the bars and holds the other end with a tight grip. I light the cigarette on the glowing end of the punk stick by holding it just below the burning part and moving it slightly towards me while "Charlie" clings to the other end and grunts impatiently as I light up then abruptly moves away and slams the shutter closed with a vengeance. The cigarette is about the size of a Camel or Lucky Strike. It is very strong, and with the first drag I feel a little dizzy.

I'm vertical, so I stay that way. It seems like about a mile across this room, in reality about 30 feet, and it appears to be a perfect square. The pajamas that I first put on about a week ago are grimy from having slept on the floor of the green room and having been sweat soaked during the process. I smell real good—a lot like something dead. The brief rinse that I had after the green room session didn't do much lasting good. Also, when I rinsed my body I removed my jockey shorts and rinsed them out. On my way back to the room next door to Ron Mastin, the guard had pointed out a clothes line and I hung my jockeys out to dry, and now they are gone from my life forever. Oh well, with no soap those jockeys were pretty much too dirty to be part of a gentleman's wardrobe.

The cigarette is soon down to a very short butt when it gives up the ghost. I deposit it on the end of my board bed. Maybe I'll eat it later.

I recline on the board bed and nap until I am awakened by the doors opening. I struggle to my feet and greet three V personnel—two guards and an unarmed man in an officer's uniform. He is a bit older than the guards, his uniform is cleaner and neater, and he speaks English. One of the guards goes over to my bunk and the officer comes along. He explains that the guard has some things for me. First, there is a pair of sandals with only one strap which goes across the toes like shower clogs. My sandals differ from the ones the V wear in that theirs have straps that go around the backs of their ankles and across their insteps. A much better fit. The militia that accompanied me on the long walk wore this kind of sandals. The peasants were mostly barefoot.

Then there is a toothbrush and a tube of toothpaste. The tube is lead alloy like the tube I grew up using—Ipana, Colgate, etc. Then there is a bar of soap and a small towel. The soap is virtually identical to the soap my mother made from wood ashes and pig fat. Then there were two changes of gray shorts and short sleeved shirts, and a second suit of the long sleeved striped pajamas. Finally there are two blankets. The officer explains that I will be issued a tube of toothpaste every ninety days and a bar of soap every sixty days. He also explains how the V expect me to fold the blankets, clothing, and mosquito net during the day.

He then shows me how to hang the mosquito net. There are two nails in the back wall spaced so as to hold the back corners of the deployed netting. He then has the guards string a long piece of string across the room at the proper height such that the two front corners of the net can be tied to the string. He instructs me to hang the net at night and to fold it neatly during the day and stow it at the head of the bunk along with the blankets and clothing. He tells me that I will leave the room to empty my "bowl" once a day, and that I will be allowed to have a bath once a day, except on Sundays. Everybody leaves.

The remainder of the day is dull. I rest as best I can throughout the day. The V bring my meals. They have to open one of the double doors at meal time and set the plate and bowl on the ground just outside the door. It's very difficult for me to pick them up, but I manage. I set the food on my bunk and eat, washing down the food with water from the earthenware pitcher that I pour into the porcelain finished cup. I eat everything they bring. It's not so tasty, but it's edible. A while after I finish the second meal, the V open the door and I set the empty dishes on the ground outside the door. The door closes and they take the dishes away. Later, as evening matures, the shutter covering the left front window bars pops open, and I get my third cigarette of the day. I arrange my mosquito net, and using the folded blankets and clothing, turn in for the night.

A lot has happened to me since my first night in the cell next door to Ron Mastin. I review some of the thoughts since my arrival here. In particular, I think about the idea of taking my life.

William Shakespeare has been a part of me nearly all of my life. When I was growing up, a seven volume hard back printing of Shakespeare's works occupied a prominent place of display in our living room. I was aware of it from my first memories. When I turned eleven, my mother gave it to me. It had been hers since she was a teen ager starting a career as a "school marm" in rural northeast Arkansas--near Luxora.

During the first year of ownership of Shakespeare, I bumped into the brightest of my seventh grade contemporaries--Thomas Jefferson Walker, Jr. Thomas Walker's grandfather was the superintendent of schools in Dyersburg, Tennessee. Like all of his ancestors, Thomas Walker was a scholar. Thomas and his older sister were valedictorians in their respective high school graduating classes.

Thomas seemed to know nearly everything and soon taught me a good deal about Shakespeare that motivated me to read Shakespeare. In particular, I was motivated to read *The Rape of Lucrece*--not for its intellectual content, but to find the scene where Tarquin sneaks down the hall to Lucrece's bedroom in the middle of the night intent on raping her. Shakespeare's description of the scene, especially the views of Lucrece in her bed, partially nude and asleep, was equivalent to modern pornography to an eleven year old. I was soon reading Shakespeare's plays but never forgot the moonlight streaming through Lucrece's window illuminating her bare breasts. As time went by, the real enormity of what Tarquin did finally fell into place in my heart and mind, and Lucrece's beauty, reputation, and suffering penetrated my consciousness. The temperance of the Roman leaders in sparing Tarquin still leaves me dissatisfied.

Later on, I read more and more of Shakespeare's works, especially his plays. Hamlet's two soliloquies that focused on his thoughts about taking his own life are interesting to all Shakespeare fans, and, at this moment I think with Hamlet how easy it would be if this "...too, too solid flesh would (simply) melt, thaw, and resolve itself into a dew." Even though I have come face to face with myself regarding the issue of suicide and know that I am too much of a coward to ever do it, the idea that if it were done for me in a painless way, it would be a blessing to be at peace.

July 16, 1967

Today is Sunday. I soon realize that the Sunday schedule is quite different from other days. The first cigarette doesn't show up until late in the morning, the bowl emptying procedure is also delayed. The camp is quieter—less people, less buzz of activity. I move about the room and inspect the wooden shutters covering the barred windows. When the shutters are closed, they are very close to the bars. I discover that there are cracks in the wood allowing a view of the outside when my eyeball is very close to the crack. I survey the outside with more than a little interest.

The buildings in the camp are arranged in an elongated trapezoidal quadrangle. There is a two story building to the left end of the trapezoid as I face the window. Slightly behind the two story building is a one story building appearing to be a row of four cells opening toward my right. If the occupants of these cells can see out, they will have a view of the length of the quadrangle. Straight across the quadrangle from me is a long one story building with fourteen evenly spaced doors. At the right hand end of the quadrangle, there is a row of three cells facing the opposite end. From my peep hole, I cannot see the extreme right end of the camp. I can only observe the entire quadrangle on my trips to empty my bowl. The honey tank where we empty our bowls is directly behind the two story building to my left. (Figure 7)

Each morning, after the first cigarette of the day, the guard comes to my door and escorts me to the honey tank. There is a brush with a long bamboo handle and a water bucket next to the tank so we can rinse out our buckets.

Today, I am privileged to watch the bo parade. As I stand at the window, the guards approach the 4 cell building to my left and open the door nearest to the two story building. Two men come out—each carrying his bo. They disappear behind the two story building for a short time, and then return to their cell. Two guards are nearly always present. The Turnkey wears a semi- automatic pistol and is accompanied by a second guard who carries an AK-47.

The second cell opens as the bo emptying process continues. There are also two men in cell number two. I recognize none of the first four Americans. Then the door to the third cell opens. I am startled to see Lt Commander Richard Stratton emerge from the room, along with a very young man, whom I do not recognize. Dick Stratton's photo on the cover of Life magazine a few months ago literally galvanized the American public, especially when accompanied by a vivid description of his actions during a staged exhibition by the V to show the world the "humane and lenient treatment" provided by NVN to the criminals who had attacked them.

One could not possibly have viewed the series of photographs, accompanied by the vivid description of Dick Stratton's behavior during the staged exhibition without concluding that something was terribly wrong. Stratton appeared drugged and incapable of thinking or acting rationally. He had a zombielike demeanor and appearance. Today, I watch him and his roommate carry their buckets. It is very warm, and they are dressed in grey shorts and matching short sleeved shirts.

Dick leads, carrying his bucket in his right hand. The younger man follows a few feet in trail. As they exit their room, each turns to his right and faces me. They can't see me as I peer out at them through the very small peep hole in the wooden shutters. I suspect that they would have been startled if they knew how intently someone was watching their every move and taking in every detail of their looks and behavior.

Stratton looks exactly like his famous photograph on the cover of *Life* magazine. He is about six feet tall with a hairline that extends forward and ends just above his eyebrows. He has sharply chiseled features--very photogenic. His room-mate is very young and heavier in physique. His shoulders are slightly rounded and strongly built. He has dark hair, as does Stratton. Stratton moves very purposefully, quick steps and a recognizable gait. The younger man moves more casually--drifts forward easily. Stratton's visage is serious and focused on doing what he has to do--carry the bucket to the honey pit and get it emptied as soon as possible. His roommate, while certainly keeping up the pace, looks about the yard and seems a bit less concerned about the purpose of their trip.

They walk toward me for a few paces and then turn right and disappear behind the two story house that serves as the administrative building for this camp. I am excited about seeing someone I recognize, even if it is only from photos. I would like very much to talk to Stratton and hear all about the events surrounding his appearance on the cover of *Life*. In a few minutes, the two emerge around the other side of the two story building and return to their cell. The other doors in the same building open in turn, and in both cases, two men emerge and complete the same round trip.

The Turnkey then proceeds to the first cell in the long building that runs perpendicular to the four-cell building and faces my cell. If the doors to this long building were numbered from my left to right, the first room being number one, the last cell--the one furthest to my right--would be numbered fourteen. The turnkey opens the number one cell. Two men emerge, turn to their right and head for the honey disposal. I watch every step they take as they disappear behind the two story building, and then wait for their return. This process continues. The turnkey, under the watchful eye of a guard carrying an AK-47, proceeds from cell to cell as each occupant, or set of occupants, make their round trip to empty their bowls. The first five cells contain one solo, three duos, and one cell with three occupants. They are all strangers to me. I try to file away a "photo" of each one.

Then the turnkey unlocks the door to cell number seven, swings the door wide open, and steps aside about four paces to the right--toward cell number eight. The guard, with the AK slung over his right shoulder, stands out toward the center of the yard, about 30 feet from the Turnkey. Two men emerge from the room. My observing eye widens in disbelief--I recognize both.

The first out is 1/Lt Ed Mechenbier, and 1/Lt Kevin McManus follows by three or four steps. They are a crew from our sister squadron--the 390th--who took a hit from AAA while attacking a rail road yard near Kep. Their airplane came off the target with an engine fire, soon went out of control, and they were forced to eject.

As Ed and Kevin parade toward the honey deposit, I follow each step they make talking to myself--"those guys sure look like Mechenbier and McManus," but my mind keeps refusing to believe it. First of all, the circumstances of their shoot down didn't leave a lot of hope that they survived. I recall that that they came off the target low and on fire after a 45 degree dive bomb attack--not a good thing. Also, I recall that no 'chutes were seen. So, there is a part of me that says "you're seeing ghosts." Nevertheless, here are two dead ringers for Mechenbier and McManus walking around, upright and mobile, right in front of my eyes, no more than 100 feet away. It finally sinks in--its them--they're alive and right here in the same camp with me!

After this shock, I keep glued to my peep hole. A host of names scroll from my memory bank: Bud Flesher, Joe Crecca, Scotty Wilson, Jim Berger, Bill Baugh, Ron Spoon, Colonel "Snap" Gaddis, Robbie Risner, Bruce Seeber, Hervey Stockman, Ron Webb, Harry Monlux, along with others who might be here--some that I knew well, some that I knew about, some from our sister squadrons, some who were my contemporaries in flying school, some from the 480th who preceded my arrival at Da Nang.

Who might step through the next door that the turnkey opens? Would it be Bud Flesher? Wouldn't that be a trip? Bud was my oldest and best friend. Last December I was his Summary Courts Officer--had the duty of dealing with his military estate believing that he was dead--had to communicate with his wife, Sue, who was like my sister, and pretend that I thought that Bud had survived, even though I was convinced that he and Jim Berger had died instantly after taking a direct hit by a SAM. Well if Mechenbier and McManus are not ghosts, then Bud Flesher and/or Jim Berger might very well step out of the next room!

I watch the rest of the bucket parade, and have soon seen all of the denizens of this camp. Bud is not here; nor are any of the others on my list. My heart hurts thinking about Bud, and thinking that there's really no way that I will ever see him pop out of a cell door here nor will I ever see him again in this world. We were like brothers. I struggle a little to move across the room and ease myself onto my board bed. It is really difficult to recline, but I manage it by using the wall and my bed itself as support. I ease my folded mosquito net under my head and gradually achieve a comfortable position. I close my eyes and think of another time, another place.

Summer 1957 has ended, Labor Day is gone, and summer vacations are over. Bud, Sue Flesher, my Sue, and I have been talking about a camping trip to the Great Smoky Mountains and have planned a time and a place and all the logistics. I have borrowed a two wheeled trailer from Sue's brother, Joel, and it's parked in our yard. One of our buddies, Captain Claude Hansen, has loaned us a tent that's now piled in the trailer. Sue and I own a well-used and weathered 1952 Ford convertible equipped with a trailer hitch. We pack up our coolers and "stuff" that we'll need and head for the hills.

We leave in the early morning and drive straight north through Atlanta into East Tennessee. Late in the day we find ourselves searching for a camping spot in the Cherokee National Forest. The sky is darkening with clouds that threaten rain. Zephyrs that precede a good rain are whispering to us that we need to make haste to set up our camp. We are having trouble finding a marked road that will take us to the lake we have chosen as a camp site. Bud is driving and our wives are in the back seat watching two fighter jocks trying to cope with a difficult ground navigation problem. We are on a narrow, unpaved road as we come around a climbing bend and sight a small country store with two rather mature men sitting on the front porch bench--one is busy whittling. Bud pulls as close to porch as he can, and the whittler looks up as Bud asks: "Can you tell us where this road goes?"

The whittler looks up the road to his left and then down the road to his right and then looks at Bud with a kind of quizzical, cynical half smile and says: "Well, I reckon it don't go nowhere. I been livin' here 'nigh on to forty years, and it's been rat 'ter all the time." The ladies and I crack up and Bud has to grit his teeth to help himself not to explode. The whittler gazes at us in a friendly quiet way.

Bud regains his composure, laughs, and tries another tack. He describes our objective to the whittler, and asks if he can offer directions. The whittler listens carefully to Bud, and then tells us exactly how to follow this unmoving road to the lake we're looking for. Bud thanks him and in about fifteen minutes we come around one of the road's continuous set of curves, and look to our left at a building open on three sides with a fire place on the single sided wall. The building sits in a mountain meadow surrounded by woods. A trail meanders from the meadow into the woods and slopes downward to the small lake we're looking for.

The Zephyrs have increased their volume considerably, along with their cooling, forceful presence now punctuated with some occasional large drops of rain. We decide to dispense with pitching Claude's tent that weighs at least 200 pounds, and to quickly arrange our stuff inside the open building. In minutes we are unpacked and busy ourselves grabbing pine needles as fast as we can to pad the concrete floor under our sleeping bags.

The structure we're under would have been the common grounds to earlier campers, but we have the whole thing to ourselves. We build a fire in the fireplace and use one of several built in charcoal grills to prepare our first feast. The scenery is spectacular. Our campsite is uphill from the small lake that has a pier. Mountain flora perfumes the air. Our condition here is even better than we had imagined during the planning stage.

We spend five days here and see only one other person. On the second day we are here, the ladies take the car for a drive to a village somewhere near the foot of the mountain we are on. Bud and I are tending camp, and Bud is making his famous Irish stew in a big pot over an open fire in one of the built in grills. The ladies have been gone for an hour or so, and a car with "pin-ball" lights and spot lights and law enforcement markings comes around the curve and halts about fifty feet from our digs. A uniformed officer opens the door and walks down toward us. Bud and I are both suddenly in a panic, waiting for this officer to tell us that our wives are rolled up in the wreckage of the Ford convertible.

The officer greets us with a smile and asks how we're doing. We breathe sighs of relief and have a pleasant conversation with a Tennessee State Trooper. He says that he comes up here sometimes and having heard that someone was up here decided to visit us. We asked him about our wives and he said that he had seen them down the road and that they were o.k. and that they should be back up here within the hour. He wishes us well on our stay and leaves. Our ladies are back pretty soon with enough ice and other supplies to last our stay.

Every time we make the trip to the lake to bathe and/or swim, at about the half-way point, I detect a slightly acrid odor that disturbs the normal aroma of the woods. The odor is familiar, but I can't place it. The day after the Trooper visited us, Bud is minding the stew while the ladies and I go down to the lake. When we return, we see Bud get up from his perch on a bench, and move around our quarters. We meander into camp as Bud pulls out his .38 Smith & Wesson from one of our bags. "Whatcha gonna do with that gun, Bud?" "I'm gonna find that copperhead that just crawled out between my feet and headed down the trail. You just walked right by him and didn't even see him."

I suddenly recognize the acrid smell we have all noticed along the trail--it's the scent of the copperhead snake, a poisonous little beggar that can sneak up on you, but is usually shy around people. However shy he may be, we would prefer his presence elsewhere, not around our camp. Bud is determined to find him in the bushes where he retreated and to kill him. Snakes are hard to spot in foliage, so we spread out a little to cover the territory, and, as circumstance will have it, I spot him in a well-covered place. Bud hands me the S & W, and I put a bullet in his head from about five feet away. Copperheads don't get very big. The biggest one I have ever seen was about two feet long. This one is close to that. Somehow we feel better that he is no longer a threat, and, from now on we are very wary when we travel to and from the lake.

Bud does nearly all the cooking. He makes a fine stew and spaghetti, along with various grilled meals.

I ease out of this reverie later in the already late morning, or maybe it's early afternoon. I don't hurt or experience any discomfort until I try to move. I recall that Walt Schrupp told me that the Doctor told him that in about six weeks he would be back to normal. I guess that I have a few days before some more noticeable improvement, but, for the moment I can't just lie here like a motionless turnip. I have important things to do.

I take my time and gradually do a reverse of lying down. In a few minutes I'm vertical and move across the room to peer out through the peephole and observe any activity in the camp. There is very little. The guards who occasionally meander across the yard are unarmed, and some are in T shirts instead of their customary military shirts. Not much action there. I retrace my steps diagonally to the opposite corner where my bunk awaits and wait for the afternoon meal. After that, there is the cigarette parade and I have the rest of the day to daydream and amuse myself as best I can. I dream about the last time I saw my little family.

My wife and son. I last saw them in June, just a few weeks ago. I had taken a leave and caught a ride to Hawaii and then bought a round trip ticket to Los Angeles. Sue and my son, Kent, met me at the airport and we went to our rented apartment at 12901 South Vermont in Gardena. For some reason that I will never fathom, one of the rules is that one could take a leave and go to Hawaii, but we were forbidden to go to the mainland. Rules are made to be broken, and fighter pilots can be frequent truants. It made more sense to Sue and me for me to travel to LA where we had all the familiar amenities.

Kent was 3 years old and was a lot of fun. My stay came to a close all too soon. A friend and neighbor, Major Archie NeSmith, took us to the airport and accompanied us to the departure lounge. We went in for some refreshments and bumped into Edgar and Frances Bergen and Jonathan Winters who were waiting for a flight to the east coast. Edgar Bergen entertained Kent with some neat magic tricks and kibitz. Jonathan Winters was friendly but reserved and rather serious--not the usual funny man we are accustomed to when he is center stage.

We had a pleasant stay with them. I will never forget a short dialogue with Frances Bergen as we were saying good-bye. She was admiring the ribbons on my tunic. When she spied the air medal ribbon which had three silver oak leaves, she exclaimed: "Oh, you have three oak leaf clusters!" Before I even thought about it, I explained that each of those oak leaves was silver and that the ribbon depicted the Air Medal with fifteen oak leaf clusters. (I was sorry immediately, and it is a bit uncomfortable now to recall that moment.) Mrs. Bergen was such a lady--she pretended to faint, and we all parted on a very friendly and pleasant note.

My mind quickly shifts from the party atmosphere created by wonderfully talented people to the malaise that I felt in my heart when I had to leave. I hope Sue and Kent are O.K. But, how can they be? A feeling of helplessness and hopelessness chills my soul. Would "...that the Everlasting had not fixed his canon 'gainst self-slaughter," not to mention that, even if I had the means, I couldn't do it. Hamlet couldn't do it for several reasons, none of which was cowardice. I couldn't do it only because of cowardice, with the excuse that living is important for the sake of my family. I've got to get away and stay away from this line of thought--but how? My heart aches for my little family. Forgive me, Sue!

The week day mornings always begin with a cigarette. Later on there is the bucket parade, which I observe every day, trying to remember all the faces. I see Ed Mechenbier and Kevin McManus nearly every day. I cling to their images as they do the same parade every day with their buckets.

Once a day we all go to the bath area. My first few baths are taken from a brick tank behind the long building across from my room. The turnkey escorts us individually to the tank. We lay our towels on the concrete ledge nearby, strip off our clothes and then use the large dipper to pour water over ourselves, and then use as little of the grandma's lye soap as possible to lather up and eliminate some of the congealed residue from our perspiration, along with the dirt. Note here that I use the plural. I have not seen any of the others bathe--just assume that they have to do what I do. What other choice?

I notice from my first bath that there is a structure, more like an ancient ruin, a few feet from the outdoor bath. It is partially enclosed by incomplete brick walls with a crude piping arrangement that ends at an overhead shower head. I think to myself that this must be the guard's place to bathe. We just pour the water over our bodies with a dipper, but they at least have the relative luxury of taking a more or less real shower, even though its cold water. The bath is a welcome respite from the total solitary of the room, even though the room is big. I am alone for 23+ hours each day, and that's no fun. Most of my time is spent with nothing but my thoughts to deal with.

I think about my response to Ron Mastin. When he asked about how the war was going, I only considered the circumstances of the war since

Ron got here about six months ago and responded: "…about the same." Now I think back on it and ruminate on my experience with Viet Nam. The "about the same" response in terms of our activity in North Viet Nam was about right. However, when considering the war in the south, I don't think we're making much progress. If you have read my remarks regarding my experience, you must have concluded that something is wrong with this picture. I don't believe the VC will ever catch us out like they did at Dien Bien Phu, I also don't believe that we're going to stop them without a considerably different effort that we've been exerting so far. I don't believe that the North Vietnamese will cease their efforts because of our air strikes. I also don't believe that we can establish a viable government in South Viet Nam. This equation yields only one result--failure.

Late July, 1967

The V pretty much leave me alone except for an occasional interview in the two story house at the left end of the compound. It's at least a respite from four walls. They want to make sure that we know that we are losing the war, and that all of us who are participants are criminals--that the U.S. is an evil country bent on International hegemony--that Ho Chi Minh is God--that …. Sometimes they offer tea and a smoke, which I gratefully accept. The officers who conduct these meetings are young and are not violent or threatening. Every time I have an interview I ask for books and ask to write a letter home. The V are always non-commital.

I am living a rather ho-hum existence. My back is improving rapidly, but my state of mind is not. Today seems strictly routine--a cigarette in the morning--a morning meal--another smoke--a late afternoon meal. Lonely and boring, except for daydreams and mental gymnastics. Then it gets dark, and about bed time, then I hear voices, truck engines, and a commotion that I soon perceive to be the opening of the big gate next to the North wall of my room. A bus about the size of the school bus that I rode 25 miles each way from my home in Chic, Tennessee to high school in Dyersburg rolls into the left periphery of my vision and stops between my window and the two story house to my left. There are guards all over the place. In a few minutes the guards begin to open the cells in the four cell building to my left and are escorting the occupants to the bus. Soon all but one of those four cells are empty--the V do not disturb Stratton and his roommate. The guards are yelling at each other, and there are two officers passing out directions.

The guards are soon opening doors in the long building straight across from my window. They begin with the first room and transfer the two occupants to one of the cells in the now empty four cell building to my left. I can't tell which room. They then proceed down the line of the fourteen cell building, opening doors randomly, skipping some and opening others. As they remove the occupants of each room, most of them get on the bus, and I watch as Mechenbier and McManis carry their "stuff," rolled up in their straw mats, across the compound and get on the bus. Soon the bus leaves with the big commotion of yelling guards, the noise of the bus engine, and the creaking and groaning of the big gate as it closes. So long Ed and Kevin. I wonder if you had a peephole somewhere in your room and are aware that I am in this camp and that I am watching you now. GBU both. Take care and God Speed.

The noise of the guards milling about and talking subsides, but doesn't go away completely. Then, the yelling resumes, the gate opens, and another bus pulls into the camp. The two officers direct the guards as the bus empties in ones and twos. The cells which were just emptied receive new occupants as the guards escort the new guys as directed by the officers who are keeping track of the movements on a clip board. It takes about 30 minutes of this ruckus filled activity to get all the new guests settled. The bus leaves and the camp gradually quiets to more or less normal. Tomorrow's bucket parade will be very entertaining. But then there is another surprise!

As soon as the camp settles down, I move to my bunk and prepare to retire. Suddenly, there is a commotion as the guards unlock my door, remove the plank that holds the double doors in place, and my door swings open. The Turnkey approaches and with hand signals and grunts, he directs me to roll up my belongings. Just outside my door, at their proper stance and distance, stand two of his buddies with their AK-47s in the usual barrel down but ready positions. I pack up my stuff and the Turnkey directs me across the compound to the sixth cell from the left end of the fourteen cell building. It's a short walk--maybe 100 feet--between the buildings. I step inside and am surprised to see that this cell only goes halfway through-- that apparently the V have made this part of the building into two rooms. The door closes behind me.

My new bunk is a replica of the one I just left--the standard wooden door supported by two saw horses. It is parallel to and against the back wall. My bucket is in the left front corner. The cell is about nine feet long, eight feet deep, with a ten foot ceiling. A small light bulb dangles from the center of the ceiling and is about eight feet up. It's high enough that I can't reach it. Above my door there is a circular hole about four inches in diameter with a sliding cover designed to be opened and closed from the outside. It is now open, and by standing on a saw horse from my bed, I can see out--a much better peep hole than in the big room I just left. The V left the rooms on both sides of me vacant. I am still in solitary.

Another strange arrangement of this room puzzles me. There is a standard wooden door between my cell, which would be number six if the cells were numbered from the end of the building which was on the left as viewed from the big room I just left, and the cell which would be number five using that numbering system. Also this wooden door has a large gap at the bottom--about 3/4 of an inch. By lying down on the floor, I can see nearly all the way across Room 5. There is nothing visible but the bare stone floor. I soon learn that Room 5 will now be a pantry. When the cooks have our meals ready, they bring the big pots to this room and ladle out the individual servings into one bowl and one plate per person. When the meals are ready to be served, the turnkey opens each cell in turn and there is a food parade as each man walks to this cell number 5, picks up a plate and a bowl and returns to his room to eat behind his closed and locked door.

When the meal is over, the Turnkey opens each cell in turn and the occupants set their empty dishes outside their doors. Eventually, the Turnkey then opens another cell that houses two or three men who are the dish washers. They go down the rows of cells, pick up and stack the empties and carry them out back to the bath area and wash them. The V rotate this KP duty, but only between the cells that house at least two.

So now I live next door to the pantry. There are two nails in the back wall, one nail in the side wall and one nail in the front wall positioned such that I can string my mosquito net. The net came with strings sewn in to the top four corners. The V provided enough string to extend the built-ins so that I can put up the net with no problem. I am soon sound asleep.

Another change occurs at this time. The next time I go for a bath, the turnkey directs me inside the structure I described earlier. There is a shower head of sorts and some piping, but no source of water for the shower. There is a brick trough, similar to the outside trough along with a bucket to dip the water and pour it over ourselves. I go in and place my dry clothes in a dry corner and take my bath. This becomes the bathing routine.

I wake up very excited the morning after the move--can't wait to watch what I can of the bucket parade. But first things first. The door to this cell is a conventional wooden cell door--a virtual replica of the door to the cell block where I "met" Ron Mastin. It has the same style of peep hole with the metal swiveling cover that is opened and closed by a lever. I am barely up when the peep hole swings open and I see a V face peering in. The face emits a grunt and is instantly replaced by a pair of fingers extending a cigarette. I grab the smoke and the glowing end of a punk stick instantly extends about four inches into the room, and I light up. One deep drag and I'm dizzy. These early morning smokes on an empty stomach, and with no coffee to wash them down, are vicious.

As soon as I finish the smoke, I remove one of the saw horses from my bunk, place it so as to step up and peer out though the vent hole above my door. I don't have the same panoramic view I had before. I am looking straight across the compound at the big room I just vacated. Of course, I can't see any of the doors in the building I am in, nor can I see any of the doors to the short cell blocks at each end of the compound. I feel much more alone here.

The parade starts with the cell block at what is now the right hand end of the camp. I can only get a glimpse of the occupants as they move around the corner to empty their buckets. I don't recognize any of the newbies in any of these cells.

July/August, 1967

The heat is just as unbearable as when I arrived here a few weeks ago. Summer is burning. My move into this small room seems to have increased the discomfort of the heat--a fact that has little effect on my overall feeling of well-being. I review my defense (or lack thereof) at my upcoming courts martial, which is certain to occur very soon after my release from this place. The heartbreak and virtually total malaise pervading my psyche from the outset of this experience are still present, although attenuated by time and the whole issue of being in prison. I am much comforted by the fact that Ron Mastin was able to teach me the tap code, even though I have not used it since my last communication. I wonder how long I will (or can) live in solitude.

The good news, if there is any, about solitary confinement is that I am learning that, during the quiet times (which is most of the time) I am able to perform mental gymnastics that I would never have thought possible--the first example was ability to use the tap code with an alacrity that I am now sure that most of "us" would exhibit in these circumstances. It may be summarized as "what else were you going to do?"

I am becoming more adept at diversions that are essential to keeping one's sanity. It might be easy to succumb to boredom, and sometimes I do just that--let my mind run in total idle--no discernible intellectual activity. This can't be healthy.

I am finished with keeping score of the flies who have perished at my hand, but still attempt to catch one live once in a while, just to prove that I can. When I am fast enough (or lucky enough) to catch a live one, I let the little pest buzz around inside my closed fist and then, mercilessly, viciously, and with great pride and gusto, slam him (it's always a *him*) into the stone floor, thus ending his nasty little life. I have learned that in the slam process, one must release the captive fly near the floor. If one releases the fly with too much altitude, the little pest can pull out of the dive and fly away unharmed. So, the release point has to be just a few inches from the stone floor. The little bugger, all in one piece, with his little legs akimbo, and his wings half spread, lies moribund on his little back. I pick him up carefully and place him in my bucket. I'm such a hero!

Today, perhaps because of my skill with flies, flies are on my mind, and one of my favorite poets occupies my time. I have always been more interested in literature than engineering, and sprinkled my formal engineering education with as much literature as was allowable. Emily Dickinson came zooming over my horizon in a survey course at Colorado. Her impact was devastating. I never was much for memorizing poetry, but took the time to memorize as much of hers as my pea sized brain would (could) absorb. Many of her poems dealt with death--dying itself or the condition of being dead. It's been a while since I have thought about any of her poems that I once knew by heart. I think of one today and begin to reconstruct it in my head.

I heard a fly buzz when I died
The stillness 'round my form
Was like the stillness in the air
Between the heaves of storm.

The eyes beside had wrung them dry
And breaths were gathering sure
For that last onset when the king
be witnessed in His Power.

I willed my keepsakes signed away
what portion of me I
could make assignable and then
there interposed a fly,

With blue, uncertain, stumbling buzz
Between the light and me
And then the windows failed, and then,
I could not see to see.

I go over and over the words to get it in some semblance of the order and rhythm imprinted by Miss Emily with her peculiar style. I recall the rhythm of the lines--iambic tetrameter alternated with iambic hexameter--eight syllables per line, then six syllables--am sure that these are the words--how could I misconstrue, even with poor memory, the power of the composition, order, and delivery?

The poet is dead and recalls her dying. Her last memory is in the stillness of her final moments she has taken care of her earthly business. She is aware of those around her who are waiting for her dying gasp when "...there interposed a fly." As the fly buzzes, her vision fails, and her final words are: "I could not see to see."

I remember the struggles I had with the exactiing demands of my favorite high school teachers--Miss Alleen Park and Miss Julia Sheaffer--and shall never forget the impact that these two marvelous women had on me. But for them, I might not have the likes of Miss Emily Dickinson to fall back on at this long moment.

This long moment. Long moment, indeed! How long would it last? I recall the sudden increases in air losses over North Viet Nam in the spring of 1965 when I was serving as a Forward Air Controller (FAC) with the Viet Namese Second Infantry Division at Da Nang and Quang Ngai. I never knew the names of the crews who were lost--only that some had died and a few were presumably taken as POWs and were up here somewhere.

I also recall a lot of the moments we experienced in the war in South Viet Nam. Successes were few and far between. Our "enemy" was a will-o-the-wisp. They showed up unexpectedly and disappeared into the *Maquis* without a trace--usually leaving dead bodies, confusion, and little else behind. Sometimes we never even caught a glimpse. It was only occasionally that these wills-o-the-wisp showed up in broad daylight where we could catch a glimpse of them--much the opposite of trying to find them in the dark shadows of night and rain. Such a day, that I described earlier, occurred on June 23, 1965. It was a good day for the good guys, and it was one of the rare times that I experienced real success.

Too bad that I had such a brief encounter with Lt Mastin. He said he thought that there were about fifty POWs here. I never got to know any of the other names--not even the Jim who was across the hall from Lt

Mastin--not to mention the others that I knew were there in the other cells in that first prison. I had asked Ron if he knew if Bud Flesher was here, and his response was that he didn't know. So, this uncertainty regarding Bud, Ron Mastin's name and shoot down date, Jim's first name, and Risner's rules constitute the sum total of all that I know regarding who is here and what this whole thing is all about, and by far, the most important of those is Risner's Rules--not that Ron and Jim were not important, but that we have a recognized leader among us who can share his courage, character, leadership, and spiritual values with us.

Wherever Robbie Risner happens to be at this moment, I now have his rules in my heart. When I think of "Risner's Rules," I think of Robbie the man--the father--the family man--the Christian--the leader--the squadron commander--the fighter ace with eight victories in Korea-- the epitome of what a fighter pilot and a gentleman should be. I wonder what he will think of me when I tell him (that is assuming I ever have the opportunity to tell him) that I only lasted a few hours in my first encounter with interrogators--that I sold out for a cup of water and a verbal threat. I guess that he will shrug and say something like "... the UCMJ will apply the cure." Oh well, on to another day.

The heat is ever present and unabated. My Bucket sits in the corner of my cell. The lid is on as firmly as it will seat. The *bo* is black. It is about 15 inches high, made from sheet metal. Hope it doesn't spring a leak!

Every day at every mealtime since moving into this room, I have placed myself lying on the floor with my feet toward the front wall and my head on the floor such that I can watch the feet of those who walk into the pantry to pick up their meals in the hope that something will interrupt the process, and produce an opportunity to talk to one of my fellows. Thus far this has not happened. However, hope springs eternal, and today, after another disappointment at the first meal of the day, here I supinate on the stone floor, feet toward the front wall of my cell, head buried in the stone floor, acutely alert and prepared to rattle my "bo" lid to convince any intruding V guard who should open my peep hole to assure my total compliance with camp rules that I am innocent by way of having to be using my "bo." I am cocked and locked.

American feet come and go. Then two pairs of American feet enter the pantry and approach the table to pick up their meal. Suddenly, there are voices--V voices-- in the yard, and then a loud response from the V who are escorting these two American diners. The V feet depart the pantry leaving these American feet standing fecklessly alone in the pantry.

I leap to my feet and do the shave and a haircut on the door. I hear a rapid two steps as one of the Americans on the other side of the door zooms to respond with "six bits." He then starts tapping--it's too fast, so we start to talk through the thin wood panel. We exchange names and other vitals. I am talking to Dick Stratton. After we exchange vitals, he asks: "How are the Yankees doing?" I am somewhat of a Yankee fan, but I wasn't as avid a fan as Dick, because I had stopped following the baseball season prior to my shoot down. To my sorrow, I had to report that I did not know. He told me that his roomie is Seaman Apprentice Doug Hegdahl. I am floored that a seaman, barely out of boot camp could make it here to the Ha Noi Hilton--no time to ask how. Dick tells me that there is a note drop under the loose brick in the south west corner of the bath. He also tells me that he is the SRO here and asks me to "keep in touch." He needn't have worried regarding keeping in touch. I will do everything I can to stay in the loop.

He parts with: "Were you tortured?" I respond: "Yes." He asks: "Were you broken?" I respond: "Yes!" His parting shot as the V close in: "Join the club!" I move away from the door and sigh: "At least I won't be alone at my courts Martial."

About three days after the encounter with Stratton and Hegdahl, I am in the bath. Stratton had told me that the loose brick covering the note drop was near the bottom corner nearest the Warehouse back wall. I look around. Then, in the cornice just inside the entryway to the bath-house, I notice a brick that is slightly displaced. After clearing the area, I move the brick and pick it up. There is a piece of tightly folded toilet paper under the brick. I grab the paper, stick it in my mouth, and replace the brick. I try not to rush my bath, but am very anxious to get back to my room to check out the note.

I return to my room and unfold the damp note and place it inside the fold of my blanket. It is not soaked, just damp, and in a short time I arrange my bedding so that I can unfold and take a look at the note. With my back to the cell door, I can look at the note while shielding it from view. If a guard suddenly pops open the peep hole, I can easily fake fold-ing and arranging my belongings such that they can't see the note. In the unlikely event that the guard becomes suspicious, I can swallow the note before they can open the cell door.

The note is written in plain text, but is worded so that only an American can read and understand it. It reads in part: "Dr. advises re-quest release. Say no to that RX. The Beak." It has to be from Stratton. I am elated to get this note and to know that someone cares.

August 11, 1967 begins just like yesterday--a strong cigarette that makes me dizzy, a trip to the honey barrel to empty my bucket, the rou-tine noises outside, a bout with the flies, the first meal of the day (soup in a bowl and a plate with vegetables and rice, and for some reason, no bath this morning. I am "relaxing" on my board bed. My back is largely healed. I can do some calisthenics. I am well, but not quite happy. Then things change with a rapidity and violence that I never expected.

I hear the V shouting to each other. A siren screams louder and longer than ever before, nearby AAA batteries shake the ground, and the concussion produces a precipitation of dust and debris from somewhere in the rafters of this building. I am amazed. Then, after a few seconds of this opening commotion, the real commotion begins--explosions, very close, very loud, and very violent. The wall shakes and my door is suddenly trying to unhinge itself. I can see outside between the violent pulses which shake the building, and for moments at a time my door looks as though it is wide open and I have a momentary view of the confusion in the compound.

Some of the guards are standing inside the concrete man-sized caissons which populate the compound--their AK47s pointing skyward. Explosion after explosion shakes the building and dirt and debris fills my cell. The building seems to move about me and I am convinced that it will collapse at any moment. I dive under my bed, seeking refuge from the impending collapse and wait for the whole thing to disintegrate around me. Will this ever end, and will I be alive when it does? Then the big concussions stop. The big guns continue the punctuation which opened this sudden maelstrom. And then--a few seconds of virtual silence. Suddenly, the guards are talking loudly, and then they move about opening the peep holes in the cells, perhaps to see if we are still there and alive. By the time a guard arrives at my peep hole, I am out from under my bed, standing in awe and wondering "Wha' Hoppen?"

I now know how it feels to be on the receiving end of a good sized air raid. There's just nothing else that could produce the scene I just lived through. I know that I am somewhere in Ha Noi, but can't guess what kind of a target invited this strike.

Tonight I shake the dust out of my "stuff," make my bed and retire a little earlier than normal, hoping to get a good night's rest. As I am trying to relax and doze off, the noise of talking guards and the opening of the main gate next to the big cell where I began my stay in this camp precedes the engine noise of some kind of big vehicle. I untuck the mosquito net from under my straw mat and grab a saw horse from under my bed and take the two steps to the door. I step up on the saw horse and I'm looking across the compound through the vent hole above my door as the school bus pulls in and the V guards begin an unloading process. I can't watch the whole thing because I have to duck away to avoid the guards spying my face as I peer out. By the sounds and movement that I am able to observe, I know that some of us are leaving, and some new ones are arriving. I know that some of the doors in the long building I am in as well as doors in the four cell building to the north have opened and closed more than once during this shuffle. As the camp quiets, I return to bed.

During the day on August 14, 1967, I wonder if I will ever have a common wall with another POW so as to be "connected" with the society of "criminals" in this place. I also wonder what would happen if the V moved someone in next door to me who didn't know the tap code. How could I ever teach him the code? I recall the frustration in not being able to tap with Ron Mastin, and how fortunate the circumstances were that made it possible for him to whisper the code to me--an apparent impossibility in this camp. I am grateful for the brief conversation with Dick Stratton, and only yearn for a more constant connection with my fellows.

I have lots of time to think and wonder and to work on some poetry that I have memorized. If I tackle a piece and can't nail it all, or am not sure of some words or phrases, I plug in the best substitute I can make up. And so it goes. Also, I try to make up and solve engineering problems. As carefully as I can, I take up the problem of dragster design and after a while I conclude that the current design with the engine very close to the rear axle, with a very short drive shaft and the front (steering) wheels extended is the best I can do. So much for that problem.

Then there is a very surprising development in my life. Several days ago the V stopped using cell number 5 as a pantry, and cell 5 has been vacant. Midafternoon, the V open the door to cell number 5. The wall that separates my cell and cell 5 still has the wooden door with a large gap at the bottom. I can hear the noises of the outside door opening and can hear movement as the V place something in that room. Soon after, I hear the door open and then close. I can hear (or imagine) someone in room five. By lying down on the floor, I can see through the space under the wooden door all the way across the floor of Cell 5, and I behold a pair of American feet! How do I know these feet belong to an American? The sandals issued to POWs are different than the standard fare worn by the V. V sandals have straps around the back--ours are strictly go-ahead. Other than that, the feet I'm looking at are very white and far too large to be found on any V. The dude that's wearing those sandals is one of us!!

Have the V made some kind of blunder? Did they park this guy temporarily for a few minutes for convenience? I'm sure that whoever owns those American feet already knows that one of us is right next door and is thinking the same things that I am. I am not going to blunder into some kind of V trap or make a silly mistake in my anxiety to speak to a fellow American. So I wait.

Some time goes by. I check outside via the vent hole above my door. The coast appears to be clear. By lying on the floor with my feet toward the outside wall near my bucket, the V can't see me. If the V were to open the peep hole in my cell door they couldn't see me, and upon hearing them, I can rattle my bucket lid and pretend that I'm using the bucket. I'm sure the man next door can do the same. I lie down so I can see under the door and call out to him. Those big feet immediately take a couple of long steps and we are soon talking and working out the ruse that I just described. Also, during the siesta period the guards are pretty lax about trying to surprise us with a sudden peep hole opening. We start to talk and agree to be cautious and not to blow this opportunity.

BILL BAILEY

My new neighbor is the first American I have talked to face-to-face since leaving Mel. His name is Lt/j.g. James ("Bill," of course) Bailey. He was shot down on June 28, 1967. He was in the back seat of an F-4B flying off the USS Constellation. The pilot was Cdr. Bill Lawrence, his Squadron Commander.

Bill Bailey has been here in this camp since just before I arrived. However, he had spent some time in the "Hilton" and learned the layout there. I describe the first room I was in, where I went after that, and the contact I had with Ron Mastin. He tells me that the first room was in "Heartbreak Hotel," that the cell next to Ron Mastin was Thunderbird 5, and that Ron was in Thunderbird six. I tell Bill about seeing the feet of the American who was in the cell directly across from me and who was wearing sox but no shoes. The cell would have been Thunderbird 4. Bill believes that the man in Thunderbird 4 with sox was Commander Lawrence.

Bill explains the entire layout of the Hoa Loa Prison. He also details the names of the buildings in the camp we are now in. The big room I was in when I came here is the "Movie Room." The cells we are now in are part of "The Warehouse," and we are in Warehouse 5 and 6. The two story building is "The Big House." The building with four cells at the north end of the camp and adjacent to the Big House is the "Gun Shed." The Gun Shed cells are numbered from west to east--the cell nearest the Big House being number one. Three cells are currently occupied. The counterpart to the Gun Shed at the south end of the compound is the "Corn Crib." The corn Crib cells are numbered from east to west--Corn Crib 1 being nearest to

Warehouse 14. There are 3 cells in the Corn Crib--none are currently occupied.

Bill tells me the names of all those he knows are here. Bud Flesher and Jim Berger are not on his list.

We talk all that we can and tell each other all of our life stories that we have time to tell. I don't tell Bill what a coward I am, nor do I tell him about my day mares re my impending Courts Martial. I know that this opportunity to talk is an accident of fate, and I don't want Bill to go away with the truth about me. It's a burden he shouldn't have to bear, and besides that, I don't have sufficient character to "own up."

I tell him that I told the V that I had flown over 500 missions over Viet Nam and that my last mission was number 564 and that it was number 106 over North Viet Nam. Bill is incredulous on two levels: One, that I had flown a lot of missions and, two that I told the V. He obviously thinks that giving them the numbers was not the thing to do.

I think I owe Bill something further. First of all, I had taken an ABC Newsman, David Snell, along with me on my 500th combat sortie. ABC had somehow convinced the Air Force to allow Mr. Snell to fly with me. I didn't like it much and neither did my Wing Commander. The "old man" (Colonel Jones E. Bolt) cautioned me to be careful and to return with Mr. Snell intact. Second, just a few days before I was shot down, I had a long interview with Reader's Digest and figured the V would soon know all about me anyway. I know that I don't have to explain all my actions to Bill, but I had no reason not to share these facts with him.

I'm sure that there's not a man up here that I wouldn't like, but I count myself lucky to have met Bill Bailey. He's the kind of a man I want for a friend. We have some things in common. Bill is from Mississippi, and I grew up on the Mississippi River about 75 miles north of Memphis.

My family roots are from Northern Mississippi. My Grandfather spent four years in the Confederate Army--the last two years in a Yankee prison camp in Ohio. He hated Yankees. Bill and I have about the same accent, like the same food, like most of the same things that Southern rural people like, and besides that Bill Bailey is just a fine man. One big difference we have is that Bill is an athlete--he played basketball in high school and college--and I am anything but athletic. We have a lot of laughs lying there on the stone floor talking through a crack between the bottom of a wooden door and the bare stone floor.

I tell Bill all about my encounter with Dick Stratton and Doug Hegdahl and about the note drop in the bath house. I have a feeling that the note drop may be a very important in the future.

During the day I spend all the time that I can safely spend standing on a sawhorse peering out at the compound. I watch the bucket and bath parades every second that it's safe. A day or so after Bill shows up, I see a man emerge from the Gun Shed area and walk up the back steps and into the Big House. I get a pretty good look at him, but it's not very close--it's probably more than a hundred feet from my vent hole to the back steps of the big House. He looks like Jim Berger. My heart almost stops. If that's really Jim Berger, then that SAM didn't finish its job, and Bud must be around somewhere!

The next time that Bill and I talk, I tell him all that I have seen during the day, and, especially about seeing a man that may be Jim Berger. I also tell him about Bud and some of our flying experiences and about how and when Bud and Jim got stuffed.

In late August, 1967, the brief interlude with Bill Bailey comes to an end. In the middle of the day, I hear the V open the door to Warehouse 5. The door is not open long--just long enough for Bill to roll up his stuff in his straw mat and follow the V out the door. Having a fellow American to talk to for a few days--even for just a few minutes a day--was more than a treat. I learned an awful lot from Bill, especially the camp layouts, but aside from that, having someone to talk to after what seems like an eternity of solitude was an awesome experience. I am very sad to see him go.

Bill has hardly passed the north corner headed for the Gun Shed when the V open my door, and the turnkey signals with his hands for me to roll up my stuff. I roll up, and with my belongings under my arm, the V direct me across the compound to my former cell--the Movie Room. It looks much like it did when I left it a short time ago, except that the bed is now in the opposite corner. When I go through the door, the bed is in the far right corner instead of the far left.

LONELINESS
I feel lonelier than I felt in the small cell in the Warehouse. I get the blues and think about my family, especially about my wife.

Before I left the 480th Squadron on my last mission, I, like all of us, deposited my billfold in a storage box at the operations counter. Among the other contents was a clipping torn from an article in Time Magazine celebrating Dante's 700th birthday, with brief excerpts from Dante's *La Comedia*--The Comedy, often referred to incorrectly as *The Divine Comedy*. One of the excerpts was Dante's thoughts when Vergil, his guide, had explained God's rules to Dante and informed Dante that God would allow him to see Beatrice.

In Dante's writing, he is in the afterlife and Vergil is his guide through the first two parts of his journey. At this time in his visit to Heaven, his most devout wish is to see Beatrice, the only woman he ever loved in his mortal existence. Dante is 35 years old, his halfway point through life. Beatrice was sixteen years when she died. Vergil and Dante are across a narrow abyss and are sheltered from Beatrice's view as they wait for her to appear. God has not granted that Dante can meet or speak to Beatrice, but has allowed Dante to see her. Dante's description of his emotional state when he sees Beatrice reaches the pinnacle of man's ability to articulate his love for a woman.

I carried the clipping in my billfold. I would sometimes, in the privacy of my room, unfold this little scrap of paper and read it. During these readings, my feelings for my wife would soar with emotion. Dante gazes at Beatrice as she moves gracefully through the Bower she currently occupies--her hair falling about her shoulders, and, forbidden to speak to her or touch her, or to in any way let her know of his presence, he expresses his feeling for her:

> *If I could lay hands on those tender tresses*
> *That are become a lash and scourge to me*
> *Seizing on them before morning prayer*
> *I would clutch through vespers and through evening bell.*
> *I would show no pity nor be courteous,*
> *But rather play at passion like a bear.*
> *And if love scourge me now because of them,*
> *I would revenge myself a thousand times and more.*
> *I would revenge myself the terror that she strikes me with,*
> *And then, I would give her peace with love.*

Tonight, in the solitude of this enormous and empty room, I relive Dante's agony. At least Dante had the real image of the only woman he ever loved--I must rely on visions of a gorgeous girl from Finley, Tennessee, who has more energy and spunk than any ten of her contemporaries, and who loves me as dearly as I love her.

BUD & JIM

Later in August, 1967, I keep an eye on the compound as best I can, but have been unable to spot any of the occupants in the Gun Shed that I know, other than Bill Bailey. I have not seen the man I thought might be Jim Berger.

Today the V take me for a bath in the afternoon after siesta. The route to the bath from the Movie Room is a diagonal line from the Movie Room door across the compound toward cell 14 at the south end of the Warehouse, then around the end of the Warehouse. The bath is almost directly behind Warehouse 8. I go inside the structure of bath # 2 (Figure 7) and stow my clothes in the corner that is dry. The water trough is near the south side of the interior wall. I keep an eye on the guards as I always do, and when I have a clear moment, loosen the brick in the corner and there is piece of folded toilet paper. I grab it and put it in my mouth and replace the brick. Unlike the previous note that I found here, it is not damp; it is soaking wet.

After the bath, I hang my wet clothes on the clothes line and return to the Movie Room. The turnkey locks the door. I remove the paper from my mouth and unfold it carefully. I straighten it and place it flat between the folds of my blanket. I will let it dry so I can distinguish the markings. I already know that it is written in tap code.

I don't want to rush this process. I know that there is a message on the piece of paper that now is safely lodged between the folds of my blanket. My biggest fear is that the V will choose this moment for a shake-down inspection and find the damp note. The result would not be good. First of all, the V would conclude, no matter what kind of lie I tell them regarding the genesis of the note, that the note, being wet, got that way because it was deposited in the bath where I picked it up. Next, I would be "punished." Next, there would be a camp wide investigation and others would be punished. And, next, and maybe not last, we would lose the only means that we have of communicating between buildings.

As calmly as I can, I wait. Another fear I have is that the V will open the shutter which covers my barred window and see me reading the note. I carefully choreograph the moves I must make to retrieve and read the note such that, even if witnessed, the V would not suspect anything unusual.

I wait as long as I can stand it. I cross the room and survey the compound. I discern a lull in guard activity and wait no longer. I move back to my bunk and begin my previously choreographed movements.

I move my folded blanket and mosquito net to the end of the bed closest to the barred window with the outside shutter that must be opened for them to look into my room. I can then sit on my bed with the window in view. If the shutter opens, I will be facing the window and will be shaping my blanket and mosquito net as if preparing to lie down. If the V are suspicious, they will have to open my door to check me out. In that case, I can easily get the note into my mouth and have it down before they realize what is happening. I open the blanket and extract the note. The markings are clear and easily readable.

```
l  l    lll   l llll l   ll llll     lll l   l llll   l l lll lll   lll lll l
lll lllll lll  ll lllll llll  llll lll     llll lll l llll   lll l ll lllll  llll lll lllll

ll l llll    ll   ll  lll    l l   llll ll l   llll
ll ll lllll    lllll llll ll    ll lllll ll  ll lllll ll
```

This is my first experience at reading Tap Code. It's more difficult than aural reception. If this message were tapped to me, I could easily read it. But, this series of marks made by a lead tooth paste tube,"sharpened" by rubbing it on a concrete floor, confuses me for a moment.

I stare at the marks and recall my original conversation with Ron Mastin when he said: "Take the alphabet, throw out the letter K, form a five letter box, A B C D E across the top, A F L Q V down the left side. To tap a letter, type down and then across. For example, the letter M is: tap, tap, tap (pause), tap, tap. Use the letter C for K...."

I visualize the box and then the marks make sense. The writer is depicting the "down" tap above the "across" tap, thus the first letter is either C or K, since we use C for K as well as for C. The next letter is also in the first row and is the 5th letter across, which is E. The third letter is the third letter across the third row--N. The first three sets of characters are in a group and are separated from the next group which is also a three letter word. Literally, the first word is "Cen," but since we use c for k, it could be "Ken." I go on to the second group of three with this logic and the translation is "Bud." Following on, the message translates: "cen bud is ok at camp one gbu jim berger." GBU always translates "God Bless You."

GBU indeed, Jim Berger, and thank God that you and Bud are alive.

It's been a while since I spent several weeks taking care of Bud's military estate. I recall noting each of his belongings on an inventory sheet. Per the Summary Courts instructions and applicable regulations, his military equipment went back into inventory, and all of his personal belongings went to his wife. It took me a while to get it all together. Of course his friends gathered about for a party to celebrate his demise, to toast him and Jim Berger, and to consume all of his "consumables," including cigars, a gallon of Bombay Gin, with some appropriate accompaniment. Later I sold his motorcycle, packed the remainder of his personalty in his "hold baggage," and sent them home to his Sue.

Ensign Roger Staubach signed the shipping order. The crate arrived at Sue's home a few days later.

I wonder who got that job for me.

If this vignette were made into a movie scene, I would direct the camera crew to segue from the translation episode to a gradual withdrawal via a near-vertical path through the roof and into the distance leaving the translator seated on the bed with the small piece of V toilet paper in his hand in a pose not much different than Rodin's "The Thinker." The music: The second movement of Mozart's 21st Piano Concerto.

LIFE CONTINUES AT THE PLANTATION

September 4, 1967 is Labor Day at home. It is also Labor Day here. It's been nearly two weeks since Jim Berger's note reached me. I have kept a close eye on the yard from my secret peephole since then. I have seen Jim Berger and Bill Bailey and their roommates from time to time when they emerge to bathe or empty their buckets. I know no one else in this camp.

Today, the morning bowl parade begins early. As soon as it ends, a group of laborers enters the camp through the gate adjacent to my cell. They are pushing a wheel barrow and a two wheeled cart loaded with bricks, cement, and tools. They meander across the yard and park in front of cell five of the Warehouse and busy themselves inside cell 5. They remove the wooden door and framing from the wall that separates cells five and six, and, although I can't see the wall from my vantage point, I know that they are closing up the wall as well. They finish the job before the day is over and leave.

September 5, 1967 is ending. All the usual activities are complete. Soon it is dark and bedtime is approaching. I hear a commotion outside and move to my peephole in the shutters to take a look outside. It is apparent that a shuffle is either occurring or about to occur. The gate opens and a small bus pulls into the camp. It parks at an angle such that I can't see the occupants, but a few, maybe half a dozen, exit. Several V guards and I watch as it expels the new arrivals.

The V busy themselves placing the newcomers and making other shuffles between the Gun Shed and the Warehouse. When they finish, the Turnkey, accompanied by two AK-47 bearers who keep their distance, moves to my door. In a minute or so he opens my door and steps inside and motions me to roll up my belongings. I roll my stuff, and the Turnkey steps aside and motions me to step outside. The AK-47s do the standard *pas de deux*, and the Turnkey motions and grunts to let me know where to stop and stand as he closes the cell doors. He then signals me to follow him across the prison yard. Several off-duty guards are sitting and standing about the big house front porch and others are moving about in the yard. Three of them are hanging out around, and on, an 85 mm howitzer that sits in the middle of the compound and was probably captured along with the French Army that surrendered at Dien Bien Phu in 1954. None of them pay any attention to us.

The Turnkey goes directly toward the open door of Warehouse cell number 6. As he nears the open door, he steps aside and motions me to enter. The bed board is positioned along the south wall, opposite the wall that had housed a wooden door when cell number 5 was a pantry and later after it had been converted to a cell and where Bill Bailey had spent a few days. The doorway is gone. The wall is now a newly finished brick and stucco, matching the rest of the building. I place my belongings on the bed and the bucket fits into the front corner of the room--the corner near the wall where the wooden door used to be. The turnkey waits patiently for me to finish, and for me to bow politely so he can close and lock the door.

I unroll my sleeping mat and center it on my bed. I then place my blankets and clothing on the end of the bed next to the inside wall. There are nails in the front, side, and back walls to support a mosquito net. I have enough string to hang the net, and soon I'm in a prone position inside the net with the edges of the net tucked under the straw mat. My back is essentially 100%. I have no problem moving about and have begun an exercise regimen that includes push-ups, sit-ups, crunches, side-straddle-hops, and just walking in circles or back and forth. I feel healthy and strong and am a good bit skinnier than when I arrived. The putative pot I was wearing when the old peasant popped me across the belly a few minutes after my capture is gone. Here's my big chance to produce some abs.

I wonder what will happen next, when I hear voices, the rattle of keys and the general set of noises that accompany the opening and closing of cell doors. The V are opening cell 5, and from the sound of things I know that I am gaining a neighbor. Up until now, I have spoken or tapped to only three of my fellows, and, with the exception of Bill Bailey, those contacts have been far too brief. I look forward to tomorrow and to learning about my new neighbor.

On September 6, 1967, the morning activity today precludes any contact with my new neighbor. I hoped to get a glimpse of him during the bucket parade by standing on one of the saw horses that support my bed. Unfortunately I only get a glimpse of his back as he rounds the corner of the Big House and then just a momentary shot as he returns. I will ask him to walk as far away from Warehouse front wall as he can so I can see him. He is medium height with brown hair and is a bit huskier than I am.

Noon comes and goes and it is time for siesta. The camp bell signals siesta time, and the guards make one final round opening the peepholes in each cell to see that we are all still here and not doing anything that we shouldn't be. The camp becomes quiet. I wait a few minutes and then move to the wall that separates my cell from Cell 5. I tap "shave and a hair-cut" on the wall and get an immediate six bits response. We start to communicate. I soon learn that I am talking to 1/Lt Loren Torkelson from the 389th TFS, my sister squadron at Da Nang. Loren was shot down on April 29, 1967.

Loren tells me that he has 170 names of POWs and asks if I want to memorize them. I say yes, and we agree that he will begin sending names at our next communication session. I am excited about having what I hope will be a steady contact and am anxious to get started with the names as well.

Loren and I begin by discussing a schedule for regular communications. Siesta time is nearly always quiet, but sometimes a lone guard will sneak around very quietly and remain very close to the front wall so that we can't see or hear him until suddenly our peep hole pops open. We develop a plan to make us look innocent in case one of us is surprised. The surprised party will bump the wall and then pretend to be doing something else. We both keep our buckets in the corner of our respective cells such that, in terms of distance, the buckets are less than two feet apart, and we are both close to our bucket. Therefore the "something else" that we will appear to be doing is using the bucket.

After we have become acquainted and I have passed Risner's Rules, Loren starts sending names. He suggests three at a time. I say ok to that, and we begin. He explains that the names are arranged alphabetically by rank and service, and that he will begin with the Air Force list. Since there were no known Colonels (0-6s), Loren begins with the 0-5 (Lt Colonel) list. It is short-- Robbie Risner. He continues with the Majors (0-4s). I begin to assimilate the names, and soon discover that I can deal with bigger batches than I expected. With nothing else to do, I soon have the names cold. I use my fingers to keep track of each batch of ten.

Loren stops to add a comment to two names. The first stop occurs with the first Navy Lieutenant Commander. We had just finished the Navy Commanders and Loren taps out the header "LCDRs." I acknowledge that we are beginning the Lieutenant Commander (LCDR) list and stand by waiting for the first name on the list. Instead of a name, he taps the following message: "The next name is a classic." I acknowledge with the standard two taps in rapid succession, and he taps the name: "Cole Black."

We complete the LCDR and Lieutenant lists and begin the Lt/j.g. list with Wendell Alcorn. The second Lt/j.g. is Everett Alvarez, Jr. I tap twice and wait for the next name, but instead here comes a message: "Shot down 5 August 64." This is the first time I have heard Everett Alvarez' name. I knew that the Navy had some losses and that at least one early shoot down was a POW, but had long since stopped thinking about it and had never known his name. Now I have a name and a date. I hesitate as my legs become a little weak, and I feel a tear welling up somewhere behind each eye, and wonder: *"How is he?--at least he's alive, or he wouldn't be on the list--how is his health? How has he survived? I've already lost several pounds and my legs have become more birdlike than ever. At this rate in another three years I will be nothing but skin and bones."* I tap twice and then sign off to take a break.

September gradually moves by and October takes its place. The Camp routine is just that--largely routine. The V occasionally "entertain" us with sessions in the Big House. The routine begins with the Turnkey showing up at the door. The door opens and the Turnkey signals with his hands that we are to put on long pants and long sleeved pajama tops. He then escorts us to a room in the Big House where we are greeted by various officers who speak English. There are usually two, but sometimes only one. They always remind us of the great generosity of the Vietnamese People who treat us humanely and leniently in spite of the fact that we are criminals. Sometimes, they offer a cigarette, and sometimes tea and cookies, and sometimes nothing. The "nothing' sessions are usually conducted by more senior and more serious hosts. These sessions are brain washing sessions condemning the American Government for waging an illegal, unjust, and cruel war against the Democratic Republic of Viet Nam.

Sometime during each of these sessions the V inquire about our health and ask if there is anything we want or need. I always ask for two things: I want to write a letter home, and I want books. They are always non-committal about both, but sometimes I have a chance to specify the books I want. I keep repeating The Bible and Shakespeare's works, hoping that by limiting my request to specifics, they just might acquiesce. As time goes by, I realize that even if the V agree to allowing any of us to have books they will never allow The Bible or Shakespeare, so I begin requesting Karl Marx's *Das Kapital* and works by other prose writers who supported the soviet revolution hoping they might allow us to read the foundation of their views on Communism. Sometimes they take notes, and sometimes they simply nod and go on to other subjects.

Some of these sessions are conducted by what appear to be total outsiders. One, whom I see on several occasions, makes me think that he may be a graduate student practicing his English. One of his sessions begins with the question: "So, what does a staff officer in the U.S. Air Force think about the illegal and unjust war America is conducting against the sovereign government and people of the Democratic Republic of Viet Nam?" He smiles as though the canary is just about to emerge from his mouth the next time it opens. The genesis of the question is that in previous conversations with this person, I have "explained" to him that my combat tour in South Viet Nam had ended and that I was a staff "weenie" who had nothing to do with combat operations. This statement was partially true. My "official" combat tour had ended. I just had to explain that I was just a few miles from Ha Noi when I was shot down because on that day there was a shortage of crews and I was "drafted" to go along on another mission. I had already told the V that I had flown more than 500 combat sorties. They seem to have gotten over that issue by acting like they never heard of it.

Since I arrived here, we bathe outside behind the Warehouse about midway between the ends of the building at bath #1. (Figure 7.) The water supply is an open trough made of brick. There is a small bucket for dipping the water and a wooden shelf to place our dry clothes and towel. The routine for bathing is to grab your soap and towel and a clean change of clothes and head for the bath area. The turnkey has made it clear that we are not to waste time. As soon I arrive at the bath, I stow my dry clothes and strip. I use the bucket to douse my body, then soap up and rinse. Then I wash my dirty clothes, get dressed and return to my room.

A railroad track runs parallel to the back wall of the Warehouse about fifty feet from the building. On more than one occasion, a train towing flatbed cars eases by as I bathe. The workers wave and stare and laugh. There are always women in the work force, and I discover that I am an exhibitionist. The women laugh and point at my nude body and the Turnkey screams at me to get dressed.

Today, when I go to the bath, the locomotive is towing a group of flatcars in the opposite direction. All the other times when the flatbeds are loaded with workers the train has been moving toward the North. Today it is headed south, and there is a long string of flatbeds behind it as it creeps by. The flatbeds are supporting a long steel truss structure, obviously a bridge span. There are workers all over the place adjusting the base supports as the train tugs the string of flatbeds around a curve, and the train has to stop every few feet to allow the workers to adjust the long span onto the flatbeds as they traverse the curve. I realize now that I know fairly exactly where I am. Until today I could not see that the railroad curved to the east as it ran north of this camp, nor did I think about a bridge. This camp is just south of the Paul Doumer Bridge that spans the Red River around the curve.

I now understand the horrible commotion on August 11. The span of the bridge is visibly damaged and the workmen are moving it for repair or maybe replacement. Our strike force did its job on August 11, and now, about two months later, here are some of the results. I return to my cell and listen to the sounds of the creeping train and the voices of the workmen nearly all day as they jockey the bridge span around the curve. It finally creeps out of range of my ears as the day ends.

Today I think about the conversation I had with Ron Mastin back in July when he speculated that we "...wouldn't be home much before Christmas." The way we have been conducting this war, the only way that we will ever get home is for the V to throw up their hands and leave South Viet Nam alone, and nobody believes that will happen. I think about the constant complaints of all the fighter jocks I know, and how the apparent stupidity, or total incompetence, among whoever is planning our strikes costs us losses that we need not incur. In particular, during today, and other days I wonder about the fate of Bill Baugh and Don Spoon and flashback to the back-to-back MigCAP missions described in "Flying the Airways," earlier in this missive.

My reverie of Baugh and Spoon plays out, and I am back at the Plantation. I wonder where Baugh and Spoon are today. Were they injured during the bail out? I wonder if they were as lucky as I was during the process of being captured.

During these days, there are occasional rearrangements between various cells, and there is one transfer in which new occupants arrive and some leave. During this process, Loren and I stay put. The transfer occurs on a week night (nearly all the movements of POWs between camps occur at night). We hear the usual commotion of the gate opening and the buses or trucks coming in and out, the guards talking, and the opening and closing of doors and look forward to the next morning to viewing the bucket parade to see the new line ups.

The morning after the new guys arrive, I am standing on my saw horse looking out the vent hole above my door as early as possible. I make two quick shifts that require some rapid movements in getting down from my saw horse perch and replacing the saw horse under the bed board. These shifts occur when the guard brings around the cigarettes, and when it is my turn to empty my bucket. Other than that, I am watching the prison yard as closely as I can. I'm sure that mine is not the only pair of eyeballs that are busy with the same surveillance.

I don't recognize any of the newbies as they parade room by room from the Gun Shed, the Corn Crib, and the Warehouse. After these are finished, the Turnkey heads for the Movie Room that has been vacant since I last lived there. I watch with great interest as he opens the door and am surprised when the second guy out of the room, carrying two buckets, is Mel. The first man out is thin and looks a little taller than I am. He has some gray hair and walks a little stiffly, as though he may be recovering from some kind of injury. He carries one bucket. I don't see the third man who must own one of those buckets and must not be able to carry his own bucket. I know that Mel must have discovered the peep hole in the shuttered window, and he must have seen me when I made the trip that he is making now. Just need to figure out a way to communicate with him and his roommates.

The day progresses and Loren and I talk when we can. He has already clued me in as to the camp line-up prior to this shuffle, and we have solid communications with all rooms in the Warehouse on a daily basis, and with the Gun Shed and Corn Crib via irregular note drops in the bath. We will still have those lines of communications, assuming that there is at least one prior Plantation dweller in both the Corn Crib and Gun Shed. The Movie Room is a problem. We don't know who Mel's third roommate is, but it's pretty certain that he is new to the Plantation, since, prior to this move, we didn't have anyone here who couldn't carry his own bucket.

There are several ways that we may be able to contact the Movie Room and inform them of the note drop, and then begin a note exchange with them. Sometimes the V allow some of us out in the Prison yard. If that happens, and if they know the tap code, we could use our hands to communicate with the tap code by flashing with our fingers. If we are assigned to sweep in the yard, which sometimes happens, we could send a tap code message by sweeping the tap code.

If they don't know the tap code, we will have to bide our time and hope that we have a creative opportunity. If some of us get the job of delivering their food, as Dick Stratton and Doug Hegdahl delivered mine, there might be a chance to place a note in their soup. Getting new guys in the loop with us is our number one mission. There might be a way to scratch some kind of signal on the wall where we empty the buckets that only an American would notice.

I watch the parade daily in the hope of seeing the third man in the Movie Room. The weather has been a bit chilly since the move. The days have been mostly overcast with little or no sun and with occasional drizzle. Then we have a cloudless day with a bright sun. The bucket parade is late and the Movie room is last. I am at my post standing on my saw horse when the turnkey opens the Movie Room door. Mel and the man with some gray hair step out and head for the honey tank. The turnkey growls at them and they stop and put down the buckets they are carrying. The turnkey stands in the door, motions, speaks to someone inside, and steps aside. Both the double doors are now open. A man on crutches hobbles into view. He is moving slowly and his right leg is in a cast covering his entire leg. He is about my height. His hair is light--not blond but more like a caramel color. He moves out into the sunlight and stops. The turnkey speaks to Mel and the man with some gray hair and follows them as they pick up the three buckets and resume their trek to the honey tank.

The man on crutches stands alone with his crutches squeezed tightly under his armpits with his upper arms. I watch as he raises his right hand to his forehead, bows his head, and stands for several minutes as though posing for a Rodin work that might be called "The Prayer."

In a few minutes, the Turnkey returns with Mel and the man with some gray hair in tow. The bucket carriers go into the room, and the man on crutches hobbles back inside. The Turnkey closes, bars, and locks the double doors to the Movie Room. I return my saw horse to its rightful place and sit down on my bed to contemplate the scene I just witnessed.

Soon we sort out the new Warehouse line up. It will take a little longer to catch up with the Corn Crib and the Gun Shed. The Movie Room, except for Mel, remains a mystery.

A week or so drags by, and Loren calls up for our first communication of the day. It is early in November and unusually chilly. Loren begins by telling me that the two strangers in the Movie Room are LtCol Swede Larson and LCDR Collie Haines. Collie Haines was seriously injured when he made a very low bail out of an RF-8. (Later I learn that Haines full name is Collins H. and that Collie is pronounced Coal E.) Apparently someone in the Gun Shed recognized them.

Swede and Collie
November 29 arrives on a cold note. There is some sun, but not the warm kind. I watch the bucket parade as always, just in case something unusual happens. We get our first meal--a bowl of soup and a plate of rice with vegetables. Not long after our meal the V begin a rare event--a room shuffle in the broad daylight of mid-day. I watch as much as I can of the few room changes in the all the buildings except the Movie room. It looks like the Movie Room will remain as is. Then, when the shuffle seems to be over, the Turnkey heads for the Movie Room with the usual

AK-47 accompaniment. He opens the door and signals with his hands and says something to the occupants and then waits at the open door for a couple of minutes. He steps back and aside, and out comes Mel carrying his rolled up belongings under one arm and his crockery water pitcher in his free hand. Mel stands in the yard while the turnkey closes the cell door, and then the turnkey directs Mel toward the Gun Shed.

Mel winds up in Gun Shed 3, and the turnkey and AK head my way. As they near my cell, I realize that I am the next transferee and scramble to replace the saw horse as the Turnkey unlocks my door. He stands in the open door and waits for a polite bow, then gives me the hand signals to roll up and prepare to move. I grab my stuff and follow him out the door and across the yard to the Movie Room, remorseful for losing contact with Loren Torkelson, but pleased to have the 170 name roster in my head.

We cross the prison yard to the Movie Room, and when we arrive in front of the Movie Room the eight foot long bar that the V use to secure the cell is standing vertical on the left side of the double doors. The turnkey moves ahead of me and swings the doors open wide. Collie and Swede are standing near the middle of the room. Swede is to my right and his bed is in the far right corner of the room. Collie is near the middle of the room and his bed is in the center of the back wall. There is a third bed to my far left in the far left corner from me. I step inside, walk across the room, and place my belongings on the bed in that is obviously to be mine. I turn and face the Turnkey who waits patiently for us to bow politely. When I face the doors I see a small wooden table and three stools in near the front wall between my bed and the wall. The table would have been to my left as I entered the room. The doors close, and I greet my new roommates. We shake hands and our initial meeting is very formal and quiet. These two are both the calm quiet type, and we don't have a lot to say. I am fairly bursting to talk to them, and want to ask a lot of questions, but attempt to meld with them in their quiet way.

Swede suggests that we sit at the table. Collie hobbles over and takes the stool nearest to his bed so that he is facing the front wall of our room. I take the stool nearest the front of the room with my back to the boarded up window and the front wall. Swede is on my right and Collie sits across the table from me. We start to talk about our last missions and how we got here, but are interrupted by the turnkey opening the door. We stand, and the turnkey motions to Swede and me to prepare to go for a bath. We each grab our towels, soap, and a clean change of clothes and head for the bath area behind the Warehouse. We bathe outside, wash our dirty clothes, and put on the clean clothes we brought with us. When we finish, we walk back toward our room and stop on the way to hang our wet laundry on a clothes line in the prison yard.

Swede is obviously not 100% in terms of physical condition. He is thin. His upper arms are deeply scarred from the rope torture in the same Green Room that we all passed through. His left arm is weak from muscle damage inflicted by the ropes. He walks a bit stiffly, but he does not complain. Swede is a tough customer. I know that I am in good company.

When we get back to our cell we all feel the cold, and soon we are all in long sleeved pajamas with our sweatshirts underneath. Collie and Swede start to loosen up a bit, and we begin sharing more details of our prior history before and after our capture.

Swede and Collie were both tortured in the Green room and wear the scars to prove it. In addition to the scars on their arms, both have other problems.

Collie's hands are partially paralyzed. He has no feeling in the two smallest fingers of both hands. In addition, he was seriously injured during the bail out. The airplane was insisting on rolling left, and Collie was giving it all the opposite correction he could find, including full right aileron and right rudder to the fire wall. Whatever battle damage his F-8 had sustained was producing more left roll signal than the remaining flight controls could overcome. With the surface of Mother Earth approaching at a quantum pace, and with his right leg holding the right rudder fully depressed, and things getting worse by the millisecond, Collie had lost the battle for control of his bird. He turned loose of the stick and throttle and reached up and back with both hands and pulled the ejection curtain down over his face. As he left the airplane his right leg was still fully extended. The result was not pretty.

Collie arrived in Ha Noi with a universal joint where his knee used to be, in a lot of pain, and soon bumped into one of the Torturer's cohorts known as "The Rabbit." At one point Collie found himself in the ropes and suffering mightily, thinking he could stand the pain no more. Unfortunately, when he arrived at this point, the Rabbit had left the Green Room and was playing a game of table tennis just a few yards away. The result was that when Rabbit returned and undid the ropes, the outside of both of Collie's hands had no feeling, and the two smallest fingers of both hands were paralyzed. After Collie had acquiesced and answered some innocuous questions, he was taken to a hospital where he underwent surgery. Now he spends hours each day massaging and shaking his hands, and his leg is in a cast from ankle to waist.

Swede's left arm is too weak to carry a bucket, and his whole body seems sore and stiff. His handsome countenance is strained from suffering. He is quiet and still most of the time and speaks with a deep chested rumble.

On his 94th Mission over North Viet Nam, Swede was leading a flight of four F-105s against a military barracks about 15 miles South of Ha Noi. As Swede came off the target, he looked around to check how his wingmen were doing. Number 2 was smoking and lagging behind. Swede made a 180-degree turn intending to escort his number two to safety. In the middle of all this, Number 2's airplane burst into flames and Number 2 ejected. At that time Swede was in a nose low turn, and his airplane took a hit from what he believed to be a SAM that he never saw. Near the speed of sound, with not enough elevator control to lift the nose to the horizon, he tried lowering the landing gear to correct the nose low attitude, but apparently the air loads were too much for the gear lowering system to overcome. He was soon supersonic, and the cockpit began to fill with smoke. A great movie scene ensued as he fumbled for the ejection handle in the smoke filled cockpit and ejected into a supersonic slipstream. This, and three weeks with Ha Noi's champion torturer, affectionately known as "The Bug," "Wall-Eye," or "The Torturer," were certainly enough to reduce the toughest of the tough to a crippled arm, a body stiff and painful to deal with, and a strained countenance.

I've landed in the room with two of our very best. What will they think of me when I tell them how long I didn't last in Room 18?

Neither Collie nor Swede is able to do anything close to a "real" workout. Swede moves about as much as he can on his feet and does as much calisthenics as he can muster. Collie spends as much time as he can hobbling about or just standing while we talk. When he stands, he rocks back and forth on his crutches. I can do push-ups and just about anything else I want to do, but I don't do nearly enough. I was doing more when I was alone, but I feel like a show off even thinking about a real workout in the presence of these two who were crippled in the same room where I caved in early and got a bye.

Swede and Collie discovered the same peephole that I had used in the shutter covering the bars in the left front window and have been keeping tabs on the bucket and bath parade just as I did. Since I am by far the healthiest in the bunch, I am welcome to become the principal look out.

The first time we are served a meal, Swede and Collie examine the main course for the presence of meat. As they move their food around in their respective plates, they explain to me what they are doing and why the presence (or lack thereof) of pork is so important. Sometime before each meal is served, they wager on the contents of the dishes. Our meals consist of a bowl of soup and a plate of some solid vegetable. The vegetables vary meal by meal, but the choices the V have are limited. Some of the possibilities are cabbage, kohlrabi (Swede and Collie have changed kohlrabi to rutabagas and shortened it to 'bagas), potatoes, greens (a green vegetable which I had eaten in South Viet Nam and grew in ponds something like water lilies and which we also called *alfalfa* because we thought that it smelled and tasted like alfalfa). Most of the time the plate with the solid dish is accompanied with rice, but, very occasionally they substitute a piece of bread.

Swede and Collie had instituted a bureaucratic procedure for establishing the wager. They take turns as to which will make the first call. For the first meal I share with them it is Collie's turn to call first. His call: "'Bagas, pork, rice, and green soup." Swede likes Collie's call. By their rules, the second caller has a right to challenge the first caller for the right to his pick. Swede challenges Collie. The call is now up for grabs. The rules require a finger throw--two out of three wins--to determine who gets the call.

The finger throw goes like this: Each player makes a fist with one hand and cocks his arm. One of the players counts "1,2,3." On each count each player "throws" his fist by extending his arm. The first two counts establish the timing, and on the third count, the fists come down to stay. As the "throw" ends each player can extend one finger, or two fingers, or a closed fist. A single finger represents paper, two fingers are scissors, and a closed fist is rock. The rule mantra is: "Rock dulls scissors, paper wraps rock, and scissors cut paper." If both players throw the same, repeat the process until they differ and apply the mantra. As an example, if the two are us are contestants, and I throw a fist (rock) and you throw one finger (paper), you win because the rule mantra is paper wraps rock. If you had thrown two fingers (scissors), I win because rock dulls scissors.

In the case at hand, Swede has challenged Collie's call and the two throw fingers, best two out of three. Swede wins. Now Swede has the "bagas. Pork. Rice and green soup" choice, and Collie has to make a different choice. He stays with 'bagas, leaves out the pork, and goes with "bagas, rice, and green soup."

The meal arrives. There's no doubt that both were on the right track. The dishes are obviously bagas with rice and green soup. This means the discriminator is whether or not there is any identifiable pork in any of the dishes. By searching carefully, Swede finds a small slither of fat and racks up a dollar. We all agree that I can join in the game if I choose. After a few meals I join the game.

To make our conversations and communications easier, we go over the names we will use for various V personnel. It is soon apparent that the vicious bugger with the wandering eyeball and the Hitler forelock is the same one that crippled Swede and Collie. He already has three names that we know of--The Bug, Walleye, or The Torturer. We decide to use The Bug because it is the shortest. We name our Turnkey "Bill." I am the only one of the three of us that met the Oxford accent, so he remains unnamed for the moment. We name others as they become important enough to deserve a name.

September is soon gone and October is slipping by as well. During this time, we share more details about ourselves. Collie was flying off the *USS Bonne Homme Richard* and had flown forty missions prior to his shoot down on 5 June--a month before me. He soon arrived in Room 18 of Heartbreak Hotel with a useless right leg. Like all who went through Room 18, he held out as long as he could before answering question number 5, and like the rest he wound up answering the ones that mattered with lies that he hoped he could remember. He doesn't complain about his partially paralyzed hands, or about the torture, or his crippled leg.

Swede was the Commander of the 469th Tactical Fighter Squadron at Korat Royal Thai Air Base--a fact that he did not wish the V to know. For a week or so, after having been broken, he kept it to himself via a series of lies. He was doing pretty well with his lies (or so he thought) when the Bug came to Room 18, placed his notebook and pen on the table along with a piece of paper with some writing on one side, placed separately on the table with the writing side down. He then asked Swede a few questions regarding Swede's prior activities, and Swede kept to his lies. After a few questions, The Bug reached for the paper with the writing, and handed it to Swede. Swede took it and read the contents: *LtCol. Gordon A. Larson, Commander, 469th TFS, Korat.*

Swede was already a broken man. The V had tortured him with the ropes until he answered Question number five. No matter to The Bug. Swede spent several more days in this torture chamber paying for his lies before The Bug spit him out into the fellowship of the rest of us "Criminals" as though he was but dross. Here was the model for a painting by Maxine McCaffrey depicting the epitome of the fighter pilot profession; a man who had taken young, would-be fighter pilots under his wing and molded them into tough professionals; who had flown "Chrome Dome" missions as a B-52 Aircraft Commander; and commanded an F-105 Fighter Squadron--one of the toughest of the tough.

Late in October a turkey shows up in the Camp. Collie has had his cast removed and hobbles a bit faster as a result, but has to use crutches to get around. Collie now shares most of the peep-hole duty with me, and the "old man" takes a look when he chooses, or when either Collie or I report something interesting or amusing or otherwise seems to be important. The turkey brings up a good bit of discussion. First, all three of us know that the turkey is native only to North America, and traditionally, we believe that the Pilgrims had turkey on their table at the first Thanksgiving Day back in 1626. So, how did this turkey get here? I had spent some time visiting provincial areas in the northern part of South Viet Nam, and had never seen a turkey anywhere--plenty of chickens, pigs, buffalos, and ducks--no turkeys. The turkey is a mix of black and white.

Christmas is coming soon--is the turkey here to be somebody's dinner at Christmas? If so, do North Viets have turkey for Christmas dinner? I have spent Christmas twice in South Viet Nam and am well aware that the Viets I knew did not have turkey for Christmas dinner. Could it be that the V would serve this turkey to us for Christmas?

We name the turkey George.

Sometimes, particularly when it's cold, I grab blankets and sit with Swede on Swede's bed. We bundle up in the Lotus position and sit like two Indian Chiefs having a personal pow-wow. Swede is an investor and would-be entrepreneur. While he was stationed in San Antonio, he looked into the business of raising chickens for food. Swede and I discuss starting a chicken business as a joint venture so that we can share the load, and take a vacation once in while without worry about the business.

There are several reasons that Swede's idea has some appeal. First of all, even if it never happens, I am learning things about business that I never thought about before. Swede explains how the business operates in the San Antonio area, which is probably about how it works anywhere. Another reason that I like Swede's plan is that while I was alone before I moved here, I had prepared a plan to raise pigs. In my head I did as complete an analysis as I could with "pretend" data. I modeled my analysis and plan after the methodology I learned while working in the advanced planning office at Air Force Space Systems Division (SSD). I recall my early days at SSD when it was....

Fall 1961

I have finished my allotted two years studying Aeronautical Engineering at the University of Colorado at Boulder, Colorado (CU) and am assigned to the Directorate which does advanced planning for military space programs. The idea is to identify the technologies necessary to execute future plans. One of those projects is a manned flight to Mars. In 1961, the nearest time in the future that Earth and Mars would be positioned so as to allow the most synergistic round trip is 1975. A launch in late 1974 will result in about four months on the surface of Mars with a return flight in 1975. At this time, this mission has virtually no priority, and we don't spend a lot of time doing details; however, we do identify "paper" numbers for sizing all the elements based on current understanding of the technologies necessary to accomplish the mission. I also worked on various reentry vehicle designs, laser technology, and hyper velocity ballistic collision research.

When an idea reached a certain point, the next step was to prepare a Proposed System Package Plan (PSPP). The PSPP would define the product and how it would fulfill a specific objective. One such plan floating around the Department of Defense (DOD) was for a comprehensive space defense system. The pricing section began with a definition of Gross National Product (GNP). Because of the projected time line for development and deployment and the extremely high cost, there was no way to put a price tag on the project. The planners could, however, estimate the percentage of national resources required to protect ourselves from missiles carrying nuclear warheads.

I decided to model my pig farm plan after the PSPP format and call it a "Proposed System for Pork Production (PSPP).

The first step in PSPP preparation was to define the system and objectives. My system definition included the objective of producing the finest pigs in the world and selling them for a profit. We had raised pigs on our farm when I was growing up, and, as a Future Farmer of America, I had shown a pig and a calf at the contests in Memphis. I didn't win any prizes, but I learned the fundamentals of how to plan and market animals for food.

I iterated several breeding cycles and developed numbers for food, water, facilities, and marketing, and juggled all the variables I could come up with, to produce what I believed to be a viable operation. I created a template that included feed prices, housing costs, transportation, and a number of other variables to test the viability of my design. There was no guarantee that my template was anywhere near an accurate algorithm for success. Even if it wasn't, if I decided to get serious about the business, I could very quickly identify the "long poles" that I would have to deal with.

Swede had done a lot of homework before he was shot down, and had fairly detailed plans for implementing the chicken business. His plan was to find a partner, and since I am the only one around to compete for that position (Collie is more interested in the automobile business), I am the prime candidate and am flattered to be considered. We plan to proceed as soon as we get out of the predicament we're in right now.

Collie is getting stronger since the V removed his cast. Inactivity does not set well with Collie. He was a varsity basketball player in high school, and after graduation from high school, he enrolled at Duke University intent on playing basketball, but didn't make the cut. I'm just as certain as Collie is certain that it was solely because of his height--or lack thereof. I am 5 feet ten inches tall and Collie is a bit shorter than I am. He must have been one terrific hoopster to have even been considered for the varsity at a perennial basketball power house like Duke.

Collie completed his first year at Duke and went home to Palmyra, New Jersey to plan his next move. Being rejected by Duke was stinging his hide, and he needed to do something to get over it and press on. During the summer, Collie met a high school friend who was enrolled at Muhlenberg College in Allentown, Pennsylvania and was now a member of the Muhlenberg varsity football squad. He urges Collie to come to Muhlenberg and try out for the football team. Having no better plan, Collie enrolls at Muhlenberg and tries out for football team. This dream came true. Collie lettered three years at Muhlenberg--1951, 52, and 53.

After joining the Navy, Collie played "Service Football" while on his way to becoming a Naval Aviator. Collie is a "jock." Now, he is doing all that he can do to stay in shape, so he moves around all that he can on his crutches, works to restore the feeling in his partially paralyzed hands, and spends more and more time at the peep hole.

As the calendar moves toward Thanksgiving, the weather is becoming unbearably cold, especially for Swede, who is still suffering from the torture he endured immediately after capture. As we talk, and I learn more about his sessions with The Bug, I am more astonished and troubled at what he has been through. It is no surprise that the V paid more attention to senior officers, and Swede's travails in the torture chamber, where all of us were systematically broken, is an example. He suffers from the cold. He spends a lot of time in the lotus position carefully bundled in his blankets trying to stay warm. I sometimes sit on his bed with him when we talk, while Collie moves about the room in between his stints at the peep hole.

Today, Swede and I are reviewing the Chicken business and other issues while Collie is maintaining watch over the goings on in the Prison yard. Collie takes a break and, and with a few adept swings on his crutches, he parks himself facing us and waits for an opportunity to get in the conversation. Swede and I soon hit a good place to pause, and focus on Collie. Collie opens up with something like: "You know, I think George is turning black." Swede and I are all ears, and Swede is somewhat amused. All three of us take turns at the peephole and all three of us are well aware of George's appearance. The turkey is obviously a mix of black and white ancestry, but is more white than black. I am incredulous that Collie has paid so much attention to George and am also positive in my own mind that George is not going to change color.

Both Swede and Collie enjoy the gambling game, and I am soon witnessing a detailed negotiating process to establish the guidelines and criteria for a wager regarding George's future either as a black turkey or a white turkey. Swede asks Collie to define the terms of the wager. Collie says that he is betting that George will have more black feathers than white feathers by the coming Christmas. Swede asks who is going to count the feathers. Collie floors me with his response: "Huge will call the shot. If, on Christmas day, Huge thinks George has more black feathers than white, I win. If Huge thinks that George is still mostly white, you win." (By this time, I have been given the alias *Huge*.)

They agree on Collie's terms, I am sworn in as the judge, and George becomes the focus of a lot of attention.

Keeping warm is a struggle, especially for Swede. He has discovered that by assuming the lotus position for an hour or so before bedtime, and by keeping his feet tucked into his groin, that he can warm his feet to the point that they will stay warm all night. I try it and it works. Collie's crippled leg is difficult to deal with, but he does his best.

I am manning the peep hole one morning after the bucket parade and before our first meal when the main gate opens, and a V peasant moves into view from my left as he proceeds into the camp pushing a two wheeled cart. He stops and lowers a rear leg on the cart, and the cart stands on two big wheels and the leg.

Several guards and the Turnkey gather around the cart and inspect its contents. I provide a blow by blow to Collie, who stands to my right and relays to Swede who is in the Lotus position on his bed trying to stay warm. The V are looking at the contents of the cart and we can't wait to see what it is. Finally, Bill (the name we have selected for our Turnkey) reaches into the cart and pulls out an Air Force blue blanket. An officer appears out of the Big House and has a conversation with the Turnkey and guards, and then waves his hands pointing around the Camp as he talks. He is soon finished and walks away. Bill talks to the peasant who pushes his cart toward the Gun Shed. He follows the turnkey to the Gun Shed and begins dispensing blankets.

In a few minutes, the cart has made the rounds and is heading for our front window. As it nears, Collie and I move away and take up positions of innocence. Bill pops the window open and hands me a blanket through the bars and, with grunts and motions, tells me to pass the blanket to Swede. I take the blanket over to Swede, and Bill hands me another blanket and lets me know to hand it to Collie. As I hand the blanket to Collie, the window slams closed and locks. Swede and collie and I are in stitches. The V sometimes show a sense of justice. It was as obvious to them and to us that Swede and Collie were having a worse time dealing with the cold than I was. I'm still not sure why we're laughing, but it is a very funny moment to us.

We all keep an eye on George. Collie believes he's getting more black feathers. Swede is quietly calm. I do my best to keep my opinion to myself until Christmas Day.

Christmas Eve 1967 is Sunday, and we spend the day trying to keep warm and Collie and I spend a lot of time at the peephole as Swede practices the Lotus position in his disguise as Chief Sitting Bull. Sunday is a "no bath" day. Thank God! A cold water bath on a cold day is a blessing in the avoidance. The sun sets and the chill does not improve. Just after dark, there is a commotion outside our room as the main gate opens, and a bus plows through and parks. I zoom to the peephole. There are several guards and officers milling around. Pretty soon the guards are opening cell doors and loading the bus. As the cells in the Gun Shed and Ware House produce their occupants who march across the yard and load on the bus, Bill breaks away and heads for our door. Collie and Swede and I assume our innocent "who me" positions as our door flies open. Bill steps across our threshold and points to Swede and tells him to come along. Swede silently moves out and gets aboard the bus a few seconds before it departs.

Swede is gone for a long time. Collie and I are certain that he has gone to a Christmas program and can't wait for his return to hear the details.

Finally the bus returns. The bus had taken Swede and about a dozen others to another camp about 30 minutes from here. There was a small auditorium and a Catholic priest presided over the mass. No one had asked about denominations, but Protestants and Catholics, and maybe an atheist or two, celebrated the Mass with total impunity. Doug Hegdahl served the Eucharist. As he passed out the bread, he asked each POW his name and passed out names and gathered names at every opportunity. He told Swede that the new kid in the Gun Shed was a Navy Ensign. Swede said that Doug had to whisper and that he couldn't understand the name clearly, but it was something like "Mawfeen." Swede is in wonder at Hegdahl's ability to deal with names so rapidly.

Christmas day 1967 is cold. We work hard to stay warm, and take turns at the peephole vigil. George is nowhere in sight. The activities are more like Sunday, except that, a little later than usual, we make a trip to the bath. The first meal is the usual--today its 'bagas rice and green soup. We take note that we have not seen George, and wonder where he could be.

As the day progresses, we are aware that there is more than the usual activity in the camp. The main gate next to our cell has opened and closed a couple of times. There are more than the normal number of civilians in the camp. We see Bill from time to time as he assists with the gate traffic and as he makes his rounds. There is something just a bit strange about it all.

And then a flurry of activity emanates from the kitchen. One of the cooks pushes a cart toward the center of the camp compound, and several helpers join him. Bill directs traffic and soon starts the door opening process and passing out food. It ain't 'bagas rice and green soup! Soon our doors open and the cook's helpers bring in our plates with meat and potatoes and the Viet version of dressing. Some of the meat is turkey and there is pork and roast beef, and bread--a feast!!

George suddenly becomes a dead issue--poor pun and all. We wade into the feast as if it came from a three star Michelin restaurant. Merry Christmas to all and to all a "Good Night!"

"Mawfeen" Sings
A few nights after Christmas, we are preparing for bed when outside noises get our attention, and soon I am at the peep hole looking toward the Veranda that faces the center of the camp. Kleig lights are lighting up

the veranda like opening night on Broadway. People are milling around and talking. The center of attention is a young American sitting on a stool, fingering a guitar, and carrying on a conversation with several V. Some of the V are the officers that we sometimes see in interviews and attitude checks. Others are strangers, but well dressed and obviously relatively important.

The group makes way for the several cameras as they zero in on the handsome young stranger. He strums the guitar and sings a song that I don't recognize. The group applauds and moves about to speak to him as though he is a celebrity at a cocktail party. I can hear his voice clearly, but can't make out what he is saying. Then in a momentary quiet, he responds to one of the dignitaries standing near him and asks, as though responding to a request: "Do you want me to sing another one?" These words were the only ones I hear with absolute clarity. He sings another song, and the party dissolves. The three of us allow as how this young man doing the singing is most likely "Ensign Mawfeen." We wonder about the young singer and what we have just seen. We have never seen him in the bucket parade and wonder where he is housed. The whole incident is strange. Soon we turn in to bed.

A day or two later, still in late December, the sun is down and the weather is cold. Swede does his Sitting Bull routine to assure that his feet are warm when he goes prone and seals himself up in his cotton blanket cocoon. We hear the guards talking loudly and hear the gate opening to allow a bus to drive into the prison yard. I am at the peephole and can only see the back of the bus. I cannot see the occupants as they disembark, but the noise and motions the guards are making tell us that the bus is unloading and that the occupants are assembling near the Gun Shed. The guards are opening and closing cells and moving the occupants around. Some of "us" wind up on the bus and it leaves. We turn in. The bucket parade tomorrow will be very interesting.

The next morning, cold and all, we are up and I am manning the peephole watching for Bill to start the bucket parade. He starts with us, and Swede and I make the round trip.

Soon, I am again at the peephole and watching Bill as he starts the Gun Shed parade. There are two stranger newbies in each of Gun Sheds 1 and 2. Gun Shed 3 opens, and a somewhat robust man with dark hair emerges carrying two buckets. Collie is standing near me, and I relay what I see to him, and he in turn keeps Swede informed. I tell Collie that since only one man emerges and that he is carrying two buckets, there must be two men in Gun Shed 3. I keep my vigil as the Cell 3 bucket carrier makes the round trip to the honey vat. He re-enters the Cell, and Bill stands aside for a few seconds. The bucket carrier emerges with a third bucket. I tell Collie that there must be three in Gun Shed 3.

When the parade is over, there are but a few of the original 20 who were there when I arrived last July.

In early January 1968, the V do a number of room changes during the day. Swede, Collie, and I wind up in Warehouse 8. We start to communicate with our fellows as soon as we can. LtCol Hervey Stockman is the SRO. He, Capt. Larry Carrigan and Capt. Bruce Hinckley are next door in room 7. Three young Turks--Capt. Tom Moe, Capt. Cliff Walker, and 1/Lt Wayne Smith--are in Room 9. We have almost instant contact with the entire Warehouse. Soon, we are able to establish note drops in the bath house, which will connect us to the Gun Shed and the Corn Crib. It is not long until we learn the identities of all the residents here and that the bucket carrier in Gun Shed 3 is Major Norris Overly and that the two cripples are Major Bud Day and LCDR John McCain.

On a day in late January, the three of us are called out to go to the bath. The baths are no longer outside. The V have constructed a brick bath house with four individual baths and doors that lock from the out-side. The turnkey locks Swede and Collie and me in bath number four. The baths have a common drain much like a street gutter that flows through the front part of each bath stall. Soon we are aware that the turnkey has placed someone in the stall next to ours--bath number 3. Since I am the most mobile, I get the job of kneeling down and whisper-ing into the drain in an attempt to talk to whoever is in Bath number 3. I make contact with Ensign David Matheny, until today known as "Mawfeen." I tell him our names and the cell we are in. Bill returns to the area, and we have to knock it off. This is the only time that Swede, Collie, and I have any direct communication with Matheny.

Tet Offensive

Every day the Viets pipe Radio Ha Noi into our rooms via speakers lo-cated in each cell. I always listen, even though we know the broadcast is all communist propaganda without a word of fact or truth. They always play some popular American songs dedicated to "American GIs," as ar-ticulated by Ha Noi Hanna, the most memorable named Su Mai. It is no surprise that in early February, Su Mai announced a great victory for the Viet Namese People in the form of a Tet Offensive that rocked all of South Viet Nam. We don't pay much attention to it, as every broadcast on the Ha Noi radio ballyhoos at least one great victory. I'm not sure of Hannah's story, but recall several incidents during my tour as a FAC that portended trouble for the South. In fact, a clinical evaluation of the situation in South Viet Nam at any time I was associated with the war would have been very pessimistic as to the outcome. I remember watch-ing newsreels of the surrender of the French forces at Dien Bien Phu in 1954, and listening to tales told by some of the few Air Force "advisors" who were in Viet Nam afterwards, as well as my own experience, that could only provide serious doubt as to any hope of success in Indo China. My personal experience amounts to participating in three years of fail-ures, and recalling the history of problems in Viet Nam since the 1950s.

In the quiet of the night, ensconced under my mosquito net, as snuggly wrapped in the two thin blankets as I can manage, I think about "Hannah's" broadcast about the Tet offensive and ruminate on some of my experiences with the ARVN 2nd Infantry Division. I could easily visualize an operation against Hue, larger in scope, but otherwise virtually identical to assaults I had personally witnessed from the air and are described earlier in this missive; e.g., see *Ba Gia July 5, 1965in this missive.*

On February 16, 1968, a bombshell explodes in the Plantation. The V release three POWS--Ensign Dave Matheny, Major Norris Overly, and Capt. Jon Black, soon to be dubbed "The MOB." We are amazed, mystified, and surprised at this news. The scene of the Big House veranda comes to mind, along with our very brief contact with Matheny in the bath. Other than that, our discussions are limited to the issue of accepting early release. We can't do that, and wonder how these three could do it. We know that there are a number of us who got here long before these three. Ev Alvarez has been here three and a half years, and a number of us have been here since 1965--more than two years. We also know that there are those here who were terribly injured, and, no doubt, a lot more than Collie and Swede whom the V have maimed and crippled. The MOB had to have had some inkling of these facts, and, even if not, all of us have been exposed to the Code of Conduct. We are disappointed that these three have accepted parole.

It is soon early March, 1967. Matheny, Overly, and Black (The MOB) have been home for two or three weeks. Swede and Collie and I are in bath number 4. Soon we are aware that one other bath is occupied and that Bill has strayed away. I get on my knees and whisper into the drain and make contact with Major James Low and give him our names. Not much else occurs as Bill returns, and we have to knock off.

We have almost real time contact most of the Warehouse occupants, in spite of the fact that the V have left some of the cells vacant, which forces the occupants to use the front or back walls and to tap louder to maintain contact between some of the rooms. John McCain and Bud Day have been in the Corn Crib since before the MOB departed. We have contact with the Corn Crib and the Gun Shed only via sporadic voice or by note drops in the new bathhouse. When we are locked in the bath, one of us reaches to bottom corner and palpates the drain plug to determine if there is a foreign object there. Sometimes there is a note carefully wrapped and sealed in a water proof plastic packet. Sometimes, these notes are a regular newspaper--a summary of goings on between the writers and the V interrogators/propaganda spreaders/ attitude checkers. Some of the alert and enterprising Criminals in this camp cadged the plastic wrapping and pencils and paper that make our underwater news system possible.

We talk to our neighbors in cells seven and nine daily. Hervey Stockman, the SRO, has assumed the leadership role with authority. His orders to us are based firmly on The Code of Conduct. After the release of the MOB, acceptance of early release is the most crucial subject we have to deal with. One would think that the issue is totally resolved by the Code, stating that as a POW "I will neither accept special favors nor parole." We have interpreted early release as acceptance of parole. The CoC provisions prohibits early release. The SROs and all the POWs that I know here would say that release in the order of capture or if seriously ill would be acceptable. Another mantra among us is: "One go, all go." Early release is clearly unacceptable.

(Comments: For a few, their medical condition could be construed as an acceptable reason to accept early release. Later on, I will learn of Ray Vohden, John McCain, Fred Cherry, Dale Osborne, Collie Haines, and Bob Fant, to name a few whom I would have no problem urging to accept early release, assuming the release was proffered based only on their state of health. I roomed with Fred Cherry and Dale Osborne and Collie Haines and Bob Fant and personally observed the results of their injuries and the failures of their medical treatments.

I saw Vohden from a distance and heard details regarding John McCain from other POWs. From personal knowledge regarding Cherry, Haines, Vohden, Fant and Osborne, I would unreservedly urge them to go if offered. However, I am absolutely certain that none of them would have accepted early release for any reason. McCain just happened to be the only one on my list to whom an offer was proffered, and John knew that the reason for the proffer was purely for publicity and had little to do with his serious injuries. Even if the V had told McCain he was going home because of his injuries, he would have refused. So would the others. These men would have died in Ha Noi before compromising the Code of conduct or their personal codes of honor in any way.)

I believe that all of the POWs at the Plantation, with the exception of eight of the nine who eventually were released early, were in complete agreement with these principles and were totally supportive of Colonel Stockman's orders to us as well as all the existing and future directives issued by the senior officers regarding early release. The ninth of the nine was Seaman Doug Hegdahl. The SRO ordered Hegdahl to accept early release if offered with no strings because of Hegdahl's phenomenal memory and intelligence, as well as his youth and enlisted rank.

Later, other issues regarding such items as letter writing, hunger strikes, and giving up smoking met with some Bronx Cheers among some of the rank and file, including myself, but there was essentially complete agreement within the main body. There was a group of about eight who openly defied the senior officer's directives regarding anything and consorted with the V. The V kept them separated from the rest of us.)

I do most of the communicating between our cell and our neighbors. We have discovered that we can talk directly through the foot thick brick walls of our cells using our tin water cups. To talk to the other room, we place the bottom of our cup against the wall and then seal the top around our mouth and speak into the cup. The listener places the open end of his cup to the wall and places an ear against the bottom. As the conversation progresses, the listener taps twice at the end of each sentence or major thought, and would tap several times rapidly to ask the speaker to repeat.

Since I am still the most physically capable of the three of us, I do most of the talking through the walls. Tapping signals are still useful when using the cup to talk directly. For example, after each complete thought the receiver taps twice and the sender then continues to speak. If the receiver does not understand the speaker or something the speaker says, the receiver taps several taps very rapidly. The speaker then can try again. These conventions work the same whether we are tapping or talking.

The brief contact with Jim Low is a significant news item. Low is living alone in the Gun Shed, and when he identified himself, I was hoping to get some current news. However, every contact, no matter how brief, especially with an occupant of one of the other buildings, was big news. Later in the day I get on line with Hervey and tell him about Low. We exchange news of our other contacts from each direction in the building. The three occupants of Cell nine (Moe, Walker, and Smith) are younger men and in general good health. They get more of the physical details like making coal balls in the kitchen and washing dishes than the rest of us. They always have interesting trivia to report. Trivia or not, we have ears for all of it as though our existence depended on it. We exchange the trivia, and then Hervey passes out his staff meeting objectives.

In late March 1968 Hervey announces a contest for all to consider. He will award prizes to each of the following: 1. Lowest bail out; 2. Fastest bail out; 3. Highest bail out; and 4. Slowest bail out. He will announce the prizes on April 1. We pass Hervey's message through our wall to the south and wait for responses. Swede thinks that he may win two of the categories--low and fast. He was about 400 feet and supersonic when he ejected. Collie, even though he was running out of altitude when he bid farewell to his crippled F-8, will concede the low prize to Swede. I am in the middle--no chance of a prize for me. I'm guessing that Swede pretty well has at least the fast category locked up.

Three days later Hervey calls. I grab my cup and listen up. "Today, I had an interview with The Bug. He asked me if I had been to survival school back in the States. I told him that I had. The Bug then told me that if I didn't order the Criminals in the Camp to stop communicating that he would put me through survival school here in Ha Noi, and that I wouldn't like it."

Having met The Bug, endured his tirades and heat treatment, and his very convincing threat to end my life if I didn't answer his questions, and after learning the details of what he did to Swede, I hope that Hervey won't have to go back through the Green Room. However that may be, Hervey is courageous and tough as he passes out his directive in response to Bug's threat: "This changes nothing. We will continue to communicate every way we can until the hammer falls." We pass Hervey's message down the line and continue to pass "news" through the walls and via the note drops. It appears that the tapping (or talking) was all the Bug knew about or suspected.

In late March, it is still a bit chilly and Swede has a cold. Sniffles and cold symptoms have plagued us all during the winter. Swede seems to be more susceptible to colds because he still hasn't fully recovered from his supersonic bail out and the severe tortures imposed on him by the Bug. Tonight we hear Hervey's cell open. We listen intently and are convinced that a shuffle is in progress. Soon it is quiet. We retire. We don't have much to say, but suspect the worst.

The next day we get a call-up from Hervey's cell. It is Larry Carrigan, one of Hervey's roommates. He tells us that the V have taken Hervey away. We pass this to all, along with the fact that Swede is now the SRO.

Our morale slumps a bit. Given the Bug's threat, we know that Hervey is being tortured. We hurt for him.

Later in the day, the V come for Swede. He rolls up his "stuff," and by some dint of circumstance, he winds up with Collie's cup lid. The lids to our cups are important to us. They not only cover our cups and keep out dust and flies, when we get a sugar ration, the safest place from ants is in the upside down cup lid sitting on top of the cup. A missing cup lid is a serious matter.

The room seems largely empty without Swede. Collie and I wonder about our fate. Will the V be happy with taking it out on Swede and Hervey, or will they dig further? If they come for one or both of us, where will they stop? They know, or at least they think they know who the next SRO is. It may be Collie. Collie is senior to me, but may not be the SRO. When this situation blows over, we'll sort it out.

We still talk to those on each side of us. The V don't seem to be any more alert than usual. The only news to pass is the absence of the two senior men in the camp.

Next day the regular schedule does not change. We have the standard bucket and bath parades. Right after the bath parade, the V show up and take Collie away. If there is any good news about Collie's going, it is that he leaves his "stuff" on his bed. I wish him well and wait for another shoe.

I am alone for the first meal. I wonder where Hervey, Swede, and Collie are, and if they are having a meal. I finish my meal and deposit my dishes outside the door where the three next door will pick them up and wash them. About an hour goes by and my door opens. Bill signals me to head for the Big House. I walk across the yard and up the steps and enter the side door. Bill ushers me in to the first room on the left. A Johnny-come-lately addition to the English speaking staff is waiting behind a table. Bill seats me on the low stool facing the table. We have named this new guy "The Camel" because he walks with the peculiar gait of a real camel. The camel is standing rigidly erect with his hands behind his back and giving me his best "you naughty boy" look. He stares and stares and finally speaks: "Where is Larson?"

"I don't know. Where did you take him?"

"Larson is a bad man."

Now seems to be a good time to keep mouth closed. Camel launches into a tirade. It's soon obvious that he needs a good deal more coaching from the Bug, but he keeps going at his Camel pace. "Larson is a Criminal and not only that, he is a bad Criminal who has disrespected the humane and lenient treatment afforded him by the people of the Democratic Republic of Viet Nam, in general, and in their venerated leader, Ho Chi Minh, in particular. Larson is now paying for this disrespectful and criminal attitude. You are here to learn not to associate with criminals like Larson and Stock Man. You are here also to confess your own crimes. You have violated rules of the camp by communicating with the other Criminals in the camp. You will confess your crimes and promise not to commit such crimes in the future." He goes on for a while--same song--same key--different verses. He does a fair job of imitating a father who is totally outdone with a juvenile delinquent son.

He finally gets to the particulars. He turns over a pad of paper and a pencil and says to me, "Now confess your crimes. Begin by writing down the names of the other Criminals in the Camp."

"I don't know the names of the POWs in this camp."

Camel does a poor imitation of The Bug by way of explaining that there are no POWs in this camp, only Criminals who are guilty of the blackest crimes. He reiterates that he knows we have been communicating and that I must know the names of all the Criminals who live in this Camp and continues to insist that I confess to communicating with the other "Criminals." He leaves the paper and pencil on the table and leaves me alone with an AK-47 armed guard just outside the door.

I pick up the pencil and begin to write. I explain that we sometimes communicate with our immediate neighbors with whom we have a common wall. I write down the names in room nine--Moe, Walker, and Smith. I also list the names in room seven--Stockman, Carrigan, and Hinckley. I explain that we communicate because we are concerned about our health and well-being. I avoid the word *criminal* because we are collectively maintaining that we are *POWs*. I also avoid using the term *POW* just to avoid the inevitable argument that will follow. I dawdle as much as I can and when finished, I put down the pencil and place the paper in the center of the table.

In due time, Camel returns to the room. He is not very happy with my "confession." He brings up the fact that there are many "criminals" in the camp, and that I must have communicated with others. I explain we have no way to communicate with others who are not near us. He insists that I write more and leaves.

I sit on the stool and do nothing. I don't believe that I will get away with what I have done, and feel some dread about what will happen next. After a while, I begin to nod off--a nap would be nice. The guard un-limbers his AK and punches me in the ribs with the butt. So much for napping.

Camel returns periodically. He insists that I admit to communicating with more than just our immediate neighbors. I try to convince him otherwise. We fence. I finally say to him that certainly he can punish me severely and force me to write just about anything he wants to dictate to me. If that's what he chooses to do, sobeit. I have written down what I have done. If that's not sufficient, then I have a problem. I tell him that I can't stop him from torturing me that I have been tortured before, and am prepared to attempt to endure whatever torture he can provide. He does not like the word *torture*, and reiterates that I am lying and that lying deserves severe punishment, and that he will apply such punishment if I don't admit the truth.

I don't want to be tortured and keep holding the line that I would be happy to name others that I have communicated with if he will provide the names. If the V had sent the Bug to do this job, I would have long since been in the ropes. I have decided that, if pushed further, rather than to take physical punishment, that I will offer up fictitious names that I can remember. Camel leaves me on the stool with the AK guard nearby.

At meal time, the guard brings my food. The day progresses into night. The stool is hard and I am uncomfortable, but I'm not in the ropes and I'm not being beaten. I nod off. Here comes the rifle butt to the ribs. This process goes on throughout the night. When I need relief, I ask for my *bo*. The guard takes me around to the back of the building to the honey well for relief. Then back on the stool. My meals come on time. I wonder where Collie is. I also wonder what has happened to Hervey and Swede and if any others of us will be called up for this exercise.

One more night on the stool. I fight as hard as I can, but get an occasional poke in the ribs as a reminder to keep my eyes open. Morning comes again. The Camel shows up and brings Collie into the room. He declares that due to the determination of the DRVN to provide humane and lenient treatment to us in spite of the fact that we are criminals, we may return to our room. He asks us if we wish to return to the same room together. We both say yes. He admonishes us that if we are ever caught communicating again that we will be "punished severely."

Bill arrives and directs us back to Cell eight. When we are safe in our room, we compare notes. We each had the same experience. There is no discussion regarding future communication--It is a given. As soon as we are rested, we contact the cells on each side of us and brief them on what went on. Other than the removal of Hervey and Swede, the Camp line-up is the same. We caution them to be careful, especially with the note drops. We got a break this time; that probably won't happen again.

After all the big excitement that included the loss of the two senior officers, life at the Plantation continues apace. Communication actually improved. The V had not discovered the bath house note drops.

It is clear from our interviews, attitude checks, and brain washing sessions that we undergo just about monthly, that the V are contemplating another early release. Jim Low's response in the bath the only time we spoke to him indicates that he must be a prime candidate. I can't get too excited about the program because I know that they will never let me go, and if they offer it, I will be obliged to refuse--but will I? I think about my little family--one wife--one little boy--not quite constantly. I can see them, especially Sue, in my mind's eye. As what must be common to all of us here, I allow images and incidents free passage through the dendrites in my brain to produce documentaries that are sometimes difficult to deal with, and drift away to another time...

It's a weekday in mid-May, 1946. The weather is warm and the Cotton chopping season is just beginning, meaning that all the county schools are closed so that the students can work in the fields. Its 5:00am, and I am just out of bed and getting ready to catch the bus that will take me for the 25 mile ride from our house in Chic, Tennessee to Dyersburg High School in Dyersburg where I am a sophomore. The 25 mile ride takes 2 hours. The driver is a neighbor, Alec Williams--Mr. Alec to his passengers.

At six O'clock I will be standing by our mailbox on the highway. Meanwhile, I heat some water on the cook stove and wash up, get dressed and have breakfast in our kitchen. We always have biscuits, ham or bacon or both, eggs, and milk. I'm not much on coffee. Three of us breakfast together--my mother, my brother Jack and I. My father has been dead a little less than a year.

The ride to Dyersburg is wasted time. It's virtually impossible to study on the bus. The constant stop start, the mischief, a 20 minute wait at the Richwoods School while the bus turns off to on a side road to pick up those who live off the main road. While the bus makes this round trip, most of us get off and stand around the store or play some kind of games. Considering this four hour ordeal each day, it's no wonder that no kid from Chic has ever graduated from Dyersburg High School.

After the stop at Richwoods, the next village is Finley. Until we arrive in Finley, Mr. Alec is stopping at individual farm homes along the highway. Finley is a real village with streets, three churches, a grammar school, a combination filling station and country grocery, a grocery store which also houses the Finley Post Office, and Tom's Café. The kids who live in Finley congregate at Tom's Café to wait for the bus.

Today, as we pull in to Finley, we are slowing down to a fast walk as we pass Don Ed Pritchett's service station and store. The weather is mild. Several of the Grade School students are milling around the front of the Filling Station. Suddenly, from the side street that runs by Don Ed's, a small group of Grammar Schoolers emerge. One is a girl. Not just any girl, but a special girl. As I watch the vignette played out by this little group, I can only see this special girl as she interacts with her contemporaries. She is beautiful, and more important than her looks, is the electricity that she exudes in her actions. I can't hear the conversation, but she talks, laughs, and moves with a vivacity that emanates from her like a high powered radio signal.

I ask some of my neighbors on the bus if they know who she is. Everybody on the bus, and all who get on the bus at Finley know this girl. Her sister is one of my classmates. These two young ladies are the daughters of the Finley Pentecostal Minister, Brother Austin. The one I am seeing for the first time is dressed in overalls and a dress. It's common for young women who work in the fields to wear a dress over their overalls. She is laughing and bantering with all around her and is clearly the center of attraction in her circle. She is now the center of attraction in my circle as well, she just doesn't know it yet. Her name is Sue Austin. At this moment, there is no way that I can, even in my wildest fantasies, contemplate the total effect this extraordinarily pretty and vivacious girl will have on my life.

The school year grinds to an end. On Friday May 24, 1946 Mr. Alec drives us home for the last time until the fall session begins. I look forward to a summer of work. My brother, Jack, has brought the farm to a good start this season. The hundred acre farm is made up of alfalfa, cotton, corn, and pasture land, some pigs and a small herd of cows. We have one tractor, one pair of mules and one mare and a young mule who work as a pair. Sometimes, Jack hires one of our neighbors to help.

I spend a summer working the hardest and having more fun than I ever thought about. I am, by natural proclivity, lazy, but something about sharing the responsibility of getting all the things done that needed doing dragged me out of my lazy shell and changed my attitude about work. Every day brings a new perspective. As one job gets done, another is waiting.

My first really important assignment is to cultivate a field of corn that is just sprouting. The corn is about six inches high. Jack helps me to prepare the tractor for the job. The first step is to install the rear cultivator assembly that contains the large plows that clear out the middles between the rows. When these plows are all installed, I start the tractor, move the plows to the up position, and then drive the tractor into the front cultivator assembly. The front assembly straddles the corn row with small plows on each side and plows the ground very close to each stalk of corn.

The tractor is a 1936 model International Harvester Farmall F-20. It has no power lift system--that came along in 1937--so lifting the plows out of the ground and lowering them to the "cutting" position is a manual operation. I only weigh 90 pounds, so I have to learn how to use my limited strength to raise and lower the plows. Jack shows me some tricks that allow the full use of my entire body and to use timing to advantage.

After plowing the corn, there is hay to cut, cure and bale. Then there is.... We work hard every day and soon the summer is gone. I think about the coming school year with ambivalent feelings, and I wonder how Sue Austin spent her summer, and how she will look when school begins. I know that she will register as a freshman. I also know that she has no idea that I even exist.

Back to the reality of life on the Plantation. The disappearance of Swede and Hervey and the rather light weight communications purge that followed has essentially no effect on the communications process. It did, however, destroy the burgeoning leadership that Hervey was exerting. There is no doubt that the V had achieved a lot by disrupting the chain of command.

During the months that follow we have the usual individual visits to the Big House. There is no set pattern. Sometimes it is for a lecture about the goals of the Vietnamese People under the leadership of Ho Chi Minh. Then there are the questions about our understanding of these noble goals. The V clearly want to hear that we side with them in their quest to reunify their country as provided by the 1954 agreement that was made right after they had captured nearly the whole contingent of French military at Dien Bien Phu.

They also talk to us about our release, which would be an early release based on our "good attitude" and by exhibiting behavior and deeds that proved we are worthy. Part of the initial showing of good attitude would be a letter to Ho Chi Minh. All of those with whom we have contact are declining to participate.

At every session that I attend, I continue to ask for reading material and to write a letter home. The V continue to ignore my requests.

Collie and I are the nexus of the communications network in the Warehouse. We relay broadcasts from each half of the building to the other half. We also spend some time talking about our plans when and if we ever got home. Bruce Hinckley, our neighbor in Cell seven, is an avid outdoorsman and fisherman who looks forward to owning something like a Ford Bronco and a full staff of camping accessories. I want a motorcycle. Cliff Walker, Cell nine, is a wild and crazy guy who has ridden motorcycles. He talks about opening up his Harley Davidson and declares that he probably won't get another bike because of the temptation to explore the limits of the performance envelope--not good for one's longevity.

For the rest of my stay at the Plantation, which will end in December 1969, the SRO situation is unclear a lot of the time. During this time, Collie Haines dispenses wisdom as appropriate to keep up morale.

As soon as we recover from the momentary shake-up, which would have drawn blood at any of the other Prisons, we get back to the contest that Hervey Stockman announced just before his demise. We do not get as far as determining awards, but we do discuss what we know. It seems that Doug Hegdahl would pick up low and slow, since he was essentially at Sea Level when he sailed over the fantail of the U.S.S. Canberra. Swede may have some competition for fast. Mel and I were subsonic when we bailed, so we are not contenders. However, on a couple of occasions we found ourselves supersonic at low level with SAMs locked up on us which could have ended in supersonic bail out. Also, Thud drivers were often supersonic in the process of getting out of Dodge in one piece. High would probably go to one of the B-66 crews who flew above 30,000 feet most of the time--in which case there would be multiple awards. Just something to think about.

March 1968 to August 2, 1968
Sometimes a young officer who seems more interested in practicing his English hosts an hour long session. He is friendly, even congenial. During one visit he describes a "holy day" that he has just taken to the sea. He is especially excited about a fish that comes up to the boat to "have a look." These sessions are boring and worth no comment.

The more senior hosts are died-in-the-wool Communists who spout the party line and remind us that we are criminals. They always tell us the bad news and ask for our opinions. They are clearly fishing for any comments from us that would indicate sympathy for their struggle against "U.S. hegemony in the world in general and the cruel, criminal, illegal, barbarous war the U.S. is waging against the people of Viet Nam."

Since our encounter with Jim Low in March, we have heard nothing directly from him. He was living in the Gun Shed when we spoke to him in the bath. Later on we hear that he has moved to the "Show Room," next door to the honey tank. Matheny and Black were in the Show Room about the time we saw Matheny play and sing for the party on the Big House veranda. Apparently, Warren Overly joined them there just before their release.

On August 2, 1968 another bombshell shakes the Plantation. The V release three more of "us"--Major James Low, Major Fred Thompson, and Captain Joe Carpenter. At this point in time, we have no steady contact with anyone senior to Collie Haines. There are other field grade officers in the camp, and we get enough news about them to know that they are here, but communications are too sparse to maintain anything like a military command structure. All indications among those who are in the communications loop are that we are all well aware of the Code of Conduct and intend to follow it. That means that none of the rest of us that we know about has any intentions of accepting an out of turn release of any kind.

Matheny, Overly, and Black surprised us and made us wonder how the V picked them for release, but somehow this second group seems different. We don't have any prior knowledge about any one of them except for Jim Low. I still remember vividly his photograph on the cover of *This Week*, and articles about him being the only Second Lieutenant ace in Korea.

As to our morale, I don't feel any differently. The V have never discussed the issue of a release of any kind, and, until they do, this whole business of early release is a moot point--why bother with it? This cavalier attitude does not prevent me from thinking and dreaming about my wife and son. The day dreams sometimes revolve around my high school days and the events that allowed the bond between Sue and me to grow and finally become strong enough that we could not sever them.

Collie and I remain in Warehouse eight. We continue to maintain contact with our immediate neighbors by tapping or talking through the wall. The note drops in the baths are occasional and sometimes surprisingly long and newsy. They are always written almost entirely in abbreviations and sometimes take a while to reconstruct. Here is an example: "yd 2 engspk host bh tlk rlse no do t n crpts cigs ..." translates to Yesterday, two English Speakers hosted in the Big House talked release we showed no interest served tea and crumpets and cigarettes.

In between all these survival activities, I ruminate about my past and spend endless hours after taps under my net, either wrapped in my blankets to stay warm, or spread eagled as possible to stay cool--seldom was the temperature just right--putting together the important stuff. My personal time and space machine takes my psyche to other times and places.

Sixteen Months at the Plantation

In August 1968 we get news that startles us. A man named Ernie Brace appears out of nowhere and is housed in the cell behind Warehouse 14. The guys in Warehouse 14 have managed to teach him the tap code, and we get a long report on Brace as they relay through the walls. Brace was captured in Laos on May 21, 1965 while resupplying a remote outpost of some kind. He had landed a Pilatus Porter at a remote airstrip, and the cargo door was open as the Lao contingent unloaded the airplane. Suddenly, he was looking down the wrong end of an AK-47 barrel, just a few inches from his face and just outside his window. He thought about pouring the juice to the Porter and, depending on the suddenness of the Porter's capability to accelerate and with a little luck, making a successful escape. Big problem: the Porter has an enormous cargo door, which was locked in the open to unload position, and the airplane could not fly in that configuration. Ernie shut down and spent most of the next three years in leg irons at Dien Bien Phu. He got here sometime last month and is the only civilian POW that we know about.

Later in 1968, Collie and I get a challenge from Cell nine to play chess. We accept and immediately begin a detailed set of communications as to how to set up chess boards and communicate moves. The board is easy. Our mosquito nets are woven with reinforcing threads which form perfect squares about three quarters of an inch on a side. By folding a net carefully, it is easy to expose a perfect 12 x 12 board. We then tear 24 small squares from a sheet of toilet paper, and mark them by using the sharpened bottom corner of a tooth paste tube. P = Pawn. Q = Queen. K = King. N =Knight. B = Bishop. R= Rook. Since our "stuff" has to be folded when not in use, it's easy to fold one net and place the pieces so we can study the board. We memorize positions as the games never end during one day. Since Cell nine is the challenger, they give us the first move. We set up as White, and the first game begins.

Collie and I stand near the foot of my bed and contemplate the first move. A pawn move that is as good as any is King's Pawn from King's 2 to King's 4. The game is on. We make our first move in the morning communications session, and they respond in the afternoon or evening session. They respond with a Pawn advance, and then Collie and I discuss our attack. I make a suggestion, we discuss options, and then Collie says something like this: "How about if we…" and outlines about three or four possible moves and responses, which may result from his suggestion. I think it over for a minute or two and soon conclude that I can't think of anything better to do, so we send the move. Cell nine responds with one of Collie's predictions, so we go right to autopilot and make our next move. Cell nine accepts our move and we don't hear from them until the next communications session.

Here comes Cell 9's response. It is the move that Collie predicted, and we respond with Collie's next planned move. Cell 9 accepts the move and Collie and I now survey our domain and talk about the next move we will make. I suggest a Knight's move and Collie goes through about four or five potential sequences, and says something like: "How about if we…" and moves a Bishop and runs through about five potential ploys that may occur. I can't think of any better plan. We send the move.

At the next Communications session, Cell nine responds just as Collie predicted they might, and since we already have discussed our plan, we send our next move immediately. Do you see a pattern developing? Every time Cell nine transmits a move, it's totally expected, and we just counterpunch. Finally it gets down to the point, that in just a few moves in the future, the game will be over. Soon into that final series, Cell 9 concedes.

I look at Collie in wonder, and realize that I don't know squat about Chess. Collie is making shots that are clear out of my comprehension.

When I move out of this room on December 10, 1969, I will have spent two years with Collie--most of it with just the two us--, and I never asked him about how he developed such uncanny prowess at Chess.

Collie and I wonder about Swede and Hervey. We joke about Swede having "stolen" Collie's cup lid. Collie intends to kill Swede the next time we see him.

Days get longer as the year ages. The Plantation would be boring but for the challenge of keeping communications going. The late autumn chill segues into the winter monsoon that brings the cold wet weather of winter. In between the clouds and chill, we have a day or two of Indian Summer--clear air and warm sunshine. On such a day, I am standing on a sawhorse peering at the outside world through the open vent above our door. It is siesta time, the camp is very quiet, and I am just about to leave my look out post, when from the far right, toward the Gun Shed, one of the turnkeys, not bill, and an AK carrying guard come into view escorting Swede toward us. I let Collie know what's happening.

As I continue to watch, the turnkey places a stool in the yard in direct sunlight. Swede takes a seat facing our door, and the turnkey and guard meander off to the side. I get down from my perch, return the saw horse to its rightful position, and go prone on the floor where I can see Swede through the space at the bottom of our door. I can also see the turnkey and guard. I move my fingers across the bottom of the door to get Swede's attention. I flash "Hi Swede" with my fingers and Swede responds.

I ask him where he has been and he says "the guard house under the gun tower at the end of the Gun Shed." I am relaying everything to Collie who is standing near me. Swede says that he has had a heart attack. Collie says: "Ask him where is my cup lid?

The V start moving around where they could see my fingers. The way Swede was signaling with one hand dangling down in front like a catcher flashing signals to a pitcher, the V couldn't see his signals, but could see my fingers under the door, and I waved Swede off.

Swede's presence was the biggest news we had during the year. We were worried about him because of his report about his heart, but he looked o.k. Swede had been through too much during his initial interrogation and was not in good health to begin with. We hoped the V eased off on him. The fact that they brought him out for some warm sunshine was a hopeful sign.

Christmas 1968

The V outdo themselves with a surprisingly tasty meal.

JANUARY 1969–DECEMBER 10 1969

The first few weeks in 1969 are uneventful. Tet comes along in February and the V try to duplicate their 1968 attacks. We have no real way of knowing how Tet 1968 went, but believe that it was mostly a propaganda coup, if anything at all. The best part of Tet for us is the food.

Tet is a very special time for everybody in Viet Nam, no matter which side. Several major historical events are tied to this holiday. I was introduced to the traditional Tet celebration dish, banh chung, in South Viet Nam. It is a complicated dish to make and delicious to eat, and probably dangerous to your health. The V make sure we have banh chung for Tet, along with all the propaganda they can pitch.

As the year progresses, there is more and more pressure on all of us to request early release. We get frequent trips to the Big House to listen to propaganda and to have an opportunity to write a letter to Ho Chi Minh which had to contain a lot of obsequious apology to Uncle Ho for killing his folks and then a real knee dragging request to be forgiven and returned home to assist in the conversion of the rest of the American people whose minds need recalibration regarding the glorious communist revolution in general and in the plight of the peace seeking people of Viet Nam who only want peace and freedom for themselves.

During this process, I continue to ask to write home and for books.

One day, I am in the Big House and this rather cultured officer that we sometimes see around the camp is the host. We have a discussion about the issue of my writing a suitable note to Uncle Ho via their "Ministry of Justice," or some such. I decide to pen a note requesting release. I'm sorry now that I did. I could never have accepted an out of turn release, and am glad that the V didn't find my request sufficient.

On August 4, 1969, the third bombshell went off at the Plantation. The V released Lt/j.g. Robert Frishman, Capt. Wesley Rumble and Seaman Apprentice Doug Hegdahl. Dick Stratton championed a directive to Doug "to accept early release," tantamount to a direct order. There was good reason for that decision by the seniors. Doug knew every name of every one of us that he had heard. Armed with a direct order to go home with his knowledge, not only of names, but also of a lot of specifics regarding torture, states of health, and overall inhumane treatment of all of us, not only could he not be censured for accepting release, he would be honored for doing his duty.

One day in the summer, it is very warm and the Camp is relatively quiet. Collie and I keep a vigil, as do the rest of the cells. There is no reported traffic to the Big House. Then, in the afternoon, Bill opens our door and signals me to come along. We go the big house and enter through the front door on the veranda. Bill takes me straight through to a large office in the back. I step through the door and there sits the Oxford speaker. He was all business in the Green room and he's all business today. He motions me to sit as Bill leaves the room and closes the door. With no further ado, he reaches into a portfolio and pulls out a small poster sized black and white photograph of a Bill Board antenna used by our "Over the Horizon" radar equipment. It's been a long time since I was a radar technician, and this technology has come along since I left the business. I am suddenly grateful that, even if I tell Oxford everything I know about this stuff, it would be less than nothing. He holds up the photo and asks: "Have you ever seen anything like this at Da Nang?"

I am looking at the photo trying to figure out where it might be. I am thinking about the settings in our Distant Early Warning (DEW) line where the background in the photo might fit--not so that I can answer any questions Oxford might have, but just of my own curiosity. I have no idea where that contraption might be, but it's not at Da Nang. So I tell him: "That's not Da Nang," without even thinking about it.

He is impatient, not like an interrogator, but like anyone might be in any kind of a conversation after having gotten an answer to the wrong question. He Says: "I didn't ask you if this is Da Nang, I asked if you had ever seen anything like this at Da Nang." I said: "There's nothing that looks like that around Da Nang." He's not quite finished: "Have you ever seen anything that looks like this anywhere?" "No." He signals Bill to come and replace me in my cell. I will never see Oxford again, but I shall never forget him. This was the shortest interview I ever had with the V.

During the year, I have several conversations with two V that I don't believe anyone else ever saw. One is a mature gentleman, about sixty years old. The other is a younger man, maybe in his thirties. Both are very cultured and speak essentially perfect English. They are well dressed, and the elder never appears in uniform. They are not much interested in the V propaganda line, but occasionally the elder of the two will talk about the general objectives of Communism, and, on one occasion, when I expressed my opinion that the U.S. would never become a Communist country, he smiled, and politely responded: "Someday the water will boil." The younger never says much, but when he joins in, his English is better than the older man's. From now on I shall refer to them as Martin and Lewis--the older as Martin, the younger as Lewis.

I think a lot about these two. I sometimes think that they are academicians who are faithful Communists and/or are either members of some governmental body, or have the blessings of the government to talk to POWs. In our communications among ourselves, we always report the details of our visits to the Big House, and I have not received any feedback that anyone else ever spoke to these two. My common sense tells me that I am wrong. Why would two really unusual V come here just to talk to only one of "us"?

Both of these men would sometimes remark on Lenin or Marx, and occasionally on other historically significant personages that support the Communist view of the world in some way. I expressed my wish for reading material. They were not as non-committal as the military people were. They always smiled and made remarks like anything might be possible. They never commented on the early release issue. They never called me by name, and I never asked theirs. I observed the standard Viet Namese social manners with these two as they did with me.

On the evening of December 9, 1969 as bedtime approaches, we hear the standard set of commotions signaling a move. We hear the guards talking and the noise of the main gate swinging open. I grab a sawhorse to stand and take a look at the yard through the vent above our door. A small bus enters the yard and spews out POWs. The V take several to the

Big House and disperse others to the Gun Shed and to some of the cells in the Warehouse.

In the middle of all this, Bill heads our way, and I quickly step down and replace the saw horse. The door opens and a young man enters with his "stuff" rolled up in his bed mat. He places his bed roll on the bed that was Swede's, turns and bows, and Bill closes and locks our door. We introduce ourselves. The young man is Navy Lt/Jg Dick Tangeman. He was flying with Lt. Giles Norrington in an RA-5 on May 5, 1968 when their battle damaged airplane exploded. They ejected through the fireball and Lt. Norrington suffered third degree burns. Miraculously, both survived, and Norrington arrived here at the Plantation a few weeks ago.

On 10 December, 1969, Tangeman, Collie, and I take a turn with the parade of the entire camp to the Big House. The V gave us an opportunity to celebrate Christmas by placing art, poetry, and greetings on a bulletin board; another obvious attempt to exploit us for propaganda. If they showed the stuff that we put on the board, their propaganda ploy would have backfired, much as Nils Tanner's writing, citing Commanders Clark Kent and Ben Casey as being anti-war proponents aboard their ship. The letter was widely disseminated in news media all over the world and Nils paid a high price for this high jink. I recall reading Tanner's remarks in Time Magazine, and wondered then if he would survive. If our display made any papers, we never heard from it. Collie wrote a beautiful satirical Higgeldy Piggeldy poem with a little help from me. We were proud of it.

Other than this unusual visit to the Big House, our day is normal. The day goes fast as we exchange our experiences.

On the evening of the 10th of December, 1969, as we prepare to turn in, the V unlock our door. We stand and Bill opens the door, with an AK carrier in the background. Bill points to me and signals me to roll up. I roll up my stuff, say good bye to Collie and Dick, and step out into the prison yard. I wait for Bill to lock up and then follow his directions to walk across the prison yard toward the Movie Room. He directs me to stand near the corner of the Movie Room nearest the gate. The guards swing open the main gate and a jeep like-vehicle made in France comes in.

I am amazed as Lewis steps out of the vehicle and moves toward me. He smiles in greeting and speaks to the guards. There are two other uniformed men with him who step out and stand near the vehicle. After a few remarks to the guards, Lewis asks me to please get into the vehicle and sit in the middle of the bench seat in the rear. I scoot into the seat and hold my bed roll in my lap as the two uniformed men sit on each side. Lewis gets into the passenger's seat and speaks to the guards. The driver turns the Jeep around and we drive through the gate and turn left into the street.

Camp Hughey

There is very little conversation as we drive through the streets of Ha Noi and head generally South West. The streets are lighted, people are moving about, and buildings are lighted. It seems like a "business as usual" evening in Ha Noi. As we near the edge of town, we drive along parallel to a trolley for a mile or so. The trolley is a small locomotive pulling two cars that are lighted and partially filled with passengers. As we continue and transition from the city to the bare countryside, street lights and the end of the trolley recede from view, and we transition to an unlighted paved highway for two or three miles.

We slow to a crawl, turn left onto a well maintained but narrow dirt road, and continue for a mile of so at a modest pace. We are in a rural area--lots of trees and a roadway lined with shrubs. The only lights we have seen since we drove out of the city are the headlights on this jeep. A group of buildings move into the range of our headlights, like ghostly shadows, and we arrive at a gate. There are some military personnel and flashlights present. Lewis and the guards sitting with me get out of the jeep and Lewis asks me to step out. I step out with my bed roll under my arm and the guards lead me away, lighting the way with flashlights. (Figure 8, Camp Hughey)

We walk about fifty yards through an open area with buildings all around, following a guide with a flashlight and arrive at a masonry wall that is about eight feet high. There is a wooden door in the wall that the leader opens. I follow him through the door into a small courtyard surrounded by the wall. There is a small cell at the right rear of the courtyard. The door to this cell is a heavy wooden structure with bars in the upper half. The flashlight leads me in. The Cell is slightly less than six feet wide and is about ten feet long. There is a barred window at the back wall that extends from about four feet from the stone floor to about seven feet up. The ceiling inside the cell is about nine or ten feet.

I place my things on a wooden bed similar to the one I just left, and the guards assist me in unpacking and hanging my mosquito net. During this process, a peasant man arrives with a small can with a screw-on top and a wick protruding from a spout on top. The wick is burning and the whole thing smells of kerosene. Lewis explains that this camp has no electricity, and that I must allow this kerosene lamp to burn all night. If it goes out, the camp cadre will come around and relight it.

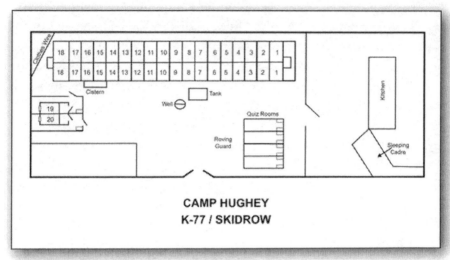

Figure 8

In a few minutes, I am organized, the V lock my cell door and depart, my bed is made, and all that remains is to turn in. I crawl into my nest enclosed by the mosquito net and go to sleep accompanied by the very slight noise made by the fluttering flame of the kerosene lamp now sitting on a small table near the wall opposite my bed--about two feet from my head.

The morning of December 11 is much like other mornings except for the openness of my cell, and the fact that there is a kerosene torch sputtering away. I might as well be outside in many respects. I stand up beside my bed, face the opposite wall, pick up the lamp, and blow it out. To my right, I peer out into the rear of the small courtyard that I could not see last night. I look across the courtyard about ten feet away to a masonry wall about twelve feet high. The courtyard is filled with small shrubs and a small tree. Standing near the rear window, I have a narrow view of a small segment of sky.

I take down my mosquito net, fold up my belongings and place them at the "head" of my bed, the end nearest the rear window.

Standing near the door to my cell, I look through the bars in the upper half of the door, and peer into the front part of the courtyard that my cell occupies. I can see an eight foot wall separating the courtyard from whatever is on the left. The wall straight ahead contains the door that I came in last night. The door is about fifteen feet away, and a brick trough sits on the ground near the outside wall to the right. (Figure 7)

In a while a guard opens the wooden door to the front courtyard. He comes to my door and hands me a cigarette through the bars. I take the cigarette and he gives me a light and leaves. I have a leisurely smoke, and soon the same Viet peasant that helped me put up my net last night comes through the gate. He is carrying a basket via a loop over one shoulder as he approaches my door. He is friendly, but all business as he points to the kerosene lamp and signals me to hand it to him. I hand him the lamp through the bars, he puts it in his basket and departs with purposeful alacrity.

The V left a bucket in my room last night. I have used it, and it now sits in the corner near my door as I wait for the camp schedule of events to play out. Soon, a very friendly Turnkey comes through the gate and unlocks my door. As he swings the door open, he signals me to bring my bucket and follow him. I grab my bucket and he signals me to set it just outside the door to my courtyard, and get a quick look at the prison yard. There is a long building on my left that extends toward the opposite end of the Camp. There are a number of doors evenly spaced the length of the building. At the opposite end of the prison yard there are other buildings and some to the right as well. I return to my room and the turnkey locks my door after me. (See Figure 8.)

Mid-morning, my courtyard door opens and the Turnkey invites me to come and retrieve my bucket from just outside my cell door. I bring my bucket back to my room, and the turnkey locks me in.

A short time later, a V peasant comes through my courtyard gate. He moves a small square topped stool from the corner of the court yard to a position just outside my door, sets the standard plate and bowl and spoon on the stool, and leaves. Soon, the Turnkey shows up, unlocks the cell door, and signals me to pick up my food and take it inside. I set my food on the small table in my room and sit down and eat. The food is the same as at the plantation.

Later in the morning, the Turnkey returns and asks me to come with him. I follow him out and we walk straight ahead after we exit my courtyard. I walk the length of the prison yard and observe that the long building to my left has eighteen numbered cells. We pass the end of the long building, and the Turnkey ushers me in to a small room with a table and chairs. Martin and Lewis stand and greet me as I enter. They smile and are pleasant.

They have tea and cookies on the table and ask me to sit and join them. Martin asks me if I have any idea why I am here. I say no. He then explains that he and Lewis recall that I have asked them for books, as well as having asked other camp officials many times in my past interviews. He then says that this camp has a small library for those who live here, and that I will be provided reading material that I have specifically asked for along with other things to read. I am excited at this prospect. He then tells me that I will get Karl Marx to begin with, and when I have finished Marx, they will furnish other things for me to read. I am overwhelmed. First, I am overwhelmed at the prospect of having something substantive for myself to read, but also to learn that, at least in this camp, all here have that opportunity.

They also tell me that while I am reading Marx I will be allowed to have pen and paper to take notes, which, because of the camp rules, I will not be allowed to keep.

Martin and Lewis do not stay long. We have some small talk, I have a small tea and a cookie, we bid adieu, and I return to my cell.

On my way back to my cell, I note that I am in cell 20 and that there is what appears to be a mirror image of my cell and court yard adjoining cell 20--must be cell 19, since the cells in the long building are numbered 1 through 18. (Figure 8) A wall separates the two courtyards. This wall is about eight feet high, the same height as the front wall that contains the entry gate to my cell. I soon discover, by listening, that cell 19 is occupied.

At meal time one of the kitchen crew comes into my court yard and places the standard two dishes on the stool, and later the Turnkey comes by and lets me out so I can bring them into my room and set them on my small table. Sometime after the meal, the Turnkey returns, unlocks my door, and I place my dirty dishes on the stool. Later, one of the kitchen crew comes through my gate and picks up the dirty dishes.

As the sun sets and dark approaches, the dude with the kerosene lamps shows up. If I don't hear him or see him right away, he grunts and thrusts the lighted can through the bars. I grab it and set it on my table. I have been instructed that if the lamp goes out, that someone will come and light it for me. If no one comes right away, I should call "Bao Cao" (pronounced Bow Cow), and someone will come. The crew at this camp is much friendlier and efficient than at the other two camps I have visited. They are not buddy-buddy, but they are also not openly hostile and demanding.

Sunday morning December 14 is my first Sunday here, and I soon learn that Sunday here is the same as the Plantation. The Turnkey shows up a bit late and I set my bucket outside my gate. Then, instead of locking me back in my cell, he lets me know that I can stay outside and get some sun. He then leaves and opens Cell 19. From my position outside, I can hear the doors opening and can visualize what is going on. I know that my neighbor is out in the courtyard the same time that I am. Sunday is also a bit of a lazy day for the camp personnel. One of the guards who has been showing up periodically at my back window doesn't come around today. I would be lonely, if I didn't have my daydreams and memories. I can't help but think about my wife and son and how it all began.

Fall 1946

Summer is over and I resume the long ride to and from Dyersburg to do my sophomore year. Sue Austin has started to high school. She rides the same bus that I ride between Finley and Dyersburg every day. As macho as I think I am about driving tractors and hunting, and doing "male" things, I am scared to death of girls, except for the ones that are just friends, which means that, at the moment, I'm only scared to death of Sue Austin. I am a very sociable person unless Sue is in earshot, and then I get lockjaw and/or a bad case of the mumbles, and my heart speeds up. I notice that Sue doesn't say much to me either, and I chalk it up to a lack of interest. It never occurs to me that she might be "suffering" just a little bit from the same set of symptoms that plague me.

The school year progresses and the bus ride isn't getting any shorter. I made it through the freshman year with minimal effort. I don't believe that any of our classmates who live in "town" have any inkling how nearly impossible it is for those of us who live on the edges of the county to get enough homework done to survive. I don't think our teachers do either. My mother is very concerned that the four hour daily commute is wrecking my academic career.

My father died summer before last, and my mother and I have been pay-ing periodic visits to the office of Lyman Ingram, the probate attorney who is handling my father's estate. My mother is entitled to a widow's part of the estate and the remainder is allocated to my brother, Jack and my Hughey sisters, Ruth, Ruby, and Catherine, and to me. It comes down to this: My mother and I get 3/7 of the estate, and each of the other Hughey children get 1/7. My mother bargains for cash, and my brother Jack buys our shares, and the estate settles not long into the school year.

I need to explain why I use the terms "Hughey sisters" and "Hughey chil-dren." Each of my parents lost their first spouse, and each had four children by their first marriage. My father did not adopt my mother's children, and, by law, my mother's four prior children were not included in my father's estate. They are the Burgher children.

My mother buys a small house in Finley and rents it out to the Tidwell family, with a provision that I can board with the Tidwells for the remainder of the school year. I suddenly have time to do my homework, to play ball after school, and sometimes to help the Tidwell's twin grade school daughters, Susie and Luzie, with their homework. I am still not hitting on all cylinders in terms of my own schoolwork, but I now live only a block away from that saucy little girl I saw for the first time last spring. Like George Gordon when he first bumped into Caroline Lamb, I am stricken, but unlike Lord Byron, I don't have the gumption to do much about it.

The house in Finley is a small bungalow. It has a living room, one fair sized bedroom, another bedroom which is just big enough for a standard size bed and a small dresser, a kitchen, and a dining room. The whole thing may be 800 square feet. Note the absence of a bath room.

There is an outhouse in the far corner of the vegetable garden in the back yard. Bathing is a choreographed event. We turn the kitchen into a bath room by taking a galvanized bath tub into the kitchen, filling it with hot water from a pot on the kitchen stove, bathing, dressing, and then crying out for someone to help carry the tub through the dining room and out the back door, passing the hand operated water pump on the back porch, to be emptied. We all are encouraged not to dally during the bathing process, and not to bathe at crucial times, as when Mama Tidwell needs to be in the kitchen preparing a meal. I soon learn the routine.

Six of us share this little house, and it works just fine. Lusie and Susie are eighth graders at the Finley school, which is just a block away. They share their parents' bedroom. Joe, their brother who is about twenty years old, shares the small bedroom with me. Lusie, Susie, and I do our homework together at the dining table. The girls are conscientious students and we work well together. Very occasionally, they have a math problem that I can help them with, but most of the time, we don't bother each other, except for small talk.

As soon as I can, I make friends with two of Sue Austin's younger brothers, Joel and Titus. Titus is a little more than a year older than Joel, but they are more like twins. They started to school at the same time, so they are in the same grade. Sue has two other siblings. Her older sister, Elizabeth, is in my class in high school, and a Johnny-come-lately brother, William, is about six years old. The idea is that having her siblings on my side can't hurt my secret cause.

Sunday December 14, 1969 continues

I think about the situation here with a neighbor, who is just inches away, and how to contact him. I try the shave and a haircut tap but get no response. Maybe there are V present that he knows about and I don't. I'll try later.

It is Sunday, after all, and on prior Sundays at the Plantation for the five months I was alone, there were lonely moments like today. I usually reviewed some past poetry or maybe a story or book, or maybe some events from my past. Today, I remember that Sue would help me memorize things by listening to me recite while she followed along with the written text. How about some Emily Dickinson? I'm in a melancholy mood anyway; How about one of her death or dying poems with some spiritual overtones? I start to work:

Safe in their alabaster chambers
Untouched by morning and untouched by noon
Sleep the meek members of the generation
Rafter of satin and roof of stone

Light laughs the breeze in her castle of sunshine
Babbles the bee in a stolid ear
Sing the sweet birds in ignorant cadence
Ah, what sagacity perished here.

Grand go the years in the crescent above them
Worlds scoop their arcs and firmaments row
Diadems drop and Doges surrender
Soundless as dots on a flake of snow

The poem begins with a totally ironic notion—the dead who are safely interred are the meek, as the meek in the beatitudes who, as Jesus put it, "shall inherit the earth." given that we arrive quickly to the notion that she is writing about the dead. These dead people--the meek members of humanity-- have inherited a position in the earth. It is theirs and they are safe. Excuse me Miss Emily, if death is safety, I'll take my chances elsewhere.

Safe, and untouched as well. The dead are untouched, and I don't like that idea either, but it has its beauty.

I walk through the rest of it--the timelessness of being dead. The motion of the cosmos, as the billions of heavenly bodies "scoop" their way along the perfectly synergistic lines defined by nature, leaving the events of this fleeting human existence to swirl in their wake. Curiously, I find some comfort and satisfaction in the fact that, even disarmed of my freedom and all material "things" other than the barest of necessities, there is a portion of me that no one can touch. The time and trouble that I took, and the willingness of my help mate to help me with the seeming folly of cluttering my brain with information that seemed to serve no useful purpose, has provided me with a buoy that keeps me afloat in this sea of despair. For a while, I am alone with this diminutive plain Jane from an obscure little no place somewhere in Massachusetts who scooped her own arc in whose wake I currently swirl.

This little prison complex is really in the sticks. The kitchen personnel, guards, Turnkey, and all of the few others have a very provincial air. I spent some time in provincial South Viet Nam and met dead ringers for everybody I see here. I like provincial people. They are closer to the earth, to nature, and to reality. They are not concerned about all the sophistications and complications that overwhelm many urbanites. Some would call them simple--I would not. The cultured urban soul would starve to death in the environment where the "simpletons" flourish with nothing much but the earth itself and what they glean from it.

Monday comes and I take a bath from the small brick trough next to the outside wall of my courtyard. It's too chilly to really enjoy a bath, but I need it. It's very different having no bucket or bath parade. I would like to spend a bit more time outside my courtyard to learn more details about this camp. I miss not seeing other POWs. Then it occurs to me that there may not be any other POWs here. There may not be a soul in the long building with numbers from one through eighteen over the doors. The camp is very quiet, and the only noises I have heard are associated with the goings on in my neighbor's area that make me know that I even have a neighbor. He may be a Viet. Then comes the dawn.

Martin and Lewis told me that this camp has a library for all to read--a clear admission that there are Americans here, since the library must be in English if they are going to share it with me as well.

About all I can say about Monday is that this place is very quiet and with no prison yard to view, it is very boring. By bed time on Monday, I am familiar with all the faces that look after my welfare here. The Turnkey is a very pleasant nonchalant man, probably about 40 years old. The peasant man who deals with the lamps is taller than most Viets and is always in a hurry. If I am not paying attention as it becomes dark, he will suddenly appear at my front door thrusting a lighted kerosene can with a burning wick through the bars.

I have only seen two guards patrolling in the vicinity of my cell. One was here only on Sunday, and I doubt that I could recognize him with any certainty if he shows up again. The other is a young man, a little taller than the average Viet, and he has shown up at my back window at least twice when no one else is around. He is quiet and friendly. He smiles, inspects my cell with a few glances, smile and leaves. I have never had a guard smile in my presence before. I have seen more than one of the kitchen personnel who bring my food and retrieve my dishes. They don't take much note of me--just do their jobs.

Tuesday is another Chilly day that promises to be boring. My big interest today is to pay particular attention to the camp noises and routine in the hope of getting a clue as to how I might contact my neighbor. I can hear his gate opening and can hear the Turnkey unlock his door, and little else.

This afternoon, the Turnkey unlocks my door and invites me out. I leave my courtyard, and he directs me toward the other end of the camp. He ushers me into the same room I had visited before, and Martin and Lewis are there. They have tea and small cookies as before. We exchange pleasantries, and they ask me to sit. They remark about the primitive nature of the camp--no electricity, a cistern water supply which I had passed on the way here, the quiet secluded country environment. They are apologetic about the physical plant, but go on to explain that they think that I would appreciate the reading material.

They have no way of knowing that I had grown up with just about the same level of accoutrements as I have here. I didn't use a bucket, but the rest was about the same. I never lived in a home with indoor plumbing until I left home to join the Air Force. We cooked and heated with wood and pumped water using a pitcher pump. My mother made her own soap from ashes and pig fat. We killed enough hogs during hog killing weather to furnish our smokehouse for more than a year. We didn't use Water Buffalo for draft animals, but mules and one horse. I never said this to them, but I could have moved in here, or into a similar village in South Viet Nam and thrived.

The visit is not long. They explain to me that later today, the camp personnel will bring to my room Karl Marx Volume 1 of *Das Kapital* along with pen, paper, and ink. I never would have believed it. My persistence paid off. I now understand the move here. Someone in their system is willing to allow some of us to read selected material that passed their test for propaganda purposes, but was, even if they didn't understand it, of interest aside from being Communist propaganda. Perhaps it never occurred to them, and I didn't tell them, that the study of economics, history, and politics virtually demand an understanding of a number of Communist writers, economists, and leaders, including Karl Marx. I thirst to read Marx' complete *Das Kapital*.

I say farewell to Martin and Lewis and return to my room. Later in the day the turnkey comes through my courtyard and opens my cell door. A young man is with him. I stand and the young man steps into my cell and places a book, a sheaf of notebook paper, a small bottle of ink, and a pen with a Spenserian nib on my table. The young man exits, and the Turnkey locks my Cell.

I grab the book and start turning the pages. This is the first time I have seen a complete text of Karl Marx. For our economics class at the University of Colorado, we read a tome that contained condensations of the works of the great economists from Adam Smith as he explained his views in *The Wealth of Nations*, through Thorsten Veblen and into summaries of the economics of Socialism and the goals of Communism. I found economics tough sledding and, given the nature of an Engineering curriculum, which kept me hopping, I didn't do the course justice. I passed the course, but left with the notion that someday I would read the subject on my own and try to master it. Since that time, which was in 1959 and 1960, I have been too busy doing other things to get back to economics. I intend to do this opportunity justice.

I have been involved in this war since March 1965. During that time I flew 564 combat sorties. Some were fun and not dangerous, but I survived several that were extremely dangerous, and my doom finally closed in on me, and here I am. During the past nearly five years, nothing much seems to have changed. Not long after I was shot down, we declared a moratorium on striking targets in North Viet Nam. In Ha Noi the air raid sirens have been silent. No bombs have exploded in earshot since I moved in with Collie and Swede. The V claim they scored a great victory in South Viet Nam during the Tet holiday in 1968. They probably did-- we won't know until we are home, assuming we ever get home.

When I told Ron Mastin in July, 1967 that the war was about the same, that statement was true, given the reference points of our shoot down dates. From January 1967 to July 1967, the war news was about the same. However, in assessing the total situation, we were steadily escalating our involvement here since early 1965 and steadily losing ground all over South Viet Nam. For example, in 1965, I lived in a house in Da Nang which my boss and I rented from Madam Nam--a refugee from Ha Noi--who owned extensive real estate in Da Nang. We ate and drank at the finest Bistros in Da Nang. The Shark's Fin soup at the Grand Hotel on the Da Nang River waterfront was the best I have ever had. That was 1965.

In 1967, two years later, Da Nang was essentially off limits. Marine MPs patrolled the streets. I borrowed my Squadron Commander's vehicle to drive into Da Nang in May 1967, not long before I was shot down. I had been unable to get off base before then because of security, but that day I had a special pass. Marine MPs pulled me over and asked me to get out of the vehicle. I remember telling the young Marine Sergeant that he was out of line for stopping a field grade officer who was minding his own business. In the best professional way that only a Marine can exhibit, the Sergeant pointed to his assistant and let me know that their job was to protect the few Americans that were allowed to be in Da Nang and to keep them alive. He then explained to me where I could and could not go. Had I not had a special pass, he would have escorted me back to the Main Gate at Da Nang Air Base.

The South Viet Namese military officers that I served with in 1965 asked me if there was something wrong with our fighter airplanes as our losses accumulated in the North. We had led these people to believe that we were invincible and would help them prosecute this war to the limit. Nothing could be further from the truth. We, as a nation, had no idea what we were doing.

Since being here, I have thought a lot about the way things had gone during my involvement from March 1965 to July 1967. It's a depressing situation. I expect to be here many years. If the V are allowing the POWs in this camp to read, they may extend it to the rest.

Interjection: Had I known what was happening to the majority of POWs while I was enduring a benign interrogation that produced no scars and a very easy stay at the Plantation, I might very well have taken a different tack to accepting anything the V furnished me to read.

There was a school of thought that demanded we not accept anything until whatever was being offered to one had to be rejected until it was offered to all. This notion broke down in a hurry when some were offered the opportunity to write letters home, and others were not. I know of no instance where any of us turned down the opportunity to write a letter home when it was offered, even when one's roommate was denied the opportunity.

It is hard to imagine the hurt endured by those who watched their roommate(s) write letters to their loved ones, while the V acted as if the non-writers did not exist. As a non-writer, I can tell you that it hurt like the dickens to know that the ones I loved were denied any news from me for three and a half years, while my room-mates wrote regularly. I wanted to scream to my fellows, "How can you do that?" as they themselves ignored my plight. If the fact that I held my tongue is offered now as proof of my holiness, forget it. I remained silent for good reasons: I had to live with these guys, and, if I had been in their shoes, I probably would have written.

On the other hand, had I known that the most important person in the world to me would remain in a state of limbo for as long as she did, I might have made some noise and risked having my roommates writing privilege cancelled in the attempt to rescue my own wife from forty-one months of the torment of uncertainty. I am writing this in real time in 2013 and am still hurting be-cause I stood by when my roommates wrote home, thinking that if I kept silent, I would soon be offered the same opportunity, not suspecting that it would take three years to come around.

Much later, when we were in Camp Unity in large groups and had fairly well established communications and a strong chain of command, our leaders came up with the hair-brained notion that if we stopped writing letters home it would somehow speed up the process of the war we were in and expedite our release. I nearly exploded with indignation that any of us could have the notion that a few hundred of us could do anything toward the prosecution of the war and flatly refused to comply with an order not to write home. I sent notice up the line that if offered the opportunity to write, I would write.

I delve into Marx and soon learn why Monks are Monks. I have more alone time than I had before during solitary. Even when I didn't have a common wall with others and had no direct communications with other POWS, I had a view of the outside and could keep track of activities outside my cell. Here I cannot see outside the confines of my cell and courtyard and am really alone. Also, this camp is very quiet, or at least from my cell, I can pick up almost no outside noises that might signal some kind of intelligence. I have nothing else to do but to concentrate on the material the V have loaned me, or to meditate or daydream.

I enjoy Marx and work through the simple equations that are intended to illustrate how capitalism works. He probably understood the capitalism of the industrial revolution better than anyone else--at least in the way he articulates his understanding.   It is clear that labor increases the value of a commodity. Corn on the stalk, lumber in the yard have a certain value, but the labor required to gather the corn and build a house from the lumber, obviously make the basics more valuable. There are a lot of arguments that come to mind about this process or any other economic theory, and contemplating other arguments is part of the fun.

When we left Ha Noi, I thought we were headed generally Southwest, but wouldn't have put a lot of money on my sense of direction. While I am absorbed in Marx, I hear loud engine noise. A big airplane with radial engines is nearby, sounds like right overhead. I get up to look out the front door and see nothing. I turn and stand at my rear window, and watch a Boeing Stratoliner move into view from my six o'clock position and moves majestically to 12 o'clock at about 3,000 feet altitude. I now know exactly where I am. This is the International Control Commission (ICC) bird arriving at Gia Lam Airport in Ha Noi from Vientienne in Laos. The heading from Vientienne to Ha Noi is 45 degrees. This Camp is on a direct southwest line form the center of Ha Noi. If I were at Gia Lam Airport and had access to an airplane, I could take off and turn to a heading of 225 degrees and fly right over this camp, just like the ICC bird does.

During the rest of my stay here, the ICC bird comes over this Camp at irregular intervals traveling in both directions. It always appears to be at about 3,000 feet.

One thing, even more important than economics right now, occupies the leading edge of wherever my synapses are traveling. That is, I want to establish communications with the neighbor next door. I try the shave and a haircut at various intervals, but get no results. This dude next door may not be an English Speaker; he may be a Frenchman who somehow got caught up in the backwater after the Viets captured the French Army at Dien Bien Phu. He might also be a Viet Criminal, or an anti-Communist dissenter who is here for "re-education." My imagination is playing tricks on me. He or, God help us, she, not knowing the tap code, and never having heard the shave and a haircut rhythm, may be as anxious to talk to me as I am to him/her, and just doesn't know yet what to do about it.

I decide to try to sing out my back window in hopes that my voice will carry over the high wall that separates us. I don't see much of the one guard that I assume makes the rounds of the camp, since he shows up periodically at my back window. I decide to keep track of his schedule and to try and dope out the best time to try my singing stunt.

After a few days, I come to the conclusion that the afternoons are most likely the best time to sing. I look and listen for the wandering sentinel, take note that the gate to my court yard is fully closed, and stand at my back window and start to sing. I make up the tune as I go along and begin. "American in the next cell, if you hear me, tap twice, tap twice on your wall." I move away from the window and wait for two taps. If that occurs, I intend to sing the same tap code instructions that Ron Mastin used. No response. I'll try again at another time.

I am aware that on each Sunday morning, my neighbor and I are in our outside courtyards at the same time while the Turnkey conducts the bucket parade for the occupants of the long building. I develop the habit of going to my courtyard gate every chance to see what I can see. Most of the time I see nothing, because the Turnkey closes the gate completely, and I can't move it without being seen or heard. The courtyard gate is substantial and when closed there are no cracks that allow me to view the outside. Once in a while, however, the Turnkey, or maybe the person who picks up my bucket, leaves the door slightly ajar. I have seen at least two other Caucasians who obviously occupy cells in the long building.

After about four weeks, I have seen enough and heard enough to be confident of the Sunday routine. The Turnkey always starts the bucket parade with me. I take my bucket from my room and set it just outside my gate. Then he opens my neighbor's cell, and my neighbor sets his bucket outside his gate. Then the Turnkey takes care of the long building. It takes a while for the Turnkey to finish the long building parade. During that while, it might be possible for me to stand on the stool, which is used to hold my food when the kitchen crew brings my meals, and get enough elevation to chin myself on the wall that separates our courtyards and to talk to my neighbor.

It's Sunday, and I give it a go. The Turnkey shows up, unlocks my door and I set my bucket outside my courtyard door. I am all ears and my heart is running a little faster than normal. I hear the Turnkey open my neighbor's cell, and I hear the door to his courtyard cycle. I wait for any other noises. Someone picks up my bucket. I wait a while and hear nothing. I grab the stool, center it next to the wall that separates us, stand on it, and reach up and grab the top of the wall and pull myself up. Suddenly, I am looking down at a man in faded yellow and blue striped pajamas and can see his closed courtyard and nothing else. He is unaware of me. I whisper to him: "Hey, there." Startled, he looks up at me, and I ask: "Are you an American?" He says: "Yes, I'm o.k." Then he looks around to his gate in alarm, points to his gate and starts to mouth something. I don't wait to try to read his mouthing--it's obviously a warning that the Turnkey is nearby. I retreat and replace the stool to its usual position.

I now know that eventually we will establish communications, and I know that he is an American. He is about my size--not quite six feet tall with Sandy hair and light colored eyes--gray or blue. He is older than I am, maybe mid to late forties. I can't wait to get him on line, just don't know how right now.

Having seen my neighbor, my zeal to contact him and pass him the tap code and be able to talk to him on a regular basis is burning. It's all I can think about. There is only one way to go about it. I have a pen, ink, and paper, and even if I didn't, I could use toilet paper and my tooth paste tube to write a note. During the week I compose a note:

"I am Major Ken Hughey, shot down 6 July 67. Here is the tap code: Take the alphabet throw out the letter K form a five letter box ABCDE across the top AFLQV down the left side. To tap a letter tap down and then across. For example the letter M is tap tap tap--tap tap. Use the letter C for K. Tap twice when you understand. Tap several times rapidly when you dont understand or want a repeat. One bump on the wall means danger. Two taps means all clear. There are more than 200 of us in Ha Noi."

I am extremely careful with this note. I roll it up in tight little bundle and shove it into the waist band of my short pants. Sunday rolls around. The routine begins. Today, I wait a bit longer to repeat my chinning exercise. I pull out the note, move the stool and up I go. My neighbor is waiting. He looks up at me as though he has been waiting. I whisper: "Here's something for you," and toss the note. It lands at his feet, and as I depart, he is bending over to pick it up. "Whew!!"

I know now that it is only a matter of time. I must be patient, because his door faces the end of the long building, and he is more vulnerable to being caught tapping than I am. He is in a much better position to observe the camp routine, plus he has been here longer than I have. I will let him call the shots.

PHIL MANHARD

I keep working with Marx and try to keep my mind off contacting my neighbor. Sunday comes and goes and I decide to try him on Monday at siesta time. Monday the camp becomes quiet in the early afternoon and sit down on my bed facing my doorway such that I can see my courtyard door. If it starts to open I can hit the wall with an elbow and assume an innocent position before the guard can see me. I tap shave and a haircut on the wall, and in a few seconds I get a soft tap tap. I start tapping slowly: "What is your name?"

"Phil Manhard"
"When were you shot down?"
"Not shot down. Captured in Hue "
Wow! What have we here? A Marine? Army?
"Your rank?"
"Civilian State Department."

Double Wow!! Judging from the brief glimpses of his countenance, I guess that he must be pretty senior. But, what was he doing in Hue? I wasn't totally familiar with I Corps, the Viet Army District that included Hue, but this makes no sense. Wonder how long he's been here.

"When were U captured?"
"Tet" and then he spells out: "nineteensixtyeight!"
This is unbelievable! So, Ha Noi Hannah's propaganda reports about the Tet offensive weren't all baloney.

It takes several weeks to get Phil's story through the wall one tap at a time, and even then I know there is a sea of missing detail. I'm guessing it would take several hours or even weeks to completely de-brief him.

As the story unfolds I learn that twenty men who were captured during the Tet offensive had accompanied Phil from South Viet Nam to this camp. They arrived here in July 1968, six months after their capture. One of these men, Tom Ragsdale, who was a Department of Agriculture employee, died not long after their capture when an American FAC spotted the group they were moving with and called in an air raid. The V allowed the group to bury Ragsdale and put up a wooden marker. Phil said that when we get home he planned to recommend Tom Ragsdale for a State Department Award.

Phil feeds me the names of his other nineteen fellow travelers and tells me that they are here in this camp. I memorize these names as a separate list from the names that Loren Torkelson gave me.

He also tells me that a day or so before I arrived here LtCol. Ben Purcell (U.S. Army) had escaped from this camp. Col. Purcell was not a part of the group that came here with Phil. He said that before Col. Purcell left the camp, he swung by his back window and tossed a note into his room. Purcell furnished details about his family and the fact that he was escaping so that Phil could, if necessary, report the incident. I wonder where Purcell is now and how he made out with his escape.

Retrospective: The years go by faster than light, and it is soon 1992, and I have been home for nineteen years when I have my first direct communication with Colonel Ben Purcell. Twenty-two years ago I took his name back to the Ha Noi complex, along with the others who traveled with him from South Viet Nam. Here is the note that Colonel Purcell folded inside a copy of the book that he and his wife wrote jointly. A squadron of Valkyrie subsequently airlifted Colonel Purcell to his place in Valhalla. His wife, Mrs. Ann Purcell, has graciously given her blessing for me to share this communication with you.

4 Sept 1992

Dear Ken,

More than a year ago I read your reaction to a blurb in the Free Press concerning my first escape in Dec 1969. Since that time our book <u>Love</u> and <u>Duty</u> has been published so now you can read the rest of the story.

I shall never forget that you took some significant risks on my behalf... by communicating with Phil Manhard at camp 77 then taking my name back to the Hilton. I was told by DIA after I returned home in '73 that I might have been killed for escaping <u>except</u> for the fact that the Vietnamese found out that my name was being circulated in Hanoi. Thanks for blowing the security of my solitary.

Hope you enjoy our book.

Regards and GBU.

Ben Purcell

I complete Part 1 of Marx and take on Parts 2 and 3 in turn. Part 1 is fun to read and easy to understand. But for the peculiar circumstance of being in prison and having nothing else to do, I would have trashed canned Volumes 2 and 3--they were just more than I ever want to try to digest.

After Marx, the V bring around a few other books, one at a time. Some are very good reading. I read four books by Maxim Gorky that I hope to read again. Three of them are his autobiography from childhood to early manhood. The folk poetry in the first book is worth the price of the book. They also have a great novel by Gorky--*The Life of Matvei Kozemyakin.* There are a few other Russian books that I had never heard of--mostly extolling Soviet propaganda. Some are well done. All are infinitely more interesting than the Viet propaganda they dropped off in our cells occasionally.

Sometimes when I am out in my courtyard to bathe, I can sneak over to my courtyard door and peek out into the prison yard, and sometimes I see another POW. One day I see a very young man, dark hair and a bit on the short side. I describe him to Phil and Phil tells me that he is the Canadian, Marc Cayer, who was working for International Voluntary Services as a school teacher. Another time I see a more mature man, six feet or so tall, with broad shoulders and narrow hips like "Big John" from the famous song. At our next tap session, I start describing him and after "broad shoulders and narrow hips," Phil interrupts me and taps s-p-e-e-d a-d-k-i-n-s. Speed worked for a construction company and, as I later learned, looked the part of who he was--a big man with big hands, big feet, broad shoulders, and a big heart.

After Marx and the other material, virtually all, except Marx, printed in the USSR, I suddenly explode into a vacuum. Then in the summer of 1970, the request that I had always included with Marx, Shakespeare's works appeared. Lewis shows up at my cell. This is the second time that I have seen him outside a "quiz" room. He steps up to my door. He is smiling as always. He has a good sized book in his hand whose cover is slightly bluer than Cambridge, but is the Cambridge Shakespeare identical to the well fingered and well marked-up version in my library at home--the same version from which I memorized more than one famous speech that wound up on the cover of a best seller by a world class writer, perhaps most notably Faulkner's *The Sound and the Fury.* It is brand new. I would bet a month's pay that this very book came in a package from my wife that I have never received.

Lewis hands me the book. He explains that this book is on loan to the camp library and, and since all of those who live here will be allowed to read it, I may have it for only 15 days. After that, he explains, it will be passed around to all who wish to read it, and each will keep it no more than 15 days. I am always happy to see either Lewis or Martin, the only real gentlemen I have met in North Viet Nam. He is genuinely pleased to be able to furnish this opportunity to me and lets me know it.

I pass this news on to Phil. I suspect that he will be the next on the list, and in any event, fifteen days hence we will know.

Shakespeare has been my bag for a long time. The seven volume hard back version in a wooden rack given to me by my mother when I was eleven years old sits on my desk at home very near the Cambridge twin to the one I'm holding in my hand. My mother purchased it in about 1916. Before I left home it was showing signs of aging, and I rarely opened any of the volumes, and, when I did it was with reverential care. I had never made any annotations in any of the volumes, and never would.

My attack on this work is simple. This collection of Shakespeare's works contains 37 plays, 154 Sonnets, the epic poem "The Rape of

Lucrece," shorter poems "The Phoenix and the Turtle;" "The Lover's Complaint;" and "Venus and Adonis." I will read each of the 37 plays twice and skip most of the rest.

I am reading about 15 hours per day, maybe more. I read at night by the kerosene light, but restrict that reading time to work on things I want to memorize, which means that I am only reading to check my memory. The only time in my life that I have ever approached a reading task with this intensity is the first time I read *War and Peace*. Sue was working long hours at her job managing a restaurant, bar, and gift shop at Los Angeles International Airport, and I took a week off to read. I wrapped myself in a blanket and read about 12 hours a day. My current task is easier because I am a Monk.

At the end of 15 days, Lewis shows up to collect Shakespeare. I thank him for the opportunity and he leaves. The next day when Phil and I talk, I begin by tapping something like "did u get...", and he interrupts with "yes." Phil and I never get around to saying anything further about Shakespeare.

May 30 falls on Saturday this year. I think about Memorial Day and particularly about some of my memories about WWll, and suddenly I'm home in Chic, and all the young men are heading off to war.

A lot of men and women have sacrificed their lives so that the rest of us can live free. My plight here is trivial compared to some. I think of several of them often on this day, as well as other days. I think of "Man Boy" Bowles who left his country village home in Chic, Tennessee --still a teen ager. I think of his parents who loved him so dearly as their youngest that they never called him by anything but his baby nick-name--Man Boy. He was a strapping six footer--handsome and shy. All the local girls eyed him hopefully.

Then, on an early morning in March 1943, he left his home in Chic for the drive to the nearest town--Dyersburg--where he boarded a bus for Memphis. His mother kissed him farewell on her dark front porch and wet his handsome face with her tears. She returned to her kitchen to sit and weep as Man Boy's father pulled out of the yard in his Model A Ford for the twenty-five mile drive to Dyersburg.

In Dyersburg, Man Boy hesitated near the door of the bus that would take him to Memphis and to his service in the US Army. His father applied a bone-crushing hug to his youngest son, turned slowly away, unable to control the tears which washed his weather beaten face. He had seen his most precious boy for the last time on this planet. Man Boy died a few months later on the beach at Salerno, Italy.

There are not enough riches in this world to adequately reward the Man Boys and the "Woman Girls" who gave their lives for the rest of us. Only God can take care of that matter. Meanwhile, the rest of us can only recall the heart-ache of their loss with gratitude and thanks. I am fortunate to be blessed in these moments of quiet solitude with the memories of this young hero whom I barely knew.

Summer moves on and it is soon August. The Turnkey shows up occasionally with a copy of "Soviet Union" magazine. It's fun to read and is very upscale in terms of quality of photographs and articles. If I were home, I would look into a subscription. That's about it. The camp's library would occupy a portion of a shelf in my study at home.

August brings along a curse--dysentery--that, for a short time, convinces me that my doom has finally tracked me down. It starts with a mild case of diarrhea. I visit my bucket at intervals, which become short-er and shorter until my bowels are moving constantly, even after there is nothing further to move. I have never experienced anything like this, but know what it is from briefings about some of the Japanese POW camps during WWII. Guys were dying like flies from dysentery. Without including all the explicit details of how a terminal case of dysentery plays out, the magic landmark was 3 days. If you were alive after 3 days, you had it made.

I keep hoping that this thing will end today, and I won't have to prove or disprove the conclusion from WWII. Late in the day, as the sun lowers, I am getting weak. I can still move around, but my legs feel shaky. I look in my bucket to see what's there, because I know that my insides have long since been empty. I have seen some blood on my toilet paper, but when I look into the bucket, there is almost nothing visible but foamy blood. I yell "Bao Cao" out my front door several times. In a few minutes, the turnkey shows up and I ask him to look into my bucket. He opens the door so he can see into the bucket. He looks in, and his face contorts into frown of worry and distress. He departs abruptly and leaves my door ajar.

In about half an hour, maybe less, the Turnkey returns with two strangers in tow. They are medics. I lie down on my bunk and one of them gives me a 10cc IV from a syringe. These guys are talking to each other and seem genuinely determined to fix the problem. They give me two pills to swallow and leave.

After about another half hour, the Turnkey returns with one of the kitchen crew with a bowl of very liquid rice--not the pile of dry rice we get in our plates, but more like a soup. The Turnkey places the rice on the table with a spoon and urges me to eat. The stuff is very sweet and tastes good. I take down all that I can.

Whatever is going on in my insides begins to subside. I lay on my bed and am able to rest. I sleep some and visit the pot some. Somebody comes by with a flashlight at more frequent intervals than normal.

Morning comes and I get another visit from the medics and another 10cc IV. The kitchen crew brings more sweet rice and I sleep a lot today. Whatever had happened to me is getting better, but I feel moribund, and still visit my "bo," but less frequently. The V medic gives me a bottle of purple pills and tells me to take one every day until they are gone. For several days, I have only the sweet rice soup, the pills, water, and sleep.

My condition improves. I am still weak, but vertical and able to walk when Martin and Lewis pay me a visit. They inform me that I will soon be returning to Ha Noi to be among my fellow Americans. They never use the words *criminal* or *Prisoner of war.* They let me know that I will never see them again. I am sad to learn that I will never again see the only friendly faces I have encountered here.

I inform Phil that I will soon be leaving for Ha Noi. He believes that I am returning to Ha Noi in preparation for release, and that all of us will soon be going home. I hope he is right. I will miss Phil Manhard. We have been neighbors for nine months, and for nearly eight months, we have shared as much of ourselves as we could by tapping through a foot thick masonry wall. We have been careful and the V apparently have never suspected that we were communicating.

When the dysentery started, I had not bathed or shaved in more than a week. After a week or so on the pills and sweet rice, the V put me back on normal rations. I am feeling almost human, but still not strong and still have several pills left in the bottle. Tonight, on Friday, August 21, it is dark, and I will soon be turning in when the Turnkey shows up with two helpers who help me pack my bags for a move. They escort me out to the gate and a Jeep-like vehicle is waiting with a driver and Lewis. We load up and head for Ha Noi. I wish that I could have tapped good-bye to Phil, but am pleased that I had enough warning to let him know that I was leaving, and that he will understand.

We are soon in the suburbs of Ha Noi, and shortly we leave the road from Camp Hughey and meander for a very short distance on suburban streets. The Jeep turns left off the street we are on, and we drive through a large gate and stop. We are parked near the end of a long building with doors that open on to a veranda. I remain in the Jeep as the guards exchange small talk with each other and Lewis walks away. One of the guards offers me a cigarette. I light up and right away I wish I hadn't. I haven't had a smoke in a few days, and soon extinguish this one. (Figure 9)

In a few minutes Lewis returns, and the local Turnkey takes charge. Lewis says good-bye, and the Turnkey escorts me up a few steps and on to the veranda of the building just a few feet away from where we parked. We step down to the third door, and I stand aside as the turnkey opens the door. When the door is open, I am facing two men dressed in American made boxer shorts and the standard issue rubber tire go-aheads. They are clean shaven, with neat haircuts, and they look great to me. I take the middle bed in the room as the Turnkey locks up, and Bob Fant and Larry Friese introduce themselves.

They look me over and try to hide their surprise at my appearance. I have not shaved or bathed or had a change of clothes in about three weeks. My blankets have not been washed for nearly a year and are filthy. I smell terrible and feel tired and ill. My last haircut was at least 2 months ago.

THE ZOO

Tonight, I learn that I am now in the Zoo and that all the buildings have names, and that we are in the Garage, Cell 3. (Figure 9)

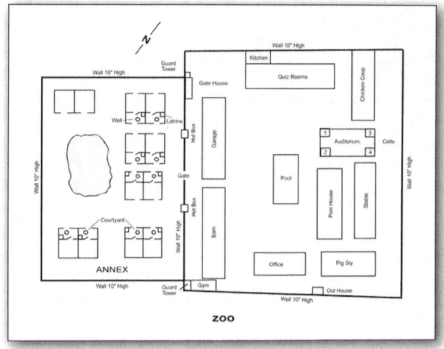

Figure 9

The next day the V take us to the bath, which is located in the space between the Garage and the Barn. I take everything I have with me. The V lock the three of us in the bath and take a break while Larry and Bob help me with my laundry. The blankets are a two person job. Bob Fant has a serious injury to his right hand and stands by as Larry and I wash and wring out my blankets. The V left a razor and I shave.

Back in room 3 of the Garage (Figure 9), I feel a lot better and the three of us exchange stories. Larry is a Marine Capt., who was in the right seat of an A-6 with Marine Capt. Jerry Marvel (no kidding!) when they were shot down on a night raid just a few miles from Ha Noi. Bob is a Navy Lt. who was in the back seat of an F-4-B with Lt. Chuck Parrish. Lt. Parrish apparently did not survive the ejection from their battle damaged F-4.

Fant is in an unusual set of circumstances regarding his personal life. He and his fiancée, Rebecca "Becky" Otts, were scheduled to be married in just a few weeks when he got stuffed. It never once occurs to him that this wedding is not still scheduled for a short time after this cruise ends--it's just that this cruise is turning out to be a few years longer than anticipated. *(I won't keep you in suspense. Becky waited for Bob, rapscallion that he is, and they married about two weeks after he was released in March 1973. This is one of those stories that's too good to be true, but it's true anyway!)*

Bob's injury left his right arm shorter than his left, and he has difficulty using his right hand. As a result, his nickname is "Fingers." Nothing much was sacred in this circle. When Friese saw Ray Vohden in shorts from our view across the prison yard, he turned to Bob and me and said something like: "He needs to trade that mess in for a prosthetic leg." If they had been face-to-face, Larry would have said about the same thing to Ray. (As it turns out, after our release, Ray kept his leg. Even though it was terribly mutilated, his medical team fixed it good enough for him to keep it.)

I soon learn that Larry Friese has an insatiable hunger for knowledge. I am nowhere near 100%, but even if I had been in the middle of extreme unction, Larry would have closed in, like an intellectual vulture, to pick my brains of anything of value before it was too late. He soon learns that I know something of Shakespeare, and that the V had let me borrow (what was probably my own anyway) Shakespeare's complete works for 15 days. He asked me if I had read all of Shakespeare's plays, and when I said yes, he asked if I could name them, and, when I said yes, he said: name them. I had never named Shakespeare's plays before, and they weren't stored in my memory bank in any kind of a file. I start with the ten histories and could rattle those off because they occur in order and are just one continuing story. The tragedies and comedies are troublesome, but, at least I know that, in the Cambridge Edition, there are ten tragedies and seventeen comedies. If I can nail the tragedies, then maybe I can take a break and dredge up the comedies.

It works. We have no place to write them down, but soon Friese has arranged them in an order that that make sense to him. He nailed the histories effortlessly. Then he arranged the ten tragedies to suit himself, by asking me some questions and thinking about it. When Friese finishes his organization, *All's Well That Ends Well* takes its place as number 37.

In return for Shakespeare's plays, Larry agrees to teach me Russian. When he was in college at the University of Washington, he studied Russian and lived for a while in Rooski Dom (Russian House, my English spelling, so watch out!) where the denizens were allowed to speak only Russian. We begin with the alphabet, and I eventually learn some valuable phrases like "I'm going to the post office to mail a letter.", and "Here is the factory, here is work.", and the complexities of the Russian use of hither, thither, and yon.

The buildings in the Zoo are scattered. We communicate with all in the Garage via the tap code, but it's a bit sporadic with the rest. Sometimes we can see others and signal with the tap code, and that's mostly it. That's enough that we know all who are here and their general state of health.

The big news is that two guys escaped from this Camp in May 1969. Those of us at the Plantation at that time were living in tall cotton and didn't know it. The situation at the Zoo was terrible before the escape and went into a state of total Hell afterwards. The escapees were back in the camp only a few hours after breaking out--a very predictable result. I am grateful that I was not here. One of the escapees, Captain Ed Atterbury, died a few days afterwards while being beaten daily. Several others were beaten nearly to death. One of the sufferers, Major Ken Fleenor, later told me that when he realized that he could not survive the beatings he was taking, he planned to overpower one of the AK armed guards and take as many with him as he could. The problem was that the V kept the AKs at enough distance that he could only hope that one of them would screw up and get too close--but it never happened.

In the meantime, my roommates tell me that the food here would be a big improvement over the fare I just left--they are right.

I soon finish the little purple pills and feel almost human again. Being clean and having clean bedding and clothes is especially nice, but the best part is the company. Not only do I have two roommates to talk to, but we have a common wall on both sides of us and communication is easy. It seems that subsequent to the aftermath of the escape attempt and the death of Ho Chi Minh, the V have become much more rational and reasonable in their dealings with us. The food here is better prepared and cleaner looking than at the Hilton, Plantation, or the Camp I just left, that soon will be referred to as Camp Hughey as shown in Figure 8.

Not long after I arrive here, I go to one of the Quiz Rooms (Figure 9) for an interview with an English speaker that I have never seen before. After a brief conversation about my health and my roommates, he asks if I would like to write a letter home. At last! He shows me a form that he says is in accordance with the Geneva Convention. He then explains that I will be given an "opportunity" to prepare a draft, which, when approved by the DRVN authorities, I will be permitted to copy onto the form and send to my wife.

I write a draft and return to my room. A few days go by and I get another trip to a Quiz Room. This time the same English speaker is there with a buddy. They explain to me that I will have to delete requests for the Bible and Shakespeare from my draft. I do another draft which they accept. It is 19 September, 1970.

Retrospective: Years later I will learn that Sue got this letter during the Christmas holidays in 1970, and that it was only then she believed that I was alive.

Soon there is a shakeup in the camp, and I wind up in the Office. The V leave our individual cell doors open during a lot of the day and we can mingle. There is an enclosed yard with trees and a bath. The Rabbit, the torture specialist who crippled Collie Haines and was a major player in the Ha Noi March, which came very close to getting a bunch of the early shoot-downs killed, shows up here for visits and to conduct "attitude checks." He is a pretty fair guitar player and loans us a guitar. Several can play it; the rest of us listen and watch.

The shakeup results in improvement in our living conditions. The V leave the individual cell doors open most of the day. We can wander around and visit other rooms and spend time in the yard and the bath. There is also a "common" room that has an ancient miniature pool table.

There are trees in the yard and some limbs are at the right height for chin-ups. Larry Friese, Bob Fant, and I remain together in the same room. We meet and see others that we never were able to see before: Tony Andrews, Gobel James, Navy Lt/jg Edwin Miller, Joe Mobley, Giles Norrington, Brad Smith, Art Hoffson, and Terry Uyeyama live in the other rooms.

We trade shoot-down stories as well as a lot of biographical information. The most interesting shoot down story comes from Tony Andrews. Tony was a member of Hotrod Flight, a flight of four F-105s who attacked a target very close to Ha Noi on 17 October, 1967. The flight leader was Major Dwight Sullivan. Three of the four pilots did not go home that day. Sullivan, Tony Andrews, and Don "Digger" O'Dell all bailed out very near the target. Capt. "Skeet" Heinzig went home alone for the second time that we know about in his combat career.

In November, several of us are in the yard working out and talking. I am talking with Tony and Art Hoffson when the gate to our compound opens, and an American carrying his stuff under one arm walks through. Tony looks up and says: "There's Digger." The guard with Digger directs him to his new bunk in one of the cells, and we gather around to welcome him.

This is the first time that Tony and Digger have had an opportunity to compare notes. Digger describes what was going on in his cockpit during the final moments of their mission. As he came off the target, his flight control system was acting up, and he was approaching Tony's airplane. He realized that he didn't have enough flight controls to avoid a collision and tried to call Tony to warn him, but his radio was gone. Digger's airplane rammed Tony's, and you already know the result. (*At this point in time, Tony and Digger had not talked to Dwight. It later came out that Dwight is certain that Digger's airplane did not ram Tony, but rammed Dwight. I do not know whether the three of them have ever spoken together about what happened to Hotrod Flight that fateful day.*)

In the fall of 1970, there was a routine shakeup. We all remained in the Zoo and had good communications between buildings and a lot of outside time when we could talk to those in our building. I found myself in the Pig Sty in the same room with Jim Pirie, Big Bill Robinson, and Norm McDaniel. During our outside time I met some "new guys" and other POWs that I had not seen before. Navy Ensign Bill Mayhew, and Ltjg Mark Gartley were newer than the rest--they were an F-4 crew taken prisoner on August 17, 1968.

Christmas creeps up on us. We discover that some among us can sing, and I am amazed at Gobel James in particular. Gobel has this dry sense of humor, and you can't always tell if he's joking or serious. I'll leave it for you to discover his intent when he responded to my wish to sing like he sings. He asks if I have ever heard Mario Lanza sing, and, of course I have. Gobel says: "Well, just sing like him." Sure, Gobel.

Most of us enjoyed good health most of the time, and most had not suffered any serious injuries during the shoot down and capture process. You have already heard about Bob Fant who was seriously injured and lost about four inches of his right arm and had problems doing things that were once easy for him. He has healed well, and can do almost anything with little or no assistance, but will be permanently crippled. Giles Norrington had third degree burns on his hands and some of his upper body, had also healed well, but is permanently scarred.

One of us will never completely heal until we leave this place. Lcdr Dale Osborne was seriously injured during his shoot-down. He is missing about six inches of bone in his lower right arm, including the wrist joint. When the V patched him up, they had to remove what was left of the bone structure and attach what was left into one piece. It was a crude job, but at least they salvaged his hand that is now attached to the lower bone and works o.k., but with no wrist.

His lower right leg is loaded with pieces of shrapnel that keep working their way to the surface and then through the skin. He lives in constant pain, as these pieces of metal keep threading their way to the surface and popping out of his body. It seems that just as the last open sore is about to heal, here comes another chunk. We suffer with him as he endures this ordeal.

Just before I came here to the Zoo, I got a package from my wife. The V had removed most of the contents and kept it for themselves, but they left a bottle of antibiotic pills and I still have them when I arrive in the same building with Dale. He is in the middle of the process in which a chunk is close to the surface and the leg is infected from the results of other pieces that have found their way out of his body. I have no idea as to the efficacy of the antibiotics on his condition, but we all figure that they can't hurt him, so, over his objections, we prescribe what I recall as the "standard" dosage, and he takes them. The problem is that, even if the pills are helping him, at the rate this stuff keeps ripping through the muscles in his leg, we would need at indefinite supply to get him through. If we were home, we're all sure that a good surgical team could locate and remove the pieces that are left, and he would heal up post haste. Dale Osborne is a tough hombre and endures his curse without complaint.

In the late summer, a small lesion opens in my scalp and soon I've got an ugly open sore. It turns out that hair cut time comes around and the V hand our barber, Brad Smith, the hand clippers. I go last and ask Brad to clip my hair as close as he can. The open sore has become a mess and in the process of the hair cut, the clippers are loaded with goopy hair clippings and pus from the running sore. The task was very unpleasant for Brad, but he hung in there and did it. I hope that those clippers were never used again, but we cleaned them up as best we could.

The V take me out of the compound later that day and quarantine me in the nearest end cell of the Barn. I can talk to the guys in the office, so I'm not in in total isolation. The V medic tells me not to wet my head or wash it. Pretty soon the open running sore expands to a spot a little bigger than my hand. It's really a mess and getting messier. I hope none of the rest come down with whatever it is. I have access to a bath area and soon believe that a thorough washing can't make it any worse, so I use up a hefty amount of V issue lye soap and hand scrub my head thoroughly when the V guard isn't looking. It feels better to be as clean as possible, and soon the whole mess starts to dry up and form a scab.

As the days go by, the scab scales away and leaves purplish new skin with no hair. I came here with a full head of hair, but it looks like that, if we ever go home, I will have replaced about a third of my head with purple skin in place of hair. The healing continues, and after a few days, fuzz starts to appear in the purple zone. Eventually I have a head of hair much like I arrived with and the purple color gradually returns to normal. I can't wait to share this ordeal with Dale Osborne--I'm sure he'll be very sympathetic.

The weather cools as winter approaches, and we will soon celebrate another Christmas in Ha Noi.

It's a cool evening on my wedding anniversary December 26, 1970. Suddenly, there is a crowd of V inside the Office compound, and they start opening our cell doors one at a time, starting with the Cell that I am in. Several V enter our room, along with the Rabbit. He orders all of us to strip, place our clothes on our beds and stand facing the wall opposite the ends of our beds. The V have a thing about nudity and have never done anything like this before. While we're standing nude, the V go through our belongings one piece at a time and confiscate everything that any of us have received in a package from home, including Friese's and Fant's boxer shorts. Then they ask for a bend over and look to see if we have anything hidden on, or in, our naked bodies. They are finished in a few minutes, and the Rabbit orders us to roll up our stuff and load into a bus that's waiting at the gate. In a few minutes we're on our way to someplace else.

CAMP UNITY

The bus takes us to Hoa Lo, and we are soon in Camp Unity, Building 3. (Figures 5 and 10). In a short time we know that there are seven Buildings in Camp Unity with thirty to forty in each room. With thirty plus people in this big room, we don't go to sleep right away. We mill around getting our nets up and getting acquainted, and then there's still a lot of talk after we get under our nets. Our "beds" consist of our straw mats lying on a raised platform that slopes upward from the edges toward the center so that our heads meet in the center and are slightly higher than our feet. I have not met the man whose head is about a foot from mine in this head to head arrangement. We introduce ourselves through the ends of our nets. He is Major Bob Barnett, an F-105 driver shot down on 3 October, 1967.

Bob Barnett is a significant addition to my circle of role models. He is a Christian man with the highest personal and moral values. At this point in my life I profess that I am an atheist, and I have never been gung ho about the issue of how to resist our captors.

Having about nearly half of the shoot downs in seven large rooms in shouting distance of each other is a more than a significant event. To say that all of us are excited wouldn't get it done. Each of the rooms sorts out the seniority issues and establishes a chain of command. The SRO in Building 3 is Navy Commander Leo Profilet. We organize like a Squadron with a Squadron Commander and four Flight Commanders. The Squadron CO is Cdr. Profilet. My Flight Commander is Major John Stavast.

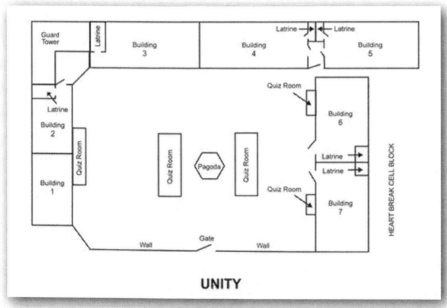

Figure 10

Refer to figure 5 to locate the Pagoda and Buildings 1 through 7 to see how this part of the Hoa Lo Complex fits in.

The earliest shoot-down in this room is the first--Navy Lt/jg Everett Alvarez, Jr. When I see him, I recall the day in October 1967 at the Plantation when Loren Torkelson tapped his name through the wall of cell number six. My knees weakened at the news that he preceded me by three years, and I wondered how. Ev looks good. He looks healthy and exhibits a quiet, controlled, mature, intelligent behavior. When we moved in here, we all just put our stuff down with little consideration of any kind of order. Ev, one of the junior men in the room, wound up sleeping next to the SRO. A lot of us were strangers to each other and had no way to know who we were landing near. We landed by chance.

Trouble began to brew for the VC the minute we arrived, particularly from Building Seven. The V know by now who the tough guys are, and have concentrated a bunch of them in Room 7. One would think that they should have known better and scattered them about. But on second thought, grouping them together might have been the smartest thing to do; these toughies might have leavened the other six buildings and spread even more trouble for our captors.

All of the Buildings hold Church services, but for some reason the V pay more attention to what Building Seven is doing than they do the rest of us and try to stop them from having Church. After a few Sundays, the situation in their Building had worsened to the point of more than one confrontation, and, on one Sunday morning, in defiance and desperation, we heard all the voices in Seven singing out in defiant unison: "We are Cell Block number seven, where the Hell is Six?" In a millisecond, Building Six responded: "We are Cell Block number six, where the Hell is five." In less than a minute the entire camp has sounded off.

For the next few days and weeks, the V are so busy pulling people out of Seven, they don't have time for most of the rest of us. They make some noises about how we should do our Church services, but we do them anyway. Just a note: the Pontifical *We* here does not include the entire room. Two of *us* are avowed Atheists, and, along with one or two others, for reasons of their own, do not participate.

I spent a lot of time with Viet Namese of all stations of life during my year as a FAC and had a lot of conversations with them regarding the state of things in their country; I never talked to a Viet that would say anything derogatory about Ho Chi Minh. During the Eisenhower administration, the media had reported that our intelligence sources believed that had the elections that were agreed upon at the peace agreement after the debacle at Dien Bien Phu been held, Uncle Ho would have carried more than 80% of the popular vote, and that Viet Nam would have been united under the Communist regime. Every time that the subject of Ho Chi Minh came up with the South Vietnamese that I knew, they would say "he is a good man, too bad he's a Communist." I never heard a harsh word spoken about Ho in South Viet Nam.

I still vividly recall the Movietone News coverage of Dien Bien Phu that was shown in theatres everywhere in the U.S. There were generally two reactions. First reaction: "Where is Viet Nam and what were the French doing there?" And the second was "Good for the Viets, Communist and all, they taught the French and the world that colonialism is no longer in vogue."

There was just one big problem that clouded our judgment about how we reacted to what was going on from 1954 until we finally found ourselves bogged down in this place we called "South East Asia" or "French Indo China." The cold war and the actions of the Communist world had somehow twisted our thinking, and we couldn't with confidence look the Communists in the eye and realize that the seeds of their destruction were imbedded in their philosophy along with enough fertilizer to assure their development and growth. The brand of Communism that was being forced down the throats of nearly a billion people during that time could not exist for any length of time.

"No Nhus is good news" typified a lot of opinions during the entire era that we supported South Viet Nam. When the South Vietnamese government didn't act like we thought it should, we simply installed another, and another--each a bigger joke than the last.

I sat in the same room with Nguyen Cao Ky in a briefing room at Da Nang Air Base when he was leading a group of A-1s on a strike into North Viet Nam. The whole mission seemed like a circus. Not long after that, Ky became Premier. He and his wife sported custom tailored flying suits and generally made spectacles of themselves. Most of us fighter jocks admired Ky for leading a strike to North Viet Nam, even if it was purely symbolic, but as head of the government, he was a good man, but a joke. Of course, one could say the same thing about all who occupied that position.

During conversations with Bob Barnett, I told him that I was the American voice that he heard reading excerpts from *The Bitter Heritage* on Ha Noi Hannah's broadcasts. Bob was not alone in questioning and condemning such an act. I explained to him that I read the book for more than one reason. One was that the only way that I would have the opportunity to read it was to read it for the broadcast. The V did not torture me, and if they had asked me to read their routine Communist propaganda on the radio, I would have refused.

The reading issue began at what I expected to be a routine attitude check, which always included a liberal (no pun intended as to my liberal lunatic friends) seasoning of North Vietnamese propaganda. Instead of the usual stuff, the English speaker simply showed me the book and asked me if I would consider reading some of it for their radio broadcast. I asked him to let me see the book so as to read some of it. He pushed the book across the table, and I picked it up and turned a few pages and spent a few minutes scanning the book. I very well knew who the author was and was impressed by this writing. My first thought was that, if the

V were smart, they would order a number of copies and distribute them to us. Another thought was that I could be tried by a General Court under the UCMJ. However all of this went down in my head at the time, I decided to do it, and I have no regrets. If we ever get out of here, I plan to add a copy to my library.

Barnett is far more gracious to me about the reading than most of my fellows would have been. There are some here who may well file charges against me, if we ever get home. I think I have a defense in that the contents of what I read was not Communist propaganda, but rather a scholarly historical piece that accurately summarized the situation we are in. Realistically, I am fairly certain that when those broadcasts of my reading were piped into our rooms in 1969 no one listened to the content and no one cared. We are regularly regaled with conversations with virtual traitors, such as the ignorami who call themselves Viet Nam Veterans Against the War (VVAW), and give them short shrift.

We have church services every Sunday morning. All but a very few attend. Two of us in Room 3 profess to be Atheists, and two or three others decline to attend for their own reasons. The participants are Christians who gain strength from the act of worship, and they are all wonderful people. When the organizers began the Church services, they were careful not to discomfit any who might not want to participate. While Bob Barnett expressed his intense disapproval of my reading on the radio to me, he never broaches the subject to anyone else, and we are friends. For that matter, we are all friends, but just as in any social group, there are different levels of bonding between groups, factions and individuals. No one goes around expressing any special feeling for others, but by gestalt, we know.

After a few Sundays go by, and the regulars at Church take turns doing the homily, Bob asks me to consider attending a Church service and doing a homily. I am surprised and flabbergasted. I reiterate my state of disbelief and that it wouldn't be possible to do it, and that it would be hypocritical. Bob explains to me that he has heard me recite parts of a long folk poem from the oral tradition of Russian peasants that Maxim Gorky wrote down in his autobiography. Bob points out that while the poem is not from the Bible, he knows that the Christian principles and values expressed in the poem are important to me, and that the Christian group would profit from my recitation. It boils down to the fact that my heart is touched by this request, and I cannot say no.

Sunday comes, Bob is emceeing the service, and I sit together with the group at one end. Bob makes some appropriate remarks that alert the audience that they are about to hear how simple people who cannot read and write, and who suffer in poverty and deprivation, approach God. I stand and find that I have to take a moment to grab some composure. I hope that the audience does not detect my discomfort, but will take it as a dramatic pause.

There are three characters in the story: Gordion, an evil war lord; Ivan, Gordion's warrior; and Miron, a hermit and holy man loathed by Gordion. Gordion hates Miron to the point that he orders Ivan to go and bring Miron's head to him. Ivan doesn't want to kill Miron, but regards his duty as "decreed of God," and goes to Miron's home intending to kill him.

Miron is on to Ivan's mission because of his faith and let's Ivan know that Jesus knows everything, including Ivan's intent to kill him. Ivan, even though ashamed of what he is to do, tells Miron to "pray for all men" and prepare to die.

Miron's prayer turns out to be a long one. Years and Seasons go by, and Miron remains on his knees, praying. Ivan dies—his armor rusts away, and vegetation covers the scene, as Miron's prayer continues to this day to "...flow like a stream to the Ocean-sea."

(For Bob Barnett's benefit, in 2013, I am having an emotional time reliving this moment. 43 years have skidded off the stage, and I am, like all of us, a far different person than then. John Fer, one of our other roommates in 1971 was my sponsor in the RCIA program in 2007 and I am now a card carrying Catholic. Without this Christian faith, I could not have endured the past two years of my life.)

Several of our senior officers are congregated in a separate area of Camp Unity. All of us are soon aware of the command structure. The seniors direct the formation modeled after a typical fighter wing. Each Cell is a squadron of four flights. Soon, there is a communication structure that designates "communications officers" for each squadron. This is a necessity in that there is just no way that thirty or forty guys could communicate with each other--we had to keep it streamlined so that the communicators could pass all the news one-on-one. In case individuals wanted to communicate with each other, the request would go through the comm officers. For example, if a person in Cell 2 had an old buddy in Cell 3, the comm officers would set up a time when to tap or speak to each other directly. This was no big deal. Everybody understood the issue and there was always plenty of time for these "special" communications between individuals.

To provide one such special communications between myself and Porter Halyburton who was in Cell 4 while I was in three, I need to discuss the issue of "POW Facts."

Among the 500 plus men there is a wealth of information that we share as best we can. Not all the "information" we share is totally reliable, and when someone doubts the accuracy of some data, the question becomes "Is this really the way it is, or is this a POW fact?" In the bit stream of the total data, there has to be some things that are at least hazy. In case somebody suspects that a certain "fact" is questionable, it becomes a "POW fact" until (and if) a corroborating and reasonable source can be found among us. For example, in my memory the biggest and best known big truck brand is *Kenilworth*. In my mind, it remained Kenilworth until Major John Stavast appeared in Cell three the night we moved to Camp Unity.

John Stavast is a very interesting man with a set of unique experiences, like all of us, and he is the only one among us who has been a professional truck driver. John has driven 18 wheelers all over the lower 48--every state and every major city. Because of this experience, John Stavast knew the lower forty eight geography better than any person most of us had ever met. He also knew big trucks--who made them, and how they worked. There is NO doubt that he knows the correct name of the big Semi Tractor that I recalled as *Kenilworth*, but whose real name is *Kenworth*.

Our biggest single thirst is knowledge. Every one of us brought something with him, some deep knowledge about something that would interest all of us. In Cell three, two men are fluent in a current foreign language. Bob Barnett is fluent in Spanish, and Kevin McManus is fluent in French. Additionally, Capt. Terry Uyeyama, whom you have already met from the Zoo, is fluent in Latin. Larry Friese lived in "Russian House" while he was at the University of Washington studying Oceanography--two disciplines in one. In another Cell Block, there is a former Thermodynamics instructor from the Air Force Academy. At the Zoo, I roomed with Charlie Zuhosky, who could do differential equations in his head.

I believe that I am the only one here who has read all of Shakespeare's plays, and apparently the group believes that also, because there is a demand for notes on Shakespeare's plays. I do my best by writing summaries of some of his plays, with some critical discussion regarding plot, characters, historical significance, etc. Along with these notes, I include all the quotes that I can remember. Some famous examples that are best known are: a couple from MacBeth, including the "sound and the fury" speech and his speech lamenting the fact that he can't sleep. And of course, the "To be or not to be" soliloquy by Hamlet, that may very well be the best known of all of Shakespeare's quotes. And here comes another "POW fact" a la Dr. Hughey, Shakespeare expert.

I jot down Hamlet's "To be or not to be" soliloquy and our communicators include it in the "newspaper" that we pass around. A couple of days later, our communicator, Joe Abbot, is under a blanket in the corner of our room talking to the communicator in Cell 4, when he comes up for air and puts out an APB for me. I ziggy over to see what he wants. He tells me that Porter Halyburton is on the other side of the wall and has a bone to pick with me regarding something about Shakespeare. I am quaking in my boots. Porter has a reputation among us as a Literature Scholar that is frightening, and his notes on "The Bishop Orders His Tomb at Saint Praxed's Church" included long quotes and detailed footnotes that were pure gold. I dread this encounter much like some junior RAF jockey would dread a set-to with the Red Baron.

Here goes. Joe hands the cup to me and says "Here's Porter." I put the open end of the cup against the "sweet spot" on the wall, put my ear firmly against the flat bottom of the cup, and tap twice to let Porter know that I'm listening. Porter begins very graciously by telling me that he appreciates my notes. I tap twice. He then says that he thinks I have omitted some words in a couple of places. I tap twice. He then says that he thinks the sentence that begins "To die, to sleep--" should read "To die, to sleep--*no more*; and by a sleep…, " I omitted the words *no more*. I immediately recall this line and give the wall two vigorous taps to signify assent. He then reads the sentence: "For in that sleep of death, what dreams may come," should be followed by "When we have shuffled off this mortal coil." I immediately recognize that I omitted that entire line and again tap twice vigorously to assent. Those were the only flaws he found. We exchange pleasantries and sign off. Given the encounter with the Red Baron, I feel relatively unscathed. I also have learned that not only is Porter Halyburton a scholar, he is indeed a gentleman and a gentle person.

Our seniors are doing everything they can to facilitate a military command structure. And, as these things inevitably go, whether in or out of prison, there is always a certain amount of dissention among the rank and file. It's not just a matter of taking orders. We are bound by the Code of Conduct to adhere to the lawful orders of those above us. Some of the directives leave some of us a bit cool. One example: the seniors direct that we eschew cigarettes. Each of the squadron commanders tell the V that we no longer want cigarettes--that we have all quit smoking. I am not the only one who is totally opposed to this as a directive.

A V officer is assigned to each of the cells and spends some time each day in his office which is adjacent to the courtyard space connected to each cell. Sometimes this officer will send for one of us for a talk, and we stand at a counter, like a reception desk.

Right after the non-smoking directive is issued, I step over to the counter, intent on talking to the officer assigned to Cell 3, who happens to be the notorious "Rabbit" who conducted the Ha Noi street march and who crippled Collie Haines' hands and Swede's arm. Some of us here have been around the Rabbit a lot at the Zoo. When I approach the counter, the Rabbit is sitting about eight feet away behind a small desk. He acknowledges my presence, and I ask him if I can have my cigarette ration. He says that our cigarette ration has been terminated because we don't smoke anymore. I tell him that I haven't quit smoking and that I would like my cigarette ration. He then tells me that I should talk to Profilet, that Profilet had told him that we had all quit smoking. Since I was out of earshot of other Americans, I could say things to Rabbit that I wouldn't have gotten away with in "public." I told him that I had never told him that I didn't want any more cigarettes. His response: "Talk to Profilet."

Commander Leo Profilet is our squadron commander. Leo is a good man, and as the senior officer in our room, he feels obligated to carry out all the orders of the senior staff, even if he doesn't agree with them. I have never heard Leo say whether or not he agreed with the no cigarettes directive. Most of us think that it is a meaningless gesture. I believe the Rabbit's response pretty much reflects the V's view of the situation as "who cares?"

The directive that rankled most of us the most was a decision to stop writing letters home. I waited three years to write a letter home. During part of that time I watched my roommates write letters home, as my heart was breaking to let my wife know that I was alive-- something she didn't learn for three and a half years. I thought about bringing up the subject to my roommates along the lines of telling the V that "we will write when you let Hughey write." I said nothing, not because I was trying to suck it up and be a hero, but because they had the same feelings about letting their families know they were alive as I did, and giving up their opportunity to write would only allow their families to suffer and wouldn't help mine. Had the current directive been: "Don't write any more letters until we all are allowed to write," I would have supported it. As it was, I sent a message to the Senior Ranking Officer (SRO), that if the V offered me an opportunity to write a letter home, I would take it, in contravention to what amounted to a direct order not to.

Retrospective from the future: I considered such an order unreasonable and unlawful as well, but did not bother to include these words in my opposition. There may be some things about my behavior as a POW that I would change, but opposing this issue about letter writing and reading Arthur Schlesinger's book on the camp speakers are two I wouldn't change.

In October, 1971, a bunch of us move back to the Zoo. Things are much the same as when we were there before. We are in smaller groups than at Camp Unity, but communications are good between the buildings. Two senior officers who are collaborating with the V live in the Office and have a fish pond and garden and are not locked up at any time as far as we can tell. We have a good command structure and the V are not bothering us.

Our Camp SRO is Major John Stavast. I am in the Stable in a room next door with LtCdr Jim Pirie (senior man in the room); Navy Lt Giles Norrington; Navy LtJgs Gary Anderson, Charlie Baldock, Bill Metzger, and Earl Lewis; Air Force Lts Marty Neuens and Hank Fowler. During our outside time, all of us who dwell in the Stable are outside together. Our bath is at the north end of the building and consists of a large brick vat and a brick yard. The V have left a fish in the bath vat. John asks them to move the fish elsewhere because we don't think it's healthy having a fish in our bath water. I'm not sure this is true, but John is the SRO, and if he wants the fish removed sobeit. The V don't move the fish. The next time we bathe, John grabs the fish and heaves him toward the Pool--a long throw. We can't see if the fish made it to the Pool, but the fish is gone, and the V don't notice.

John Stavast has now made his final flight into the sunset. I look forward to seeing him again somewhere in eternity where I can tell him how much I love him and appreciate him.

We entertain ourselves in the evening by telling stories. Our stories were almost always a movie or a book, but sometimes they were personal experiences. The V also let us have Nina Potapova's four volume set of Russian Language texts. Several of us work on Russian.

Later on, the V move us around and I wind up in the Pool House in the room with Air Force Capt. Joe Shanahan: Air Force Lt Darrel Pyle; Navy Ltjgs Charlie Zuhosky, Charlie Baldock, Brad Smith, Joe Mobley, and Earl Lewis; and Navy Lt Giles Norrington. We continue to entertain ourselves in the evening by telling tales from books we have read, movies we have seen, and sometimes life's experiences. We share our shoot down experiences as well.

Brad Smith has seen nearly every movie released before he was shot down, and is always handy with one that none of us has ever seen. Also, sometime in his sordid past here, he roomed with John Borling and memorized some of John's poetry. In particular, a poem called "Boneyard" was very popular. (*John Borling came home, continued his career, and eventually retired as a Major General. He has published a book of his poetry--*Taps on the Walls. *It's a good investment.*)

Christmas 1971

The V arranged a Christmas program every Christmas that I was in Ha Noi. Swede Larson went in 1967 to the first one that I knew about. You have heard about that already. Each of these programs allowed us to communicate with people from other Camps and to at least see others. The only one I made was in 1971. All of us there were able to talk to some of the others.

"Pop" Keirn sat in on the bench directly in front of me and I was able to whisper to him and to let him know the names of those who were there from the Zoo. A group who were now housed in Hoa Lo sang Carols and Quincy Collins sang "O Holy Night." When Quincy arrived at the last line in the last verse, he substituted the words *Keep your chins up, we're soon going home* for the original. If any of the V caught his change, they kept it to themselves.

PHOTO 13

*Christmas 1971. Numbering the pews from 1 through 5,
Pew 1 being at the far left, the occupants are:*

Pew 1: Major Richard "Pop" Keirn, USAF.

Pew 2: from right to left: Major Ken Hughey, USAF; Capt. Joe Shanahan, USAF

*Pew 3: from right to left: Capt. Terry Uyeyama, USAF; Lt/
jg Robert StClair Fant, USN; Major Gobel James, USAF.*

*Pew 4; from right to left: Lt/jg Joseph Mobley, USN; Major
Fred Cherry, USAF; Major Richard Vogel, USAF.*

*Pew 5; from right to left: Major John Stavast, USAF; LCDR
James Pirie, USN; Major James Clemens, USAF.*

BACK TO HOA LO

We move back to Unity in early 1972 and soon develop a command
structure that goes to the seniors who are kept separate from us but are
able to communicate well. The bulk of us are housed in Buildings 1
through 7. The senior officers are separate and isolated in the "Rawhide"

area (Figure 10). They are able to communicate using notes delivered by the dish washing crew and Thai and Viet Nam POWs who are allowed to work in the kitchen and to do clean-up work throughout the Camp. Each of the Buildings is organized along the lines of a combat fighter squadron with a Command staff and four Flight Commanders. The commander in Room 3 is Navy Commander Leo Profilet. My Flight Commander is Major John Stavast.

Things are better than when we were here before. The V let us have playing cards and we can arrange bridge tournaments. Bill Bailey is in the room with me and turns out to be the best bridge player in the room. I am clearly the worst. I learned about the game during my first stay at the Zoo, and am a total tyro, but I am eager to learn and willing to take the inevitable abuse. Bill Bailey is not an excitable person, but he is a bit serious about bridge.

One day, Bill and I were partnered in a duplicate tournament. Navy Lt Ed Estes, and others, came to me and told me of a plan to pull a joke on Bill. They explained how the hand was laid out--Bill and I would wind up playing the offense at a bid of four spades. There would be a point in the play of the hand that Bill would lead an Ace in another suit, a suit I would be void in. One of the fundamental axioms in bridge is: "One never trumps partner's winning card." When it's my turn to play, I am to say: "It's time for me to take charge of this game," and trump Bill's Ace. I make the play, and Bill almost faints. The non-playing observers break out in laughter, and never convince Bill that it was a set-up.

There is much serious business in the organization. Our seniors, who live together in isolation from the seven cell blocks, communicate daily with us by every means possible. They promulgate the creation of a military organization named "The Fourth Allied POW Wing--" an appropriate label in that the "fourth" signifies the four major wars of the 20th

Century--WWI, WWII, Korea, and Viet Nam. The "allied" signifies the fact that we had allies in all these wars who fought with us. In this war, *allies* represent a Viet Namese fighter pilot, three Thai army personnel, and extends to the civilians who are here as POWs.

The senior officers publish directives called *Plums* that are intended to govern our behavior and activities as POWs. The V are still harassing many of the "hard-liners" and meting out physical torture in an attempt to modify their behavior. One of the plums goes like this: "If you're broken, remember that you are an American and bounce back in the next round and win."

We were all aware that there were a few guys who had betrayed the values of the Code of Conduct. A lot of us were aware of the historical miss-steps we had made in this part of the world and the horrible ineptitude exhibited by the top leadership in our country. During much of our stay, we suffered under a country bumpkin school teacher who somehow magnetized enough voters, including those who rose from their alabaster chambers in the local cemeteries, to vote for him. At least he was smart enough to step aside and alleviate some of the pain by letting someone else run for the office. This awareness did not deter our patriotic feelings for our country.

There are a few who are openly supporting the VC propaganda machine, and in at least two cases, accepting special favors from our captors. The last plum issued had to do with our behavior in regard to those: "Remember that a man's reputation is his most prized possession. After our release don't say anything derogatory about a fellow POW except to an official board of inquiry." In spite of this rule, there were those who preferred charges against some of their fellow POWs after we came home. Eventually, the Department of Defense dropped all charges against all but two. These two were issued letters of reprimand and allowed to depart their respective services. The general consensus seemed to be that pursuing the offenders, as Huck Finn put it, "...*would only make trouble and wouldn't do no good.*"

As to violating the Code of Conduct, all of us who came home alive certainly violated the Code by answering question number five, whatever it was, and, further questions as well. Except for a small group, we did so to avoid pain and suffering. There were some who took a lot more pain and suffering than others--the toughest of the tough. Several have written books about the POW experience containing graphic descriptions of every torture tool the VC used, as well as the crippling results. As to that very small group who openly sided with our captors, I seriously doubt that the VC got anything of value from any of them, including positive benefits from the propaganda.

Military secrets? The VC weren't interested in any "military secrets" other than, perhaps, something to do with our aircraft performance, which they knew by observation anyway. Their gunners that hung out in our entry and exit routes already knew our published routes and altitudes. The classic example is the case of Bill Baugh and Don Spoon who took battle damage at the same location and altitude two days in a row. They were lucky the first day, in that they made it home on one engine. The next day didn't work out so well--they soon checked into the Ha Noi Hilton for a six year stay. (*The last time I saw Bill and Don was the day they were shot down. Bill Died in 2010, after completing his career in the Air Force and serving his community and his country in retirement. Don Spoon went to medical school after we came home and continued to practice medicine after retiring as a Colonel. He now lives in retirement.*)

After my brief encounter with the Bug and his associates, I was convinced that some had died in the Green room. I felt terrible about caving in, even though everything I told them, except my base, which they already had to know, was lies. I am now convinced that the Bug told all of us that he met that he would kill us if we didn't "talk," and that, except for Lance Sijan, we all caved in somewhere down the line. I believe that Lance Sijan is the only one of us that held the line and gave up his life rather than to violate any part of the code. If there were others who "went to the wall," we would have known about it, unless it happened during the initial interrogation, in which case they died in room 18 before getting into "the system."

In September 1972, the VC release another three POWs to a Communist Party led visiting "delegation." One of the releasee's is the son of one of the so called *delegation* member--His mother has come to ha Noi to take him home. The other two releasee's were late shootdowns that we had never heard of until the VC announced their names on the PA system in all the cells.

In mid-December 1972, late in the evening, an air raid interrupted our sleep. SAMs blazed from horizon to horizon, and we could see explosions in the sky through the tall bars on the south. I was asleep in my spot on the north side of the pedestal, and turned so I had a clear view of the outside as the sky continued to light up with fireworks, and bombs shook the earth. A large mushroom shaped explosion blossomed amid the smaller pieces of the display, high in our view, and I said to myself: "Well, Hughey, the shock wave will be here momentarily." As I continued to watch, the mushroom changed shape to big oval of fire, and descended vertically. Another big flash joined it and both continued to descend until they disappeared. It wasn't long before all of us realized that the B-52's had arrived. In a day or two, we saw some B-52 crewmen who had bailed out and were now among us. The B-52s kept coming at night.

After the second day, a high ranking VC officer with an entourage, including an interpreter, visited each of the cell blocks and spoke to us all. He explained that the air raids might continue for an indefinite period. He asked us to obey the guards if we were outside and they asked us to return to our cells. He also asked us not to antagonize the guards, and explained that the guards were somewhat on edge, and might do us harm. He further explained that our "humane and lenient treatment" would not change.

The raids continued for several days, and then ceased.

During the year, Bud Flesher had moved into Cell Block number 2. By standing in the middle of the large raised pedestal that we slept on, we could talk to others in Cell 2 by flashing the tap code with our fingers. The general M.O. was for one of us to ask our designated communicator to arrange a one-on-one conversation between individuals in either of the two Cells that we talked to directly.

One night in early January, 1973, just before bed time, the door to our cell block opened, and in walks Bud Flesher with his rolled up belongings under one arm. We find a spot for him in my flight. We talk as long as we can after getting under our mosquito nets, and turn it off until tomorrow.

Bud and I have a lot of catching up to do. I brief him in detail about handling his estate, and thank him for the gin, cigars, and sausages on behalf of myself and all the partyers. We have a lot of good laughs about the whole thing. Bud and I had always had the habit of philosophical discussions, and continue here. We trade the stories of our shoot downs and internment in great detail. Bud had spent several months in Camp Hughey during 1972 before coming here, and reiterates some interesting details about his stay there.

At this time, our senior officers have ordered a letter writing moratorium. I am totally against it and eventually send a message through channels to our SRO explaining my concerns about such an action. Because of constraints on the number of bits our communication has to be as succinct as possible, and I cannot, in a few words, express some details that, to me, are of paramount importance. I know that my view will not be popular, but I don't care. If I am allowed to write a letter, I will disobey this directive. I don't believe that a General Court will care either.

A day or two later, Bud and I are walking around the room and talking, as are several others. The subject of the letter moratorium comes up and Bud is in complete agreement with me. When I tell Bud that if given the opportunity to write a letter to Sue, I will do it, and he asks me what I plan to say to her. Without thinking or blinking, I respond: "Dear Sue, Bob Markum's mother came and got him." We both crack up.

Soon after this conversation, I move to the plantation, and stay there until early February. There are several in each room, and our rooms are open for several hours a day. I soon learn that I am in the room with an expert Backgammon player--Major Ken Fleenor. He agrees to teach me the game and succeeds in teaching me to execute the simple rules of the game, but is a total failure at teaching me enough to have a prayer of beating him. He polishes me off repeatedly with the same aplomb that Gwendolen Chelm employed in the famous chess game in *Beat the Devil*. He would be carrying on a continuous conversation with several people, while I fretted over every roll of dice and still lost.

Ken Fleenor was at the Zoo in 1969 and endured the aftermath of the escape attempt by two of his fellows who managed to get outside the camp in the evening with the very predictable result--they were returned before the next day's first meal. The V beat one of them to death, and beat several others to about the same extent, Ken being one of them. As the beatings continued on a daily basis, Ken soon realized that if they went much longer, there was no way he would survive. At that point he made up his mind to keep a lookout for the AK bearing guards to offer an opportunity for him to grab a rifle and at least take a few V with him. The V guards kept their wariness and distance, and Ken never got the opportunity. The beatings finally stopped, and Ken survived.

Later our seniors issued a directive that there would be no more escape attempts without the assurance of outside help. This restriction essentially eliminated the possibility of any further attempts, since the only outside help that was in the least bit likely was another Commando raid--a rescue, not an escape.

Shortly after we arrived at the Plantation, the V Camp Commander asks us to assemble in the Prison Yard. We line up in military formation and Colonel John Flynn gives all the commands as we remain in formation, listening to the terms of the recently concluded peace agreement. We stand in silence until the SRO gives the dismissal order, and then quietly return to our rooms. Of course, we are excited, but nobody exhibits any emotions to the V. A part of the peace agreement included the requirement for the V to provide certain portions of the agreement in English. The V comply by providing printed copies to us, and the planned release dates by groups. We will be released in the same order we arrived.

Soon after, the SRO sets up an appointment system and has private conversations with each of us. He is impressive. We chat about alternatives in continuing our careers. I tell him that I plan to request appointment as an AFROTC Professor of Air Science after completing an advanced degree in English. As far as I know, we all had very cordial conversations with him.

In early February, 1973, I move back to Hoa Lo into Cell Block 3. The V divide us into groups based on shoot down dates, and we are counting down to February 12, the date the first group will depart. The V issue the first group their "release" package--a small zippered carry-on bag, one pair of boxer shorts, one pair of cotton pants, one cotton dress shirt, one undershirt, one pair of leather shoes, one belt, and one zippered cotton jacket. February 12 comes and the first group departs.

March 4, 1973 is a dreary Saturday. We rise in time to take a bath. I don't bother. I don't like cold baths, and I firmly believe that wherever we spend tonight at Clark Air Base, there will be plenty of hot water and plenty of time and enough soap to get *really* clean.

We get into our release clothes, complete with a leather belt and shoes, and a full pack of Dien Bien cigarettes to stick in our bag. I pack up a suit of prison clothes, along with the tin cup and spoon I've use for a while. Some (maybe most) leave everything behind.

We walk across the camp yard and out to the street where a row of camouflage painted buses are waiting at the curb. We load up and make a slow drive across Ha Noi to the Gia Lam airport. We pass a lot of debris and destruction left by the B-52s, including a lot of railroad tracks piled and laying around with ends pointing all directions, and arrive at Gia Lam under a solid overcast with what looks like about a 200 foot ceiling. We move into an open shed and stand around waiting for the three C-141s to arrive. I am thinking, as most likely all of us are, that the only navigation we know about up here is the low frequency broadcast station. I'm guessing that the C-141 has more sophisticated radar than we had in the F-4, as to dealing with finding landmarks on the ground. I am also wondering, if they don't show up today, will they come tomorrow?

It's pretty quiet among this small crowd. I am sure we're all thinking the same thoughts. Then, (do these things always happen suddenly?) suddenly there is a C-141 on final under the overcast. Not much noise, it just sets down right where the numbers would be, if there were any--can't tell from here. It rolls well down the runway and, as soon as it's slow enough, it makes a 180 degree turn and taxies back to the approach end of the runway. It seems that there is no parallel taxiway.

It comes off the runway and taxies right up near us--a big beautiful airplane with an American flag painted on the tail. Just as it parks and stops, a second C-141 appears on final and rolls down the runway and makes a 180 degree turn. As it taxis back toward the approach end, the third bird breaks out of the overcast, headed for the numbers. We watch as the third airplane adds power and disappears into the overcast. We can hear the thunder from its engines as it flies the missed approach.

The next few minutes slog by as the number two airplane takes its place on the ramp near the first one and stops and we wait impatiently for the third C-141 to reappear. Soon it pops out of the overcast and repeats the wonderful show just completed by its two predecessors.

We gather in three groups and form up into military formations. The airplanes load in turn and soon Mel and I, the last two to load on the number three airplane, are at the head of line. Someone calls my name, and I step forward and salute the best looking, best dressed Air force Colonel I have ever seen. As he returns my salute, Colonel James Dennett reaches his right hand for mine, and says: "Welcome home, Colonel Hughey. Look to your right, there's someone over there who wants to take your picture." With that Colonel Dennett continues to hold my right hand firmly in his and looks to his left, no doubt anticipating me to follow his instruction. I flunk that course, never look at the photographer, just turn and step toward an officer in a flight suit who salutes me and grabs my left elbow in his right hand and says: "Welcome home, Colonel Hughey, step right this way," as he gently guides me to the rear steps of the waiting C-141.

Mel is right behind me. We are leaving in the same order we arrived.

PHOTO 14

Outlaw Lead, aka LtCol Ken Hughey, and Colonel James Dennett at the Gia Lam Airport in Ha Noi, March 4, 1973. Colonel Dennett has just advised me to look to my right as someone wanted to take my photo. I was so enthralled with shaking hands with this wonderful man, perfectly dressed in a "Class A" USAF uniform that I didn't pay attention to what he said after his first words: "Welcome home, Colonel Hughey."

Colonel Dennett left us in 2013. See his impressive obit on line. It was no accident that he was chosen to join the negotiating team that brought us home.

I look up the back steps of the C-141 and see several faces looking down--all are smiling, laughing, joking, reaching to welcome me aboard as they have all the others, and will in a few seconds do likewise for Mel who is right behind me. This is almost as good as my first flight alone in the T-28.

It seems that there are nearly as many crew members on the airplane as there are of us. During their de-briefing at Clark, the two groups that had preceded us had informed the homecoming team of our general health. One of those on the airplane with me has exhibited symptoms of a heart problem for some time. When he came aboard, the team greeted him, and then a cardiologist took him aside and hooked him up to an EKG machine. There were enough bunks in the rear of the airplane to accommodate all (or at least most) of us. When I came aboard, he was reclining in a bunk talking to the Cardiologist.

Soon the celebration winds down, and we take our seats and strap in for departure, and I find myself sitting next to Colonel Dennett. We chat during some of the flight, but as soon as we are safely airborne, all of us are wandering about, talking to each other and the cabin crew, and taking turns visiting the flight deck. When it was my turn, I stepped onto the flight deck and was greeted by two brand new college graduates wearing Captain's bars. We had a too brief, but very pleasant, conversation that soon got around to how they managed to find Gia Lam in a low solid overcast ceiling. They summarized the entire mission.

When they launched from Clark, there were more than three airplanes heading for North Viet Nam. There was at least one spare in case any of the primary three had a problem. Somewhere near the coast of North Viet Nam, the spare turned back, and the three primaries continued. The Aircraft Commander said that with the equipment they had on board, they were prepared to break a 200 foot ceiling, and after he spoke those words, he turned in his seat, looked at me, flashed a bright Ipana smile, and said, and I QUOTE: "But, sir, we were coming to get you!" His smile and the tone of his voice spoke volumes.

In just over two hours, we are on the ground at Clark disembarking. We exit the airplane in the same order we boarded--in order of our shoot down date. There are cameras and broadcast crews filming us, and a cheering crowd in the background. Each of us steps down the boarding stairs, salutes, and shakes hands with the senior officer who greets us.

We soon discover that our own forces have a more secure detention capability than our captors. As soon as we disembark, we were directed ("herded") onto buses that transport us to the Clark Hospital, in the order that we arrived. Hospital personnel, including nurses, lead us to elevators to take us to the level where rooms and personal escorts were waiting for us. I soon find myself in an elevator with about half a dozen of my fellows along with one female nurse who was our guide at the moment.

She selects a floor, the elevator jerks and begins to move, and then jerks and stops somewhere between floors. So now this young lady is trapped in this cubicle with a bunch of guys who haven't seen an American woman in years, haven't been near any kind of woman in years, and whose foremost dream in all those years has been to get back to the woman of their lives, or, in case of the bachelors, to begin the search for the woman of their dreams. We all look at each other, and I'm sure we're all thinking the same thing--"If I were in her shoes, what would I be thinking?"

Whatever she is thinking, she pulls the emergency telephone from its storage box, and soon someone on the other end gets the elevator to go where it's supposed to go and we exit into a foyer where each of us meets his personal escort. The nurse introduces us by name and, when my name is called, an Air Force major, carrying a brief case in his left hand, greets me and introduces himself. His name is Ted Newcomer.

Ted explains to me that he is my personal escort and that we will be joined at the hip for the next few days, and at the moment, I have a private room waiting for me just down the hall. He leads me there and shows me about the room and suggests that if I choose, I might want to get a shower and change into pajamas and robe for my own comfort. A hot shower, a shave, and clean garb make me feel better.

When I'm finished, we sit down together, and he tells me that he has my personnel records with him, and that we can spend a few minutes reviewing the last five years and eight months of my life. I agree.

He opens his brief case and begins with my last mission on July 6, 1967. Post-strike intelligence sources show that we did a good job on the target, and that I was awarded a second Silver Star as a result. He reviews my pay records, accrued leave time, current pay, and notes the date of my promotion to Lieutenant Colonel.

During our last few months we all had fantasized about what we would do about various things, including the leave time we had accrued during our stay in prison. When I was shot down, I had very close to the maximum accrued leave time and now had an additional 170 days. I had the notion that the Air Force would allow the 170 extra days, in spite of the fact that most was not allowable by regulation, and that I could use it as an extended vacation. I was wrong. The government has ruled that we will be paid for leave time accrued while in North Viet Nam and a payment for the appropriate amount based on our salaries would be issued forthwith.

We get back to the subject of my family, and Ted asks me if I would like to talk to my wife. I had been waiting for this question, and we are soon on our way to the elevator that takes us to the basement where there are several private offices. We pick an office, go in, and close the door. There is a desk, some chairs, a telephone, a pad, and pens. Ted picks up the phone and dials a number he has written on a piece of paper. He waits a few seconds and says: "Mrs. Hughey? This is Major Newcomer.

Your husband is here with me, would you like to talk to him?" A second goes by, Ted hands me the phone, leaves, and closes the door. My conversation with Sue is very short. Before the call, I thought we might talk for hours, but after a few minutes, we ran out of topics, declared our love for each other, and hung up.

I open the door and Ted comes in. He hands me a piece of paper with a long series of numbers and explains that this is Sue's phone number and that I could come here any time I pleased to call her and could talk as long as we wanted.

The next step is the chow hall. The hospital has a big kitchen and dining room, and Ted explains that it is always open and we can come here any time we choose and the chefs will prepare any dish we order. Some of the young Turks have already arrived and, contrary to the instructions that nursing staff has passed on about eating too much rich food, several have already devoured more than one large T-bone, followed by some heavy duty deserts. They all survive. I order a steak.

Back in my room, Ted lets me know what to expect for the next few days. We will all get thorough physicals tomorrow, and will be fitted for uniforms. The BX will be opened at night tomorrow night from about 6 P.M. until we are finished shopping. Finance personnel will be present to pay for whatever we choose to buy and will deduct the payment from our leave reimbursement later. We will have a brief debriefing session with an officer who will show us a particular ID. Ted shows me an actual sample of the ID card and tells me that I am not to talk to any-one else until after I have spoken to one who exhibits this particular ID. We are not allowed to leave the hospital until we are released to go home to the States. I listen carefully to this and all other details, and Ted says he'll see me at breakfast tomorrow.

After Ted leaves, I pick up a pad and pen and slip off to the basement and call Sue. We talk a bit longer this time and I bring up the subject of travel during my "rehabilitation," including a trip to Acapulco. It's still not a very long conversation, and I'm soon in bed dreaming of sugar plums.

The next day is Monday, and I join Ted at breakfast. After breakfast, we "make the rounds" of appointments that Ted has on his calendar. I see a dentist, who cleans my teeth and makes notes in my dental records. I lost one tooth in captivity, and my teeth need a good bit of attention. I visit a doctor and as dietitian--both marvel that all of us seem so healthy, excluding those who were seriously wounded and who will receive appropriate attention later on. We stop in at the tailor's shop and order a set of uniforms, including ornamentation such as rank and service ribbons.

In between these things, Ted takes me back to the basement to a private office, and I meet an Air Force Captain who shows me the distinctive ID. He has an assistant and the first thing he wants to know is the names of all the POWs that I knew were in the "system." He has a list of names that I use to refresh my memory. It doesn't take as long as you might imagine. He's mainly interested to know if I bumped into others that are not on his list. Some of the names of the people that Phil Manhard gave me are the only ones that the other POWs had little or no contact with during our stay.

During the day I slip aside to the basement and chat with Sue. We're getting a bit more accustomed to "ourselves," and this conversation is a bit longer. We talk more about where we would like to go during my "rehabilitation" and about our son, Kenny, and our families.

Tonight we're in the BX like a horde of locusts. Everybody gets a camera and at least one change of Civvies.

On the fourth day, I get up, breakfast, pack up and eventually check out of the hospital and head for the flight--line to board a C-141 for McClellan AFB, near San Francisco. The flight will stop at Hickam AFB in Hawaii and we will meet a few brave souls who will come out in the middle of the night--about 2:00 AM-- to meet us for a few minutes while the airplane refuels. Major General "Boots" Blesse is among them. General Blesse was the Deputy Commander of Operations in the 366th TFW when I flew my last mission. He is anxious to hear a brief on the shoot downs for everyone aboard, and in particular a couple of us from the 366th that he had flown with. We are soon on our way to McClellan, and get back into sleeping gear and fall into a bunk for the ride.

We wake up and freshen up during the let-down and are soon gawking out the windows as the crew circles the San Francisco area at low altitude before we land. We aren't on the ground very long at McClellan as we all disperse to our final destinations to meet our families. I board a C-9 "Nightingale" and land at March AFB in Riverside, California. We land in a light rain and the reception that was originally planned to take place on the ramp occurs in a hanger. The crew pulls in as close as they can and Sue and Kenny wait as I step down the stairs and walk a few feet into the hanger.

It's been a long eight years dealing with the Viet Nam "War." If you want to feel the character of our reunion, just put together the longest string of trite expressions intended to characterize Rip Van Winkle/ Robinson Crusoe experiences you can imagine and multiply by infinity. The bottom line is this: if you haven't had a similar experience, don't even try to understand what it's like.

WAR IS HELL
A day or two after I joined the 480th TFS in October 1966, my old friend Bud Flesher and I are talking about the war and what we are doing.

Sometime during the conversation the following quote pops out of Bud's mouth: "It ain't much of a war, Hughey, but it's the only war we've got." This statement echoes a patriotic profundity that needs explication.

Bud and I grew up with the millions of youngsters who, like us, followed WWII with their own feelings of pride and patriotism and dreams of what they would do if only they could. The exploits of major commands, war maneuvers, battles, and individual exploits of our individual heroes permeated the news. The news even covered the heroics of those who reported the news. Our nation mourned men like Ernie Pyle who risked their lives, and sometimes lost the wager, to assure accurate reporting of the heroics that occurred in combat.

I, along with a number of my contemporaries, followed the combat careers of our aerial aces, and many had their personal favorites. Sometimes we would argue the merits of our favorites, much like sports fans defending their favorite athletes. And of course, in typical boyhood fashion, we attributed superhuman qualities to our favorites, elevating them to prequalified passage and Valkyrie escorts to the halls of Valhalla.

After I met Bud Flesher and we flew together and, for a time, spent most of our social time together, we discovered that we were brothers under the skin in terms of our overall feelings of loyalty and patriotism for our country. Without articulating a lot of specifics, we both knew that that both of us were living in hope that our country would someday need us to replicate the exploits of our star fighter pilot heroes from WWII and Korea.

We wouldn't express a hope for war or the ravages of war, but hoped that if hostilities occurred, we could participate fully. Bud's joking remark "…it's the only war we've got," was an echo of the feelings among the group of young officers who listened to General William Tecumseh's "War is Hell" speech.

To understand what Bud was talking about, we need to look at some history and to speculate a little about General Sherman's impassioned caution to a group of young officers about allowing feelings about war and personal accomplishment and glory to lead them astray, when he said to them:

I've been where you are now, and I know just how you feel. It's entirely natural that there should beat in the breast of every one of you a hope and desire that some day you can use the skill you have acquired here.

Suppress it! You don't know the terrible aspects of war.....I tell you, War is Hell.

The "war" we participated in was not the same Hell General Sherman was referring to, but it was another brand of Hell.

In the air, we didn't suffer the sight of our comrades bleeding to death from horrible wounds, or listen to the screams of pain from the mutilated bodies of the dying. Our losses were more distantly impersonal. The Hell created by losses began for me just three days after my first combat sortie as a straphanger with Bill Campbell, when he wound up in a battle damaged airplane in an impossible situation that left him and a fellow commando dead in an A-1 at the Can Tho Airport. From then on for the next eight years our air losses were a steady stream of ones or twos as the Ha Noi Hilton registered guest list steadily increased, and others didn't make it to the registration desk.

Our ground casualties were much more numerous, and much more personal. Most of the final tally of 58,000 plus names engraved on a black marble wall on the Mall in our nation's Capitol, were ground losses, not much different from the Civil War.

While these numbers pale when compared to the casualties in major ground engagements, such as Cold Harbor, during the Civil War when six thousand Union soldiers died during one day's engagement, other aspects of the happenings in Viet Nam created a different brand of Hell--A Hell that has affected our country for decades thus far, and still smarts in the recall of the macabrely comic blunders that propelled us through it.

Viet Nam wasn't a numbers game, nor was our Union at stake. At least General Grant had the courage to admit that he had made a mistake in that the thousands lost at Cold Harbor "gained no advantage." I have never heard any such admission on the part of any of our government leaders who drug our country through the Hell that lost more than 58,000 of our best and not only "gained no advantage," but resulted in the most embarrassing moment in the history of our country. General Grant had every right to claim some advantage gained at Cold Harbor, in that he had, at least, weakened the Confederacy and pushed the cause of preserving our Union a little further down the road. Conversely, the 58,000 casualties we suffered in Viet Nam, not only resulted in an ignominious failure, but caused a rift in our Union.

The War is over, and with that, so ends that portion of my life. In 1975, I watch the coverage of our final withdrawal from Viet Nam. I laugh as I recall the Movietone coverage of Dien Bien Phu from 21 years ago--the haggard French soldiers herded by the same group that are rolling into Sai Gon and will soon rename it Ho Chi Minh City. Somewhere in Viet Nam, Vo Nguyen Giap must be facing East waving an extended middle finger--if he isn't, it's just because he has other ways of savoring the moment, and has other issues to deal with now that he has ousted the United States of America from his country just as he ousted the French.

I close this chunk of my memoir with a 477 word write up that appeared in *The Beach Reporter* in Manhattan Beach on December 26, 2013, our 60th Wedding Anniversary, just to let you know how it's going with Mimi and me.

Sincerely,
Outlaw Lead

Happy 60th Anniversary
Mimi and Ken Hughey

Long ago in a galaxy far, far away, two star-crossed lovers met when they were barely in their teens. Unlike, the protagonists alluded to here, these two were not thwarted in their quest to spend their lives together. They married in an Antebellum style home in Tennessee on December 26, 1953. The young bride came down the spiral staircase to her betrothed, a dashing young fighter pilot, who was quaking in his boots at the sight of the most desirable woman he would ever meet.

On December 26, 2013 these two--the bride as beautiful as ever, who still fits into her original wedding dress--the groom, white hair and bit of a paunch, as dashing as ever--will celebrate sixty of the years they dreamed of as teenagers. Sue, now known as Mimi, and Ken Hughey have lived the equivalent of several lifetimes during their sixty years together--some sad, some glad, some heartbreaking, some ecstatic, all wonderful years. Fifty-one of those years as residents of the South Bay.

In 1961, Sue took a job with Interstate Hosts and soon became the Manager of the Restaurant, Bar, and Gift Shop in Satellite 7 at LAX, then the total domain of United Airlines. Can you imagine a 5 foot two inch Hour glass 100 pound female firing a 220 pound bartender for drinking on the job?

Ken, at that time, was active in the design and procurement of advanced space systems for the Air Force at Space Systems Division in Inglewood, Ca.

Their only surviving child, Kenny, was born in Inglewood in 1964. Kenny and his family now live on the Riviera in Redondo Beach with their two daughters--Ashley, a sophomore at UC San Diego, and Courtney, a senior at Mira Costa High. Their daughter, Kelly Susan, infant, is buried in Boulder, Colorado.

The years in between have been filled with a lot of adventure for both. Ken accumulated a lot of combat experience in Vietnam, including 564 combat sorties and nearly six years in prison in the Ha Noi Hilton. Sue kept the little family together for all that time, including three and a half years of not knowing if Ken was alive.

After the family was reunited in 1973, Sue worked in the retail clothing business with two of her friends, and was the mainstay in caring for the elders on both sides of this family during their final days. Ken continued his career in the Aerospace business, and graduated from law school in 1967, after he had passed the California bar. He served as a Criminal Prosecutor for the City of Los Angeles until 2011. He currently practices law as a Defense Attorney.

This is the 477 word version of a Saga that would rival War and Peace. Ken and Mimi expect to spend another lifetime in the South Bay.

PHOTO 15

Made in the USA
Charleston, SC
12 June 2015